Visual Culture in Shanghai
1850s–1930s

Published and Forthcoming by New Academia Publishing

Visual Culture, Popular Culture, and Cinema

SUPER HEROES: From Hercules to Superman, edited by Wendy Haslem, Angela Ndalianis, and Chris Mackie.

SHOPPING FOR JESUS: Visual Culture and the Marketing of Christianity, edited by Dominic Janes.

EVERY STEP A STRUGGLE: Interviews with Seven Who Shaped the African-American Image in Movies, by Frank Manchel.

HERETICAL EMPIRICISM, by Pier Paolo Pasolini.
Ben Lawton and Louise K. Barnett, trs., eds. With Ben Lawton's new Introduction and the first approved English-language translation of Pasolini's essay, "The Repudiation of the 'Trilogy of Life'."

IMAGING RUSSIA 2000: Film and Facts, by Anna Lawton.

BEFORE THE FALL: Soviet Cinema in the Gorbachev Years, by Anna Lawton.

Visual Culture in Shanghai
1850s–1930s

Edited with an Introduction by
Jason C. Kuo

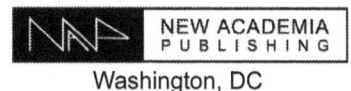

Washington, DC

New Academia Publishing, 2007

Printed in the United States of America

Library of Congress Control Number: 2007921396
ISBN 978-0-9787713-5-5 paperback (alk. paper)
ISBN 978-0-9787713-8-6 hardcover (alk. paper)

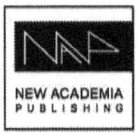

New Academia Publishing, LLC
P.O. Box 27420
Washington, DC 20038-7420
www.newacademia.com - info@newacademia,com

In memoriam
Wai-kam Ho
Frederic E. Wakeman, Jr.
Nelson I. Wu

Contents

Illustrations

Chapter 4

Chapter 5

Chapter 6

Chapter 7

Chapter 8

Chapter 9

Chapter 10

Acknowledgments

Visual Culture in Shanghai, 1850s–1930s and *Modern Chinese Poster-Calendars: History, Art, and Culture* (also edited by myself and forthcoming) have grown out of the US-China Cooperative Research Project, "Art in Shanghai, 1850–1930," which I directed with the generous support of two grants from the U.S.-China Cooperative Research Program at the Henry Luce Foundation.

As the principal investigator of this project, I organized a series of research conferences in College Park (University of Maryland), Beijing (the Palace Museum and the Central Academy of Fine Arts), Shanghai (the Shanghai Museum), and New York (Institute of Fine Arts at New York University) from 1993 to 1998. Participants in this project included scholars and advanced graduate students from the University of California at Berkeley, The Ohio State University, the Institute of Fine Arts at New York University, the Freer and Sackler Galleries in Washington, DC, Rice University, the University of Maryland, the University of London, the Palace Museum, the Shanghai Museum, the Shanghai Art Gallery, the Shanghai Academy of Social Sciences, and the Central Academy of Fine Arts in Beijing. A comprehensive exhibition on the Shanghai School of Painting was held at the Palace Museum in Beijing from June to September 1995. Two special issues of *I-yuan tou-ying* (nos. 53–54, June 1995), one of the most important art magazines in China, and one special issue of *I-shu-chia* (no. 243, August 1995), the most important art magazine in Taiwan, were devoted to this project. I am most grateful to all participants in this project for their support and contribution.

In addition to the generous grants from the U.S.-China Cooperative Research Program of the Henry Luce Foundation, support for this project has been made possible by the College of Arts and Humanities, the General Research Board, and the Department of Art History and Archaeology, University of Maryland. I am most grateful to my colleagues in the Department of Art History and Archaeology, University of Maryland, for their generous support. I also would like to thank Joel Kalvesmaki for his patient and careful copyediting, and the four anonymous reviewers for their comments and suggestions.

Jason C. Kuo

Introduction

Jason C. Kuo

As a powerhouse for China's modern transformation Shanghai was a city of tremendous importance and enormous complexity. In the half century after 1843, when the Treaty of Nanjing opened it to trade with the West, Shanghai rose to become China's largest city and its leading center for finance and industry, as well as for art, printing, publishing, journalism, popular entertainment, and higher education. Home to the conservative Sino-Western comprador merchants of the nineteenth century, Shanghai in the Republican period (1911–49) was nonetheless the birthplace of radical ideology, mass demonstrations, anticolonial nationalism (with economic nationalism), and political organizations of all stripes, including the Chinese Communist Party.

Although in the last twenty years the city's social and political institutions have been better understood, not enough has been learned about the cultural milieu of Shanghai as it emerged from a middle-sized county seat to become a cosmopolitan metropolis.[1] We now know a fair amount about the highly differentiated urban society of Republican Shanghai, with its professional classes and modernist values distinguished from the rest of the country, but historians have only roughly sketched out the city's drastic social and cultural changes brought on after the Taiping Uprising of the mid-nineteenth century. As a result, we can recognize the far-reaching consequences of Shanghai's cultural developments in the late nineteenth and early twentieth century, yet, given the long process, singularly marked by tension between tradition and modernity, between China and the West, we remain uncertain about where to locate the dynamics of these changes.[2]

One of the best ways to understand the cultural history of modern Shanghai in general and the history of Shanghai School painting in particular is through the study of visual culture in Shanghai. Several scholars have recently attempted to define the term "visual culture" relative to visual images. According to Norman Bryson, Michael Ann Holly, and Keith

Moxey, in their introduction to *Visual Culture: Image and Interpretations*, art is "actively engaged in organizing and structuring the social and cultural environment."[3] They argue against the practice of a traditional art-historical approach: "It is, in fact, art history's continuing adherence to a theory of immanent aesthetic value that has prevented historians from fully examining the way in which the work is related to all other institutions and practices that constitute social life."[4] Although, as W. J. T. Mitchell has cautioned us, "one cannot simply graft a received notion of visual experience on to a received notion of culture," it is clear that we can no longer ignore the challenge of the approach of visual culture. As Mitchell has argued, "From the standpoint of a general field of visual culture, art history can no longer rely on received notion of beauty or aesthetic significance to define its proper object of study. The realm of vernacular and popular imagery clearly has to be reckoned with, and the notion of aesthetic hierarchy, of masterpieces and the genius artist have to be redescribed as historical constructions specific to various cultural place-times."[5] Recent efforts by scholars such as Julia Andrews, Ellen Johnston Laing, Kuiyi Shen, and Leo Ou-fan Lee have begun to address the production and circulation of vernacular and popular imagery in early twentieth-century China.[6]

A part of the field of Chinese history, the study of the cultural history of modern Shanghai has been flourishing. Yet until recently, as in so much of Chinese art history, the study of art in Shanghai has remained, with some rare exceptions, confined strictly to connoisseurship and authentication of traditional Chinese painting. This has been unfortunate, because the production, circulation, reception, and consumption of the visual arts lend themselves particularly well to art historians, cultural historians, social historians, and literary historians for integrative and interdisciplinary study. For instance, the term *Haipai* ("Shanghai School" or "Shanghai Style"), used as both a noun and an adjective, gained wide usage in Chinese around the turn of the century, both to denote the particular artistic taste and style of life associated with Shanghai's comprador merchants, and to be contrasted to the *Jingpai* ("Beijing School" or "Beijing Style") of the established bureaucratic elites. Identified originally with Shanghai's operatic theater and art market, the term *Haipai* was extended to include styles of entertainment as well as patterns of consumption. While it was a matter of status among many of Shanghai's mercantile elites to live up to the expectations of *Haipai*, the term in fact carried negative connotations outside the arriviste social circle as a symbol of bad taste and dubious significance. After the 1920s, *Haipai* also became an object of denunciation by cultural bureaucrats appointed by the Nationalists and later by the Communists. The form and practice of *Haipai* thus occupied a contested terrain between social classes and cultural allegiance. A study of formal and informal meanings of *Haipai*, as seen through the paintings of the Shanghai school as well as other media of visual representations, provides us a point of entry into the nexus of relationships that structured the encounter between China and the West as experienced by the treaty-port Chinese in their everyday life. Exploring such relationships gives us a better sense of the ultimate significance of Shanghai's rise as China's dominant metropolitan center.[7]

Continuing Stella Yu Lee's earlier work on art patronage in Shanghai in the nineteenth century,[8] Kuiyi Shen's essay, "Patronage and the Beginning of a Modern Art World in Late Qing Shanghai," deals with the social and economic contexts of the Shanghai School of Painting. Like the rapid development of the Chinese economy, particularly in port cities, the patronage of art changed greatly during the late Qing dynasty. Especially in Shanghai, as it was transformed into a new modern metropolis and the hub of southern China's cultural and artistic activities, art patronage of a new kind emerged from a new class of art buyers, and was associated with a dramatic increase in the number of shops selling paintings, the emergence of new types of artists' associations, and the establishment of a thriving market for contemporary art. These features, part of the rapid commercialization of society, changed the styles and subject matters of paintings in Shanghai. By examining these changes in late nineteenth-century Shanghai, this essay suggests that the changed nature of art patronage represents a key feature of modernity in the culture of late Qing Shanghai.

Late nineteenth-century Shanghai witnessed an increase in the available technologies of image production, including photography and lithography. Paralleling this, there was an even greater expansion in the number of subject matters considered worthwhile. In her essay, "Uncommon Themes and Uncommon Subject Matters in Ren Xiong's *Album after Poems by Yao Xie*," Britta Erickson focuses on Ren Xiong's 1851 album, which, now in the Palace Museum in Beijing, is the largest extant Chinese painting album, containing 120 leaves; this album presages many of the fin de siècle developments just mentioned, since the variety of subject matters and styles assembled in the album is absolutely unprecedented in the history of Chinese painting. Stylistically, the leaves vary dramatically, from detailed, fine-lined brushwork, to bold and expressive brushwork, to archaistic styles. Ren Xiong's openness to new ideas is reflected in his renditions of unusual subject matters, such as machines and exotic foreigners, and in the likely influence Chinese printed books, European illustrated books, and Japanese prints and paintings all had on him.

Ren Xiong's album also exemplifies art patronage in the Shanghai School of Painting. The album was a cooperative venture between the artist and his primary patron, Yao Xie. Yao Xie selected a line of his own verse as the subject for each leaf, and Ren Xiong responded with a painting. Yao Xie thus initiated each leaf's direction, and was responsible for choosing some of the unusual subjects, such as people of exotic ethnicity. He also injected political content into the album, by inscribing lines of verse describing the Opium War, sometimes critical of the Manchu imperial army. Erickson argues that, in expanding and exploring the limits of style and content, artist and patron may have been motivated by more than just intellectual gratification, because the album could have exemplified the possible kinds of paintings that the patron could commission from the artist.

At the height of his artistic career in 1888, Ren Bonian (1840–1896), one of the best-known artists of late nineteenth-century Shanghai, painted a twelve-leaf album on the subject of beautiful women. In "Deliberate Looks: Ren Bonian's 1888 *Album of Women*," Roberta Wue explores the artistic context of the album by highlighting a range of issues significant to Ren Bonian at this time: his relationship to old masters, his development of a more calligraphic style, and his challenging of narrative conventions in painting. She also explores personal issues and themes the album may have had for Ren Bonian during this period, and the possible self-identification of the male artist with his female subjects.

The essay "The Traditionalist Response to Modernity: The Chinese Painting Society of Shanghai," coauthored by Julia F. Andrews and Kuiyi Shen, looks at the institutional, social, and economic aspects of Chinese painting, specifically artists' organizations. The essay focuses on the activities of one of the most important traditionalist painters' organization in Shanghai, the Zhongguo huahui or Chinese Painting Society. Established in 1931 on a culturally nationalist agenda, the group claimed as members many, if not all, of the most important traditional painters in the city. Its members participated in the cultural debates of the period, upholding a traditionalist cultural agenda while remaining fully engaged in the life of modern Shanghai.[9] Andrews and Shen argue that its members' traditionalism was active, not passive; further, they argue that the promotion of traditional Chinese painting by members of the Chinese Painting Society in Shanghai in the 1930s, in the face of Western influences, might be considered not a reactionary but a progressive and "modern" activity.[10]

In his current research, Jonathan Hay has been concerned with interpreting visual culture in Shanghai in terms of modernity.[11] In his essay, "Notes on Chinese Photography and Advertising in Late Nineteenth-Century Shanghai," he focuses on the development of photography and advertising and argues that forms of a commercial mass culture in general and visual culture in particular in Shanghai in the first half of the twentieth century were first worked out in the late nineteenth century on a relatively small scale through experimentation with new, but limited, technology. He has attempted to reconstruct the social, economic, and cultural context for the Shanghai art world, of which the Shanghai School painters only formed one part: other professional artists of the time included illustrators, photographers, artisan painters, wood-block print artists, and commercial artists specializing in backdrops and technical illustrations. Hay's essay demonstrates clearly that, from about 1860 to 1895, Shanghai served as an experimental laboratory for the development of China's modern commercial mass and visual culture. He further argues that, through an expansion and intensification of preexisting Chinese visual practices on the one hand, and experimentation with imported technologies on the other—an intersecting process also seen in pictorial journalism and the mechanical reproduction of paintings—a new and distinctive orientation for visual culture came into being.

The essays by Yingjin Zhang, Carrie Warra, and Shu-mei Shih, by focusing on the representation of women, further examine the new ways images were produced and received through new visual technologies in a rapidly changing, culturally hybrid, cosmopolitan Shanghai. Zhang's essay, "Artwork, Commodity, Event: Representations of the Female Body in Modern Chinese Pictorials," deals with the complicated ways in which the visual representations of the female body circulated and functioned in Shanghai in the late Qing and early Republican period. He focuses on two principal sources: Wu Youru's lithographs from the *Dianshizhai huabao* and numerous images from the pictorial *Liangyou*. To situate his study in the broader context of Chinese visual culture, Zhang also briefly refers to contemporary literary works (e.g., modernist poetry and fiction) as well as other pictorials (e.g., *Beiyang huabao*) and cartoon magazines (e.g., *Duli manhua*). He approaches the pictorial representations of the female body in three distinctive modes: as artwork, as commodity, and as event. As artwork, the female body was regarded as embodying the essence of feminine beauty and male aesthetic taste. In this mode, the female body worked to solicit a "privatized" aesthetic gaze and eventually to confirm the male viewer's self-confidence in erotic connoisseurship. As a commodity, female bodies were offered in graphic form for public consumption and, obviously, to increase the circulation of the pictorials. Consistent inclusion of photographs and paintings of female nudes in *Liangyou* thus worked both to promote sales of the magazine and to build the magazine's reputation as a vanguard in modern Chinese art. As an event, the female body was inserted in a threshold where the traditional was forced to admire the modern and the weak fantasized to beat the strong. Inevitably, the female body in this third mode served as a surrogate for the male body and seemed to provide a certain amount of comfort in the latter's discursive negotiation and symbolic confrontation with the West. Drawing on films and art theory to analyze visual representations in terms of the look, the gaze, and the screen, as well as their exhibitionism, voyeurism, and sadomasochism, Zhang offers a close reading of a select number of pictures and concludes that the female body in the pictorial representations constitutes both a sight for visual consumption and a site for articulating public anxiety and private fantasy in the metropolis of Shanghai.

Carrie Waara's essay, "The Bare Truth: Nudes, Sex, and the Modernization Project in Shanghai Pictorials," looks at the representation of the female nude by studying its presence in *Meishu shenghuo* (*Arts & Life*), a prominent art periodical, and other pictorials published in Shanghai. Western fine art nudes as well as paintings, sculpture, and photographs of nude subjects by Chinese artists frequently appeared in these magazines as part of their modernization project: to foster "a commanding view of the world" in order to develop the human ability to control things in terms of truth, rational calculation, authenticity, and/or beauty. Representations of nudes thus secured for the editors vivid credentials of their expertise in translating Western modernity for Chinese society.

Yet this new convention of portraying women in China also presented problems of spectatorship for middle-class women readers. Historically, the female nude presumed the dominant spectatorship of men, long associated with sexuality, voyeurism, and power.[12] The nude's association with uncontrolled sexuality, prostitution, and the social degeneracy of urban entertainment districts also conflicted with the magazines' ideology of domesticity. Nonetheless, the editors suggested that the vitality of human sexuality might revivify Chinese art and culture. The treatments of the human subject, clothed and unclothed, by *Meishu shenghuo* and other periodicals were part of a project to create a new, modern cultural identity that redefined Chinese middle-class femininity and masculinity. Waara's essay constitutes a new understanding of the construction of gender by pictorial magazines produced in Shanghai from 1912 to 1937, when the rise of the pictorial press underscored the power of representation and its relation to Shanghai's visual culture.

In her essay, "Shanghai Women of 1939: Visuality and the Limits of Feminine Modernity," Shu-mei Shih explicates the relationship between Chinese modernity and gender by examining the representation of women in advertisements in the 1939 issues of *Shanghai shenghuo* (*Shanghai Guide*). She distinguishes between two forms of modernity: masculine and feminine. When modernity was articulated as a nationalist resistance to imperialism, the empowerment of the modern nation-state of China, it was often presented in masculine terms. But when modernity was articulated in terms of everyday practice, women often embodied it through their dress, manners, and lifestyles. Within this realm of feminine modernity, modern women were encoded as objects of desire by advertisements encouraging their active participation in consumer activities. Thus, modern women were caught between the supposedly liberating potentials of modernity and the traditional expectations of native patriarchy. Furthermore, as illustrated by the advertisements that encouraged women to buy native Chinese products, their role appears to be restricted only to that of consumer. Shih therefore argues that, whether represented as "Westernized-sexualized-therefore-modern" women, or as patriotic housewives, their advertised images suggest the limits of feminine modernity.

The essays by Ellen Johnston Laing and Lenore Hietkamp look at the hybrid aspects of visual culture in Shanghai. Soon after the Exposition Internationale des Arts Décoratifs et Industriels Modernes, held in Paris in 1925, strong simple shapes; geometric designs; intersecting squares, circles, and triangles; angular chevrons and zigzags; smooth curves; and stylized representations began to dominate the decorative arts. Art Deco, as it came to be called, quickly became international, appearing particularly in the decorative arts and architecture of Europe, the Unites States, and Asian cosmopolitan centers such as Shanghai and Tokyo. In her essay, "Art Deco and Modernist Art in Chinese Calendar Posters," Laing identifies and discusses the influence of Art Deco on the popular calendar posters (*yuefenpai*) of the 1920s and 1930s, focusing on the decorative borders, the typographic designs, and the domestic interiors rendered as backgrounds for depictions of modern women. Artists designing the calendar posters, which served primarily as advertisements, but eventually as popular art for mass consumption, incorporated not only elements of Art Deco (crisp lines, geometric forms, and flattening of pictorial space) but also patterns and motifs found in traditional Chinese decorative arts. The very presence of Art Deco motifs and modernist styles in the calendar posters brought abstract art forms directly to the streets and homes of Shanghai for all to see.

The calendar posters are an accurate and concrete visual gauge of popular acceptance of cultural developments because, exhibited and sold at street corner stalls, they reached all classes of Chinese society. At another level, by 1930, several art schools in the Shanghai area had established design departments, some with Chinese instructors educated in Paris. When these artists' designs were published in Chinese popular art magazines, they helped bring the aesthetic ideals of Art Deco to a Chinese art world already sympathetic to Western and modern art styles. Movies also helped spread Art Deco in China. For the ordinary person, the sumptuous and elegant Art Deco clothing and furnishings seen in movies probably represented a level of luxury perhaps admired but acknowledged as unattainable.

Since most of the calendar posters advertised commodities, they embodied the intriguing relationship between commodity culture and modernity. As Garry Leonard has argued, "commodity culture is modern, in part, because it relies on technological advances in visual presentation, such as photography, and improved methods of printing, such as lithography. These advances permitted, in turn, cheap production of the plethora of images and advertising that provided the infrastructure of what we now call 'mass media.'"[13] Leonard's comments belong to his study of James Joyce, but are applicable to Shanghai in the late nineteenth and early twentieth century. Two other essays in this book, those by Shih and Hay, also touch upon advertising, and other scholars, such as Leo Ou-fan Lee and Sherman Cochran, have turned to Shanghai poster calendars in their studies of modern Chinese cultural history. But studies remain to be undertaken on how the mass-produced poster calendars embodied transformations in modern Shanghai: the reconfiguration of desire and pleasure; the social construction of reality, identity, and gender; and the redefinition of the "borders of art."[14]

The Park Hotel in Shanghai, built in 1934, was a powerful symbol of 1930s China. Designed by the Hungarian architect Laszlo Hudec (1893–1958) and visually compelling from excavation to completion, it far surpassed its rivals on the Bund in height and modernity. At eighty-seven meters (284 feet), it was the tallest building at the time outside of North America, and, until the early 1980s, towered above Shanghai's cityscape. Hietkamp's essay, "The Park Hotel in Shanghai: A Metaphor for 1930s China," is based on a firsthand study of the monument and on drawings, photographs, and newspaper clippings held in the Laszlo Hudec Collection at the University of Victoria, Canada. The combination—Chinese owners, Hungarian architect, and Western style—reflected the cosmopolitan nature and complex social structure of Shanghai in the 1930s. In its height and services, the Park Hotel can be classed with the great American skyscraper hotels. The potential visual impact of the tall structure on Shanghai residents informed the design and the choice of the site for the Park Hotel. Stylistic sources for the hotel can be traced, not only to the contemporary streamlined Art Deco style, but also to the more conservative New York skyscrapers. Hudec was educated in the Beaux Arts tradition of Austria and utilized central and eastern European ideas throughout his career. The hotel's façade filtered all these influences. The hotel is therefore an important receptacle of stylistic confluences of modern architectural ideas from around the world. The hotel, furthermore, was a symbol not only of the Chinese owners' ability to help finance the modernization project, but also of the optimism for the future shared by the wealthy Chinese and Westerners in Shanghai.[15] Furthermore, China's efforts to modernize during the Nationalist regime are echoed clearly in every aspect of the hotel.

Wen-hsin Yeh's afterword, "The Shanghai Gaze: Visual Culture and Images of Modernity," gives a thought-provoking overview of the relationship between cultural history and visual culture in Shanghai. The complexity and richness of visual culture in Shanghai, as she sees it, compel us to ask serious questions as we explore the visual dimension to understand Chinese modernity: "How was the Shanghai gaze disciplined either to revere or to dismiss, to engage or to avert, to support or to subvert emerging systems of power? How, conversely, did commercialization and industrialization, colonialism and nationalism, manifest themselves in a new visual culture?" As she puts it, "To make sense of the visual culture in the city, one must thus not only keep in sight the incessant struggles between the high and the low, the near and the far. One must also confront the fragmented nature of the myriad images that were but parts of an evolving whole, and were gleaned from a variety of perspectives." In short, this volume explores how visual culture in general and painting in particular in Shanghai from the 1850s to the 1930s embodied China's search for a modern identity, and how Shanghai emerged as the center of Chinese cosmopolitanism.

Notes

An earlier version of this introduction was presented under the title "Visual Culture and Shanghai School Painting" at the International Symposium on Shanghai School Painting, December 2001, Shanghai, and published in *Haipai huihua xanjiu wenji* (Shanghai: Shanghai Shuhua Chubanshe, 2001), 1004–24.

1 For a succinct summary of recent scholarship, see Wen-hsin Yeh, "Shanghai Modernity: Commerce and Culture in a Republican City," in *Reappraising Republican China*, ed. Frederic Wakeman Jr. and Richard Louis Edmonds (Oxford: Oxford University Press, 2000), 121–40.

2 An excellent example of recent scholarship on the cultural history of Shanghai is Leo Ou-fan Lee, *Shanghai Modern: The Flowering of a New Urban Culture in China, 1930–1945* (Cambridge, MA: Harvard University Press, 1999). For a useful bibliographical survey, see John Clark, "Modernity in Chinese Art, 1850s–1990s," *Journal of the Oriental Society of Australia* 29 (1997): 74–169. The following recent studies are useful for understanding the visual arts in Republican China in general and art in Shanghai in particular: Ralph Croizier, *Art and Revolution in Modern China: The Lingnan (Cantonese) School of Painting, 1906–1951* (Berkeley: University of California Press, 1988); Michael Sullivan, *Art and Artists of Twentieth-Century China* (Berkeley: University of California Press, 1996); Julia Andrews, Kuiyi Shen, et al., *A Century in Crisis: Tradition and Modernity in the Art of Twentieth-Century China* (New York: Guggenheim Museum, 1998); and John Clark, *Modern Asian Art* (Sydney: Craftsman House, 1998). See also Jo-Anne Birnie Danzker, Ken Lum, and

Zheng Shengtian, eds., *Shanghai Modern, 1919–1945* (Ostfildern-Ruit: Hatje Cantz, 2004), the catalog accompanying a major exhibition held at the Museum Villa Stuck in Munich in 2004. A more comprehensive study on visual culture in early twentieth-century China remains to be undertaken.

3 (Hanover, NH: University Press of New England, 1994), xviii.

4 Ibid.

5 "What is Visual Culture?" in *Meaning in the Visual Arts: Views from the Outside,* ed. Irving Lavin (Princeton: Institute for Advanced Study, 1995), 208–10. For other attempts at defining the term "visual culture," see John A. Walker and Sarah Chaplin, *Visual Culture: An Introduction* (Manchester: Manchester University Press, 1997), and Malcolm Barnard, *Art, Design and Visual Culture: An Introduction* (New York: St. Martin's Press, 1998).

6 See, for example, Lee, *Shanghai Modern* (n. 2 above) and papers given at the session "Commercial Art and the Publishing Industry in Old Shanghai," Association of Asian Studies Annual Meeting, 1997: Julia Andrews, "Judging a Book by Its Cover: Book Cover Design in Republican Shanghai"; Ellen Johnston Laing, "Commodification of Art through Exhibition and Advertisement"; Kuiyi Shen, "Comics, Illustrations, and the Cartoonist in Republican Shanghai." Also see Julia Andrews and Kuiyi Shen, "The Modern Woodcut Movement," in *Century in Crisis,* 213–25; Kuiyi Shen, "Comics, Picture Books, and Cartoonists in Republican China," *Ink, Cartoon and Comic Art* 4.3 (November 1997): 2–16; Kuiyi Shen, "Lianhuanhua and Manhua: Picture Books and Comics in Old Shanghai," in *Illustrating Asia,* ed. John Lent (Richmond, Surrey: Curzon, 2001); and Kuiyi Shen, "Publishing Posters before the Cultural Revolution," *Modern Chinese Literature and Culture* 12.2 (2000): 177–202. For a useful collection of studies on comics and picture books, see Lin Min and Zhao Suxing, eds., *Zhongguo lianhuanhua yishu wenji* (Taiyuan: Shanxi jenmin chubanshe, 1987). An excellent study on book cover design can be found in Yang Yi and others, *Ershi shiji Zhongguo wenxue tuzhi,* 2 vols. (Taipei: Yeqiang chubanshe, 1995). Also see Harriet Evans and Stephanie Donald, eds., *Picturing Power in the People's Republic of China: Posters of the Cultural Revolution* (Lanham: Rowman & Littlefield, 1999).

7 For a recent study of *Haipai* and *Jingpai* in literature, see Yang Yi, *Jingpai yu Haipai bijiao yanjiu* (Xi'an: Taibai wenyi chubanshe, 1994).

8 "The Art Patronage of Shanghai in the Nineteenth Century," in *Artists and Patrons: Some Social and Economic Aspects of Chinese Painting,* ed. Chu-tsing Li et al., 223–31 (Lawrence, KS: The Kress Foundation Department of Art History, University of Kansas and The Nelson-Atkins Museum of Art, Kansas City, in association with University of Washington Press, 1989).

9 For recent studies on tradition and modernity in Chinese painting, see Jason C. Kuo, *Transforming Traditions in Modern Chinese Painting: Huang Pin-Hung's Late Work* (New York and Bern: Peter Lang, 2004); Ralph Croizier, "Post-Impressionists in Pre-War Shanghai: The Juelanshe (Storm Society) and the Fate of Modernism in Republican China," in *Modernity in Asian Art,* ed. John Clark, 135–54 (Broadway, Australia: Wild Peony, 1993); Kuiyi Shen, "A Debate on the Reform of Traditional Chinese Painting in Early Republican China," *Tsing Hua Journal of Chinese Studies,* n.s., 26.4 (1997): 447–69; and Kuiyi Shen, "Traditional Painting in a Transitional Era, 1901–1950," in *Century in Crisis,* 80–95. For an excellent study of calligraphy in

the twentieth century, see Chen Zhenlian, *Xiandai Zhongguo shufashi* (n.p.: Henan meishu chubanshe, 1993).

10 For female artists and their organization, see the insightful study by Julia Andrews and Kuiyi Shen, "Traditionalism as a Modern Stance: The Chinese Women's Calligraphy and Painting Society," *Modern Chinese Literature and Culture* 11.1 (Spring 1999): 1–29.

11 For example, see Jonathan Hay, "Painters and Publishing in Late Nineteenth-Century Shanghai," in *Art at the Close of China's Empire*, Phoebus: Occasional Papers in Art History 8, ed. Ju-hsi Chou, 134–88 (Tempe, AZ: Arizona State University, 1998).

12 For recent scholarship on spectatorship as a historical phenomenon produced in a particular cultural moment, see Vanessa R. Schwartz, *Spectacular Realities: Early Mass Culture in* Fin-de-Siècle *Paris* (Berkeley: University of California Press, 1998), 8–12.

13 *Advertising and Commodity Culture in Joyce* (Gainesville, FL: University Press of Florida, 1998), 21–22.

14 Ellen J. Laing, *Selling Happiness: Calendar Posters and Visual Culture in Early-Twentieth-Century Shanghai* (University of Hawaii Press, 2004); Lee, *Shanghai Modern*, esp. 43–81 (n. 2 above); Sherman Cochran, "Marketing Medicine and Advertising Dreams in China, 1900–1950," in *Becoming Chinese: Passages to Modernity and Beyond*, ed. Wen-hsin Yeh, 62–97 (Berkeley and Los Angeles: University of California Press, 2000); Ng Chun Ping and others, comps., *Chinese Women and Modernity: Calendar Posters of the 1910s–1930s* (Hong Kong: Joint Publishing, 1996); Jason C. [Chi-sheng] Kuo, ed., *Xiandai Zhongguo Yuefenpai: lishi, yishu, yu wenhua* (Taipei: SMC Publishing, forthcoming). Also relevant are the following unpublished papers: Francesca Dal Lago, "Modern Looking and Looking Modern: 'Modern Woman' as Commodity in 1930s Shanghai Calendar Posters," given at the symposium "Visual Cultures and Modernities in China and Japan," Institute of Fine Arts, New York University, October 26, 1996; Martha E. Huang, "Calendar Girls: The Chinese Advertising, 1914–1939," given at the session "Modern Fashion/Fashioning Modernity: The Politics of Clothing in Twentieth-Century China," Association of Asian Studies Annual Meeting, 1999. For a study of changing boundaries of fine and commercial art in the United States in the early twentieth century, see Michele H. Bogart, *Artists, Advertising, and the Borders of Art* (Chicago: University of Chicago Press, 1995). For a study of advertising, "progress," and modernity in the late nineteenth and early twentieth century, see Pamela Walker Laird, *Advertising Progress: American Business and the Rise of Consumer Marketing* (Baltimore: Johns Hopkins University Press, 1998).

15 For an introduction to German architecture in Shanghai, see Torsten Warner, *Deutsche Architektur in China* (Berlin: Ernst and Sohn, 1994), 84–139.

1

Patronage and the Beginning of a Modern Art World in Late Qing Shanghai

Kuiyi Shen

Along with rapid development in the economy, particularly in port cities, the patronage of art changed greatly during the Qing dynasty. Especially in Shanghai, as it was transformed into a new modern metropolis and the hub of southern China's cultural and artistic activities, art patronage of a new kind emerged from a new class of art buyers, and was associated with a dramatic increase in the number of painting and fan shops, the emergence of new types of artists' associations, and the establishment of a thriving market for contemporary art. These features, which appeared in the context of a rapidly commercializing society, resulted directly in changes of subject matter and style in Shanghai painting of the period.

Treaty-port Shanghai was significantly different from other Chinese commercial cities, both those of the past and those of more recent times, such as the cultural centers of Suzhou and Yangzhou. Population growth, rapid development of the economy, and establishment of a pluralistic culture contributed to laying a rich foundation for the city's cultural and artistic growth.

In contrast to those of Shanghai, the Yangzhou merchants involved themselves in cultural life to be taken seriously by circles of Confucian scholars, gentry, and officials. The merchants often invited poets, calligraphers, and painters to their beautiful gardens to establish their own reputation as people of good taste, and to elevate themselves into these circles.[1] For example, the salt merchant Lu Zhonghui established the "Hanjiang shishe" [Han River Poetry Society] in his Rangpu garden. Many literati, such as the scholars Li E, Quan Zhuwang, Hang Shijun, the painters Gao Xiang and Wang Shisheng, and the calligrapher Ding Jing, often gathered in his garden.[2] The gardens of other salt merchants, including the Ma brothers' Xiaolinglongshan Guan [Small and Exquisite Mountain Garden], Wang Tingzhang's Wang Yuan [Wang Garden], Cheng Mengxin's Di Yuan [Di Garden], Zheng Xiaru's Xiu Yuan [Xiu Garden], were also places the literati often met.[3] In organizing this kind of scholarly gathering, the merchants developed relationships with painters and calligraphers.

Art patronage in Shanghai continued the Yangzhou tradition in certain respects, that is, the Shanghai merchants, like their counterparts in the previous century, not only managed the local economy, but also involved themselves deeply in many aspects of cultural life. Shanghai merchants, like those in Yangzhou, were the major patrons of art in the city, but the relationship between merchants and artists in Shanghai did not develop in the same way as in Yangzhou. By the late nineteenth century, the scholar-officials had lost most of their status because wealthy merchants could purchase high positions, without having to pass the imperial examinations.[4] With the arrival of commercialism, many officials engaged in trade, and found that business in the city was the quickest way of getting rich.[5] With the declining importance of scholars, the boundary between the scholar-official and the merchant almost disappeared.[6] On the other hand, treaty-port industry and commerce, with its foreign companies and banks, further affected the role of Chinese workers, especially in Shanghai. Relying on the foreigners' extraterritorial power, Chinese who worked for these companies and banks formed a new, powerful social class, and lived in luxury as if they were nobility.[7] Among the newly prosperous merchants, there were many who were enthusiastic art connoisseurs and collectors, yet "even greater numbers of social climbers who mingled with the men of letters and posed as art lovers, spending huge amounts of money purchasing art without any true knowledge or appreciation of the works."[8]

Shanjianzhuang: Art Shops

There is little evidence that Shanghai merchants, unlike successful merchants in earlier times, needed to gain esteem by buying social position. They did not use money to establish direct relationships with literati or artists in order to enter scholar-gentry-official circles, as Yangzhou merchants had done. As for the patronage of art, they seemed to depend much more on an increasingly anonymous art market.

Their interest in acquiring culture resulted in the opening of many antique and art shops to collect and sell antiques, paintings, and calligraphies. A modern Western-style art gallery system never took hold in China, but the fan shops and other Chinese-style art shops in Shanghai were apparently new and distinctly modern developments. Although such shops did not entirely replace the three major traditional modes of acquiring a painting—direct contact between patron and artist, an indirect approach made through a mutual friend or other intermediary, and sponsorship of a resident painter—nevertheless, they absorbed the second and third of these functions, serving as both nonexclusive agent and place of lodging for the artist.[9] Fan shops offered clients easy places to buy a painting, free of the stresses of personal obligation involved in many premodern transactions. At the same time, they helped establish the artist's fame and price structure and thus also a celebrity that might lead to direct business between patrons and artists.

By the first year of the Xuantong reign (1909), there were as many as 109 art shops registered in the *Shanghai huashanghang minglu* [Record of Shanghai Chinese companies]. The earliest fan shop to be opened in Shanghai may have been the Manyunge [Silken Cloud Pavilion] on Jiujiang Road.[10] During the Tongzhi reign (1862–74), there were more than a dozen fan shops, mounting shops, and antique shops in business. Among them were Guxiangshi [Chamber of Fragrant Antiquity], Qinglianshi [Chamber of Blue Lotus], Jinruntang [Luxuriant Hall], Yilantang [Orchid Hall], Lihuatang [Magnificent Hall], Xihongtang [Hall of Sporting Wild Geese], Feiyunge [Flying Cloud Pavilion], Laotongchun [Evergreen Hall], and Deyuelou [Moon-Possessing Tower]. At least twenty-five shops were established in the Guangxu reign (1875–1908), including Jiuhuatang [Hall of Nine Splendors] (fig. 1), Liyunge [Pavilion of Glorious Clouds], Duoyunxuan [Cloud Blossom Studio], and Wangxingji [Wangxing Fan Shop]. According to a guide book written by Ge Yuanxun in 1876, "Guxiangshi, Manyunge, Lihuatang, and Jinruntang were the best in the foreign concessions, and Deyuelou, Feiyunge, and Laotongchun were famous in the old city."[11]

Shanghai, in which there were few artists before, suddenly became a vitally strategic place for art activity and the cultural center of southern China. It attracted the attention of artists who were not refugees but professionals in search of active consumers. The Qing writer Zhang Mingke recorded in his *Hansongge tanyi suolu* [Essays discussing art from the Cold Pine Pavilion]: "Since the ban on maritime trade was removed, prosperous trade became typical of Shanghai. The people who lived on their painting all came here and tried to sell their works."[12] Artists who moved into Shanghai outnumbered the natives. Among the more than six hundred artists whose names were recorded in the authoritative *Haishang molin* by Yang Yi for the late Qing period, at least 338 came from other provinces.[13]

For those newcomers who depended for their living on painting but had yet to make their names, the most urgent thing when they arrived in the new metropolis might be their basic needs, especially lodging and food. Such artists were largely unfamiliar with their surroundings and the local populace. To accept someone's hospitality and to serve as a private artist-in-residence was not new for impoverished Chinese artists. As James

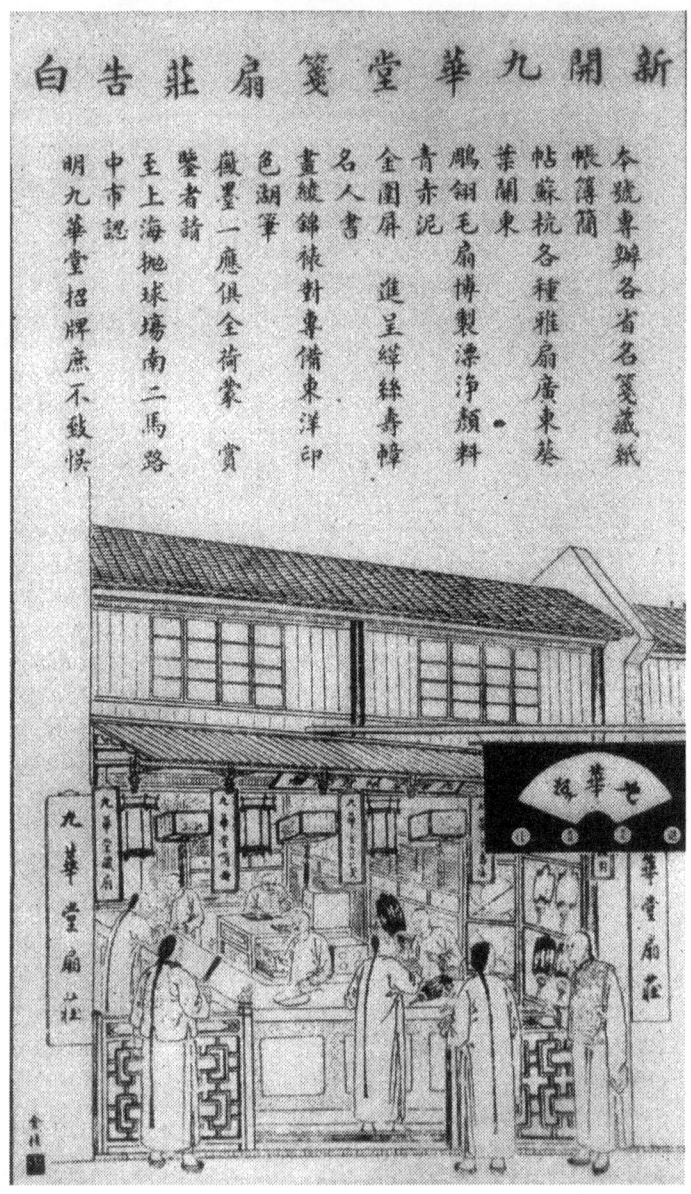

Fig. 1. Jin Gui, 1889 advertisement for the Jiuhuatang letter paper and fan shop. After *Dianshizhai huabao* (1897; reprint, Guangzhou: Guangdong renmin chubanshe, 1983), 2:736.

Cahill has described, accounts of painters spending periods in residence with a patron begin as far back as the early Song period, and include many famous names, such as Guo Xi and Yi Yuanji of the Song, Zhou Chen, Qiu Ying, and Tang Yin of the Ming, and Wang Shimin and Wang Hui of the Qing Dynasties.[14] But in late Qing Shanghai, instead of individual patrons, some newly established art stores and fan shops, presumably the mediator between artists and patrons, served as venues for artists to make a living and build their reputations. They offered food and lodging to those impoverished newcomers, as well as steady commissions or consignment opportunities. For example, when Pu Hua (1830–1911) arrived in Shanghai from Jiaxing, he became an artist-in-residence at the fan shop Xihongtang, working during the day and lodging in the upper story of the shop at night.[15] When Ren Bonian (1840–1896), one of the most important Shanghai School artists, arrived in Shanghai in 1868, the price of his paintings was quite low. In Zheng Yimei's *Yishu sanye* [Art jottings], it is said that Ren Bonian only earned three *jiao* for a fan painting, which would have made it impossible for Ren Bonian to support his family.[16] With the aid of Hu Gongshou (1823–86), an authority in Shanghai painting circles, and with strong support from merchant society, Ren Bonian entered the fan shop Guxiangshi as one of its artists-in-residence. The shop provided him painting supplies and steady commissions. Through the help of the fan shop Guxiangshi, Ren Bonian's art began to be appreciated by many patrons, especially the wealthy Cantonese merchants who comprised the majority of the Bankers' Society membership. These Cantonese patrons later became the most important promoters of Ren's art and spread his name widely.[17] Later Ren Bonian got to know many famous merchants, such as the owner of the art shop Jiuhuatang, Zhu Jingtang, and the banker Tao Junxuan (fig. 2). Even after he became one of the most famous painters in Shanghai, every year Ren Bonian would return to Guxiangshi to paint several paintings for the owner to repay the hospitality and kindness he received early in his career.[18]

Kinder fan shop owners were willing to go even a step further to help the artists out of their difficult predicaments. When young Zhang Daqian (1899–1983) went to Shanghai in 1919 to seek his career, he wanted to learn calligraphy. However, he was unsuccessful at finding a good teacher in this unfamiliar place. It was only through Duoyunxuan's introduction that he came to study calligraphy and poetry under the famous calligrapher and painter Zeng Xi (1861–1931). In this case, Duoyunxuan played a crucial role in the development of this artist.[19] Such practices of art dealers promoted not only individual paintings but the painters' careers.

These shops also set the prices for artworks. The relationship between artists and patrons was more than ever straightforwardly commercial, as

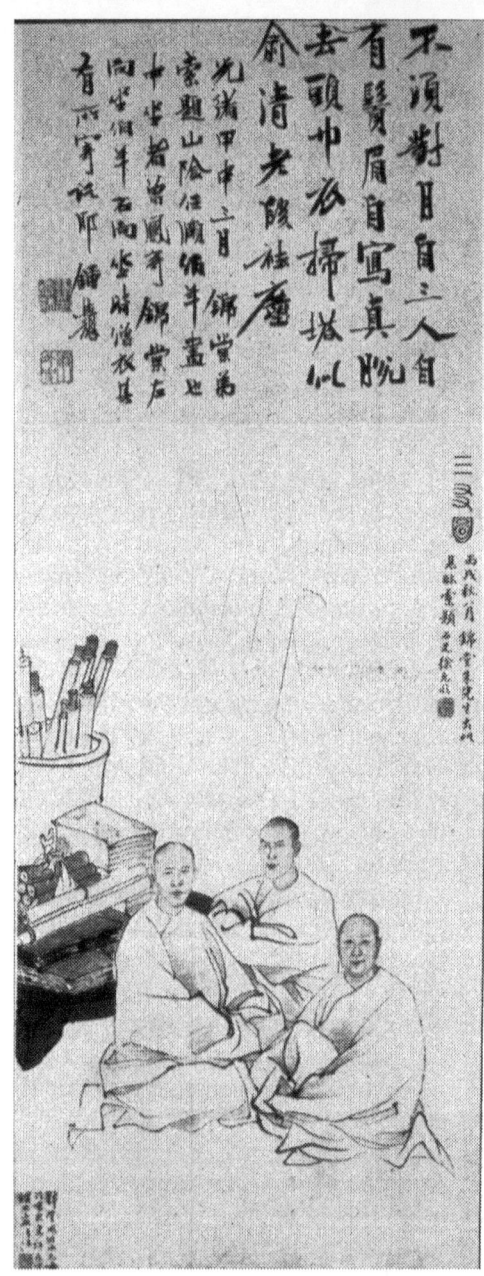

Fig. 2. Ren Yi, *Three Friends: Self-Portrait with Zeng Fengji and Zhu Jintang*, dated 1884. Hanging scroll, ink and color on paper. Palace Museum, Beijing. After Shan Guoqiang, *Ren Bonian* (Taibei: Taiwan Mac, 1995), 89.

Xugu stated in one of his poems: "In my leisure time [I] write three thousand sheets [of paintings], with which I beg my bread."[20] In this sense,
both patron and artist became much more independent. Undeniably, the
Western concept of market value influenced the cultural life of Shanghai
and the buying and selling of paintings.

New Patrons

Shanghai painters' patrons were not limited to Shanghai. Because Shanghai became the center of international trade, many merchants came from
southern China and Japan. These merchants also became important patrons of Shanghai painting. The "big merchants from Min [Fujian] and
Yue [Guangdong]" clustered in the eastern part of the city's port area.[21]
    A letter written by a Suzhou calligrapher Li Hongyi (1831–1885) to
painter Gu Yun (1835–1896) indicated that French buyers started to collect his paintings in the Shanghai area during the 1880s.[22] The Japanese
tradesmen, however, might have been the earliest foreign buyers in the
art market of Shanghai.[23] As early as 1872, many Shanghai artists, such
as Zhang Xiong (1803–1886), Zhu Cheng (1826–1900), Hu Gongshou, and
Ren Bonian, became quite famous among Japanese who resided in the
city.[24] According to a Japanese source, in the fortieth year of the Meiji reign
(1907), there were only four Japanese artists, and sixty Japanese bookstore
and art-supply merchants in Shanghai; but by the fourth year of the Taisho
reign (1915), the number of Japanese dealing with art in the city rapidly
increased to hundreds, including fifty-three artists and two hundred antique shop owners.[25] Their involvement in buying art in Shanghai was also
noted by Yang Yi in his *Haishang molin*:

> Xu Fangzeng, a native of Pinghu, lived in Shanghai in the early
> Tongzhi period (1861–74). He was good at clerical script callig-
> raphy and copied Han stele script everyday; the Japanese were
> wildly enthusiastic about his calligraphy, bought a great many to
> take back to Japan.[26]

In the twenty-sixth year of the Guangxu reign (1900), the Japanese
Tanaka Yasutaro, owner of the art shop Bunkyudo in Tokyo, and calligrapher and seal carver Kawai Senrō (1871–1945) came to Shanghai and were
introduced by Luo Zhenyu (1866–1940) and Wang Kangnian (1860–1911)
to Shanghai painter Wu Changshi (1844–1927; fig. 3).[27] In 1903, Nagao
Uzan came to Shanghai and worked in Shanghai Commercial Publishers
as editor and translator. He was introduced to Wu Changshi by Matsuzaki

Tazuo, a Japanese dealer in Shanghai. Both Kawai Senrō and Nagao Uzan became the earliest foreign members of Xiling Yinshe [Xiling Seal Carving Society] when it was established in 1904. Wang Yiting (1867–1938) also introduced many Japanese patrons to Wu Changshi, including Mizuno Sobai in 1910.[28] Moreover, the Japanese restaurant Musaen (Liusanyuan) in Shanghai was where Wu Changshi, Wang Yiting, Zhu Zongyuan, and other Shanghai painters often gathered. Through the owner of the restaurant, Shiroishi Musaro, an admirer of Wu Changshi, many Japanese, among them Tomioka Tessai (1836–1924), Nakamura Fuori (1866–1943), Naito Konan, Saionji Kobo, and Tanaka Yasutaro, bought Wu's painting and calligraphy. They organized several exhibitions for him in Tokyo, Osaka, and Nagasaki, spreading Wu's name in Japan.[29]

Besides Japanese patrons, many Koreans also admired Wu Changshi's art. It is said that during the early 1910s, Wu Changshi carved more than three hundred seals for a Korean patron.[30]

Painting Societies

Although the gatherings of painters held in eighteenth-century Yangzhou were informal and intended for exchanging painting skills and making friendly contacts, the commercial dynamic in Shanghai gradually transformed painting groups into something like guilds. Few characteristics of the scholar-official ideal remained by the end of the Qing dynasty as the artists coordinated their sales and commercial activities for mutual benefit. From 1839 to 1911, at least eleven formally organized painting societies were established in Shanghai.[31]

In the early and mid-nineteenth century there were several active painting clubs in Shanghai to which professional painters belonged, but documentation for any commercial activity has not yet been found. Xiaopenglai shuhuahui was established by Jiang Baoling (1781–1841) in the old town of Shanghai in 1839, and attracted many artists who were active in the city, including Li Yunjia, Fei Danxu (1801–1850), and Yao Xie (1805–1864).[32]

In 1851 the Pinghuashe (Duckweed Flower Club) was established in the Guanwangmiao (Temple of the Lord Guan) in the western part of the city by Wu Zonglin. The activities of the society were documented in a colophon of 1864 by Wu Zonglin in 1864 on the now-lost painting "The Elegant Gathering of the Pinghuashe," which was painted by members Qian Huian (1833–1911), Wang Li (1813–1879), and Bao Dong (active 1849–1866).[33]

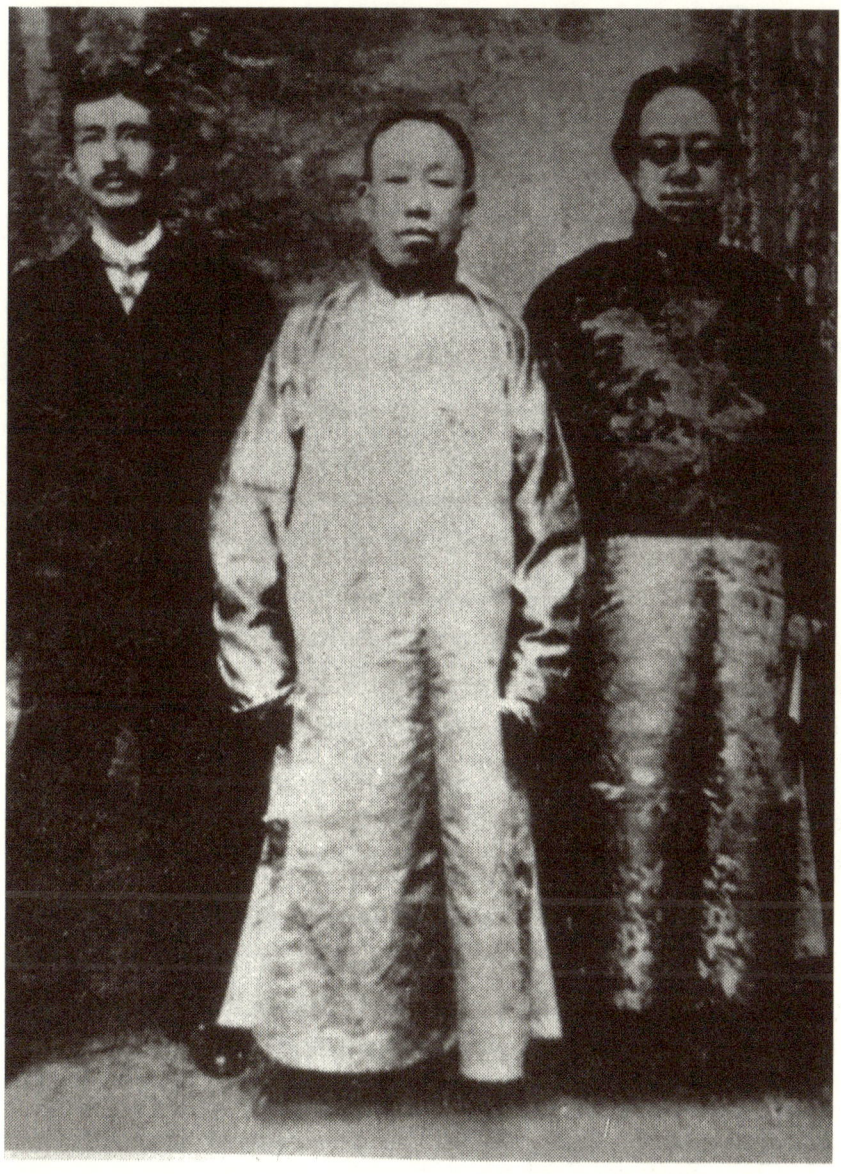

Fig. 3. Anonymous, photograph of Kawai Senrō (1871–1945), Wu Chang-shi (1844–1927), and Wu Cangkan (1876–1927; left to right). After *Huiyi Wu Changshi* (Shanghai: Shanghai renmin meishu chubanshe, 1986), 58.

By the second half of the century, the commercial function of the societies became more evident. Feidange shuhuahui was active in the old town of Shanghai during the Tongzhi and Guangxu reigns (1862–1908) at the original site of the Deyuelou Fanshop in the Yu Garden (fig. 4). The members of the society included almost all famous Shanghai painters of the time, such as Gai Qi, Hu Gongshou, Ren Xiong, Ren Xun, Ren Bonian, Zhang Xiong, Pu Hua, and Wu Changshi. Yin Baohe, the son of the fanshop owner, was a member of the group, and he turned over the Deyuelou building to the club, which used it to meet and sell their paintings. It also provided lodgings to painters from other places who wished to temporarily stay in Shanghai. Ren Bonian is believed to have stayed there frequently even before he permanently settled in Shanghai in 1868.[34]

The Seal-carving, Calligraphy, and Painting Institute of Haishang Tijinguan (The Tijin hall of Shanghai), established in the 1890s, set the price of paintings for members and provided a place where members could study and trade old paintings and antiques. It is said that more than one hundred painters, calligraphers, and seal carvers joined the group. Wang Xun (d. 1915), Wu Changshi, Ha Shaofu, and Wang Yiting were its successive directors.

A decade later, the Yuyuan shuhua shanhui (The Yu Garden Calligraphy and Painting Charitable Society) was founded in 1908 at Deyuelou. This artistic and literary group soon became a quasi-commercial cooperative organization, with a formal, written charter that stipulated that all work, except calligraphy, be collaborative. It accepted on its members' behalf public commissions and orders for art, and the members shared the profits. The name of the group, Calligraphy and Painting Charitable Society, was selected because half the price of work sold would be returned to the artists, the other half would be invested in a Chinese-style bank (qianzhuang), with the interest used for charitable purpose.[35] Its directors included Qian Huian, Gao Yong, Yang Baoguang, Ma Ruixi, Shen Xinhai, Wang Yiting, and Wang Xun. Many important Shanghai School painters, such as Wu Changshi, participated throughout their lives in these art societies' activities, which came, in the twentieth century, to include group exhibitions.[36] This phenomenon reflected the artists' self-coordination to set the prices of Shanghai School art, and demonstrated the power of self-help. These professional painters realized their value not only as individuals but as a group.

The changes in patronage and in the livelihood of artists were reflected in their artistic productions. First, their subject matter shifted to include more themes from popular culture. Along with the reduction of the power of the scholar-official class, landscape painting, which was regarded as the

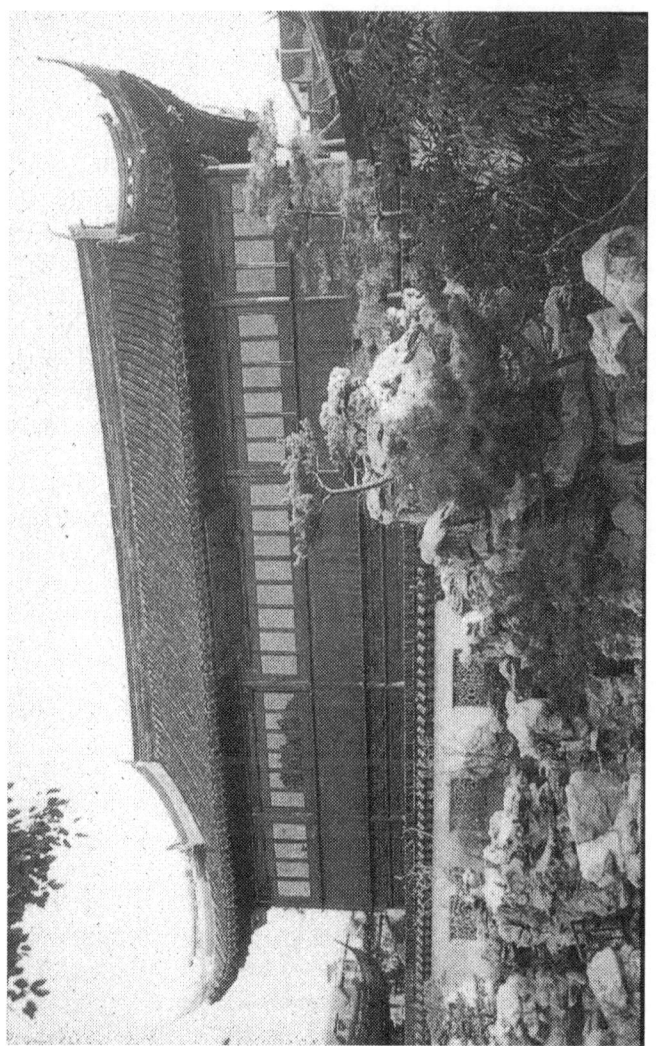

Fig. 4. Anonymous, photograph of Deyuelou in the Yu garden of the old Chinese city, Shanghai. After *Survey of Shanghai, 1840s–1940s* (Shanghai: Shanghai renmin meishu chubanshe, 1994), 30.

highest category of Chinese painting by most literati, also lost its attraction. Actually, these trends emerged first in Yangzhou School painting, but in the Shanghai School became much more obvious.[37] Therefore, the subjects chosen by most Shanghai painters were primarily figures and birds & flowers, with only occasional painting of landscapes.

Conclusion

This paper focuses on two institutional structures as they developed in the art world of late Qing Shanghai, the painting society and the shanjianzhuang, or as we prefer to call it, the art shop. The new types of painting societies that emerged during the late nineteenth century, with their charters, price lists, and sales to the new merchant elite, were an organized response to the needs of professionalized painters living in this new modern metropolis, and reflected the strong influence of a Western-oriented modernization in both their organizational and economic structures. Similarly, the art shops of late nineteenth century Shanghai transformed earlier kinds of trade in art into commercial structures that rivaled modern Western galleries. They set the prices for artists' work, took commissions and received orders from buyers, and sold art by displaying it in their shops. They provided anonymous buyers, including foreigners who existed outside any previously known Chinese social structure, easy access to the market of contemporary painting.

Although we are arguing for the modernity of these innovations, it is important to recognize that they nevertheless developed within a cultural continuum, and that these shops retained many local or traditional aspects. The social pattern of the artist living in residence at the art shop, for example, is a unique combination of premodern conventions of private patronage and the new commercial structure. Similarly, while the art shops offered a public space for an anonymous, and even foreign, clientele, they continued to provide necessary goods and services to the Chinese public. The art shops mounted paintings and calligraphy, decorated fans, and printed elaborately decorated stationary, sometimes to special order. They did a thriving business in writing brushes, ink cakes, and ink stones, as well as in a variety of other supplies for painting and calligraphy. We thus find that while the old elites were greatly transformed by the new situations; the new elites were more influenced by existing traditions than might first be assumed.

The modernity reflected in late Qing Shanghai may be summed up in theoretical terms by Shmuel N. Eisenstadt and Wolfgang Schluchter: "The cultural codes of modernity have not been shaped by the evolutionary potentialities of societies, nor by the natural unfolding of their traditions, nor even by their placement in a new international setting. Rather, they have been shaped by the continuous interaction between the cultural codes of these societies and their exposure to new internal and external challenges."[38]

Notes

1 See Ginger Cheng-chi Hsu, *The Eccentric Painters of Yangzhou* (New York: China House Gallery, China Institute in America, 1990); "Merchant Patronage of the Eighteenth Century Yangchou Painting," in *Artists and Patrons*, 215–22 (intro., n. 8); "Patronage and the Economic Life of the Artist in Eighteenth Century Yangchow Painting" (PhD diss., University of California, Berkeley, 1987).

2 Wang Shisheng, *Caolin ji* [Collections from the grove], n.d.

3 An Qi, *Moyuan huiguan: Duanfang xu* [The survey of calligraphies and paintings: The preface of Duanfang]; *Yangzhou huafang lu* [Records of Yangzhou painters] (repr., Taipei: Xuehai, 1969), 406. Among those gardens, Xiaolinglongshan guan of the Ma brothers, Ma Yueguan and Ma Yuelu, was most popular.

4 According to *Man Han wenwu guansheng mincilu* [Index of Manchurian and Han civil and military officials], in the third year of Jiaqing reign (1798), there were more than one thousand four hundred lower rank official positions in the capital and three thousand positions at local levels purchased by the rich. See Liu Guangjing, *Jingshi sixiang yu xinxing hangye* [New ideas of business and new professions] (Taipei: Lianjing, 1990), 302–3.

5 Xiao Yisan, *Qingdai tongshi* [The general history of the Qing dynasty] (Taipei: Taiwan Shangwu yinshuguan, 1980), 3:1607.

6 Yu Ying-shih, *Zhongguo jinshi zongjiao lunli yu shangren jingsheng* [Religious principles and merchants' consciousness in modern China] (Taipei: Lianjing, 1992), 106.

7 Xiao Yisan, *Qingdai tongshi*, 3:1607.

8 Wang Tao, *Yingruan zazhi* [A collection of jottings on miscellaneous subjects relating to Shanghai] (prefaced in 1876; repr., Shanghai: Shanghai guji chubanshe, 1995), 4:73.

9 See James Cahill's discussion of the painter's livelihood in *The Painter's Practice* (New York: Columbia University Press, 1994), 32–70.

10 *Ming Qing shuhuajia chidu* (Shanghai: Shanghai shudian, 1996), 2:378. Here I quote from Zheng Wei's unpublished paper, "A Record of Old Shanghai Fan Shops, from 1821–1960." Also see *Shenbao*, March 25, 1872 and September 26, 1880.

11 Ge Yuanxun, *Huyou zaji* [The record of flourishing Shanghai], preface dated 1876, chap. 2, p. 2.

12 (Preface dated 1908; repr., Shanghai: Shanghai People's Fine Arts Publishing House), 6:150.

13 Yang Yi, *Haishang molin* [Shanghai's forest of ink], a collection of biographical notes on Shanghai artists, issued in at least three editions, preface 1919, first supplement 1921, second supplement 1928 (repr., Shanghai: Shanghai

guji chubanshe, 1989), juan. 3, pp. 55–90, "Yuxian."

14 Cahill, *Painter's Practice*, 67.

15 According to the interview with Peng Renpu, who worked for Jiuhuatang, Duoyunxuan, and other fan shops during the first half of the century conducted by Zheng Wei. Here I quote from Zheng Wei's unpublished article, "A Record of Old Shanghai Fan Shops from 1821–1960."

16 In *Zheng Yimei xuanji* [Selected writings of Zheng Yimei] (Ha'erbin: Heilongjiang renmin chubanshe, 1991), 3:20.

17 Zhu Yin, "Rediscovery of Ren Bonian's historical documents," *Mingjia hanmo* 28.5 (1992): 104; the fact was also mentioned by Chen Banding, whose oral memoir was recorded by Ning Ren in "Ren Bonian he ta de hua" [Ren Bonian and his painting], *Meishu* (May 1957): 42–44.

18 See the inscription written by Ren Yi on his painting of 1885, which is collected in Chicago Institute of Art. Shanghai collector Qian Jingtang also heard same story from Ren Jin (1881–1930), Ren Bonian's son. See Ding Xiyuan, *Ren Bonian: nianpu, lunwen, zhencun, zuopin* [Ren Bonian: chronology, thesis, photographs and inscriptions, works] (Shanghai: Shanghai shuhua chubanshe, 1989), 65.

19 Yan Ci, *Duoyunxuan shihua* [A brief history of Duoyunxuan] (Changchun: Jilin Sheying Chubanshe, 1997), 6.

20 Xue Yongnian. "Yangzhou Baguai he Haipai de Huihua Yishu" [The Painting of the Yangzhou and Shanghai School], in *The Great Treasures of Chinese Fine Arts Painting* (Shanghai: Shanghai People's Fine Arts Publishing House, 1988), 11:13.

21 Wang Tao, *Yingruan Zazhi*, preface dated 1853, 1:9 (n. 8 above).

22 Unpublished correspondence between Li Hongyi and Gu Yun, collection of Shanghai Library.

23 Chin Shunshin, *Chugoku gajin den* [Biographical notes of Chinese painters] (Tokyo: Shinjosha, 1984), 182.

24 Tsuruta Takeyoshi, "Raipaku gajin kenkyu: ron O En" [A study on foreign painter Wang Yin], *Bijutsu Kenkyu*, no. 319, p. 68.

25 *Zai Shina honbojin shinsei kairon* [A brief report of the development of Japanese in China], Nihon Gaimusho Tsushokyoku, November of the fourth year of the Taisho reign (1915). Here I quote from Ding Xiyuan, "New Space: The Unity of Chinese and Western Art," *Zhongguohua Yanjiu*, no. 7, p. 104.

26 Juan. 3, p. 66 (n. 13 above), biographical notes on Xu Fangzeng.

27 Interview with Wu Changye, grandson of Wu Changshi, by the author in August 1994, and October 1995 in Shanghai; also see Zhang Zhengwei, "Wu Changshi de huaping yu renping" [The characteristics of Wu Changshi's painting and personality], in *Wu Changshi zuoping ji, huihua* [Works of Wu Changshi, painting], Shanghai: Shanghai renmin meishu chubanshe, 1984, n.p.; Zhu Guantian, "Wu Changshi yu riben youren zhi jiaoyou" [The friendship between Wu Changshi and his Japanese friends], in *Huiyi Wu Changshi* [Memory of Wu Changshi] (Shanghai: Shanghai renmin meishu chubanshe, 1986), 69–71; Ding Xiyuan, "Wu Changshi nianbiao" [Chronicle of Wu Changshi], in *Mingjia hanmo* 38, p. 70. Luo Zhengyu was a calligrapher and seal carver. Wang Kangnian was a famous newspaper publisher in the late Qing period and published *Shiwu bao* in Shanghai and *Chuyan bao* in Beijing.

28 Zhang Zhengwei (see previous note); Ding Xiyuan, "Wu Changshi

nianbiao," 75; Zhu Guantian, "Wu Changshi yu Riben," 72.

29 Interview with Wu Changye, grandson of Wu Changshi, by the author in August 1994, and October 1995 in Shanghai; and also see Zhu Guantian, "Wu Changshi yu riben," 73–75.

30 Zheng Yimei, "Wu Changshi wangshi" [The past of Wu Changshi], in *Yihai yishao* [A scoop from the sea of art] (Tianjin: Tianjin guji chubanshe, 1994), 102.

31 See *Zhongguo meishu nianjian* [The yearbook of Chinese art, 1947] (Shanghai: Shanghai shi wenhua yundong weiyuanhui, 1948). *Shiliao* [Historical documents], 2–3; Xu Zhihao, *Zhongguo meishu shetuan manlu* [Records of Chinese art societies and groups] (Shanghai: Shanghai shuhua chubanshe, 1994), 1–22.

32 Yang Yi, *Haishang molin*, juan. 3, p. 5b (n. 13 above; reprint of 1897, Shanghai: Yuyuan shuhua shanhui), biographical notes on Jiang Baoling; Xu Zhihao, *Zhongguo meishu shetuan manlu*, 3–4.

33 Yang Yi, *Haishang molin*, juan. 3, 61–62, biographical notes on Wu Zonglin.

34 Xu Zhihao, *Zhongguo meishu shetuan manlu*, 7.

35 Yang Yi, *Haishang molin*, juan. 3, pp. 72–74, biographical notes on Qian Huian.

36 Unpublished correspondence between Wang Yiting and Ha Shaofu, collection of Shanghai Library.

37 See Ginger Cheng-chi Hsu, "Merchant Patronage,", 215–22 (n. 1 above).

38 "Introduction: Paths to Early Modernities—A Comparative View," *Daedalus* 127.3 (Summer 1998): 5.

2
Uncommon Themes and Uncommon Subject Matters in Ren Xiong's Album after Poems by Yao Xie

Britta Erickson

A mermaid riding a rainbow, refined scholars brewing tea, the Madonna and child, soldiers classed as "drunkards, gamblers, and smugglers," figures impaled in hell, elegant court ladies playing on a swing: all of these strange and wonderful personages appear together in the *Album after Poems by Yao Xie* [Yao Xie shi yi tu ce], painted by Ren Xiong (1823–1857) in 1851. Not only are the subjects of this album's one hundred and twenty leaves varied and unusual, so too are the artist's styles and techniques. The variety of subject matter and style assembled in the album is absolutely unprecedented in the history of Chinese painting. Depicting such a wide range of subjects did not become a regular feature in Chinese visual culture until the pictorial magazine *Dianshizhai huabao* began publication in Shanghai in 1884. Late-nineteenth-century Shanghai witnessed an increase in the modes of image production due to the import of photography and lithography from the West. Paralleling this, the range of subjects considered worthy of depiction greatly expanded. Ren Xiong's *Album after Poems by Yao Xie* seemingly presages such fin de siécle developments.

How did Ren Xiong come to create such an unusual and all-embracing work of art? There was a happy confluence of circumstances. First, the artist was by nature daring and unconventional. Second, in 1851 he was eager to learn and embrace the new, having recently abandoned a stifling apprenticeship. Third, the patron for whom he painted the album, Yao Xie, pushed him toward new subjects and opened his eyes to new techniques and compositions.

Ren Xiong's Unconventional Beginnings and Personality

Besides possessing a high degree of personal creativity and technical ability, Ren Xiong was determined and unconventional. His artistic career began in his native Xiaoshan with the study of portrait painting under the town instructor, but he soon found this genre's restrictions untenable. As Chen Dingshan (1897–1989) relates in his book of reminiscences, "From the town's instructor Ren Xiong studied portraiture, commonly known as 'buying an ancestor.' However, when he was young, he liked to toy with things, so his paintings never stayed within the norm. They would show someone missing a leg, or blind in one eye, lacking a limb, with a cleft palate, or any of a hundred kinds of uglinesses or peculiar manifestations. The town instructor became angry and drove him away, and Ren Xiong fled."[1] Thus, as a young man the artist shed the constraints of life in his hometown, leaving it for a riskier but more rewarding existence in the larger and more culturally active cities nearby. Although his education was incomplete, he learned quickly and was enthusiastically adopted into elevated artistic circles.

What do we know of Ren Xiong besides the bare facts of his existence? The various accounts of his personality and actions suggest that he had great mood swings and many admirable qualities, but also that he had a less attractive side. His friend, patron, and biographer, Zhou Xian (1820–1875), emphasized the talents he possessed appropriate for a literatus, such as archery, painting, epigraphy, composing and playing music, drinking, and tea connoisseurship. At the same time, he stressed Ren's physical nature, which led to his physical engagement—where possible—with the culturally elevated activities already mentioned, for example obtaining and working the raw materials to craft his qin and flute. According to Zhou, "He could ride swiftly on horseback; could draw a bow, letting the arrow fly in a flash to hit the target; and wrestled for sport. He was good at incisive painting and epigraphy. He could cut down a paulownia tree to make a qin, and cast iron to make flutes; he could play them, distinguishing all the various musical intervals, and could compose his own pieces for the qin."[2] Countering Zhou's praise for Ren's noble qualities, the publisher Wang Ling (dates unknown) noted negative traits such as Ren's arrogance, as related in his preface to Ren Xiong's illustrated book, *Biographies of Knights Errant* (1856): "Weichang [i.e., Ren Xiong] was eccentric and highly talented. He never followed fashion and was contemptuous of conventionality. People were angry with his arrogance, but were fond of his amazing technique in painting."[3] Ren's arrogance and unconventionality may have been part of a public persona that appealed to his patrons and associates; Wang Ling, for one, excused them as the foibles of an exceptionally talented man. Such characteristics frequently are attributed to geniuses, and indeed are part of the myth that has built up around Ren's early life.

The Creation of the Album after Poems by Yao Xie

Ren Xiong met Yao Xie, a renowned poet and intellectual with a high pro-file in Shanghai literary and artistic circles, in about 1850.[4] He stayed at Yao Xie's Ningbo residence, Great Plum Mountain Hall (Dameishanguan), for a portion of 1851. During that time he painted the *Album after Poems by Yao Xie*, completing it on the fifteenth day of the first month of the first year of the Xianfeng reign period (equivalent to February 15, 1851). In a lengthy inscription on the album, Ren describes the creation of the album:

> Living on the brush in Mingzhou, I have been residing at Mr. Yao's Great Plum Mountain Hall. Exchanging thoughts on epigraphy with my host, Fuzhuang [i.e., Yao Xie]; being very fond of Fu-zhuang's poetry, and Fuzhuang being very fond of my painting, it's like the blending of water and milk [i.e., perfect harmony]. In his leisure time, Fuzhuang himself would select a few lines, and hand them to me to illustrate. Making a sketch beneath the lamp and adding color upon arising in the morning, after two months I had completed one hundred and twenty leaves.[5]

According to the artist, the album was a cooperative venture: Yao Xie selected a line of his own verse as the subject for each leaf, and Ren re-sponded with a painting. Yao Xie thus imparted each album leaf's initial direction, and would have been responsible for the choice of some of the unusual subjects. He also injected political content into the album, by in-scribing lines of verse describing events of the Opium War, sometimes critical of the imperial army. The inscriptions on all one hundred and twenty leaves are excerpted from Yao Xie's own book of poetry *Fuzhuang shiwen* [The poetry of Fuzhuang (Yao Xie); 1848].[6]

Stylistically, the leaves in the *Album after Poems by Yao Xie* vary dra-matically, ranging from *gongbi* (detailed, fine line brushwork) to *xieyi* (ex-pressive brushwork) and *mogu* ("boneless"). The distribution of subject matter in the *Album after Poems by Yao Xie* is approximately as follows: twenty leaves of *shengui* (ghosts, spirits, and immortals), forty leaves of *renwu* (figures), twenty leaves of *funu* (female figures), twenty leaves of *fengjing* (scenery), and twenty leaves of *cao mu niao shou* (flora and fauna).[7] Ren Xiong's approach to the different themes is often refreshingly original: his genre scenes treat children and the lower classes with almost unprec-edented sympathy; he (at times) invests beautiful women with strength and individuality; and he infuses his bird and flower paintings with un-usual power by presenting the subject amid an arresting composition, or by employing jarring color schemes.

The Album: New Sources for Subjects and Styles

Ren Xiong's openness to new ideas is reflected in the likelihood that he was influenced by printed books, European illustrated books, Japanese paintings, and Japanese prints. He would have been first exposed to some of these sources by Yao Xie: one of the many advantages of residing at Yao's home was having the opportunity to study his collection of paintings and use his extensive library, renowned as comprising "tens of thousands of volumes all of which, if examined carefully, were edifying."[8]

The precisely rendered machines in such leaves from the *Album after Poems by Yao Xie* as "The white maiden and her loom" and "The Han women of the inner courtyard are playing on their private swing" suggest that Ren Xiong had consulted printed books employing detailed line drawings to draw such things. "The White Maiden and Her Loom" depicts a woman weaving on a large floor loom, the warp and weft, treadles, and heddle all clearly delineated. "The Han Women of the Inner Courtyard Are Playing on Their Private Swing" features an elaborately structured swing, capable of accommodating several women and suspended from the top of a rectangular framework. Both the loom and the swing are so detailed that it is clear the artist either was drawing on personal familiarity with such machines, or more probably was basing his paintings on other images he had seen. Because such detailed renderings of machines are unique to this album, Ren may have culled the images from prints he had seen in Yao Xie's library: books on the popular themes of plowing and weaving, for instance, featured illustrations of looms. Ren Xiong experimented with such detail just this once. Apparently, he was not interested enough to employ it later.

The leaf illustrating the line "The immortals decanting from above mete out the thick fluid, and upon hearing their cries, the fox spirit comes to pour a cup" is populated by an assemblage of strange beings, some with hairy bodies and a single, very long, leg, and others combining human, animal, and bird features in different ways. Such creatures are reminiscent of *Shanhai jing* [Classic of mountains and seas], with its numerous illustrations of peculiar hybrids, such as bird-people and bird-animals, and single-sided people (i.e., with but one arm and one leg). While we can safely assume that Yao Xie's library housed various standard publications such as *Shanhai jing*, we can also speculate as to what rarities he had assembled there. Clearly, Ren Xiong had access to European illustrated books, as evidenced by the leaf, "A woman with loosened hair [appears] like a comet, riding the rainbow of seduction" (fig. 1). The dominant features of this leaf are a rainbow—unprecedented in the history of Chinese art—and, perched atop, a woman swathed in drapery and holding her breast in a gesture of plenty, typical of sixteenth- or seventeenth-century European art. Another leaf includes the reworked image of the Madonna and child, bespeaking at least second- or thirdhand knowledge of European imagery.

Judging from the content of the *Album after Poems by Yao Xie*, we can surmise that Yao Xie had acquired one or more books printed with the illustrations of Katsushika Hokusai (1760–1849). Hokusai was a prolific book illustrator, whose numerous sketchbooks and drawing guides were woodblock-printed in relatively inexpensive editions, beginning in 1814 and 1812, respectively. While we can only guess the extent of Hokusai's influence on Ren Xiong, it should not be underestimated, and may range from general approaches to subject matter to specific ways of representing particular subjects. Ren Xiong's light-hearted scene of many goats frolicking on a wooded mountain side in "On a flat mountain ridge, a disorganized, simple-minded herd of goats is playing" (fig. 2) catalogs the different poses of goats, just as Hokusai depicted the many characteristic poses of horses in pages from his drawing guides. The same connection can be made between those of Hokusai's drawings that exemplify the many poses of human figures relaxing and Ren Xiong's album leaf "The men and women sit with their clothing stripped to a minimum, and the blind singer sets out his pottery gourd instrument," showing country people of all ages enjoying themselves as they relax under a vined lattice. An undated album leaf in the Shanghai Museum (fig. 3) links Ren Xiong particularly closely with Hokusai. It depicts a man astride a horse, the animal represented *en face*, very similar to the horse in Hokusai's *Bareki*, from 1817 (fig. 4).

Other probable sources for new subjects and styles in the *Album after Poems by Yao Xie* are Japanese paintings (note the puddled ink in "The gleaming conical-legged animal vessel and the wide-mouthed *fu* vessel together blaze and shine" [fig. 5]), and Japanese prints. "Behind the slender bird, the smoky kingfisher, the bits of straw are as numerous as the hairs on a rabbit" (fig. 6) is the leaf that most obviously reflects Japanese influence, with its striking background of parallel oblique lines (representing a bamboo blind).

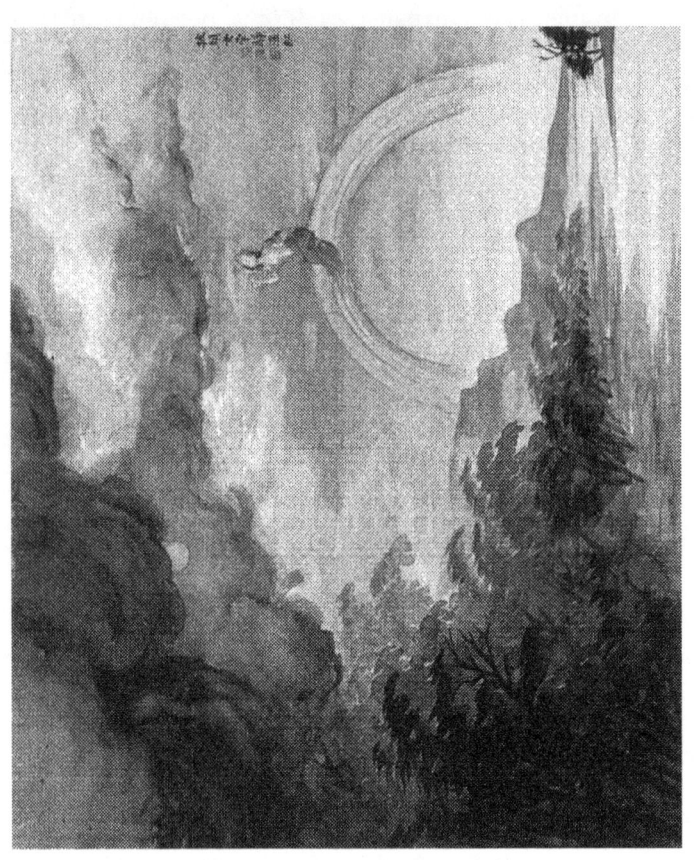

Fig. 1. "A woman with loosened hair [appears] like a comet, riding the rainbow of seduction." Ren Xiong. *Album after Poems by Yao Xie*, dated 1851. Ink and color on silk, 27.3 × 32.8 cm. Palace Museum, Beijing. After Julia F. Andrews and Kuiyi Shen, *A Century in Crisis: Modernity and Tradition in the Art of Twentieth-Century China* (New York: Guggenheim Museum Publications, 1998), catalogue number 3-4.h.

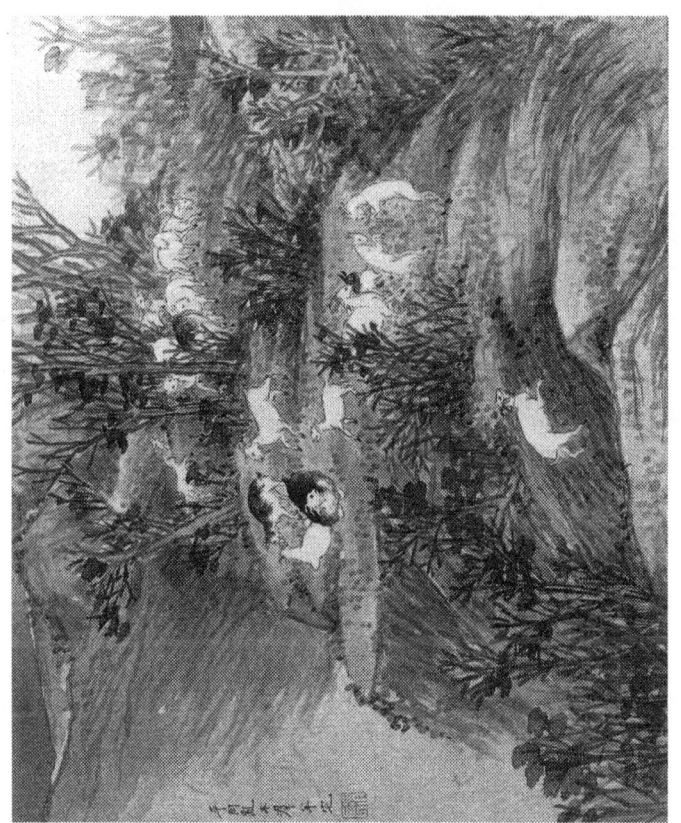

Fig. 2. "On a flat mountain ridge, a disorganized, simple-minded herd of goats is playing." Ren Xiong. *Album after Poems by Yao Xie*, dated 1851. Ink and color on silk, 27.3 × 32.8 cm. Palace Museum, Beijing. After *Haishang ming jia huihua* [Paintings by famous Shanghai artists] (Hong Kong: Commercial Press, 1997), plate 11.1.3.

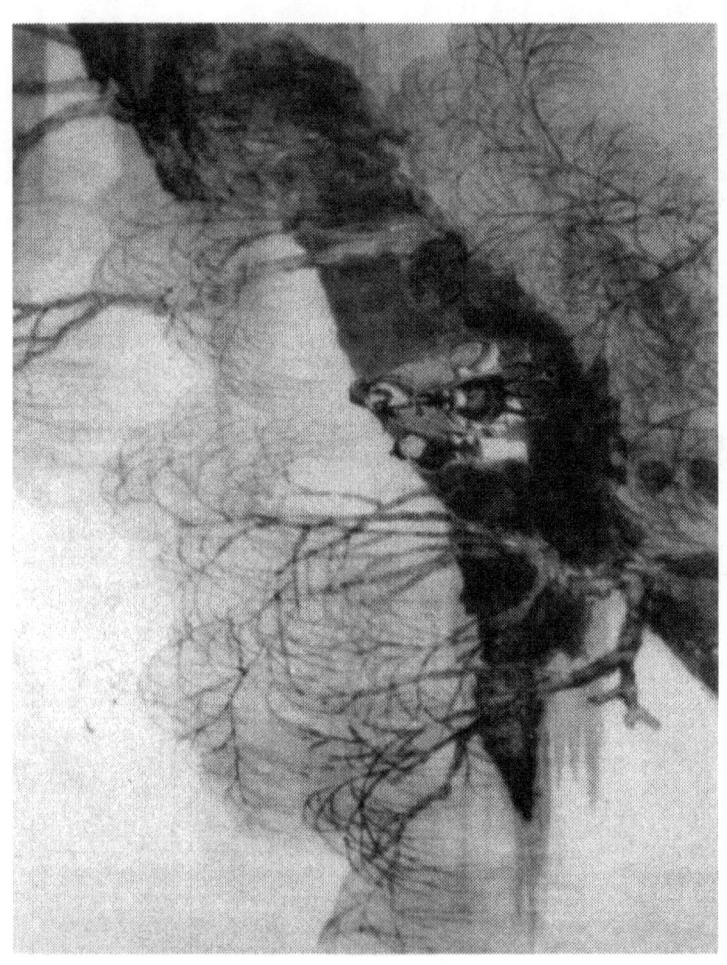

Fig. 3. Ren Xiong. *Album of Figures and Landscapes*, n.d. Ink and color on paper, 29.2 × 34.3 cm. Shanghai Museum. After *Ren Weichang renwu* [Figures by Ren Weichang], vol. 1 (Shanghai: Shen Xiu Book Society, 1930).

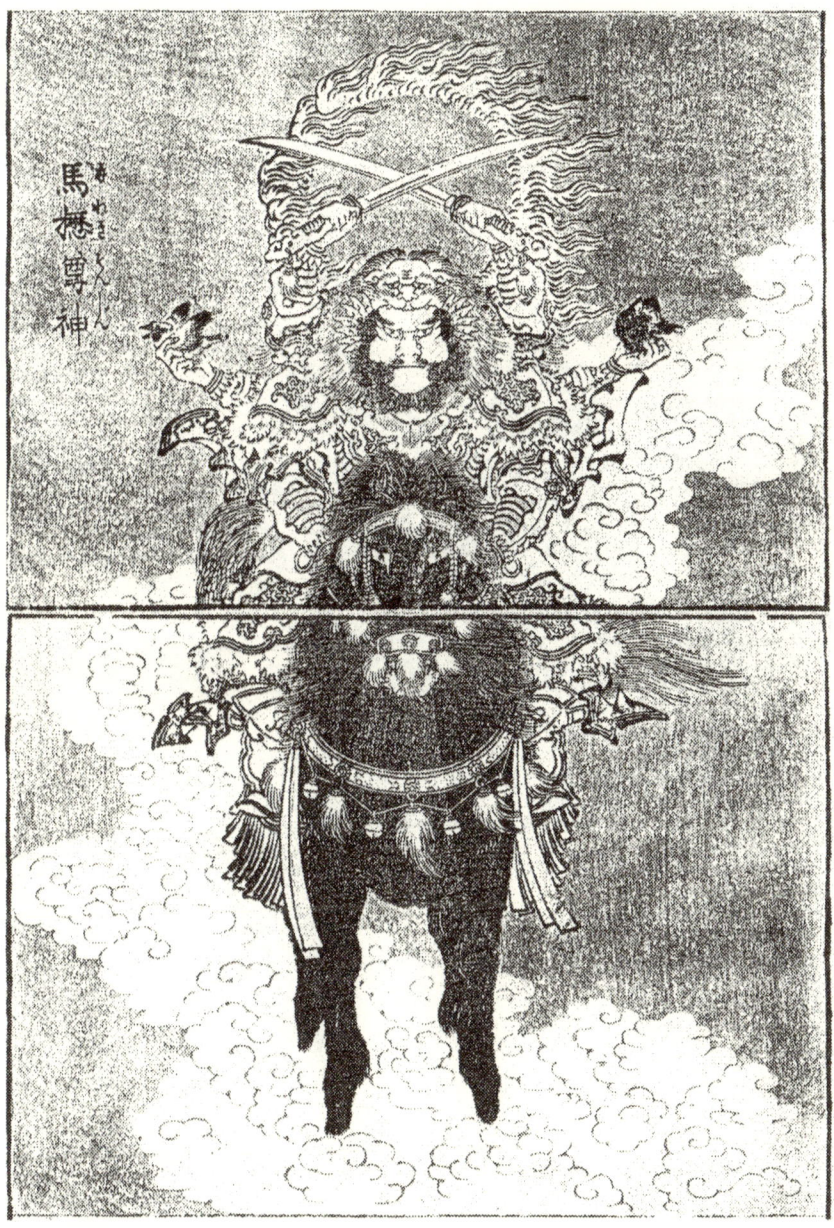

Fig. 4. Hokusai. *Bareki*, page from *Hokusai manga*, Series 6 (1817). After Richard Lane, *Hokusai Life and Work* (New York: E. P. Dutton, 1989), plate 141.

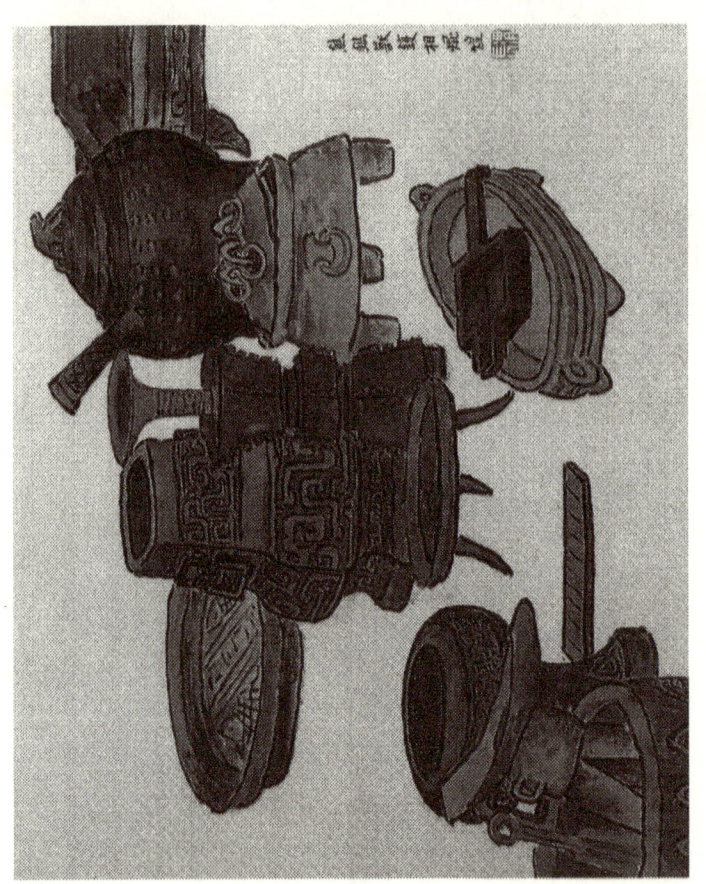

Fig. 5. "The gleaming conical-legged animal vessel and the wide-mouthed *fu* vessel together blaze and shine." Ren Xiong. *Album after Poems by Yao Xie*, dated 1851. Ink and color on silk, 27.3 × 32.8 cm. Palace Museum, Beijing. After *Haishang ming jia huihua*, plate 11.1.2.

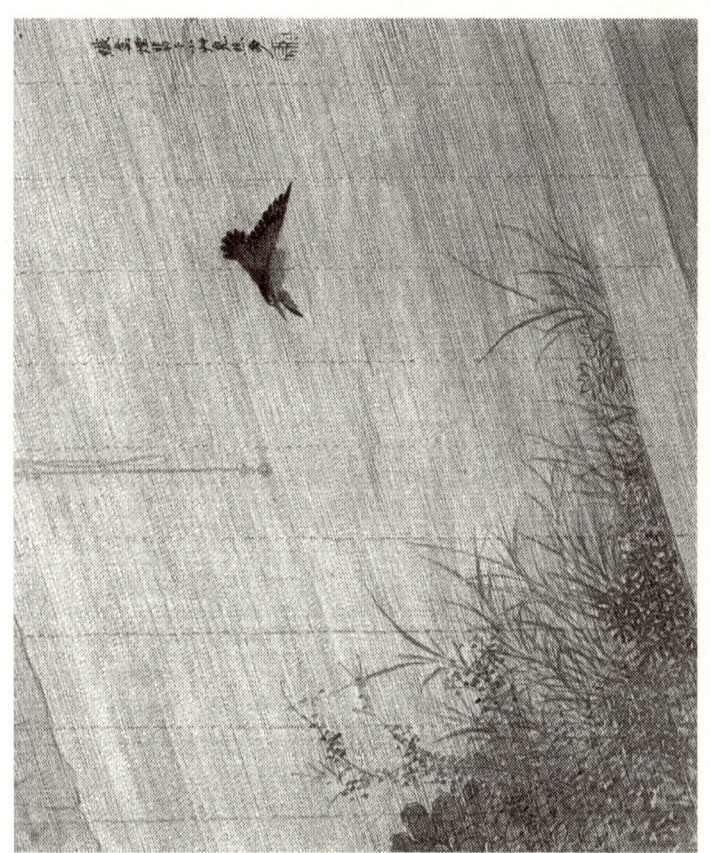

Fig. 6. "Behind the slender bird, the smoky kingfisher, the bits of straw are as numerous as the hairs on a rabbit." Ren Xiong. *Album after Poems by Yao Xie*, dated 1851. Ink and color on silk, 27.3 × 32.8 cm. Palace Museum, Beijing. After *A Century in Crisis*, catalogue number 3-2.b.

Uncommon Subject Matter: Still-Life Arrangements, Machines, and Exotic Ethnicities

Although many of the subjects appearing in the album are common throughout the history of Chinese painting, a few are not. Three subjects appearing in the *Album after Poems by Yao Xie* either are unique to the album or are unusually well represented there. These subjects—still-life arrangements, machines, and exotic ethnicities—were dictated by the lines of poetry, which indicates that they were of interest to Yao; however, they did not captivate Ren Xiong or they would have appeared elsewhere in his oeuvre. Nevertheless, the artist was challenged by these subjects and inspired to seek inventive solutions, particularly in the case of still-life assemblages.

Ren Xiong painted very few still-lifes. I know of just ten, including six hanging scrolls and four album leaves. Three of the album leaves belong to the *Album after Poems by Yao Xie*, and most of the other works similarly date from early in Ren's career. For the most part Ren's still-lifes are quite different from the occasional works in this genre that later Shanghai artists painted, and therefore cannot be seen as their direct precedents. The typical Shanghai School still-life portrays an assemblage of flowers or food; it conveys a felicitous message through widely understood symbolism, and perhaps balances the showy array with genteel accouterments, such as ancient bronzes or porcelains. Ren's still-lifes, however, focus on items redolent of gentility. "The gleaming conical-legged animal vessel and the wide-mouthed *fu* vessel together blaze and shine" portrays a group of ancient bronzes, and "An intricate display of food items including preserved vegetables and fruits: presenting the harvest as a gift makes for morally correct veneration" includes a bronze pitcher and some rolled-up scrolls, along with the vegetables and fruit called for by the inscription. "Alone at night, the trembling, fluttering shadows: the solitary lamp, this you know" contains a green lampstand with a burning wick placed behind a bowl of ink narcissus, emblem of purity. The titles of three of the other still-lifes Ren painted indicate the extent to which they, too, dwelt on scholarly accouterments and eschewed items of showy display: *Still Life with Teapot, Palm Fan, Vase, and Fly Whisk* (1848), *Plum Blossoms and Lamp* (1851), and *Yixing Teapot and Cup, Candle on a Bronze Stand, Rose and Mirror* (1852).[9] Two others, *Fragrant Bamboo Steamers* (1853), and *Fat Crabs, Beautiful Chrysanthemums, and a Jar of Wine* (1856), comprise everyday items, avoiding the vulgar without being as overtly genteel as earlier still-lifes by the artist.[10]

Ren Xiong demonstrated his openness to experiment in his still-lifes, a genre that exists apart from his general range of subject matter. For example, in "The gleaming conical-legged animal vessel and the wide-mouthed *fu* vessel together blaze and shine" he employed puddled ink to depict the heavy patinas of a group of ancient bronzes. In *Yixing Teapot and Cup, Candle on a Bronze Stand, Rose and Mirror*, which belongs to another album, he used shading resembling Western chiaroscuro to create the effect of three dimensions.

Through his presumed influence on the choice of inscriptions, Yao Xie dictated that Ren Xiong depict two exotic figures. Because the non-Han women Ren Xiong painted existed outside the bounds of polite society, he had license to render them as freed from the conventional limpid beauty and pose of ennui, just as the lower class figures mentioned earlier were exonerated from an unemotional and passive state. In "The Liaodong girl rides a camel," an interesting woman, engaged with the world, wears an orange coat and pointed hat (presumably Liaodong costume) as she sits atop a camel. A woman apparently alone in the wilderness with her horse, as no proper Han woman would ever be, plays the *pipa* in "Dismounting the horse to play a barbarian tune; suddenly, there is thunder."

Uncommon Themes: Social and Political Commentary

A theme crossing all genres and styles is that of social and political disaffection. A significant number of leaves from the *Album after Poems by Yao Xie* present themes of social and political commentary. Although these leaves may be appreciated for their overt subject matter, a deeper reading suggests they be interpreted as commentary on society and government. Such commentary likely reflects both the artist's and the poet's discontent regarding the status quo. In these leaves the questions of style, of the relationship between poetic and visual imagery, and of the patronage relationship come together particularly tightly (examples are discussed below). The friendship between Ren Xiong and Yao Xie was based on more than a shared appreciation of the arts: both men were distressed by the state of their country, which was racked by war and rebellion during the mid-nineteenth century. The Jiangnan area in which they lived was particularly traumatized by the Taiping Uprising.

The Opium Wars profoundly affected Yao, as is evident from his poetic oeuvre. Many poems scattered throughout *Fuzhuang shiwen* comment on the wars, the desolation they wrought, and the ineptitude of the Chinese army. *Fuzhuang shiwen*'s juan 21, 22, and 23 in particular focus on war. The titles of some pieces from these juan include the dates and locations of the battles about which Yao Xie wrote, at times followed by notes concerning the exact incidents upon which the piece is based. At one point during the Opium Wars, the British embarked on a strategy to divide and weaken China by controlling a vital traffic route, the Yangzi. In 1841, at the beginning of this campaign, they captured Yao Xie's hometown of Zhenhai as well as his town of residence, Ningbo. Yao recorded his reactions as the battle progressed, writing, "Done as a hasty notation and explanation of events at the prefectural town on the twenty-sixth day of the eighth month [equivalent to October 10, 1841]: at noon on this day I heard the foreign troops captured the city of Zhenhai. At dusk our lord started to resist the ten thousand, and I was joyful and relieved. So as to recount what I have heard and seen, I write this poem to record it" (*Fuzhuang shiwen*, j. 22, p. 5b). The British attacked Zhenhai and captured it on October 10, 1841, the day Yao wrote these lines.[11] The relief the poet says he felt as he wrote this piece must therefore have been extremely short-lived as the British prevailed, contrary to Yao's expectations. "War to the south of the city" (*Fuzhuang shiwen*, j. 4, p. 20a) makes it clear that the poet understood fully the destruction of war, and thought it senseless: "Bones lean against the mountains, blood seeps into the earth, the wind and thunder cry out silently, and the sun and moon are without life. For what?" In many other poems Yao Xie recounts the course of specific battles, and describes his horror at the suffering and destruction left in their wake, always conscious of the pain of the individuals whose lives were ruined.

Some of the lines Yao Xie chose for illustration in the *Album after Poems by Yao Xie* may be interpreted as reflecting his dissatisfaction with the Chinese army's performance, and his sympathy for people affected by war. Ren Xiong's disaffection is suggested by the way his responses to his patron's inscriptions contribute to their interpretation as expressive of alienation from society. Expressions of discontent occur later in Ren Xiong's oeuvre, but were first encouraged by Yao Xie.

Some leaves are difficult to categorize with assurance as containing social and political commentary. Others, however, are not. For example, "The soldiers defending the military post can be divided into the drunkards, the gamblers, and smugglers" is very clearly a condemnation of the military, even without Ren Xiong's image of soldiers drinking and gambling on the ground beside a tower, where they presumably are meant to be keeping watch. Another leaf depicts the idleness and frivolity of officials by portraying a game of arrow tossing. Surrounded by antiquities, one figure throws an arrow over his shoulder into a vase, while an imposing senior figure in a large fur coat stands by, holding more arrows ("The one wearing the sable is the best at the game of throwing [arrows] into the wine pot"). If we translate *shangxiang* as *prime minister* ("The sable-bedecked prime minister plays the game of throwing [arrows] into the wine pot"), the message becomes particularly scathing, since the arrows—and the prime minister's time—could certainly be put to better use. A leaf that most likely comments on the emperor himself depicts a peacock—symbol of the emperor—spreading its tail in the midst of a beautiful garden. The inscription, "Blown by the wind, the peacock lowers its silver, muddies its skirt," also could be translated, "Blown by the wind, the peacock puts down its wealth, submitting to female influences," intimating that the emperor is wasting his silver due to a woman's influence.

Some leaves reflect the opinion that the country is in a bad state. Several examples follow. Yao Xie wrote, "Alas! The tallow tree is tall, the palm tree is short; in vain do the yellow chickens peck, relying on the grains left behind [i.e., after harvest]" (fig. 7), perhaps suggesting that it is useless for anyone to try to survive on what is left in the wake of the Taiping rebels. Searching for further clues to this inscription's meaning within the *jueju* from which the inscription was excerpted, we find that the balance of poem supports this interpretation. The inscription is the first half of the second *jueju* of "In Stillness, Two *Jueju*" (*Fuzhuang shiwen*, j. 32, 2a). The second half reads, "I know for certain that the guests have dreams of returning home, and as the sun slowly reaches the western wall and fades out, they cry." We know that the chickens are the guests referred to here, because the character for *to cry* is one used for birds in particular. Many people fled their homes as the Taiping army advanced, and would have yearned to return, as the chickens do in the poem. The loss of the sunlight could represent the loss of civilization. Ren Xiong's response to the line of verse heightens the sense of the futility of the struggle for survival by portraying the chickens as isolated and oblivious to the approach of winter, a difficult season under any circumstances.

"The gate at the frontier of Chu is lofty; the horses leaving through the gate are many" (fig. 8) is another leaf that may be construed as critical of the state of the country. In it, throngs of people and horse-drawn carts depart through a gate: such a mass exodus would occur only if dire problems plagued the realm. According to "The Gates of Chu, Five Parts" (*Fuzhuang shiwen*, j. 11, p. 1a):

> The gate at the frontier of Chu is lofty;
> The horses leaving through the gate are many.
> The setting sun makes the open fields
> And the horses' backs red.
> The great river and mountains darken,
> And below is the lonely city.
> The forlorn city is like a *dou* [large wine container],
> And above willows are to be seen.
> The carts are urged forward,

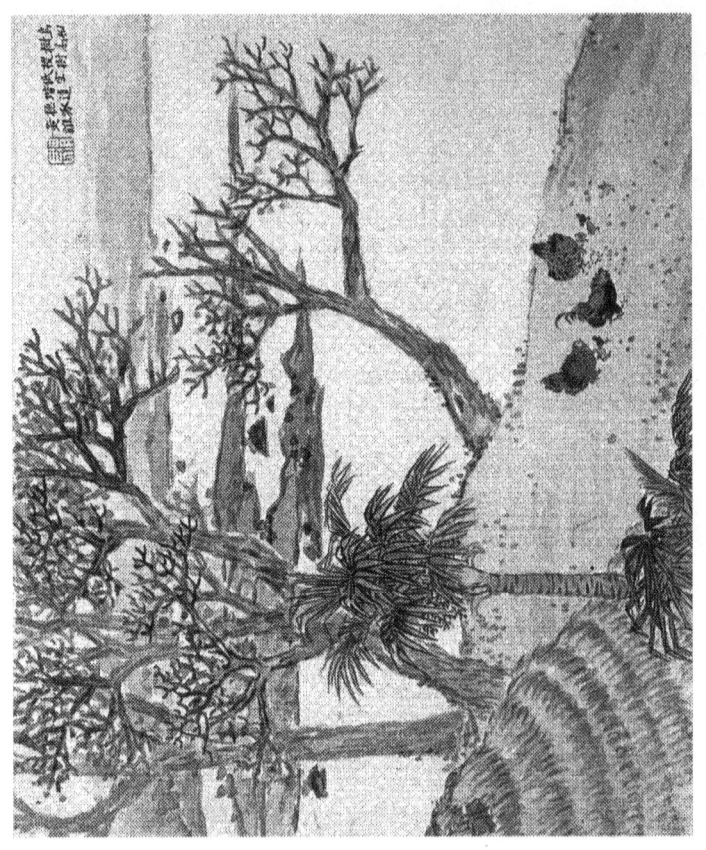

Fig. 7. "Alas! The tallow tree is tall, the palm tree is short; in vain do the yellow chickens peck, relying on the grains left behind (i.e., after harvest)." Ren Xiong. *Album after Poems by Yao Xie*, dated 1851. Ink and color on silk, 27.3 × 32.8 cm. Palace Museum, Beijing. After *A Century in Crisis*, catalogue number 3-2.i.

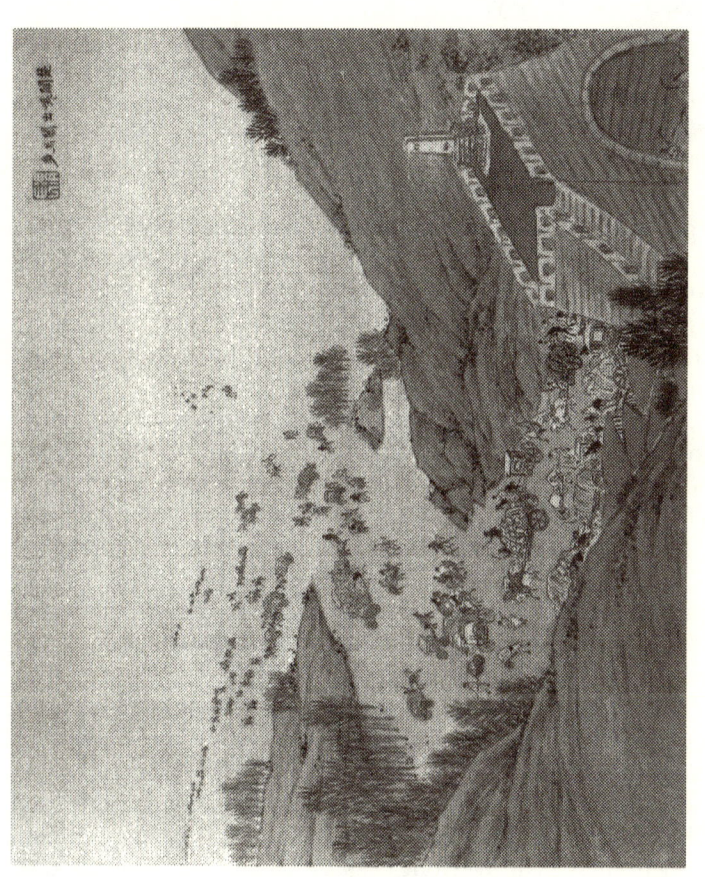

Fig. 8. "The gate at the frontier of Chu is lofty; the horses leaving through the gate are many." Ren Xiong. *Album after Poems by Yao Xie*, dated 1851. Ink and color on silk, 27.3 × 32.8 cm. Palace Museum, Beijing. After *Zhongguo lidai huihua: Gugong Bowuyuan cang hua ji* [Chinese painting of the dynastic period: Volume of the Palace Museum's painting collection], vol. 8 (Beijing: People's Art Press, 1991), p. 98.

But my horse will not speed.
The horse hurries but has no strength,
So I drive him only as is proper [i.e., not more than the horse can
tolerate].
Evening dew lies on the grass,
And washes away [i.e., revivifies] my dryness.
The new moon is in the sky;
The wild geese fly eastward.
To the east the geese cross the mountains;
To the south horses enter the gates.
I traverse a thousand *li*—
When will it end?

The wild geese mentioned toward the end of the poem are a "symbol of the people, who know how to leave [a government] not based upon the Dao to go to one that is."[12] Paralleling the geese, the former city residents travel eastward (the setting sun reddens the horses' backs), confirming the assumption that political trouble has catalyzed the mass departure. Other horsemen, no doubt invaders taking advantage of the situation, enter the city through the south gate. Interestingly, both this leaf and "The soldiers defending the military post can be divided into the drunkards, the gamblers, and smugglers" are among the four whose inscriptions were altered for reproduction in a later woodcut version of the album, *Ren Weichang Yao Meibo shihua hebi*, doubtless to eradicate their negative implications.[13]

If we equate an exodus of geese with faulty government, then even "The river of fog prevents the wild geese from descending to the sea; the bare willows at the city gate mean there will be frost" (fig. 9) might be critical political commentary. By depicting the geese as separated from the city, Ren Xiong hinted that the government was not functioning properly, augmenting Yao's message.

Ren Xiong added to his patron's remark through both composition and style in "Innate friends sit facing one another. Why do they not play the qin?" The poetry may bear overtones of societal discord, for in an ideal Confucian society, circumstances would not arise to keep gentlemen who are innate friends from playing the qin together. The artist divided the space between the two gentlemen with a tree and enhanced the message of social distress through his choice of a hard-edged style related to that of Chen Hongshou (1598–1652).

The decision as to exactly which beautiful-women paintings provide social critique is difficult, but some definitely are. In "The young girl collects the fallen red [petals]," for example, the artist highlights the poverty of

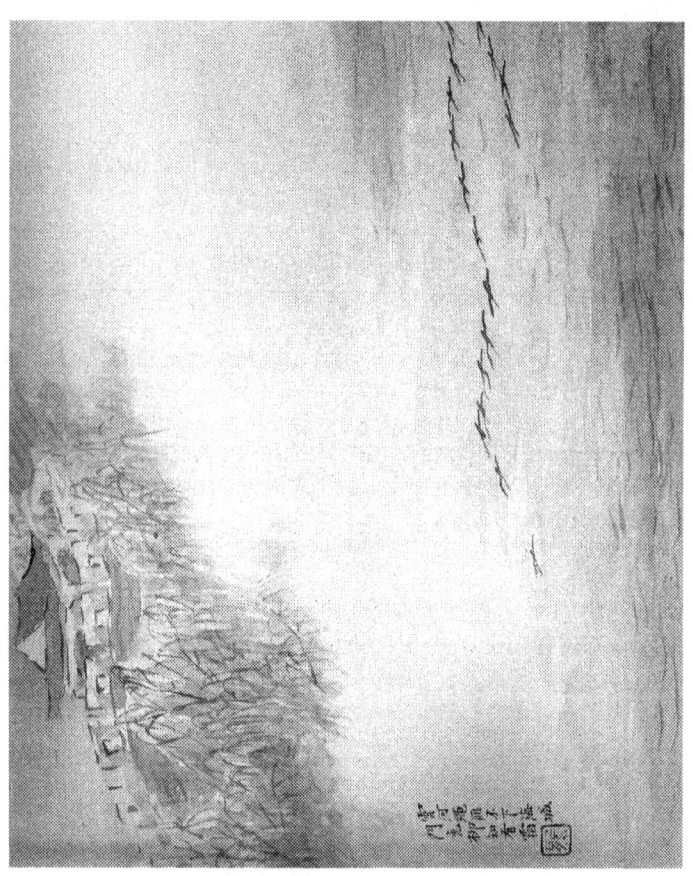

Fig. 9. "The river of fog prevents the wild geese from descending to the sea; the bare willows at the city gate mean there will be frost." Ren Xiong. *Album after Poems by Yao Xie*, dated 1851. Ink and color on silk, 27.3 × 32.8 cm. Palace Museum, Beijing. After *Haishang Si Ren jingpin* [Masterpieces by the Four Rens of Shanghai] (Hebei and Hong Kong: Hebei Art Press and Yazhou Fine Arts Press, 1992), plate 27.

the woman through the innocent gesture of the young girl who offers her petals, which are beautiful but which will not ameliorate her difficulties. Dramatically contrasting the opportunities of the rich and poor is "The senior unmarried woman of the house has her head bedecked with pearls and kingfisher feathers, but the peddler woman shouldering a burden on a bamboo pole is as lice in a pair of trousers [i.e., her world is excessively narrow]," which depicts an upper class woman sitting adorned with jewels at a moon window, looking out at a young itinerant peddler passing by (fig. 10).[14] The women are of comparable age and beauty, but the peddler is handicapped by her poverty, forced to concentrate her energies on earning a living. The wealthy woman has the time and opportunity to obtain a wider view of the world although, ironically, she is confined within the walls of her home.

Finally, the following painting could be construed as critical of the position of women in late Qing society, or it may simply represent a female archetype with no criticism intended: "So quiet as to avoid the parrot's awareness, standing exposed, the twilight passes," which portrays a woman alone in an enclosed garden (fig. 11). The woman possibly substitutes for the parrot mentioned in the inscription, her similar role as a beautiful creature kept for entertainment, rendering the substitution feasible. Also complicating the interpretation of this album leaf is that Ren's image refers to the *Dream of the Red Chamber* [Hongloumeng] illustrations depicting the book's heroine, Lin Daiyu (Black Jade). In particular, his painting of the woman relates to Gai Qi's (1774–1828) depiction of Daiyu as reproduced in woodblock illustrations for the book, with similar pose and clothing. Both artists depicted the woman in a garden setting, with the suggestion of a building in the background. Unlike Ren Xiong, however, Gai Qi showed Lin Daiyu surrounded by bamboo—her garden residence was called the Bamboo Retreat. Furthermore, Gai Qi included a parrot above Daiyu, to her right. Ren Xiong's figure gazes to her right, but Ren confined the parrot's presence to the line of verse. The parrot was associated with Daiyu, and appears in later illustrations to this classic novel, for example Wang Yun's (active late nineteenth century), published by the Dianshizhai in 1882.[15] Yao Xie was particularly interested in *Dream of the Red Chamber* (so much so he wrote a commentary on it), and would have appreciated Ren's visual reference to Gai Qi's illustrations. Ren could well have first seen the Gai Qi edition of *Dream of the Red Chamber* in Yao's library.

We know from colophons added to the *Album after Poems by Yao Xie* that Yao Xie showed the album to many of his acquaintances. As James Cahill has noted concerning other paintings with political content, they could "serve to communicate mutually held views among like-minded people."[16] Perhaps Yao Xie welcomed the possibility of this album facilitating an

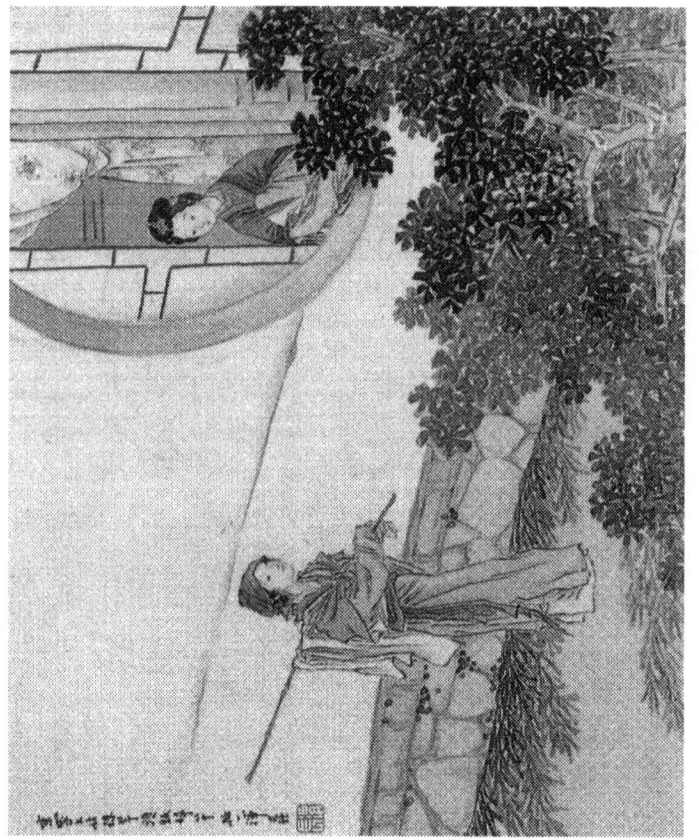

Fig. 10. "The senior unmarried woman of the house has her head bedecked with pearls and kingfisher feathers, but the peddlar woman shouldering a burden on a bamboo pole is as lice in a pair of trousers." Ren Xiong. *Album after Poems by Yao Xie*, dated 1851. Ink and color on silk, 27.3 × 32.8 cm. Palace Museum, Beijing. After *Haishang ming jia huihua*, plate 11.10.5.

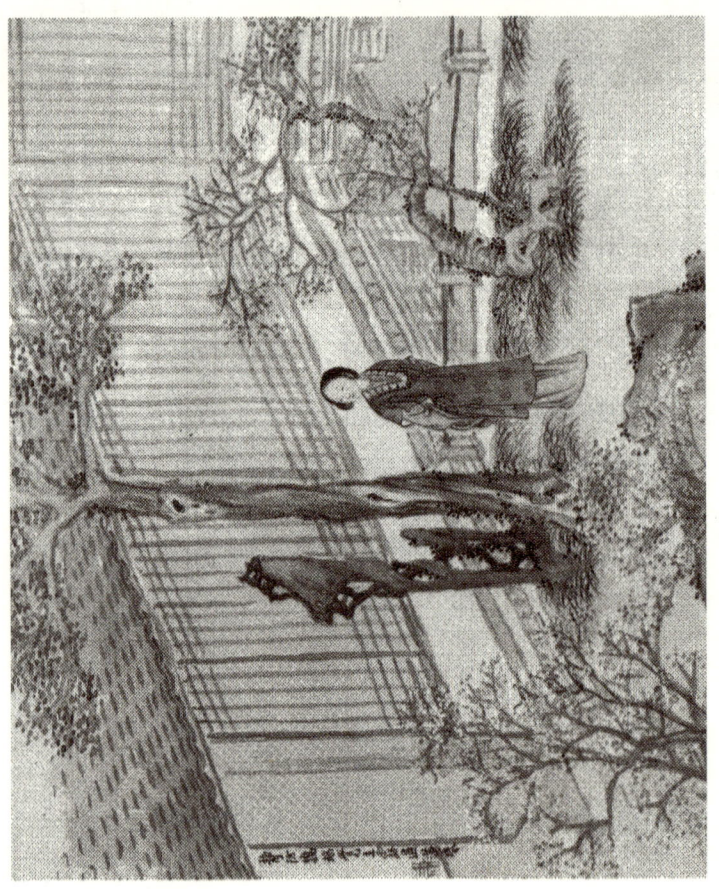

Fig. 11. "So quiet as to avoid the parrot's awareness, standing exposed, the twilight passes." Ren Xiong. *Album after Poems by Yao Xie*, dated 1851. Ink and color on silk, 27.3 × 32.8 cm. Palace Museum, Beijing. After *Haishang ming jia huihua*, plate 11.10.11.

exchange of social and political views. Although the relevant album leaves are scattered throughout the album, discontent with the status quo is a recurring theme, and is manifested quite blatantly in a number of leaves.

Motivation for Creating the Album

As already noted, for an album to be either so large or to include such a wide range of subject matter is extremely unusual. The *Album after Poems by Yao Xie* is the largest extant Chinese painting album, twice as large as its closest rival, Hongren's (1610–1663) sixty-leaf album of Huangshan (*Huangshan tu*).[17] Unlike Ren Xiong's album, however, Hongren's is stylistically and thematically unified: each leaf depicts in Hongren's characteristic style a particular site on Huangshan. Few other albums comprise more than twenty-four leaves, an exception being Lu Zhi's (1496–1576) forty-leaf *Pictures of Huashan* [Huashan tu], once again a thematically unified work.[18]

In expanding and exploring the limits of style and content, artist and patron may have been motivated by more than just intellectual gratification. Since it catalogues the possibilities of visual representation, the *Album after Poems by Yao Xie* could have served to exemplify the kinds of paintings that could be commissioned from Ren Xiong via Yao Xie. There is evidence that Yao promoted Ren's interests, and acted as a go-between for the artist. According to Chen Dingshan's retelling of a traditional anecdote, Yao introduced Ren's talent to his friends by inviting them to a banquet and surprising them with the presentation of a new set of drinking tallies, *Water Margin Drinking Cards*, designed by his protégé. As Chen relates, "The guests were . . . surprised that the cards had been painted by a contemporary, and they all ordered paintings from Ren Xiong. Soon Weichang's name became popular in [Jiangsu and Zhejiang provinces]."[19] Inscriptions appended to the *Album after Poems by Yao Xie* demonstrate that Yao did, indeed, introduce Ren's work to his circle of friends: Yao Xie and eighteen of his friends inscribed their names at the end of the album after viewing it during mid-autumn, 1851.[20] Later, on December seventh, Yao showed the same album to another group of friends: as a patron with influence in artistic and literary circles, Yao Xie was extremely important to Ren Xiong.

According to Wang Tao (active late nineteenth century), Yao was an avid acquisitor of art. Wang says that in his later years, "whenever [Yao] made some money through his writing, he would squander it all immediately. Aside from buying paintings, there was nothing he wanted from anyone."[21] Yao may have been motivated to promote Ren Xiong to earn cash with which to purchase paintings for his own collection. If Yao Xie wished to use the album as a model book, to display Ren Xiong's multifaceted talents as a painter to potential clients, he would have encouraged the use of a variety of styles.

As a final note considering the patron's motivation for arranging for the album's production, it is intriguing to speculate that he may have believed an impressive set of paintings based upon his recently published book of poetry would have encouraged interest in the book among his circle of acquaintances. It also would have opened up discussion of his poetry. As we know from inscriptions appended to the end of the album, Yao Xie showed the album to many people. Whereas suggesting to his friends that they discuss his new book would be immodest, sharing a magnificent album would be seen as a generous act, even though it most likely led to a discussion of his own poetry.

Ren Xiong and Shanghai School Aesthetics

Ren Xiong was a dynamic individual who altered the course of Chinese painting within the decade of his abbreviated career. During those ten years, he went beyond established idioms to create fresh and inventive works, some of them startlingly original. His reconceptions of traditional themes mark the first wave of Shanghai School painting, and make him a founding leader of this school, arguably inaugurating the modern era of Chinese painting. Disregard for long-established conventions typifies quintessential Shanghai School art, and the scope of conventions flouted includes suitable subject matter and the interpretation thereof. Ren Xiong was among the first to defy conventions so.

Notes

1 *Dingshan lunhua qi zhong* [Seven discussions of painting by Chen Dingshan] (Taibei: Shijie wenwu chubanshe, 1969), 114–115; this is a collection of reminiscences published in 1969, based on stories Chen had heard in his youth in Shanghai early this century.

2 "Biography of Ren the Recluse" [Ren chushi zhuan], in *Writings Left Behind from the Thatched Hall of Fan Lake* [Fanhu Caotang yikao] (Published after 1875), j. 1, pp. 18a–18b.

3 Trans. by Stella Yu Lee, "The Figure Paintings of Jen Po-nien (1840–1896): The Emergence of a Popular Style in Late Chinese Painting" (PhD diss., University of California, Berkeley, 1981), 72.

4 The artist dedicated a round fan, *The Tong Que Palace Deep in Spring* (Tianyige Collection, Ningbo), to Yao in August. The following month he signed a painting,

Beautiful Woman and Plum Blossoms (Shanghai Antique Store Collection), as having been painted at Dameishanguan; and he dated a set of four hanging scrolls of *Birds and Flowers* (Suzhou Museum) to autumn of the same year, also painted at Dameishanguan.

5 Zhi Kan, "Ren Xiong he Cai Zhao" [Ren Xiong and Cai Zhao], *Yilin conglu* (Hong Kong: Commercial Press, 1962?), 10:163.

6 For the location within *Fuzhuang shiwen* of each line of verse inscribed on the album, see Britta Erickson, "Patronage and Production in the Nineteenth-Century Shanghai Region: Ren Xiong (1823–1857) and His Sponsors" (PhD diss., Stanford University, 1996), app. V.

7 Xi Bo, "Ji Ren Xiong Dameishanmin shi zhong huace" [Notes on Ren Xiong's album after the poems of Yao Xie], *Yilin conglu* 10:257–60.

8 Wang Tao, *Yingruan zazhi*, j. 4, p. 16 (chap. 1, n. 8).

9 *Still Life: Mingren shuhua* [Calligraphy and paintings by famous people] (Shanghai: Commercial Press, 1922–),20: no. 1–10. *Plum Blossoms*: Xiaoshan Culture Bureau Collection. Gong Chanxing, "Ren Weichang nianbiao" [A chronology of Ren Weichang's life], *Meishu shilun congkan* [Art historical theory periodical] (1988), no. 2, p. 82. *Yixing Teapot*: reproduced in *Ren Weichang huaniao ce* [Album of birds and flowers by Ren Xiong] (n.p., n.d.), early twentieth-century (?) Chinese reproduction album.

10 *Fragrant Bamboo Steamers:* Ink and color on paper, 127 × 43.2 cm. James H. Soong and Jung Ying Tsao, *Chinese Paintings by the Four Jens: Four Late Nineteenth Century Masters* (San Francisco: Far East Fine Arts, 1977), 23. *Fat Crabs:* Tianjin Art Museum. Gong, "Ren Weichang nianbiao."

11 Arthur Waley, *The Opium War through Chinese Eyes* (Stanford, California: Stanford University Press, 1958), p. 158.

12 Quote from Zheng Xuan's (active Eastern Han Dynasty) commentary on the *Book of Odes*, trans. by Albert Donald Holzman, "Yüan Chi and His Poetry" (PhD diss., Yale University, 1953), 45.

13 *Ren Weichang Yao Meibo shihua hebi* [Ren Xiong's paintings and Yao Xie's poems together] (Shanghai: Shijie shuju, 1926).

14 Ruan Ji (210–163) ridiculed gentlemen (*junzi*) who could not see beyond their own small world, by comparing them to lice inhabiting a pair of trousers, astonished when they discover the enormity of what lies outside. This is the source of the expression equating people with a narrow world view with lice in trousers.

15 See *Qing Wang Yun jie renwu tu* [Illustrations of people by Wang Yun of the Qing] (Shanghai: Shanghai Calligraphy and Painting Press, 1987), 1.

16 "Political Themes in Chinese Paintings," *Three Alternative Histories of Chinese Painting* (Lawrence, KS: Spencer Museum of Art, 1988), 22.

17 Palace Museum, Beijing. Reproduced: Jason C. Kuo, *The Austere Landscape: The Paintings of Hung-jen* (Taipei: SMC Publishing, 1990), pls. 65–124 (fifty leaves only); Su Zongren, comp., *Huangshan congkan*, 8 vols., (Beijing: Baiyiyanzhai, 1937), vol. 2 (sixty leaves).

18 Ink and color on silk, 33.9 × 49.4. (Shanghai Museum.) Reproduced: *Zhongguo gudai shuhua tumu* [Illustrated catalogue of selected works of ancient Chinese painting and calligraphy] (Beijing: Wenwu chubanshe), 3:93–100.

19 *Dingshan lun hua qi zhong*, 115, as translated by Lee, "Jen Po-nien" (n. 3

above). These drinking cards do not survive, and Chen contradicts this story else-where by stating that Ren created the *Water Margin Drinking Cards* as the bride price for his wife. (Chen Dingshan, *Chunshen jiuwen* [Old tales of Shanghai] [Tai-pei: Shijie wenwu chubanshe, 1978], 131.) Still, the essence of the story, that Yao promoted Ren among his friends, is true.

20 Xi, "Ji Ren Xiong," 256 (n. 7 above).

21 *Yingruan zazhi* (chap. 1, n. 8).

3
Deliberate Looks: Ren Bonian's 1888 Album of Women

Roberta Wue

Tour-de-force painters have it rough. The visual joys and pleasures of their works are often beyond words, impossible to articulate and describe. This must have seemed true to the contemporaries of the painter Ren Bonian (1840–1896), whose effortless technique and visual bravado have come to epitomize the later-nineteenth-century Shanghai School. Indeed, the few accounts written of the artist during his lifetime invariably mention his matchless technique.[1] Ordinarily, Ren's relatively low social status as a professional painter would have excluded him from the written record; however, his virtuosity ensured the attention and admiration of his colleagues in the art world.

This can be seen in several poems by Wu Changshi (1844–1927) dedicated to Ren Bonian; Wu used metaphors of nature and supernatural forces to characterize his friend's painting powers. In one poem from 1886, he comments, "When he applies his brush his strength is enough to lift a heavy metal *ding* / He uses enough water for painting to drain the Wusong River." In another poem of the same year Wu writes that when Ren painted, "water, wind and thunder rise."[2] And although Ren Bonian and the celebrated literati landscape painter Yang Borun (1837–1911) hardly traveled in the same social circles, in the last line of his 1882 treatise on painting Yang admiringly compared the sound of Ren's brush to the sweeping, rushing sound of dry banana-palm leaves.[3]

Ren Bonian arrived in Shanghai in 1868, and quickly established a reputation for his versatility and his dazzling skills. By the 1880s, the decade from which Wu Changshi and Yang Borun's accounts date, Ren had begun to substantially rethink and reevaluate his style and approach. Previously he favored a boldly detailed *gongbi* or "fineline" style, learned from his early models, Chen Hongshou (1598–1652) and Ren Xun (1835–1893). This style relied on elegantly mannered brushwork that flaunted the artist's control and technique. By the 1880s, his *gongbi* style was seldom in evidence. Instead, Ren employed a sweeping and immediate *xieyi*

mode (literally "writing the idea"), a style generally associated with literati painting.

It is Ren's *xieyi* style that both Yang Borun and Wu Changshi appear
to describe. Unlike *gongbi* painting, the *xieyi* mode did not rely on large in-
vestments of time and handiwork; its speediness and drama made it well
suited for painting performances during elegant gatherings. One such
work painted for an audience is Ren's 1889 dramatic image of a glower-
ing cat, *Cat and Rock* (fig. 1). Painted for the owner of the Xu Garden in
Shanghai, Xu Dishan, Ren's inscription noted that "this was painted at Xu
Garden's first gathering."[4] Eyewitness accounts testify to the speediness of
Ren's execution. Cen Tongshi, whose portrait Ren painted at the age of 62
sui in 1888, observed Ren's painting process:

> Last year I sojourned in Shanghai. Mr. Ren Bonian and I cooked
> snow [to make tea] and had an evening chat. Bonian seized this
> happy moment by painting my portrait for me. It was the time of
> the second drum, and we could already see the base of the candle.
> Still, he spread out the paper . . . holding it with his left hand,
> while with his right hand he took up the brush. In less than an
> instant, it was finished.[5]

These descriptions of Ren painting are intriguing on several levels.
They are of interest particularly because the physical act of painting is so
rarely described in this period, doubtless because of its anxiety-inducing
proximity to manual labor. It may have been Ren's low social status
that made such descriptions possible; such accounts applied to a literati
painter would have been unimaginable. Moreover, in descriptions such
as Wu Changshi's and Yang Borun's, Ren is metonymically reduced to a
brush, albeit one whose skills are simultaneously magnified to forces of
nature. Such descriptions naturalize Ren's act of painting as an effortless,
unpremeditated performance, a magical process that completely captivates
the audience.

In both Wu and Yang's accounts, the focus is on the expressionistic
fluidity of Ren's technique in the 1880s; they do not address two other
notable developments in his work of this period: first, Ren's accelerating
interest in the works of older masters, and second, his conscious efforts to
expand the content of his paintings. These transformations in Ren's work
interlocked, spurred probably by Ren's often-commented-upon interest
in Bada Shanren (1626–1705). Yang Yi, in his 1920 history of Shanghai
painting, *Haishang molin* [Shanghai's forest of ink], notes that later in his
career Ren "obtained an album of Bada Shanren's paintings, and was even
more awakened to the use of the brush."[6] Others have also noted Ren's

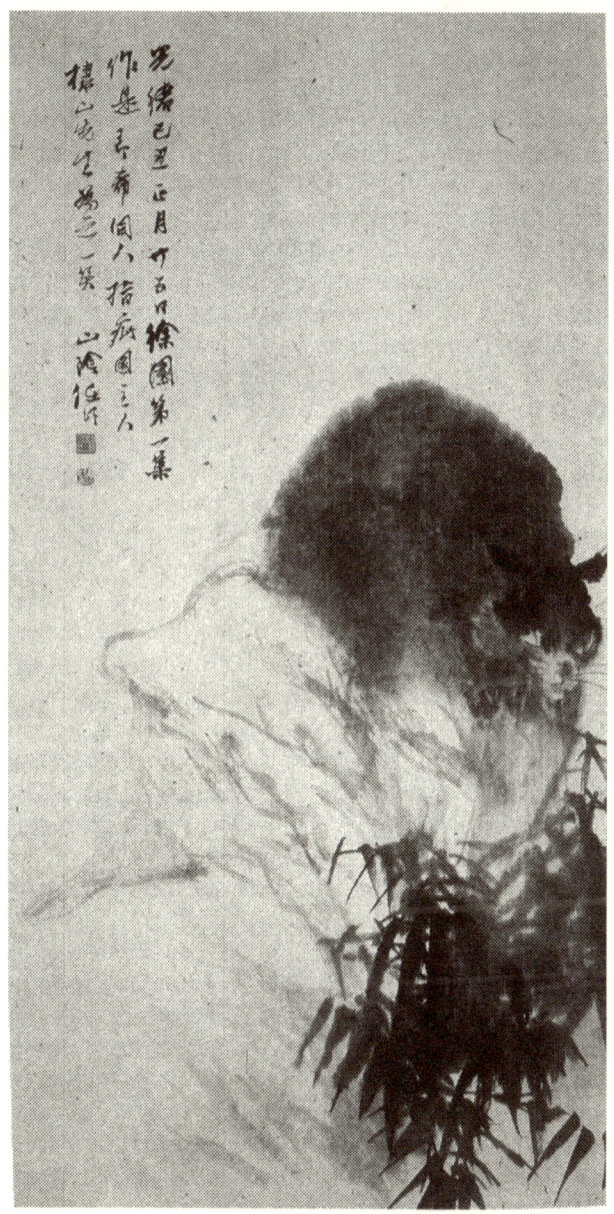

Fig. 1. Ren Bonian, *Cat and Rock* (1889, Suzhou Municipal Museum). After Zhao Guide and Wu Shouming, eds., *Ren Xiong, Ren Xun, Ren Yi, Ren Yu jingpin* (Shijiazhuang: Hebei meishu chubanshe, 1995), 214.

increased interest, like his Shanghai colleagues, in eighteenth-century Yangzhou school painters such as Jin Nong (1687–1763), Luo Ping (1733–1799), and, in particular, Hua Yan (1682–1765).

Although old master sources are frequently used to explain Ren's changing technique, less explored is why Ren chose the models he did, or how these models related to substantial changes in the content of his work, specifically a greater interest in psychology, interiority, and personalized themes. Ren was not an art-historical painter; rarely did he directly copy other works. But his choice of models in the 1880s may explain his interest in a heightened psychological mood, particularly his copies after Bada Shanren and Hua Yan. Ren's 1886 copy (fig. 2) of Bada Shanren's 1692 *Two Mynas on a Rock* (Han Pei-yuan Collection) focuses on the preternatural self-awareness of two birds on a rock. Similarly, Ren is known to have executed at least four versions of Hua Yan's 1732 *Jingu yuan* [Golden valley garden] (fig. 3) in 1888, where the relationship between the two protagonists is embodied in a loaded gaze, a motif that would be thematized again and again by Ren in the 1880s.[7]

Ren's 1880s oeuvre reveals that not only was he looking back to carefully chosen models and reforging his style into a more expressive tool, but he was reexamining his earlier themes to fit his new interests. He moved away from his illustrative approach of the 1870s to more allusive and emotionally freighted interpretations. He also began to take on new themes: a poem by Wu Changshi tells us that Ren liked to read strange books behind closed doors.[8] This perhaps explains numerous paintings of this period based on idiosyncratic, esoteric, and unidentified sources that, judging by their reiteration in his oeuvre, clearly held strong and as-yet-unexplained personal associations for the artist.

Within this period of change, towards the end of the decade in 1888, Ren produced a twelve-leaf album of images of women, formerly owned by the 20th-century painter Wu Hufan and now in the collection of the Palace Museum, Beijing. Each leaf is inscribed with simply the date and the artist's name, or merely his name. The album belongs firmly in the genre of *meiren* or "beautiful women" painting, a longstanding genre that gained popularity and currency during the Qing. One reason for its appeal was its highly conventionalized and straightforwardly decorative nature. *Meiren* painting showed idealized women, occasionally historical figures but usually anonymous beauties, engaged in aestheticized feminine activities.

By the nineteenth century, such images were so fundamentally ornamental, so utterly geared towards the viewer's visual pleasure, that they were virtually empty of meaning. Paradoxically, this emptiness conferred a great flexibility on the genre. Hung Wu describes these *meiren*

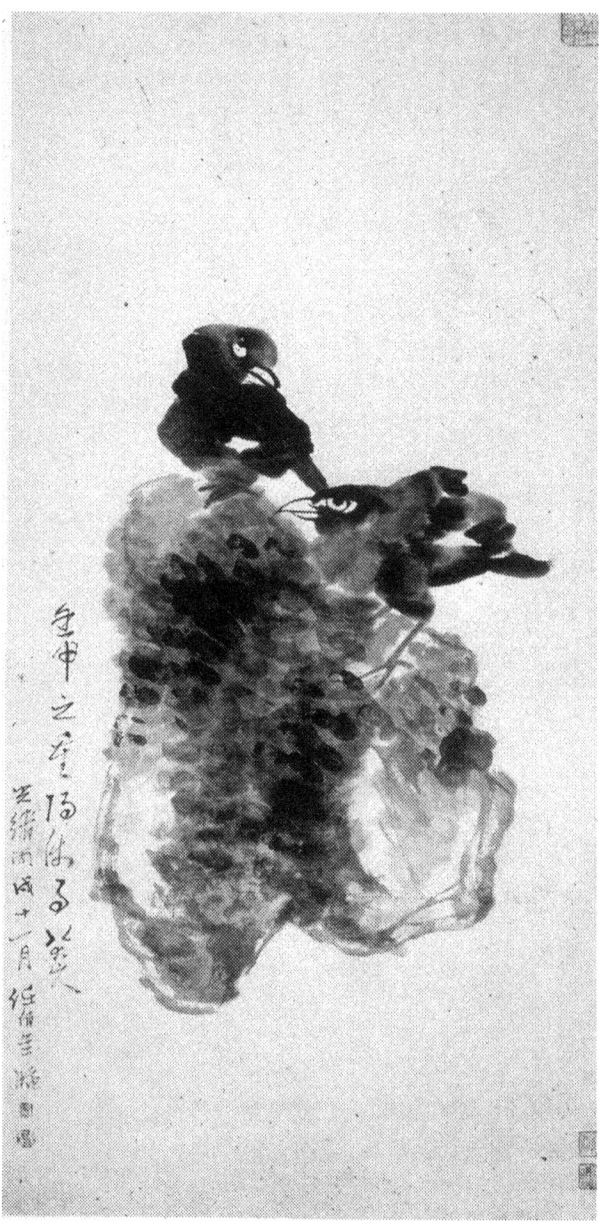

Fig. 2. Ren Bonian, *Mynahs after Bada shanren* (1888, The Palace Museum, Beijing). After He Baoyin ed., *Haishang si Ren jinpin* (Shijiazhuang and Hong Kong: Hebei meishu chubanshe and Yazhou yishu chubanshe, 1992), 89.

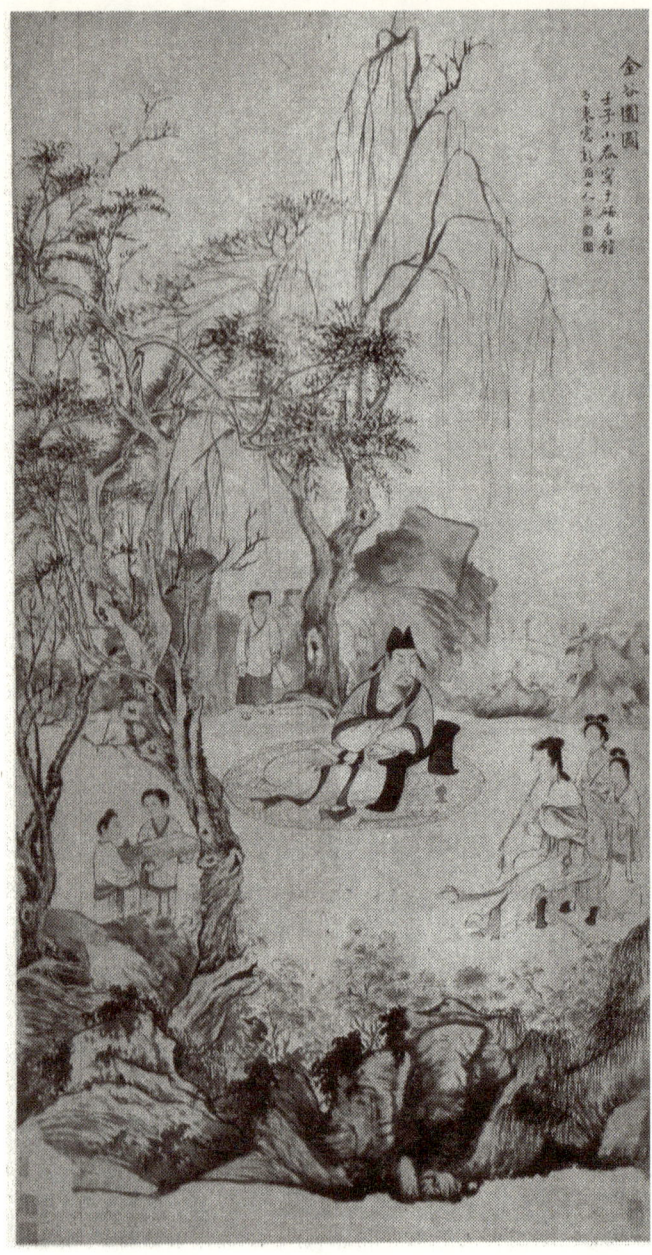

Fig. 3.   Hua Yan, *Golden Valley Garden* (1732, Shanghai Museum). After Shan Guolin, ed., *Hua Yan shuhua ji* (Beijing: Wenwu chubanshe, 1987), 6.

as "signifiers without a focus of signification," which could alternatively be described as "empty-vessel syndrome." In other words, the elasticity of the theme meant that it could take on any number of meanings for its viewers. For example, representations of the sad beauty have been associated with the *shidaifu*'s own sense of loss at his economic and social displacement; or, as Hung Wu has shown, the *meiren* is put to use by the Qing court in representing the submissive Chinese nation.[9]

As for Ren Bonian, the genre of *meiren* or beautiful-women paintings was not new to him. Many of Ren's early works from the 1860s were *meiren* paintings; his early career was characterized by his interest in overtly decorative themes and modes, and the influence of painters such as Fei Danxu (1801–1850), the great *meiren* painter.[10] However, this album of two decades later diverged markedly from the style and goals of his early work. It was much more ambitious in its breadth and emotional scope. Ren had never executed an entire album dedicated to this genre. I believe that the subject was not lightly chosen. Since Ren was then so thoroughly engaged in reinventing his art, this album can be considered a statement of purpose, one that touched on his artistic heritage, gave him the chance to revisit a number of subjects close to his heart, and, above all, gave him the opportunity to thematize issues of looking. He may have chosen *meiren* because this genre is essentially about the pleasures of looking. For a painter of few words, but of maximum pictorial intelligence, this genre and these images offer a range of visual strategies that subvert and problematize the genre's very function, namely, the engagement of the viewer's visual pleasure.

In his twelve leaves Ren combines a number of subjects from history and popular legend with more generic images of feminine activities. In some of these images he repeats favorite subjects from his repertoire; other subjects are unique to his oeuvre. The first image belongs to the latter category (fig. 4). It depicts the shepherdess San Liang, daughter of the Dragon King of Dongting Lake. According to legend, she was mistreated in her marriage to a cruel river prince and forced to tend sheep. She finally met a young scholar named Liu Yi, who, by conveying a letter to her father, rescued her from her unhappy situation.[11]

That Ren Bonian addresses the tradition of *meiren* painting as whole is clear from the appearance of several works from this album in the four-volume, 1888 revision of the *Jieziyuan huazhuan* [Mustardseed garden manual of painting]. The new, revised manual included a large selection of reproductions by "masters past and present," and Ren is prominently included. Although the final volume on figure painting was not published until 1897, a year after Ren's death and nine years after the first three volumes were issued, it is likely that Ren's contributions for this final

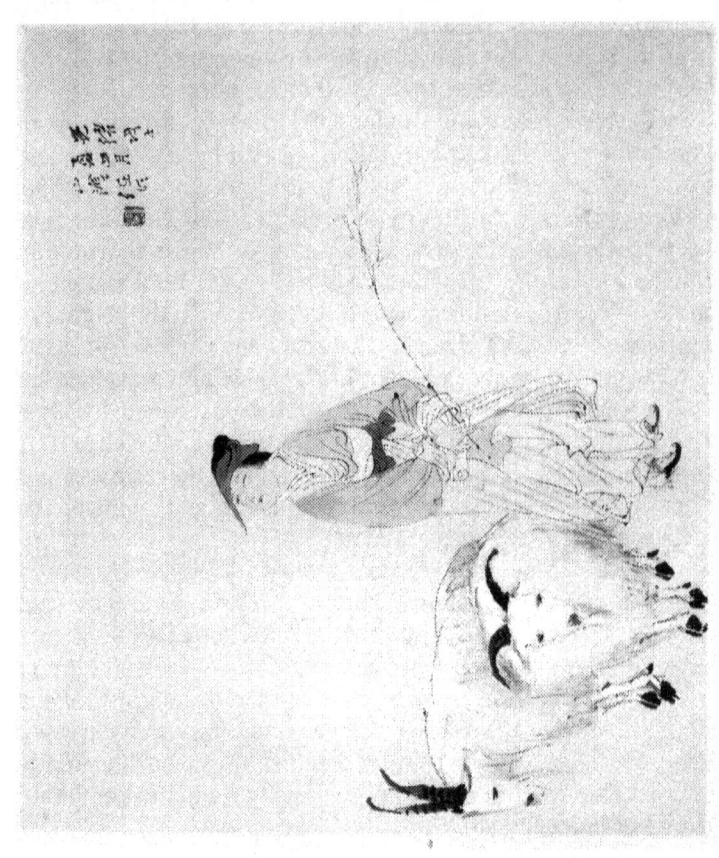

Fig. 4. Ren Bonian, *San Liang* (1888, from *Album of Women*, The Palace Museum, Beijing). After *Ren Yi "Shinu tuce"* [Album of Ren Yi's Paintings of Beautiful Women] (Beijing: Wenwu chubanshe, 1986), 4.

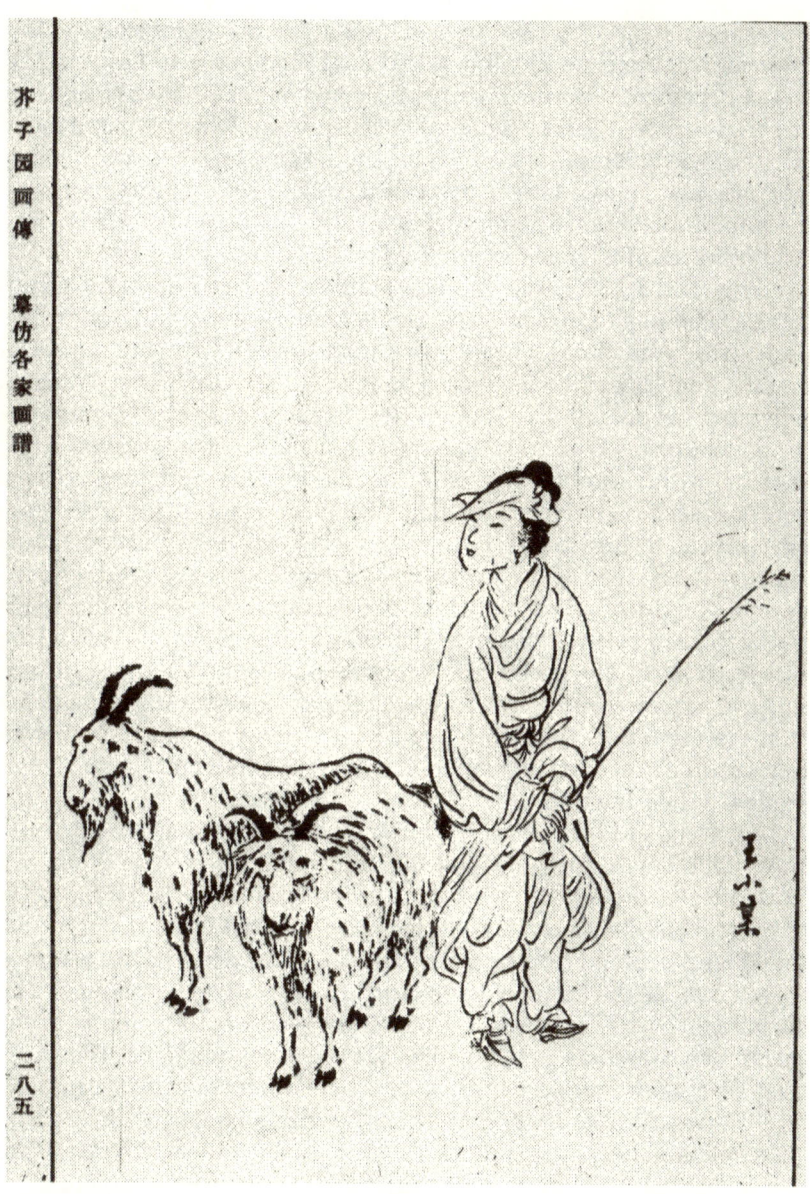

Fig. 5. Wang Su, *San Liang* (*Jieziyuan huazhuan* [Mustardseed garden manual of painting], 1893, 4:285)

volume were in place by 1888. Indeed, providing images for a new edition of this most famous of all Chinese painting manuals may have spurred Ren's engagement with the history and conventions of the *meiren* genre. The composition of San Liang tending sheep is not Ren's own, but is that of Ren's older contemporary from Yangzhou, Wang Su (1794–1877) (fig. 5). Wang was known as a late follower of the eighteenth-century Yangzhou School tradition, and had a reputation as a *meiren* painter. Ren may have found his work of interest for both reasons.

Wang died in 1877, but the new edition of the *Mustardseed Garden Manual of Painting* reproduced this single example of his work. Ren stuck closely to the Wang image; however, he made several small but significant changes. Ren substantially altered the figure of San Liang: Wang Su heightened her femininity through details such as dainty earrings and bound feet, details Ren chose to eliminate. As she holds her letter to her father, her switch droops dejectedly, her body and head facing opposite directions, seemingly frozen in place. Ren also changed the orientation from vertical to horizontal, crowding the figures into the left half of the page. The vacant space on the right exerts a pressure on the figures sideways and downwards, halted only by the frame. Moreover, the figures are destabilized by their placement atop a small implied hill, down from which each slips. The sheep are not Wang Su's sleepy animals. Instead, they have become almost humanly aware, with one now staring squarely out at the viewer, its hooves just touching the bottom edge; the second sheep's profile has been adjusted so that it just parallels and acknowledges the edge of the paper.

This is the only image in the album to be completely stripped of a setting. This device brings to life the almost palpable sense of absence that permeates the album. Most conspicuously missing is the narrative. The protagonist does not play her role, she does not enact her story. San Liang does not attend to the viewer; instead, paralyzed in place, she fixes her gaze outside the frame of the picture. Its object, like her thoughts, are thus inaccessible. That the viewer does not hold her attention is driven home by the conscious gaze the foremost sheep returns to us. The sheep, in fact, seems to have a firmer grasp of the situation than either San Liang or the viewer. Furthermore, if we trace the narrative of the image from right to left, the sheeps' triangulated bodies are stopped short by the blank lower-left corner. Movement and progression are effectively stoppered up, frustrated by the framing of the picture.

In contrast to the outdoors life of San Liang and her sheep, a more scholarly subject is the depiction of Su Shi's concubine, Wang Zhaoyun (fig. 6). According to legend, Zhaoyun was a prostitute in the Qiantang area who became Su Shi's concubine. She was illiterate until Su Shi taught her to read, and together they would discuss Buddhist matters. Her loyalty was proven by being the only one of Su Shi's wives to follow him into exile. Ren Bonian shows her with hair unbound and flowing down her back, dressed in Buddhist-style robes. The round fur prayer mat, stack of books, and garden rock provide a minimal setting. As with the leaf of San Liang, this image appropriates another picture from the *Mustardseed Garden Manual of Painting,* in this case, one by Luo Ping (fig. 7). Ren alters Luo's weighty, even iconic presentation of the woman to a figure that is less corpulent, more dematerialized. By further inclining her head, she appears more deeply absorbed in thought, and attention is deflected from her scholarly associations by the closed covers of the books beside her.

Ren's most significant changes were to reorient the composition from vertical to horizontal and to pull the viewpoint back to incorporate the garden rock in its entirety. Unlike Luo Ping's rock, Ren's rock appears oddly alive, if insubstantially so; suspended in mid-air, it appears weightless and wraithlike. The juxtaposition of rock and woman makes it appear as if the rock emanates from the center of the woman, giving shape to her thoughts, or alternatively, as if in lieu of Su Shi, she has self-created another near-human presence. The sense of the rock as a mysterious alter ego is reinforced by the suggestion of two eyelike holes, and by its mirroring her form. Signaled by the sexual message of her unbound hair, some intimate, unknowable communion seems to be in process, one that can be visualized but not verbalized.[12]

The presence of a nonhuman alter ego is the similar premise of a leaf based on the story of the Duke of Mu's daughter, who, according to legend, fell in love with a panpipes player (fig. 8). Together they made such beautiful music that it attracted a phoenix; the magical bird carried the pair off to heaven. Of all the leaves, this may have the most detailed setting: it shows the Duke's daughter holding her panpipes, seated on a terrace that faces the phoenix across a rushing stream. The tubby phoenix appears to be waiting to hear her play.[13]

As with the leaf of Wang Zhaoyun, the man central to the narrative is excluded, and the romantic male-female basis of the tale is replaced by a much stranger bird-female dynamic. The orange and green bird resembles more an outsized parrot, traditional symbol of the female quarters, companion and pet to a palace lady, than it does the mythical phoenix. And here it dominates the scene, standing stern watch over the woman. The phoenix-cum-parrot overlays this image with another strategy of Ren's in the album, whereby the narrative is merged with the stereotype of feminine activities, here one of the beautiful woman playing with her pet. However, neither the narrative nor the generic activity explain the charged tête-à-tête between woman and bird. The relationship between

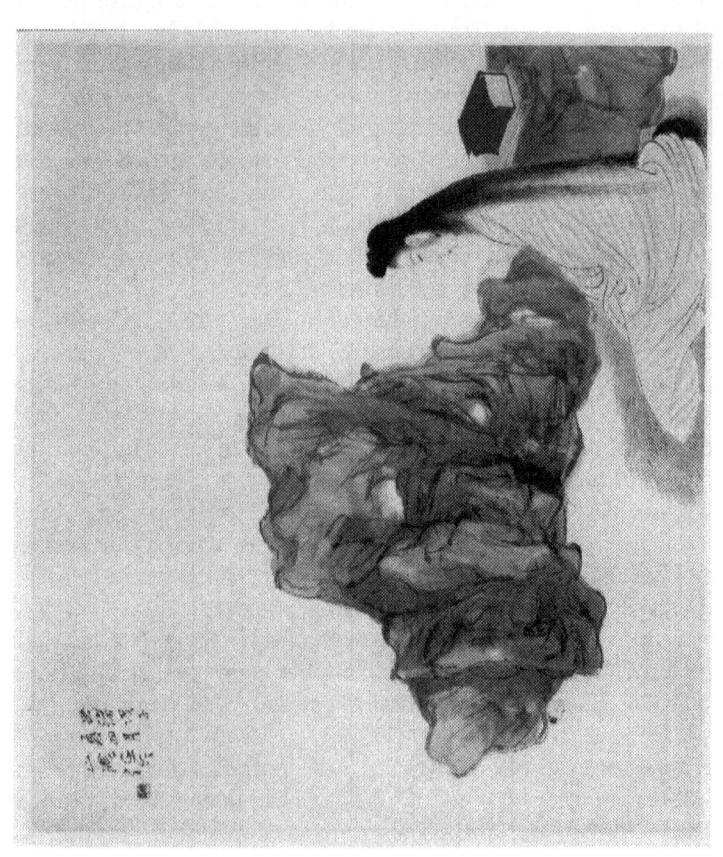

Fig. 6. Ren Bonian, *Su Dongpo's Concubine* (1888, from *Album of Women*, The Palace Museum, Beijing). After *Ren Yi "Shinu tuce"* [Album of Ren Yi's Paintings of Beautiful Women] (Beijing: Wenwu chubanshe, 1986), 6.

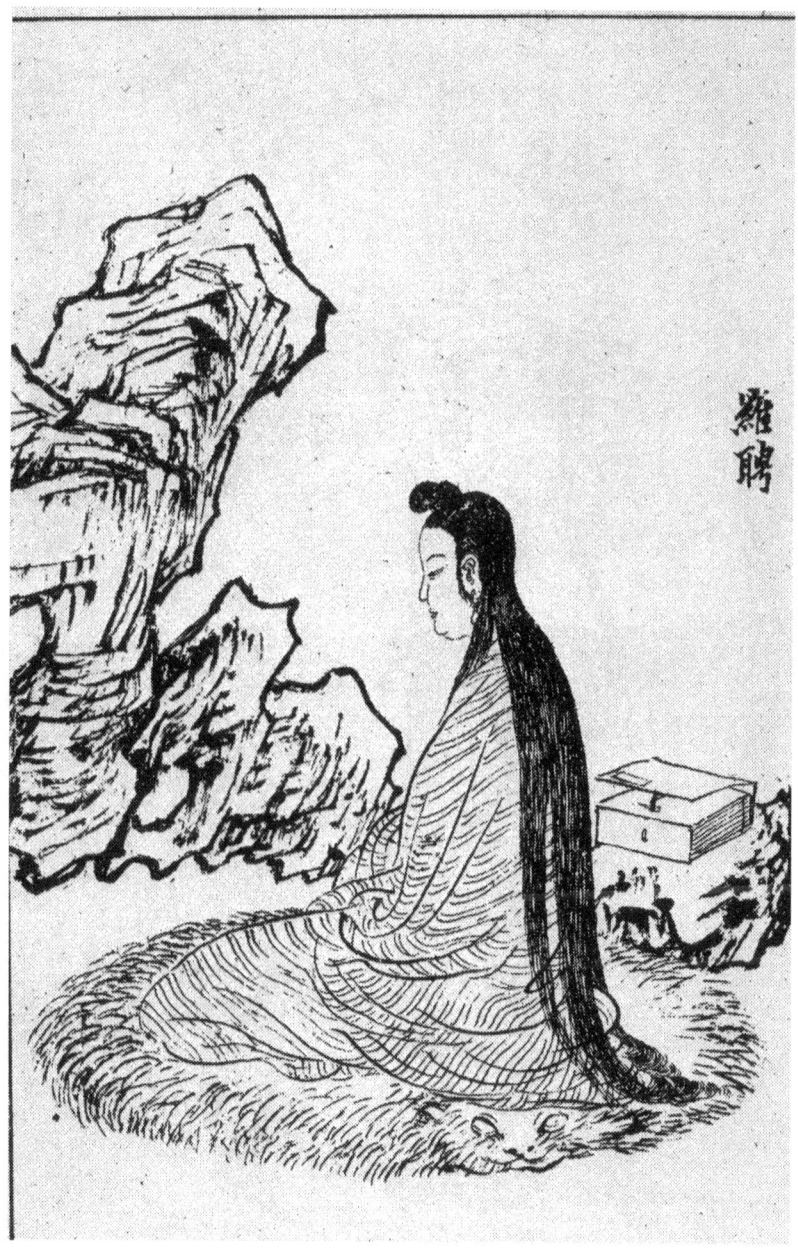

Fig. 7.   Luo Ping, *Su Dongpo's Concubine* (*Jieziyuan huazhuan* [Mustardseed garden manual of painting], 1893, 4:247)

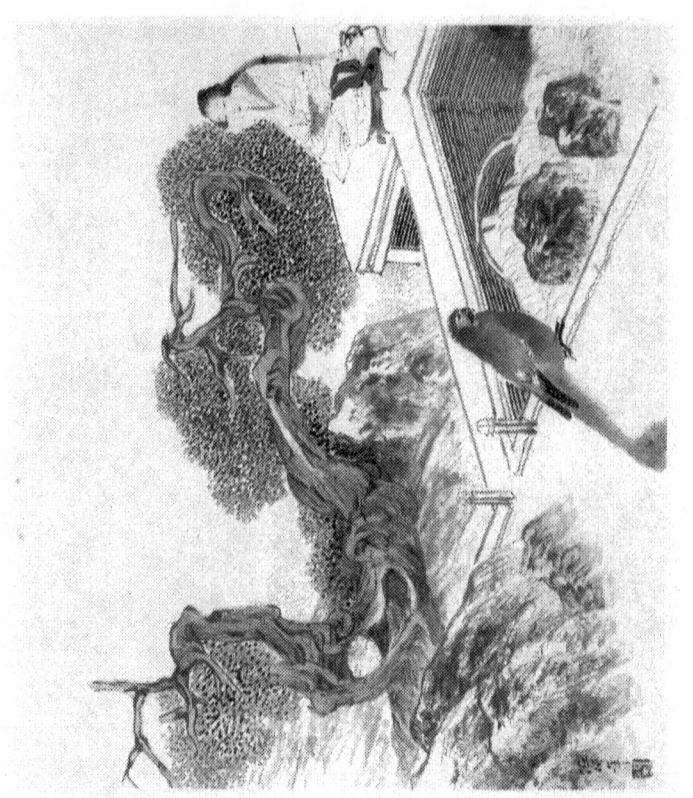

Fig. 8. Ren Bonian, *Duke of Mu's Daughter* (1888, from *Album of Women*, The Palace Museum, Beijing). After *Ren Yi "Shinu tuce"* [Album of Ren Yi's Paintings of Beautiful Women] (Beijing: Wenwu chubanshe, 1986), 8.

the two protagonists is given visual form by the dynamic diagonals of bridge and twisting cypress tree, and the nature of their bond is echoed in the agitated tree and rushing water. As with other leaves, the primary relationship of man and woman conveyed in the overt narrative is undermined by an unexpected relationship with a nonhuman object, one whose nature is ultimately inaccessible to the viewer. Through such inexplicable twists, the ostensible narrative is stopped dead in its tracks.

The next leaf depicts Xishi washing silk, a tale that Ren depicted several times before (fig. 9).[14] This is a traditional tale of an empire toppled by a woman's beauty. A servant to the lord of Yue discovers Xishi washing clothes by the riverside. Struck by her unusual beauty, the lord of Yue maneuvers her to become concubine to the usurping lord of Wu. Because she distracts the lord from his official responsibilities, Yue succeeds in bringing down the state of Wu.

The setting is minimalized, barren, and bleak. Standing on a narrow river bank, backed by a screen of branches, Xishi is accompanied by a maidservant and a basket of washing. The figure is forced up to the picture plane by the flattened screen of the thorny thicket, yet cut off from the viewer by the barrier of the river. We can see how the two figures have entered the scene from the right but there is no way onward. Isolated, the figures are on a narrow triangle of land that points nowhere.

Xishi glances sideways at the viewer. This is in fact one of the few leaves where the woman directly acknowledges the audience. The viewer is also presumably a stand-in for her discoverer, the lord of Yue's servant. However, there is no message of invitation and accommodation to the viewer, so standard to the *meiren* genre. Rather, hunch-shouldered and shrouded in black, Xishi's guarded pose and unsmiling gaze convey her withholding. Rather than being enticed, the viewer is challenged, even rebuffed by her self-possession.

The final image I examine is that of the female horseman, a theme that crops up repeatedly in Ren Bonian's 1880s oeuvre. This figure is usually identified as Hua Mulan, the filial daughter who disguised herself as a man to take her father's place when he was drafted by the army (fig. 10). Undiscovered for twelve years, Mulan rose to become a successful general before returning to her place in the family. Ren's images invariably eschewed depicting Mulan as the filial child or even the triumphant general; instead, he always chose to show her alone with her horse, at the farthest reach of her travels, often gazing away from the viewer into the distance. Here she is shown in her cross-dressing disguise, back fully turned and face barely visible, leaning on her black horse and resting a spear across the saddle.[15]

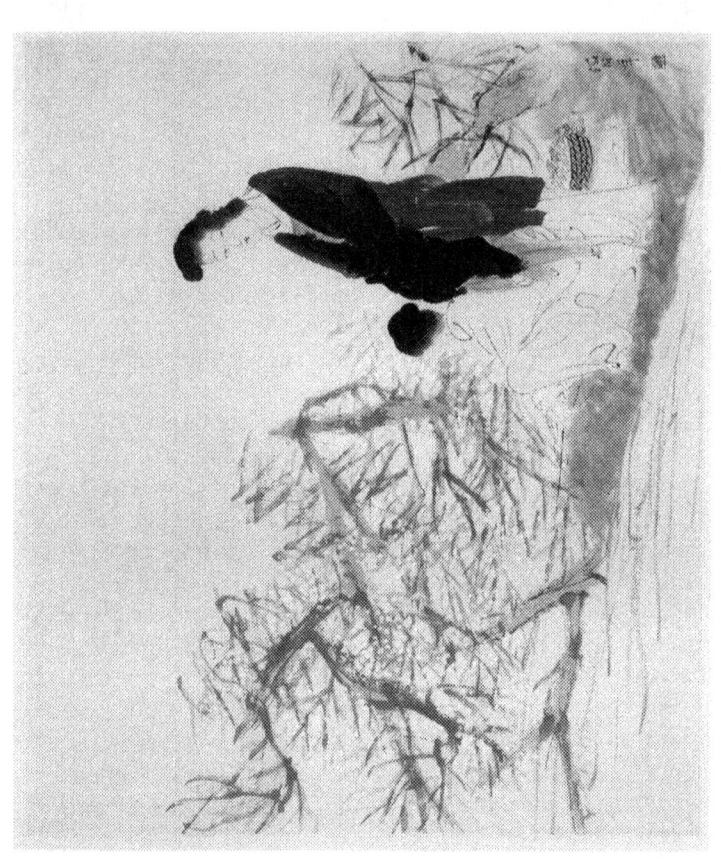

Fig. 9. Ren Bonian, *Xishi* (1888, from *Album of Women*, The Palace Museum, Beijing). After *Ren Yi "Shinu tuce"* [Album of Ren Yi's Paintings of Beautiful Women] (Beijing: Wenwu chubanshe, 1986), 9.

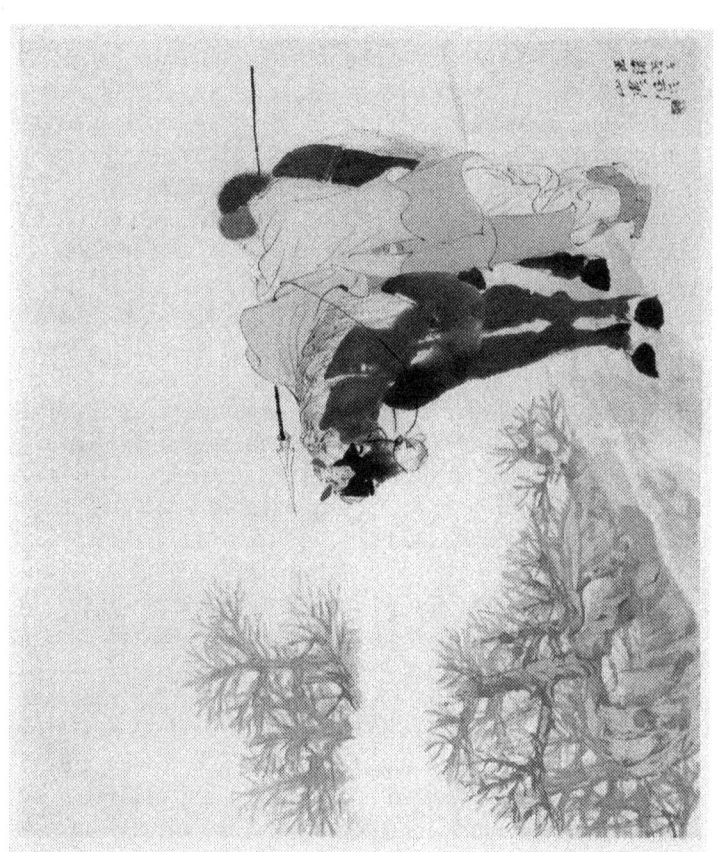

Fig. 10. Ren Bonian, *Hua Mulan* (1888, from *Album of Women*, The Palace Museum, Beijing). After *Ren Yi "Shinu tuce"* [Album of Ren Yi's Paintings of Beautiful Women] (Beijing: Wenwu chubanshe, 1986), 10.

Her informal pose, with its shift of weight, indicates her complete unawareness of the viewer's presence. Instead, the force of her thoughts and look is given form in the straight line of the spear, and a band of fog through a barren thicket provides a visual exit for her mental energies. Like the other figures, Hua Mulan has seemingly retreated from her narrative role to take a moment for herself. Once again the object of her attention is withdrawn from our view and knowledge: it is literally out of the picture. However, right under Mulan's nose, we find a more conscious actor in her companion, the black horse, who looks directly out at the viewer. The unconscious state of the woman contrasted with the aware gaze of the dumb beast is curiously unsettling. Like Ren's image of San Liang and her sheep, a strange ménage à trois of gazes is established: ours at Mulan, Mulan's into the distance, and the horse's back at us. Again, this play of looks displaces and denaturalizes the narrative, and even replaces the obvious story with one that is unknowable. The viewer is a necessary presence that puts the dynamic of the image in motion, but in the end, must remain the baffled third wheel.

Although only five of the twelve leaves in Ren's album have been examined, it is clear that Ren repeatedly employs pictorial strategies that summon then shrug off narrative, action, and convention. He subtly manipulates the audience: its expectations and involvement are engaged only to be rebuffed over and over again. In all of these images, Ren has also consciously deployed what could be termed a tactics of absence, in which every marker of the *meiren* genre is implied then evaded, leaving behind a palpable sense of loss. The visually accessible woman, the opulent settings, the romantic narrative are all denied the viewer.

Particularly conspicuous is Ren's equivocal relationship to the narrative. In his depictions, Ren invokes popular and historical stories that needed no introduction for his audience. Yet he systematically undermines the viewer's expectations of these stories, challenging both premise and outcome. As we saw in the Hua Mulan and Xishi leaves, Ren does this sometimes by placing the figures in a compositional cul-de-sac, cutting off the forward movement of the story. He also thwarts the narrative by "making strange" the romantic relationships underlying each story. Not only does the male protagonist never appear (not unusual in *meiren* images), but he also estranges each heroine from her story, usually by replacing the male with a nonhuman object.

Since the raison d'être of the beautiful-woman genre is the act of looking, it is only appropriate that Ren's subversive weapon of choice is the gaze. Throughout the album, in contrast to the otherwise-static compositions, glances fly back and forth. The women's looks are consistently directed out of the picture or sunk in introspection; when figures look out from the paper, their gaze is resistant and guarded. Again and again, their interest lies in something deliberately outside the viewer's knowledge, whether out of the painting or within the figures themselves. The tables have been turned: the gaze of possession and knowledge has been wrested from the viewer and granted to the painted women. Ren's fascination with psychological situations and interior states must have drawn strength from his interest in Bada Shanren and Hua Yan. The anthropomorphized birds and animals of Ren's album are unimaginable without the example of Bada. Echoes of Hua Yan's *Jingu yuan* are also evident, particularly Hua Yan's use of the gaze to embody the relationship between man and woman.[16]

However, if Ren has conferred his *meiren* with self-awareness and self-possession, they have little else. Confined in their surroundings, fixed and paralyzed in their circumstances, it is as if they can escape only in their unknowable thoughts. What may lie behind Ren's decision to separate his heroines from an overt, rational narrative—in other words, from the burden of producing, of putting out—may be linked to the issue of the missing man. In yet another image from the album reproduced in the *Mustardseed Garden Manual* (this time one of Ren's own contributions), he depicts a solitary woman spinning alone by lamplight (fig. 11). In both versions, she is barricaded by her small house and garden, and we catch only a glimpse of her, wielding an outsize spindle. However, the subtext is made clear in several lines from a Song poem inscribed on the published version only:

> Yesterday I went into the city,
> Coming home, tears drench my kerchief.
> She whose body is covered in silks and gauze,
> Is not the one tending the silkworms.

The poem, with its contrast between happy consumer and oppressed worker, puts an unexpected spin on the commonplace *meiren* iconography of female activities and the melancholy woman. There is also an unavoidable element of self-identification with the solitary spinner, for her situation is echoed in Ren's personal circumstances of this period, namely, his weariness at being the constant producer and maker, at the beck and call of a demanding, impatient market. We know this because in 1886, Ren had taken on a new sobriquet among those in his artworld circle, and for this reason Wu Changshi carved for Ren a seal with the characters *huanu* or "Painting Slave." Wu's poem to Ren on the side of the seal describes a harried Ren: because he felt incessantly hounded by clients, he chose to take on the ironic persona of "Painting Slave."[17]

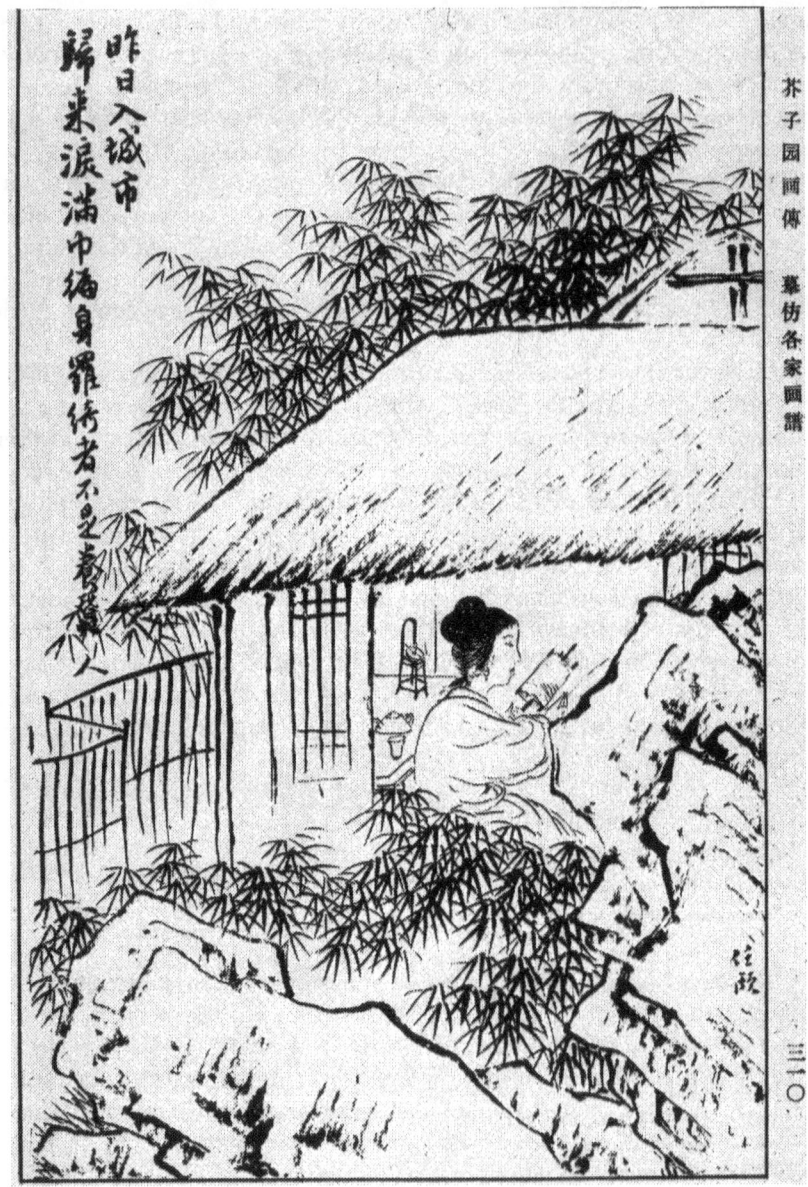

Fig. 11. Ren Bonian, *Woman Weaving At Night* (*Jieziyuan huazhuan* [Mustardseed garden manual of painting], 1893, 4:310)

In his poem, Wu suggests that Ren felt misunderstood by his audience, and concludes by saying that Ren had not yet found the perfect viewer who could fully appreciate his painting. That Ren's literary or pen name (*hao*) of "Painting Slave" was not a private joke limited to himself and Wu Changshi is evident from a New Year's gift painting of 1886, *Still Life with Inkstone*. Dedicating the painting to his friend Gao Yong (1850–1921), the calligrapher and collector, Ren refers to himself as *huanu*, and in turn addresses Gao by his artworld pen name, the "Calligraphy Beggar," or "Calligraphy Peddlar."[18] In the inscription, Ren describes Gao Yong as hiding from the demands of painting and calligraphy dealers. In the painting, he combines the iconography of the New Year—a vase of sweet osmanthus—together with a still-life of the artist's tools, namely an inkstone, book, fan, and small oil lamp. We know again from Wu Changshi that it was Ren's habit to work through the night, painting by lamplight.[19]

Both the seal and the painting highlight how much the pressures and exigencies of business impinged on the Shanghai art world, coloring even the private personae of its inhabitants. Thus, it is perhaps not surprising that Ren Bonian chose that most commercial of genres, *meiren* painting, to express his own position, and employed the *meiren*, the empty vessel, as an equivalent for his own situation. If so, not only is the missing male protagonist found, but the strong element of self-projection may explain Ren's reiterated strategy of not giving what is demanded or expected, of holding back from absolute visual possession. For Ren, identifying with his heroines who, though trapped in place, refuse to make meaning, may have been his only way to answer the demand for endless production.

Notes

1 The best biography on Ren Bonian is Ding Xiyuan's excellent monograph and chronology, *Ren Bonian* (chap. 1, n. 18).

2 The first poem is taken from a cycle of twelve poems titled "Twelve Friends," dedicated to Wu's friends in art circles. See Wu Changshi, *Foulu Shi* [Poems from the Pottery Hut] (1893), juan. 2, p. 14a. Though this collection of poems was not published until 1893, for unknown reasons, Ding Xiyuan dates the poems of "Twelve Friends" to 1886. The second poem is from a seal carved for Ren by Wu. Rubbings of this seal and the inscription on its side are reproduced in *Wu Changshi yinpu* [Wu Changshi's seal manual] (Shanghai: Shanghai shuhua chubanshe, 1985), 69. For transcriptions of its inscriptions, see Ding Xiyuan, *Ren Bonian*, 79, 81.

3 *Yushizhai huashi* [Painting knowledge from the studio of the speaking stone], 15a, published as part of Yang's *Nanhu caotang shiji* [Collected poems from the Thatched Hut of South Lake] (Shanghai, 1882). Yang writes, "'When it does not rain, the standing banana palms sigh and sough [literally, make a sound like "sousou"],' is a line from Song poetry. When Bonian applies his brush, there is the

sound of sighing and soughing." The "sousou" sound Yang describes can also denote the sound of wind and rain and suggest speed.

4 For a transcription of the inscription, see Ding Xiyuan, *Ren Bonian*, 95–96. Xu Garden (formerly located on Tiantong Road and Shanxi North Road, destroyed in a 1945 fire), a well-known private garden, was built by the businessman Xu Dishan, and was a gathering place for local Shanghai literati.

5 This painting is now in the Shanghai Museum, and has never been published. For a transcription of the inscription, see Ding Xiyuan, *Ren Bonian*, 93.

6 Yang, *Haishang molin* (chap. 1, n. 13, above). It is often assumed that Ren Bonian saw Bada Shanren's works in the collection of his friend Gao Yong, who considered himself a follower of both Bada and Shitao. For more evidence on Bada's contemporary reputation, see several Wu Changshi inscriptions on Bada's paintings in Wu Dongmai, ed., *Wu Changshi tanyilu* [Wu Changshi's discussions on art] (Beijing: Renmin meishu chubanshe, 1993), 69–71.

7 See Ding Xiyuan, *Ren Bonian*, 89. According to Ding, Ren made at least three copies of Hua Yan's painting in 1888, one of which is now in the China Art Gallery, Beijing. *Jingu yuan* appears to be the basis for several other romance themes that preoccupied Ren in the later 1880s, including "Flute-playing in Dongshan," "Xiaohong sings softly while I play the flute," and "Su Shi discussing Chan."

8 *Foulu Shi*, juan. 2, p. 14a (n. 2 above). Also see Ding Xiyuan, "Ren Bonian renwuhua zongshu" [Ren Bonian's figure painting], *Mingjia hanmo* 28 (1990): 48–87.

9 Hung Wu, "Beyond Stereotypes: The Twelve Beauties in Early Qing Court Art and the *Dream of the Red Chamber*," in Ellen Widmer and Kang-i Sun Chang, eds., *Writing Women in Late Imperial China* (Stanford: Stanford University Press, 1997), 306–65. Also see He Yanzhe, "Cong Jia-Dao shinu hua kan Qing houqi shenmei xintai wenhua guannian ji huajia jingyu zhibian" [Examining later Qing changes in aesthetics, culture, attitudes, and artists' circumstances in Jiaqing and Daoguang era paintings of women], unpublished paper, presented at the symposium New Interpretations of Ming-Qing Painting Studies, December 1994, Beijing.

10 It has been said that Ren's early *zi*, "Xiaolou" was taken on in homonymic homage to Fei Danxu, whose *hao* was Xiaolou. Fei's influence can clearly be seen in Ren's *meiren* paintings of the later 1860s.

11 There are no other known versions of this subject by Ren. However, it can be considered a female variant to Ren's numerous depictions of the patriot Su Wu, who is often depicted as a shepherd.

12 Ren did another version of this subject in 1888, now in the Zhejiang Provincial Museum. The album version bears interesting similarities to Ren's depiction of *Nuwa and Rock*, also of 1888, of which two versions exist, one in the Xu Beihong Museum, Beijing, the other in the Minneapolis Institute of Arts.

13 This is a subject seldom executed by Ren. Another version from much earlier in his career dates from 1870 and is now in the collection of Tianjin People's Art Publishing House.

14 One of the most interesting versions, for its use of Western-style perspective, shows Xishi deep in the woods. Painted in 1885, this work is now in the Nanjing Museum.

15 Hua Mulan is a theme Ren returned to repeatedly in the 1880s; like the theme of Su Wu, it has strong nationalistic overtones. His Hua Mulan paintings

usually employ the same composition, showing Mulan from the back, looking into the distance. Ren painted similar versions in 1883 (Tianjin People's Art Publishing House) and 1885 (Nanjing Museum); a variant of this image is also found in *Jieziyuan huazhuan* (Shanghai, 1888–93; repr. Hong Kong: Zhonghua shuju, 1986), 4:309.

16 "Jingu yuan" refers to the story of Shi Chong of the Jin dynasty and the lavish Golden Valley Garden he built, as well as his favorite concubine, the flute-playing Green Pearl, and their doomed love. This story may well have had contemporary currency for Ren Bonian and his audience. As Jonathan Hay observes, "Golden Valley"—with its associations of literary romance and luxury—was also the name of the performance hall at Yeshi yuan, Shanghai's premier female storytelling house. The vogue for *shuyu*, or female storytellers and singers was at its height among Shanghai's elite in the 1880s. For an illustration of Yeshi yuan, see Wu Youru, *Shenjiang shengjing tu* [Shanghai's famous sights illustrated] (Shanghai: Shenchang shuhua shi, 1884), 30. On *shuyu*, see Gail Hershatter, *Dangerous Pleasures: Prostitution and Modernity in 20th Century Shanghai* (Berkeley: University of California Press, 1997), 42–43.

17 *Wu Changshi yinpu* (Shanghai: Shanghai shuhua chubanshe, 1985; repr. 1995), 69. For a transcription, see Ding Xiyuan, *Ren Bonian*, 79. Written in late 1886, Wu Changshi's dedication on the side of the seal reads, "Mr. Bonian's painting achieves an extraordinary flavor, / Those seeking his paintings hound his heels, / Without a moment of spare time, / He changes his *hao* to "Painting Slave," / He is good at comparing himself [to a painting slave]. . . ."

18 Ren Bonian, *Still Life with Inkstone* (1886, location unknown; sold at Sotheby's HK, 18 May 1989, #99). Gao Yong was a prominent figure in the late 19th-century Shanghai art world. An amateur calligrapher, seal carver, and painter, Gao Yong was also a collector and patron. He organized the first Chinese professional association for artists in 1909, and in 1920 commissioned a history of Shanghai painting, Yang Yi's *Haishang molin* [Shanghai's Forest of Ink] (chap. 1, n. 13). Ren Bonian painted a portrait of Gao Yong in the role of a calligraphy peddlar (1887, The Palace Museum, Beijing).

19 See the seal Wu carved for Ren in *Wu Changshi yinpu*, 118. For a transcription of Wu's dedicatory poem, see Ding Xiyuan, *Ren Bonian*, 95.

4

The Traditionalist Response to Modernity: The Chinese Painting Society of Shanghai

Julia F. Andrews and Kuiyi Shen

Historians of Chinese art have tended to suggest, either explicitly or implicitly, that the great heritage of Chinese painting will survive against all odds in modern society. This viewpoint assumes a natural continuity in the tradition, and takes no account of the radically altered economic, social, and physical environment in which artists of the twentieth century worked. We argue in this essay that the continued practice of quasi-traditional Chinese painting in modern China is not natural, but instead may be an active, idealistic, self-conscious, and even modern phenomenon.

Publications of the Republican period tell a story that is complex, both for individual *guohua* artists and for *guohua* as a whole. Within the artists' lives, passed as they were in what may have been the most complicated times in China's history, one may observe fascinating transformations of both art and artists' beliefs about their purpose in twentieth-century society.

Traditionalist artists in the Republican era, most of whom were born and educated in imperial China, faced fundamental questions about their position and the survival of the art of *guohua* in the modern era. What was to be the role of traditional Chinese painting and the artists who produced it? What would be traditional painting's economic position in modern China, specifically in China's modernizing cities? To what extent could or should its ideological underpinnings be incorporated into modern society?

Of particular significance for answering these questions, despite their absence from the public record after 1949, are the proliferating private groups and societies in Republican China that were dedicated to the promotion of traditional Chinese painting. Whereas Western-style institutions, most notably schools but also modern organizations such as publishers, promoted primarily Western-style art, traditional art flourished mainly outside such modern, state-sponsored institutions. It was supported by a hybrid art market that combined traditional and modern sales methods in a uniquely Chinese manner. A publication from the end of the Republican era, the *1947 China Art Yearbook*, makes clear that throughout the first half of the twentieth century, private art groups were the most important organizations for the preservation, promotion, and development of Chinese painting.[1]

The necessity of private art groups for the functioning of the world of *guohua* of the Republican period led us in our preliminary research to concentrate on a select group of art societies. Our first project was a brief study of the Chinese Women's Calligraphy and Painting Society, founded in Shanghai in 1934.[2] Here we continue that project by considering the Chinese Painting Society, founded in Shanghai in 1931. The size and quality of its membership, its idealistic ambitions, the significance of its publications, and finally its recognition by the government, suggest that this group was one of the most important of its kind in the modern era.

Although the Chinese Painting Society had ambitions greater than other contemporary societies did, it had roots in previous groups. Painting societies were extremely fashionable in the Chinese art world of the 1930s, but they were certainly not new. As has been well documented elsewhere, informal cultural societies of all sorts flourished in imperial China. The authors of the *1947 China Art Yearbook*, apparently relying in part on Yang Yi's 1919 *Haishang molin*, document several important Shanghai groups, including gatherings hosted by Li Weizhuang at Pingyuan shanfang between 1792 and 1806; those hosted by Jiang Baoling at Xiao Penglai in 1839; and those hosted by Wu Zonglin at Pinghuashe shuhuahui between 1851 and 1874, which involved artists such as Qian Huian and Wu Qiuyuan.[3]

The authors of the yearbook comment that all of these gatherings were assembled by a private individual, and were in the nature of the "elegant gathering," but were certainly not "organizations." The first organized calligraphy and painting society may have been the Haishang Tijinguan. It is not clear when the group began, but it ceased functioning in the autumn of 1926, after about thirty or forty years of operation. Based on the activities of its first director, Wang Xun, it is estimated that the group was founded in the mid-Guangxu era.

After 1911, many retired Qing officials moved to Shanghai; most liked calligraphy and painting. The Haishang Tijinguan became a sort of club for them, especially in the evenings. The old gentlemen would talk not only of painting and calligraphy but also about politics of the bygone era. The group also served an important economic function: they maintained a price list for each member and acted as agent for painting and calligraphy sales. According to the yearbook, most painters newly arrived in Shanghai would present themselves to these gentlemen to establish a price list and to obtain their backing. For example, in 1916 Haishang Tijinguan elders Di Pingzi, Xuan Guyu, Deng Qiumei, and Mao Zijian published on the front page of *Shibao* [Eastern times] a pricelist for their colleague Huang Binhong, as follows:

> Huang Binhong has researched the Six Laws [of Painting] for many years. He excels in Northern Song styles. This richness and vitality are rarely found in recent work. Huang Binhong has recently produced some excellent work that can satisfy the desires of collectors. If interested, please contact Youzheng Bookstore on Wanping Road or any fanshop. Prices are as follows:
>
> *Tangfu* [full-size hanging scrolls]: 4 feet high, 8 yuan; 5 feet, 12 yuan; 6 feet, 20 yuan; 8 feet, 40 yuan
>
> *Hengfu* [horizontal panels]: double the price above
>
> *Pingtiao* [narrow vertical paintings]: half the above price
>
> *Lizhou* [hanging scrolls]: seventy percent the above price
>
> Fans and album leaves: 2 yuan each
>
> Hand scrolls: 2 yuan per foot
>
> Blue-green color and double inscriptions [i.e., dedication as well as signature]: double price[4]

The first director of the Haishang Tijinguan was Wang Xun, with Wu Changshi as his vice-director. Funding was said to have come from the wealthy official and compradore Sheng Xuanhuai. The group's meeting place was on Si Malu (Fourth Avenue) next to the Sanshan huiguan. In 1917, after the death of Wang Xun, Wu Changshi succeeded him as director, and Ha Shaofu and Wang Yiting became vice-directors of the group. Wu Daiqiu moved from Beijing to Shanghai at that time to become resident manager of the club facilities.[5] Notable members of that organization who were later important to the Chinese Painting Society included Wang Yiting, Huang Binhong, He Tianjian, and Qian Shoutie.[6]

A second group important for our purposes is the Yu Garden Calligraphy and Painting Charitable Society, founded in 1908. It was headquartered at the Deyuelou of the Yu Garden in Shanghai, and the charter stipulated that all work, except calligraphy, be collaborative. Half the price of work sold would be returned to the artists; the other half would be invested in a Chinese-style bank (*qianzhuang*), with the interest used for charitable purposes—hence the name. The cause to which the money would be contributed was decided by a meeting of the group. In winter they usually bought rice and in summer purchased medicine. They donated to areas of Gansu, Zhejiang, Shandong, and Henan that suffered from floods or droughts. The founders of the group were Yao Hong, Huang Jun, Wang Kun, Gao Yong, and Yang Yi. Its date of disbandment is not known, but an attempt to revive it in 1928 was not successful. As was the case with the Haishang Tijinguan, some of the members of this group became influential in the Chinese Painting Society.

A spin-off from the Haishang Tijinguan, the Guhuan Jinyushe, was founded in 1926, after internal conflicts caused it to collapse. The old Tijinguan group welcomed new members. As was the case in the Tijinguan all expenses were paid by a private individual, this time Wu Youqian of the Xiling Seal Carving Society, and membership dues were not required. The group met nightly from six to ten, and held additional dinners, usually monthly, that were hosted by its members in rotation. Some members, including Qian Shoutie, Ding Nianxian, Wang Yiting, Ma Qizhou, Shang Shengbo, Zheng Yue, Wang Geyi, Ma Mengrong, and Fang Jiekan went on to form the Chinese Painting Society. The group disbanded in 1930.

These three groups, which flourished in the 1910s and 1920s, had particular importance, not only socially but economically. They greatly emphasized the promotion of traditional painting by controlling the prices and marketing methods.[7] A somewhat differently oriented group was the Chinese Epigraphy, Calligraphy, and Painting Study Society (Zhongguo jinshi shuhua yiguan xuehui), founded in late 1925 by Huang Binhong and others and based at Youzheng Bookstore on Weihaiwei Road.[8] This group met once every season, and one of its primary purposes seems to have been publication of its scholarly journal. The manifesto for the group, possibly composed by Huang Binhong, makes clear the culturally nationalistic goals of the society:

> With the communication of all nations in recent times, all civilized countries wish to actively cherish their nation's native products, and thus those scholars who investigate the past are increasingly numerous. The powerful countries of Europe and America have museums and exhibitions everywhere, and thus can further expand their [people's] learning, create elegant arts and crafts, firmly maintain their ambition and moral fortitude, and cultivate lofty dispositions. Now, any gentlemen or ladies of our nationality may be members of our society. The goal of the society is to collect epigraphy, calligraphy, or painting; research the arts of calligraphy, painting, and seal carving; create opportunities for people to meet to pool their collective wisdom and absorb useful ideas; promote Chinese art to a perfect realm; and attract more artists with the same ideas.[9]

The mission statement of the society further states that it will "preserve the national essence and develop national glory; research art to inspire in people loftiness of mind."

The immediate progenitor of the Chinese Painting Society, according to the *Yearbook of Chinese Art*, was the Bee Society, founded in 1929 by Zheng Wuchang, Wang Shizi, Zhang Shanzi, Xie Gongzhan, He Tianjian, Lu Danlin, Sun Xueni, and other painting friends.[10] Qian Shoutie, Li Zuhan, and Ma Mengrong are listed as additional founders, and other administrators include Xu Zhengbai and Zheng Yue.[11] The membership reached over a hundred before the group transformed itself two years later into the Chinese Painting Society.

The group sponsored lectures on *guohua*, published a journal called *Bee Pictorial* and other occasional publications, including titles such as *Mifeng huaji* and *Dangdai mingjia huahai*. It had a fairly complex written charter, a published member's list, formal monthly meetings, and an annual exhibition. In its clubhouse, where members could gather at their leisure, were to be stored antique paintings and calligraphy for study. Among other notable members were Xie Yucen, Qian Shoutie, Yu Jianhua, Wang Geyi, Xiong Songquan, Xie Zhiguang, Wang Yiting, Ying Yeping, and Zhang Daqian, as well as some of the subsequent founders of the Women's Calligraphy and Painting Society, including Wu Qingxia and Li Qiujun.

With its exhibitions and publications, the Bee Society seems to have had a modern structure, but it was not until 1930, when, according to the published history, Ye Gongchuo enlisted the ideologically sharper writers Huang Binhong and Lu Danlin to assist in organizing a new group, that the society attained its national and modern character. The opening statement of the new group, "Guohua artists must unite" (*Guohuajia jiying lianhe*), was drafted by Lu Danlin in the last issue of Bee Pictorial.[12] The group's manifesto was far more ideological than any that preceded it:

Origins of the Chinese Painting Society, 1930
In the current situation of comparison between the cultures of the world, there is nothing that fails to give us a feeling of indignation and shame. Particularly, the decrepit state of our art world makes us feel that our responsibility toward the future is even greater, and we cannot shirk it by shifting this burden to others. Regardless of which country in Europe or America, there is not one that does not promote and develop its traditional culture for the purpose of displaying its national character. Painting is certainly the most valuable way of displaying culture. By its basic nature, it is the site where the most elevated aspects of human morality may be lodged. Because of this, in most civilized nations, which are driven by their heaven-bestowed characters, there is no one who doesn't know to seriously promote their tradition of painting, so as to develop in the people harmonious sentiments.

Japan is the descendent of our nation's culture, although because of differences of natural character it never fundamentally resembles us. It, however, always presents itself to the world as the patriarch of Oriental art. This should be enough to arouse us to reproach ourselves. Originally our nation's art, such as painting and sculpture, was by the Six Dynasties era acknowledged as reaching greatness. And this greatness expressed the genius and subjective feelings of its makers; this resembles in some ways the symbolist art that is current today. But there is lack of concrete systematic research, and to this point it has never been made clear and promoted. People today advocate a new culture that absorbs foreign thought, but they have not established any goals, and without any selection they follow, in a daily increasing flood, trends such as "mechanization" (*chanye zhuyi*) and "materialism" (*lizhi zhuyi*). Our nation's people suffer the constraints of mechanization, and lose their inherent human freedom; this blind following of foreign thought is one reason for the decline of our nation's painting. In recent decades, we have suffered continuous civil war and constant political coups, those in power were always concerned with solving these problems and never paid attention to art. This is the influence of politics on our nation's art, and why it has not been actively promoted. Another reason, from the point of view of society, is that today, when material power surpasses all else, the life of the masses gradually has lost the stable bonds that tied it together; the taste and appreciation for art cannot correspondingly increase, and the situation of art, with its subjective expression, cannot avoid suffering direct setbacks. From the point of view of the painters themselves, most suffer the constraints of their surroundings, and thus divine genius and human effort cannot come to fruition. Add to this another reason, that there are no permanent organizations to unify the artists, then the very survival of art has lost its foundation. If we thus know the harmful causes, but do not try to put them right, we have failed in our responsibilities.

We have heard that there is not a single country in Europe, to say nothing of our eastern neighbor, Japan, that does not have painting organizations; among them there are groups of different natures, some public some private, some organized by painters with supplemental assistance from the government, some organized at governmental behest by painters, or in some the painters are given the opportunity to unite by society's power, or some in which the painters simply take action to organize themselves.

Therefore, they are able to solve appropriately questions of international status and specialized professional problems. Reflecting on the situation of our painters, although there are a few organizations, their characters and goals are little different from clubs or entertainment centers; as for "the whole organization" or "united development," as in countries east and west, this has not yet been seen. How can we not feel shame? We thus feel, based on this observation, that in order to respond to this practical need of today, organizing the Chinese Painting Society cannot be delayed. The mission of the society is: (1) to develop the age-old art of our nation; (2) to publicize it abroad and raise our international artistic stature; (3) with a spirit of mutual assistance on the part of the artists, to plan for a [financially] secure living. Our capabilities are limited, but with human help and the grace of heaven, there is nothing that cannot be accomplished. To do this with people of like mind and to promote the development of our nation's art, this is our common aspiration."[13]

The society's primary administrators were, in succession, Qian Shoutie, He Tianjian, and Wang Yachen. Others listed as important organizers were Zhang Yuguang, Zheng Wuchang, Sun Xueni, Lu Danlin, Ma Gongyu, Zhang Daqian, Ding Nianxian, Wang Shizi, Chen Dingshan, Li Zuhan, Xie Gongzhan, Wang Yachen, Chen Shuren, Jing Hengyi, Zhang Shanzi, Wang Yiting, Xiong Songquan, Wu Hufan, and Huang Binhong. Beyond its idealistic, culturally nationalistic, and practical aims, the group was quite proud that it eventually was registered with the government. Although the significance of the request is not yet clear, the group was asked to fulfill some quasi-governmental functions, such as to organize the Shanghai section of the 1935 Hankou Exhibition.

Among the activities for which the Chinese Painting Society sought to be remembered are their publications. *Guohua yuekan*, published in 1934 and 1935 under the editorship of Huang Binhong, He Tianjian, Lu Danlin, Wang Yachen, Zheng Wuchang, and Xie Haiyan, was a professional journal that was often quite ideological, especially in its cultural nationalism. Other publications included reproduction albums, including *Xiandai zhongguo huaji*. They also held exhibitions, both domestically and abroad, and facilitated what we would today describe as networking among artists. The group had about three hundred members, reaching as far north as Beijing and as far south as Hong Kong.

A key factor in the society's importance was the number of first rate artists who were members. Equally important were its key theorists. Several of them are of special importance here.

Huang Binhong (1864–1955), who has been well-studied elsewhere, was an extremely important theorist.[14] Of relevance here is his intensive involvement with writing and editing traditionalist art theory and in organizing traditionalist art societies. Among his editorial contributions may be listed the monumental *Guocui xuebao, Shenzhou guoguang ji* (1908–1918), *Yiguan* (1926–1928), *Meishu congshu, Huaxue yuekan* (1932), and *Guohua* (1930), to say nothing of his work on publications directly connected to the Chinese Painting Society.[15] He reflected in the inaugural issue of *Guohua yuekan* that Chinese scholars needed to reexamine themselves rather than focus on the strengths of others, and that they could not maintain the honor of their tradition without studying it earnestly. For this reason, his calling in life was to conduct research on "the national essence" and to popularize traditional Chinese culture.[16]

Huang was also instrumental in organizing like-minded scholars of the period into societies. In addition to those we have already mentioned, he was one of the initiators, along with Wang Yiting, Wu Daiqiu, and others, of the Shanghai Chinese Painting and Calligraphy Preservation Society (Shanghai Zhongguo shuhua baocunhui) in 1929, which aimed, like the later Chinese Painting Society, to preserve the national essence and promote art.[17]

He Tianjian (1891–1977), who served as editor-in-chief of *Guohua yuekan* beginning with the fourth issue, is justifiably well known as a painter. Like Huang Binhong, he was very active in traditionalist theoretical circles. In 1920, he and Hu Dinglu founded the Mount Xi Calligraphy and Painting Society (Xishan shuhuahui) in their native Wuxi, into which they invited painters active in Shanghai, such as Zhang Daqian, Wu Hufan, Xie Gongzhan, Shang Shengbo, and Lai Chusheng. During his tenure at *Guohua yuekan* He Tianjian published in its pages a number of pointed articles, including "The Theoretical Principles of the Chinese Painting Society," "Calligraphy and Painting Societies: Their Right and Wrong Ways of Operating," "The Morbid State of Chinese Landscape Painting Today and the Way to Heal It," "About Painting Standards," and so forth.[18] He also made his opinions known in the popular magazine *Meishu shenghuo* in such articles as "My Opinion on Chinese Painting," and in the theoretical journal *Huaxue yuekan*, to name only a few publications.[19] His first solo painting exhibition, according to a contemporary magazine article, was held April 3–5, 1936, at the Ningbo Native Place Society.[20]

Qian Shoutie (1897–1967), also from Wuxi, was active in earlier Shanghai societies such as Haishang Tijinguan and Guhuan jinyushe. He founded a group called Red Leaf Calligraphy and Painting Society in Shanghai in 1922, and went on to be involved in establishing the Bee Society in 1929. He was a key figure in both the administrative and social life of the Chinese Painting Society and went on to have substantial influence as an editor of the magazine *Meishu shenghuo*.

One of the key figures in establishing the Chinese Painting Society, Zheng Chang (also known by his *zi*, Wuchang; 1894–1952), remained extremely active in publishing and theoretical circles until shortly before his suicide, in 1952. His painting, particularly that of the late 1940s, is noteworthy, as well. He worked as art director of China Book Company (Zhonghua shuju) in the 1920s and 1930s. In 1929 he was instrumental in establishing the Bee Society, and went on to edit its journal. A founder of the Chinese Painting Society, he was an editor and contributor to *Guohua yuekan*, contributing such essays as "The Responsibility that Today's Chinese Painters Should Assume."[21] He went on to be active in a small art group, the Society of Nine, with Zhang Daqian, Zhang Shanzi, Tang Dingzhi, Lu Danlin, Xie Yucen, and others, and in 1936 began editing the Chinese Painting Society's theoretical journal, *Guohua*. After the war, he was a founder of the Shanghai Art and Tea Society (Shanghai meishu chahui), a large and active group that was instrumental in the editing and publishing of the *1947 Yearbook of Chinese Art*.[22] He also published a number of books about Chinese art history, including *A History of Chinese Art*, *Research on the History of Chinese Mural Painting*, *An Interpretation of Shitao's Huayulu*, and *A General History of Chinese Painting Theory*, some of which were still in print as late as the 1960s.[23]

We believe that between 1931 and the fall of Shanghai to the Japanese the administrative structures of the Chinese Painting Society allowed it to function in a very modern way. To do this, it brought together various disparate modern trends developed by earlier Shanghai art groups, particularly those to which its organizers had belonged. The economic and social functions of the Yuyuan Calligraphy and Painting Charitable Society and Shanghai Tijinguan were combined with the increasingly sharp ideological stances promoted by Huang Binhong, He Tianjian, and Lu Danlin, thus leading to a complex multiplicity of promotional activities.[24]

The diversity of their activity is shown by their publications alone. *Guohua yuekan* was devoted to scholarly debates, and in some cases, as in the series devoted to Eastern and Western views of the landscape, published the views of radical modernist oil painters, in this case Ni Yide, alongside those of strident traditionalists.[25]

Guohua yuekan also published a newsletter-like section that reported such news as:

> Wang Yiting is ill; Wang Yiting has recovered and is resting at home; Wang Yiting is painting and praying to the Buddha on a daily basis.

Xu Beihong has returned from Europe and resumed his professorship at Central University.

Wu Hufan, Zhang Shanzi, Zhang Daqian, and Peng Gongfu held a four-man show in Beijing.

Wu Qingxia and her father Wu Zhongxi were guests of the industrialist Luo Liqin at West Lake for two weeks.

Feng Wenfeng has returned from Hong Kong and plans a solo show in Shanghai next year.

Sun Xueni is now editing *Shengsheng yuekan* and *Julebu.*

Nine artists, including Zhang Shanzi, Zheng Wuchang [Zheng Chang], and Zhang Daqian, have established the Society of Nine.

Huang Binhong is holding classes at his home three times a week.

Qian Shoutie traveled to Japan to visit Hashimoto Kansetsu at his home in Kyoto.[26]

The journal also began publishing members' price lists, including those of Huang Binhong, Yu Jianhua (fig. 1), and lesser painters, both male and female.

A significant activity of the core group, but interestingly not included in the Yearbook, is its domination of the editorial board of the mass media *Meishu shenghuo* [*Arts & Life*] (fig. 2). In addition to the aestheticist or family-oriented features, the magazine publicized, through feature articles and pictures, exhibitions of the Chinese Painting Society as well as those of related groups, such as Chinese Women's Calligraphy and Painting Society. The inaugural issue of April 1934 included an editorial statement by Qian Shoutie and a feature about the Chinese Painting Society's Exhibition, with reproductions of works by Feng Chaoran, Ying Yeping, Qian Shoutie, Wang Geyi, the female artists Gu Qingyao and Lu Xiaoman, and others. A notice soliciting new members was printed on the same page, along with a reordered version of the three principles enumerated above, and a specification that no gender distinctions were made for membership. Modern publishing, at both popular and professional levels, was thus used to promote various aspects of the group's goals, which included study of classical paintings and classical painting theory, promotion of the status of *guohua,* and promotion of the professional careers and economic status of individual *guohua* artists.[27]

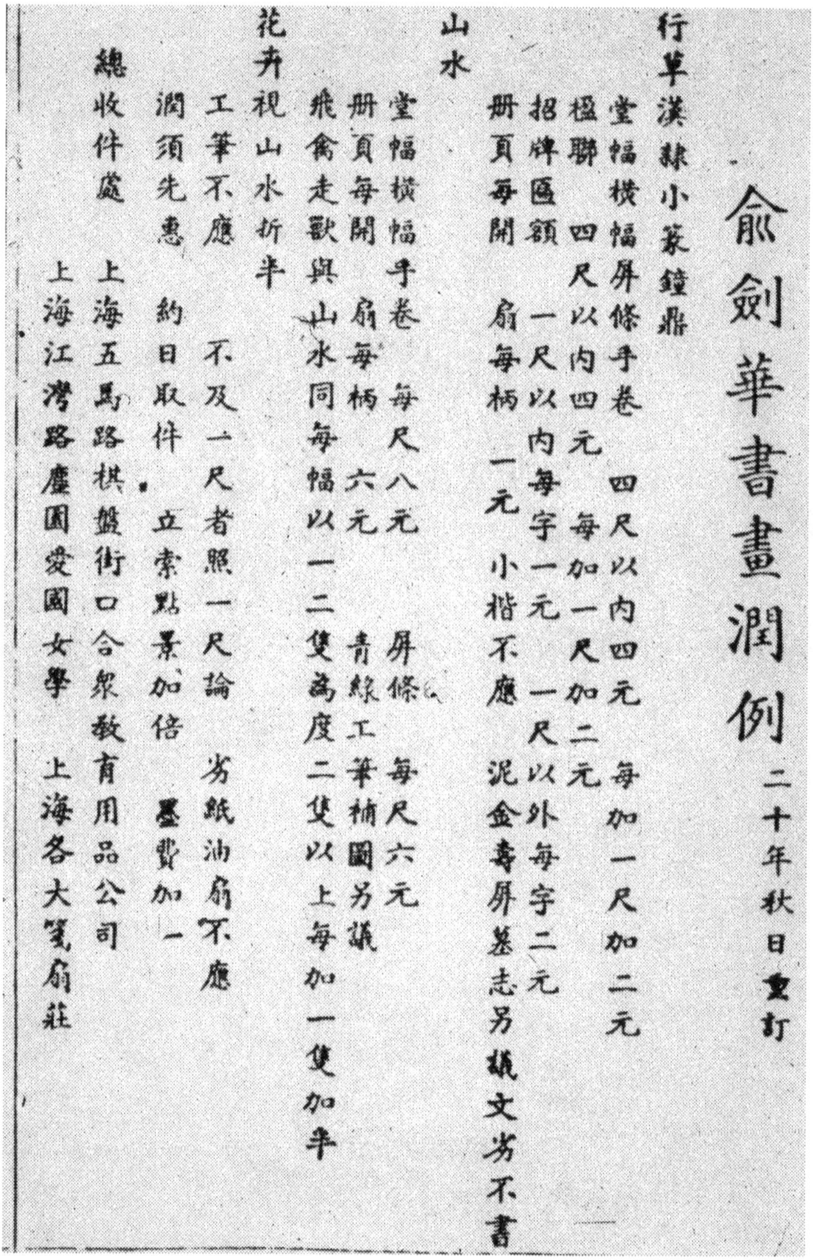

俞劍華書畫潤例　二十年秋日重訂

行草漢隸小篆鐘鼎

堂幅橫幅屏條手卷　四尺以內四元　每加一尺加二元

楹聯　四尺以內四元　每加一尺加二元

招牌區額　一尺以內每字一元　一尺以外每字二元

冊頁每開　扇每柄　一元　小楷不應　況金壽屏墓志另議文芳不書

山水

堂幅橫幅手卷　每尺八元　屏條　每尺六元

冊頁每開　扇每柄　六元　青綠工筆楠圓另議

飛禽走獸與山水同　每幅以一二雙為度　二雙以上每加一隻加半

花卉　視山水折半

工筆不應　不及一尺者照一尺論　芳紙油扇不應

潤須先惠　約日取件　立索點景加倍　墨費加一

總收件處

上海五馬路棋盤街口合泉教育用品公司

上海江灣路廬園愛國女學　上海各大箋扇莊

Fig. 1. Yu Jianhua, pricelist. After *Guohua yuekan* (1931).

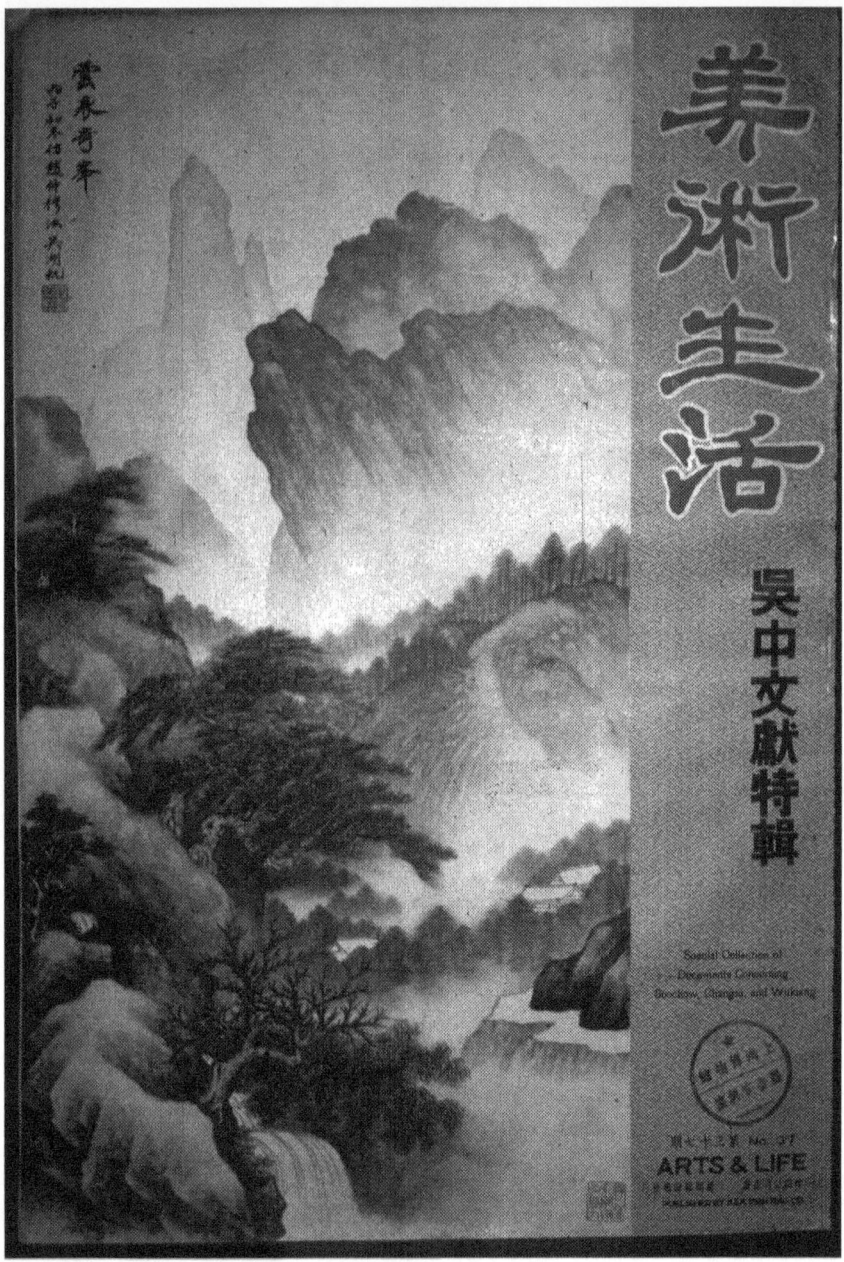

Fig. 2. Cover of *Meishu shenghuo,* no. 37 (1937).

Conclusion

Art historians and artists favorably disposed to traditional Chinese painting have suggested that the great literati painting tradition, which had flourished since the fourteenth century, simply continued, as if automatically, either until it was uprooted in the 1950s or until today. Antipathetic writers, particularly radical Westernizers inside and outside the Communist party, made similar assumptions about the natural continuity of the tradition when they castigated *guohua* painters for their blind adherence to the standards of a long-defunct cultural past.[28] Although strands of uncritical and reflexive traditionalism may indeed be found in the Republican period, as in virtually all periods of human history, the proliferation of journals and painting clubs devoted to the preservation and development of traditional Chinese art in the 1920s and 1930s suggests that, at least in some important circles, the continued practice of Chinese painting was a much more difficult task and had somewhat more complicated implications than has been previously assumed.

What it meant to be an artist in China was radically transformed, like most aspects of Chinese cultural life, by the collapse of the Qing dynasty and the classical norms of education that had supported the imperial system. Moreover, the rapidly changing economic situation between about 1900 and 1937, especially in urban China, required each artist to chart a career that had no precedent in China's imperial past. With the foundations of traditional art under attack, the choice of traditional painting as the preferred form of artistic expression could no longer be assumed. As Ralph Croizier, Mayching Kao, Zhu Boxiong, and others have described, many talented young artists rejected traditional art in favor of Western styles.[29]

Nevertheless, many painters chose to work in traditional forms. The evidence of the Chinese Painting Society of 1930s Shanghai suggests that traditionalism was, to some important artists, an active, not passive, theoretical position. A preliminary survey of the critical literature of the period makes clear that many of these traditionalist groups defended their endeavors in quite idealistic and patriotic terms. When the anonymous theorist for the Chinese Painting Society quoted above wrote that the human freedom of the Chinese person was threatened by the bonds of Western-style industrialization, he or she argued for an active response. Promotion of traditional Chinese art, artistic patterns, and, by implication, native cultural patterns, might be described as a progressive activity for its time. We have not been able in this brief introduction to do more than suggest the multiplicity of solutions proposed by *guohua* painters as they struggled with the cosmopolitan culture that threatened and, despite their efforts, ultimately overwhelmed many of the arts of traditional China. The traditionalist response to modernization, with its explicit rejection of the international dominance of Western culture, continues to be an important East Asian phenomenon, and remains relevant for any study of the art of the twentieth century.

Notes

This paper was initially presented in Chinese as part of the three-year "Painting in Shanghai" project, funded by the Luce Foundation, and in English, in a slightly different form, at the College Art Association Annual Meeting in 1997. In addition to the stimulating presentations of fellow members of the Luce Foundation project, we profited greatly in the early stages of our work from our conversations with Ellen Johnston Laing, Chang Hao, and Barry Keenan.

1 *Zhongguo meishu nianjian* (Shanghai: Shanghai shi wenhua yundong wei-yuanhui, 1948). We are indebted to Ellen Johnston Laing for drawing this book to our attention and making a photocopy of it available to us. In recent years, two scholars in Shanghai, Huang Ke and Xu Zhihao, have elaborated upon this invaluable source to write histories of modern art groups: Huang Ke, "Shanghai de meishu yuanxiao he meishu shetuan," *Shanghai meishu tongxun*, Aug. 30, 1994, Nov. 25, 1994, and Feb. 15, 1995; and Xu Zhihao, *1911–1949, Zhongguo meishu qi-kan guoyanlu* (Shanghai: Shanghai shuhua chubanshe, 1992), and *Zhongguo meishu shetuan manlu* (Shanghai: Shanghai shuhua chubanshe, 1994).

2 First presented in Chinese at the Luce Foundation project meeting in 1995, a preliminary version was published: An Yalan and Shen Kuiyi (Julia F. Andrews and Kuiyi Shen), "Zhongguo nüzi shuhua hui" [The Chinese women's calligraphy and painting society], *Duoyun* (Shanghai) 47 (Dec. 1997): 45–57. For the English version, see "Traditionalism" (intro., n. 10).

3 Yang Yi, *Haishang molin* (chap. 1, n. 13).

4 *Shibao*, Dec. 1, 1916, 1. Di Pingzi (Di Baoxian) was the publisher of *Shibao* and owner of Youzheng Bookstore. See Joan Judge, *Print and Politics: "Shibao" and the Culture of Reform in Late Qing China* (Stanford: Stanford University Press, 1996), 42.

5 *Shibao*, March 28, 1917, 6. Among members in frequent attendance at that time were He Shizi, Huang Xuchu, Gao Shengbo, Cheng Zhang, Ye Zhifa, Shen Moxian, Hu Yanqin, Yin Junzhai, Wang Mengbai, Wang Yimin, Hu Boxiang, Yan Yongsan, and Xu Zhuxian. The newspaper reported that Wu Changshi frequently wrote poems on the paintings of these colleagues. Excellent works were always displayed on the walls, with free admission to the public.

6 Wang Xun, *zi* Yuanruo; Wu Changshi, *ming* Junqing; Sheng Xuanhuai, *zi* Xingsun; Wang Yiting, *ming* Zhen; Huang Binhong, *ming* Zhi; Ha Shaofu, *ming* Lin; and Qian Shoutie, *ming* Ya.

7 See Kuiyi Shen, "Shanghai Society of the Late Nineteenth Century and the Shanghai School of Painting," *Studies in Art History* 1 (1995): 135–59.

8 *Zhongguo meishu nianjian*, shi 5, transcribes the group's charter and records that it was founded in the spring of the fifteenth year of the republic (1926) by

Huang Binhong. According to Xu Zhihao, the group was established at the end of 1925, reached a high of two hundred members, and met at Shenzhou guoguangshe at the same address, 309 Weihaiwei Road. According to Xu, the journal *Yiguan* was published between February 1926 and February 1929. See *Zhongguo meishu shetuan manlu*, 76 (chap. 1, n. 31).

9 *Zhongguo meishu nianjian*, shi 5.

10 Ibid., shi 9.

11 Ibid., shi 6.

12 This article, published in *Mifeng huabao* 11–12, is cited in *Zhongguo meishu nianjian*, shi 6.

13 *Zhongguo meishu nianjian*, shi 6.

14 Studies include Jason C. Kuo, *Transforming Traditions in Modern Chinese Painting: Huang Pin-hung's Late Work* (New York and Bern: Peter Lang, 2004).

15 The results of this activity are discussed in Xu, *Zhongguo meishu qikan guoyanlu*, 34–35, 49, 86, 112–17, 136–37 (n. 1 above).

16 Huang Binhong, "Zhizhi yi wenshuo" [About the relationship between culture and country] *Guohua yuekan* 1, no. 1:6.

17 See Xu, *Zhongguo meishu qikan guoyanlu*, 49 (n. 1 above), and *Zhongguo meishu shetuan manlu*, 99–100 (n. 1 above); also *Guocui yuekan* 1.

18 He Tianjian, "Zhongguo huahui lilun shang zhi yanshu," *Guohua yuekan* 1.2 (1935): 3–4; "Shuhuahui yu zuofeng zhi shifei," *Guohua yuekan* 1.2 (1935): 20–21; "Zhongguo shanshuihua jinri zhi bingtai jiqi jiuji fangfa," *Guohua yuekan* 1.5 (1935): 100–103; "Huihua zhi biaozhun lun," *Guohua yuekan* 1.9–10 (1935): 184–88.

19 *Meishu shenghuo* 3–4 (1934) and *Huaxue yuekan* 1 (1932).

20 *Shidai* 9.8 (1936): 4, 5.

21 Zheng Wuchang, "Xiandai zhongguo huajia ying fu zhi zeren," *Guohua yuekan* 1.2:17.

22 According to the account in *Zhongguo meishu nianjian*, 12–13, the group involved more than two thousand Shanghai artists who worked in all media and two hundred members from other parts of China.

23 For example, *Zhongguo meishu shi* (Taipei: Zhonghua, 1962).

24 See Kuiyi Shen, "Shanghai Society" (n. 7 above).

25 *Guohua yuekan* 4–5 (Jan.–Feb. 1935).

26 From *Guohua yuekan* 1–10.

27 Carol Lynne Waara's dissertation, "Arts and Life: Public and Private Culture in Chinese Art Periodicals, 1912–1937" (University of Michigan, 1994), provides an overview of *Meishu shenghuo* and its staff. See also chap. 7 of this book.

28 For further discussion see Julia F. Andrews, *Painters and Politics in the People's Republic of China 1949–1979* (Berkeley: University of California Press, 1994).

29 Ralph Croizier, "Post-Impressionists" (intro., n. 9); Mayching Margaret Kao, "The Beginning of the Western-Style Painting Movement in Relationship to Reforms in Education in Early Twentieth-Century China," *New Asia Academic Bulletin (Xinya xueshu jikan)* (Hong Kong) 4 (1983): 373–79, and "China's Response to the West in Art, 1898–1937" (PhD diss., Stanford University, 1972); Zhu Boxiong and Chen Ruilin, *Zhongguo xihua wushinian, 1899–1949* [Fifty years of Western-style painting in China] (Beijing: People's Art Press, 1989).

5
Notes on Chinese Photography and Advertising in Late Nineteenth-Century Shanghai

Jonathan Hay

Although Shanghai's key role in the creation of China's modern visual culture has long been recognized, attention has focused largely on the first half of the twentieth century. Yet, there is little in the visual culture of that period that is not anticipated in the late nineteenth century—provided we always take into account the obvious differences in technology and scale of production. Late nineteenth-century Shanghai may be fruitfully characterized as a laboratory stage, where the future forms of a commercial mass visual culture were first worked out on a relatively small scale through experimentation with new, but as yet limited, technology. Elsewhere I have explored in some detail the interactions between artists and the Shanghai publishing industry during the same period, when photolithography made possible both the first pictorial journalism and the first widespread commercial exploitation of paintings, involving very large numbers of artists.[1] The present article explores in a very preliminary way two other aspects of the late nineteenth-century Shanghai laboratory: the beginnings of its Chinese photography industry and the transformation of Chinese advertising.

Chinese Photographers and Photographs

Although both foreign and Chinese photographers worked in Shanghai from the 1850s onwards, by the 1870s at the latest the foreigners were far outnumbered by their Chinese colleagues.[2] In contrast to the recent, highly detailed research on photography in Hong Kong during the same period, very little systematic work has yet been done on either foreign or Chinese photographers in late nineteenth-century Shanghai.[3] The following brief discussion focuses on *Chinese* photography in the city, leaving aside questions of photographic technique, which I am not competent to discuss.

As pointed out by Huang Shaofen and others in their history of photography in Shanghai, Chinese photographic businesses were among the first to publish advertisements in the city's main Chinese-language newspaper, *Shenbao*, as early as its second issue, in 1872.[4] A well-known and often-published photo (undated) shows the premises of two of the most famous businesses, Su Sanxing and Gongtai (fig. 1), which were among a number concentrated in the area of San Malu (Hankou Road) and Si Malu (Foochow Road) in the British Concessions.[5] By the 1880s at the latest there were probably many smaller enterprises as well. According to the Shanghai guidebook *Shenjiang mingsheng tushuo* (1884): "Photographic companies in Shanghai number in the dozens."[6]

At least two representations exist showing the photographers at work in their studios. The first, in *Shenjiang mingsheng tushuo*, depicts three courtesans having their picture taken in a photographer's studio (fig. 2). The accompanying text mentions Su Sanxing as the leading company of the day. Somewhat later, in the early 1890s, the pictorial magazine *Feiyingge huabao* published a similar representation, of a photographer's studio set up for portraiture, an image subsequently reprinted in *Wu Youru huabao* (1909; fig. 3).[7] The photographers also worked outside their studios. For example, the most famous pictorial magazine of the day, *Dianshizhai huabao*, founded in 1884, included in one of its issues of that year an image of a photographer taking a photograph in the street.[8] Other images in the *Dianshizhai huabao* over the following fifteen years showed photographers taking group photographs in gardens and buildings. Surviving photographs prove that Gongtai, for example, was also willing to send its photographers outside Shanghai.[9]

Who constituted the Chinese photographer's public and clientele? Given the small size of the Shanghai foreign population and the presence of foreign photographers working in Shanghai, it seems likely that most Chinese photographers would have tended to work for a Chinese public. However, the leading Chinese photographers (like their foreign colleagues) had mixed clienteles. Surviving albums of photographs brought back from China by Western visitors often include photographs acquired from Chinese companies in Shanghai such as Gongtai, as well as others acquired from foreign photographers.[10] These photographs often have labels printed in English, giving the name and address of the photographer, for example, "Ye-chong. Photographer and Painter on Canvas. No. 24, Foochow and Kiangse Roads, Shanghai."[11] (Early Chinese photographers had often started out as painters working in Sino-Western modes of oil painting and watercolor.)[12] Equally relevant, the illustrated magazine *The Far East*, published in Shanghai from 1876 to 1878, used Chinese as well as foreign photographers (see below). And the Shanghai

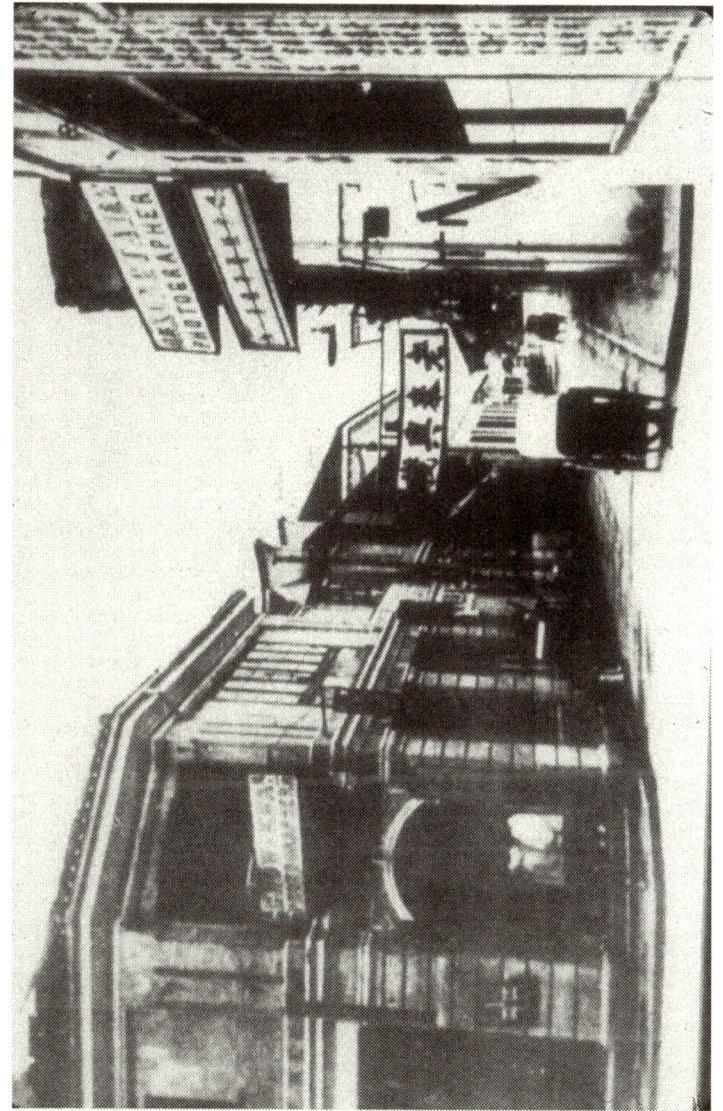

Fig. 1. Unidentified photographer, *Su Sanxing (Chow-Kwa) and Gongtai Photography Studios, Shanghai*. After Ma Yuanzeng et al., *Zhongguo sheying shi* [History of Chinese photography] (Beijing: Zhongguo sheying chubanshe, 1987), fig. 23.

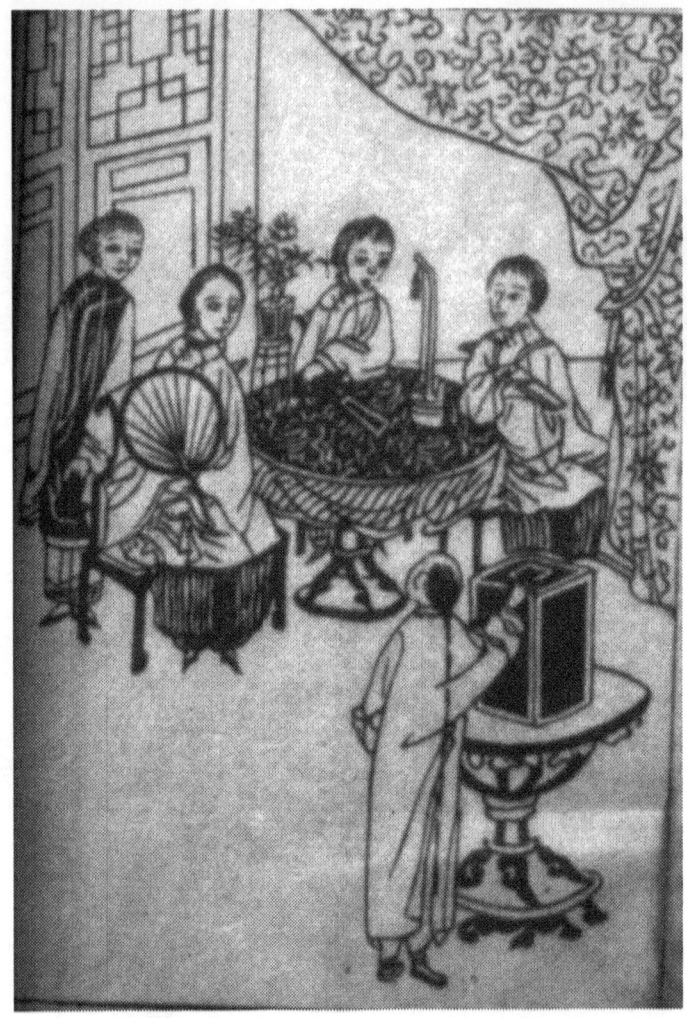

Fig. 2. Unidentified artist, *A Visit to a Photographer's Studio*.
After *Shenjiang mingsheng tushuo* (1984).

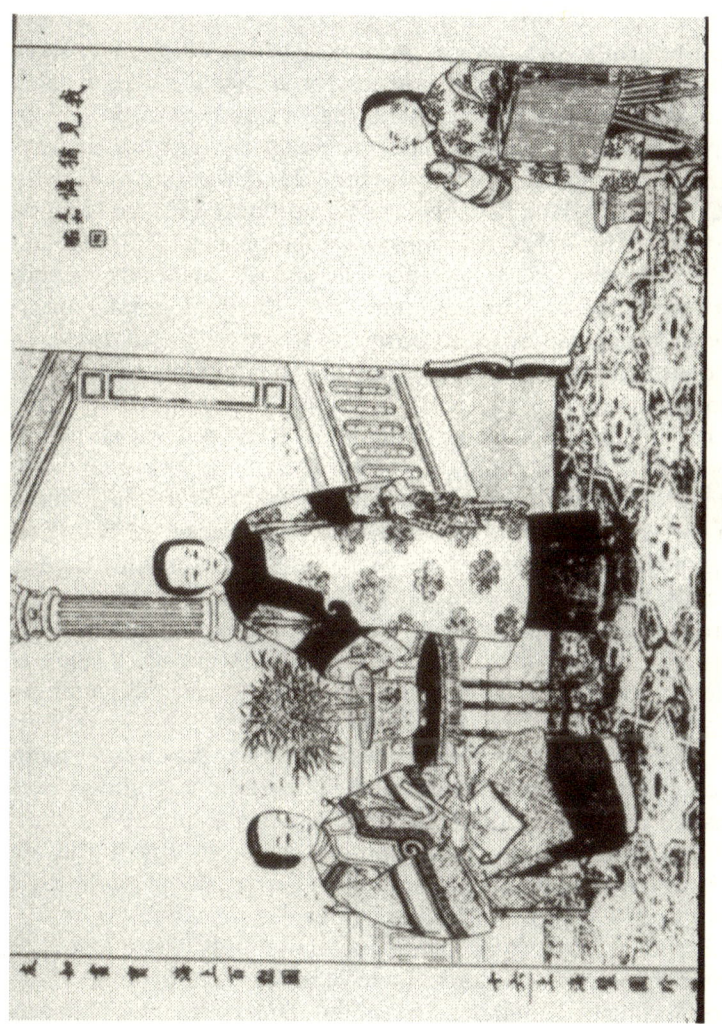

Fig. 3. Wu Youru, *A Visit to a Photographer's Studio*, originally published in the pictorial magazine *Feiyingge huabao* in the early 1890s, later reprinted in *Wu Youru huabao* (1908).

Photographic Enlarging Co. on Foochow Road (Si Malu), a Chinese-owned company founded in 1890 that was the subject of a laudatory article in the English-language newspaper *Shanghai Mercury*, anticipating a mixed clientele, proudly advertised two waiting rooms, one for foreigners and one for Chinese.[13]

While the archive of work by Chinese photographers in Shanghai may eventually prove to be vast, at present we are still at the rudimentary stage of identifying the relevant material. Fortunately, as noted earlier, in some cases the photographer attached a printed label or inscribed the mount, in English or, presumably, in Chinese. One notable example among many is a twelve-part albumen-print panorama of the "Shanghai Bund," formerly in the Lau Collection, which its label says was produced by the Gongtai company in 1881.[14] The works of Chinese photographers in Shanghai that were published between 1876 and 1878 in *The Far East* constitute a second, smaller, but very interesting, body of material.[15] The photographs (original) are often accompanied by explanations, in which the photographer is sometimes identified as Chinese; in the case of one group of photographs, originally commissioned by the Daotai of Anqing in Anhui province, the photographer is identified as Gongtai (fig. 4).[16] However, the vast majority of surviving Shanghai photographs of this early period have no documentation to establish their provenance, and can be attributed to Chinese rather than foreign photographers, and to photographers in Shanghai rather than elsewhere, only on the basis of internal evidence, which, in the case of portraits, includes the sitter's clothes and hairstyle. One group of portraits can be attributed to an as-yet-unidentified Chinese photographer in Shanghai on the basis of a striking similarity to the scene of a photographer's studio represented by Wu Youru in his *Feiyingge huabao* illustration, from the mise en scène to the clothes of the two women.[17]

Gongtai's 1881 twelve-part panorama of the "Shanghai Bund" demonstrates that, like their foreign colleagues, Chinese photographers produced tourist views for visitors to Shanghai. Another example, less typical, is a series of Sichuan landscapes published in *The Far East* in the late 1870s (fig. 5). The magazine had commissioned an unidentified Chinese photographer to take pictures in Sichuan; however, the editors were disappointed that he returned with landscape views, only a few of which they published.[18] Somewhat different (since it is not really a tourist view) is the view of Anqing by Gongtai, taken for the Daotai of the area.[19] In earlier times the Daotai would have asked a painter to paint a series of views of the area for which he had responsibility; now he could call on a photographer. It is worth noting that both the cityscapes and the landscapes follow closely the style of contemporary foreign photographers working in China.

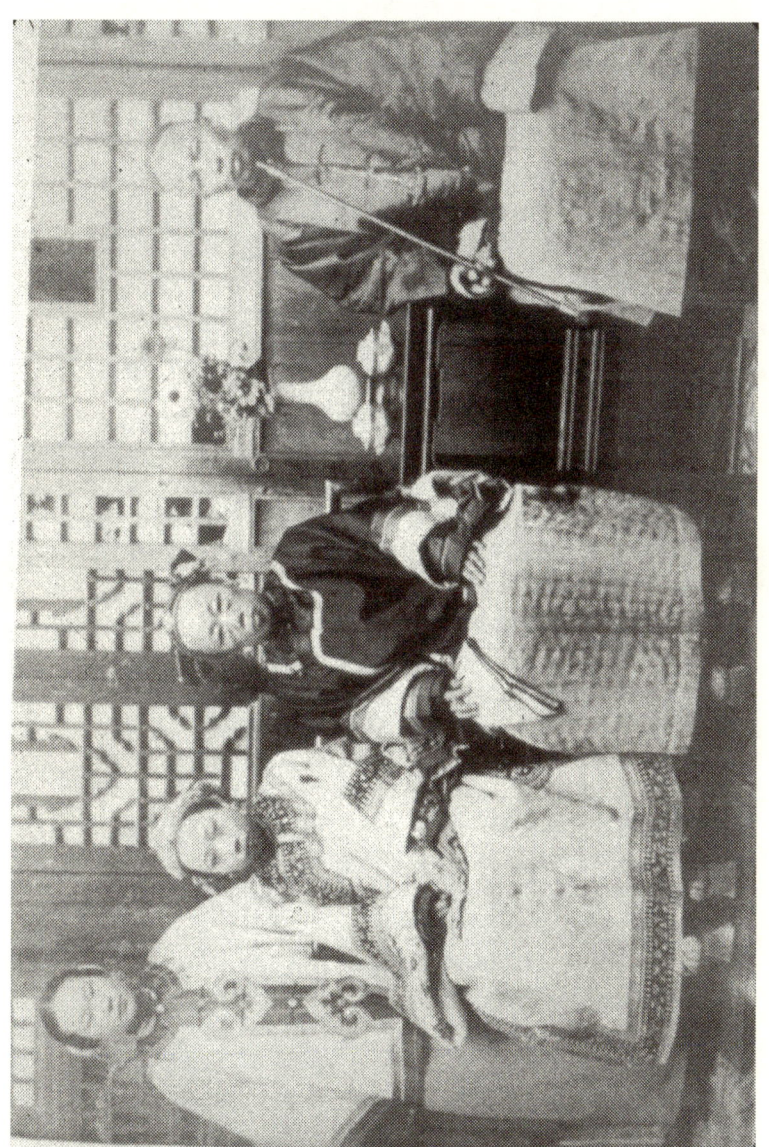

Fig. 4. Gongtai Photography Studio, *The Daotai of Anqing and His Family. After The Far East 5* (1878).

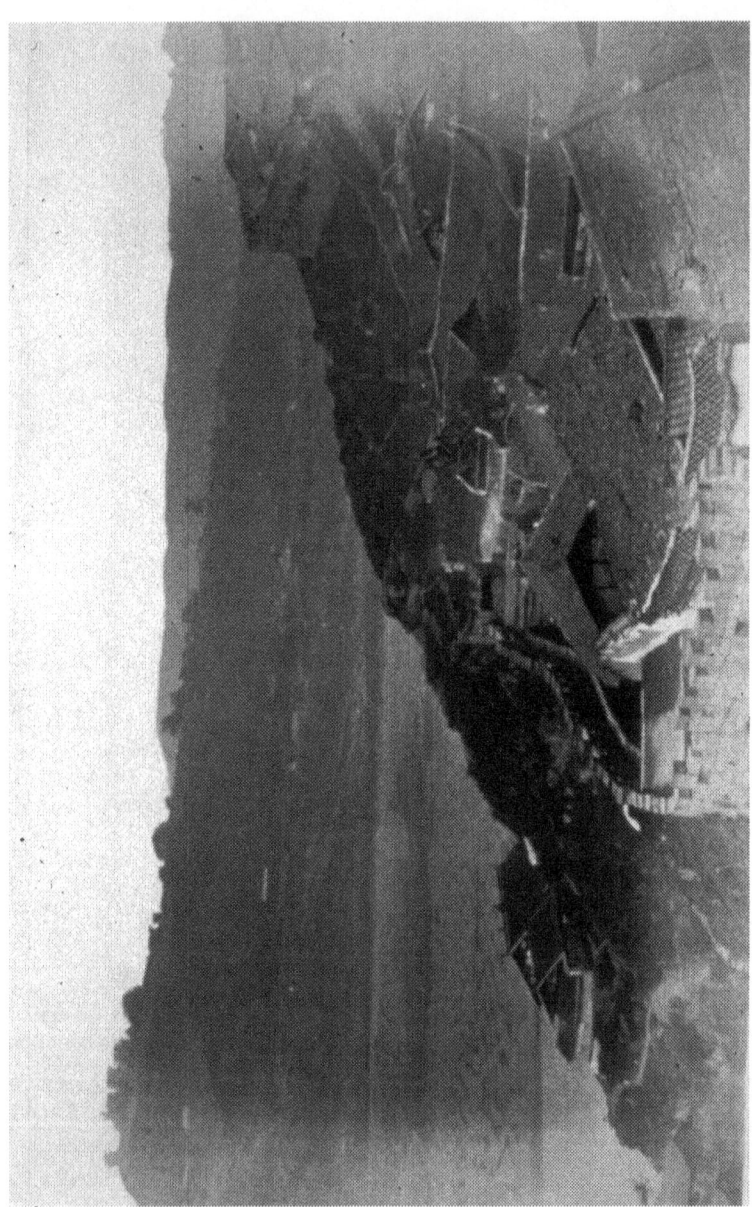

Fig. 5. Unidentified Chinese photographer from Shanghai,
Sichuan Landscape. After The Far East 3 (1877)

Similarly, Chinese photographers followed the lead of their foreign colleagues in taking journalistic photographs to commemorate special occasions, such as the opening of the Shanghai-Wusong railway in 1876. On that occasion, a commemorative photograph was offered for sale to its readers by *Shenbao*.[20]

There also existed a lucrative market for photographic images of "the Chinese," construed as a series of stereotypes. The market for photographs of this kind, aimed at foreign visitors, was initially dominated by foreign photographers, who used staged scenes. However, in Hong Kong the Chinese photographers, too, supplied such pictures, and there is no reason to think that their Shanghai counterparts would have proceeded differently.[21] In some case they may have recycled portraits as generic pictures of Chinese people. This seems likely to be the case for at least two photographs by Chinese photographers published in *The Far East*, one titled "Theatrical Group" and the other a "Pekingese Lady."[22] But there was also an equivalent demand on the part of the Chinese public for images of foreigners, paralleling the exotic imagery available in the peep shows of the day. In 1890, for example, it was discovered that certain amusement stands offered as prizes "lucky bags," in which portraits of individuals in the foreign community were to be found. Presumably the photographers who had taken the portraits had later supplied copies to the amusement-stand owners as generic images of foreigners.[23]

There is little doubt that the portrait was the major specialty of Chinese photographers in Shanghai. One of the most revealing texts on photographic portraits is to be found in an 1884 guide to the world of Shanghai prostitution, *Haishang yeyou beilan*:[24]

The Westerners have created the art of photography, with which one can use chemical fluids to make a complete portrait of a person on a rectangular piece of paper. It is lifelike and perfectly resemblant. Wherever there are prostitutes, they fight to have their portrait taken, hanging it on the wall or making a present of it to clients. Recently [photography] has spread to distant provinces and is available everywhere. As for the few most famous courtesans, they always keep the original glass plate at the [photographer's] shop, in order to have photographs printed as necessary to sell to people. They can truly profit from it indefinitely.

Although the text is brief, it nonetheless reveals several entirely different uses of individual photographic portraits. One is a private use: when the prostitute hung her own picture on the wall she was doing the same thing that many other private individuals did in this period, although they might have rather placed the photograph on a table (cabinet portrait). The practice of hanging portraits on the wall is well documented in *Feiyingge huabao*, and framed portraits of this kind still exist today in their original frames (fig. 6).[25] The second use of the portrait image was professional, as a *carte de visite* given to clients.[26] Actors, too, used portraits professionally as *cartes de visite*. According to *Shenjiang mingsheng tushuo*: "There is not a beauty of the willows and alleys, nor an actor of the 'pear garden' who does not have small photographs printed for the pleasure of giving them away."[27] A third use of the photographic portrait was as an entertainment commodity. The courtesan used the negative to have multiple copies printed for sale to others. In this way portraits of courtesans (and actors) circulated publicly. An 1876 poem comments on courtesans' photographs: "Clients pursuing spring pleasures compete to buy them / Hoping to use the pictures to guide them in their search for a beautiful girl."[28] Needless to say, group portraits were also popular. The *Shenjiang mingsheng tushuo* illustration of a photographer at work (fig. 2) shows a group of three courtesans, and certain *Dianshizhai huabao* illustrations show photographers taking pictures of much larger groups. At least one group portrait in the same journal is clearly based directly on a photograph (fig. 7). A number of unidentified group portraits, in both studio and outside settings, some of which may be the work of Shanghai photographers, exist today in Western collections.

Finally, a few speculative remarks may be made on the stylistic features of portrait photographs by Chinese photographers in Shanghai, although these features are probably shared with the work of Chinese photographers more generally in this period.[29] One may be struck, for example, by the photographers' need to create an environment for the sitter. Most commonly, simple groups of objects (a table, a vase of flowers, a book, and so on) function as metonymic signs to evoke a domestic interior. Striking, too, is the importance of Western or Westernizing elements, whether in the furniture or in the painted, illusionistic backdrops, with their suggestions of a Western architectural setting. The portrait then does not simply record; it creates an imaginative displacement that is not so easily found in portraits by foreign photographers. Formally, certain images are striking for their rhythmic treatment of solid and void, light and dark. One notices also the care with which the photographer leaves the objects clearly isolated, which contributes further to the graphic effect. Moreover, the photographer has his subjects pose so that their bodies, or rather their silhouettes, are aligned with the surface of the image. All of these elements are reminiscent of Chinese painting, and at the same time are alien to the approaches of foreign photographers working in China. Finally, when it was necessary to express a domestic hierarchy, the

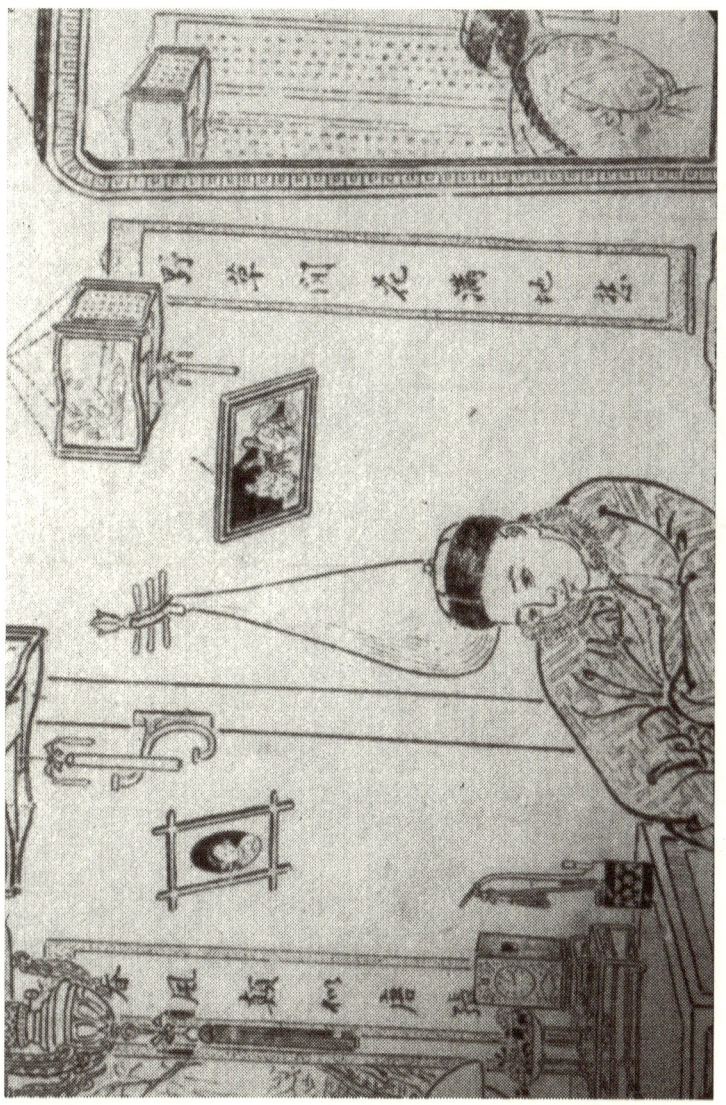

Fig. 6. Detail of the wall of a courtesan's bedroom, from an illustration by Wu Youru originally published in *Feiyingge huabao* in the early 1890s, later reprinted in the *Fengsu zhi* section of *Wu Youru huabao* (1909).

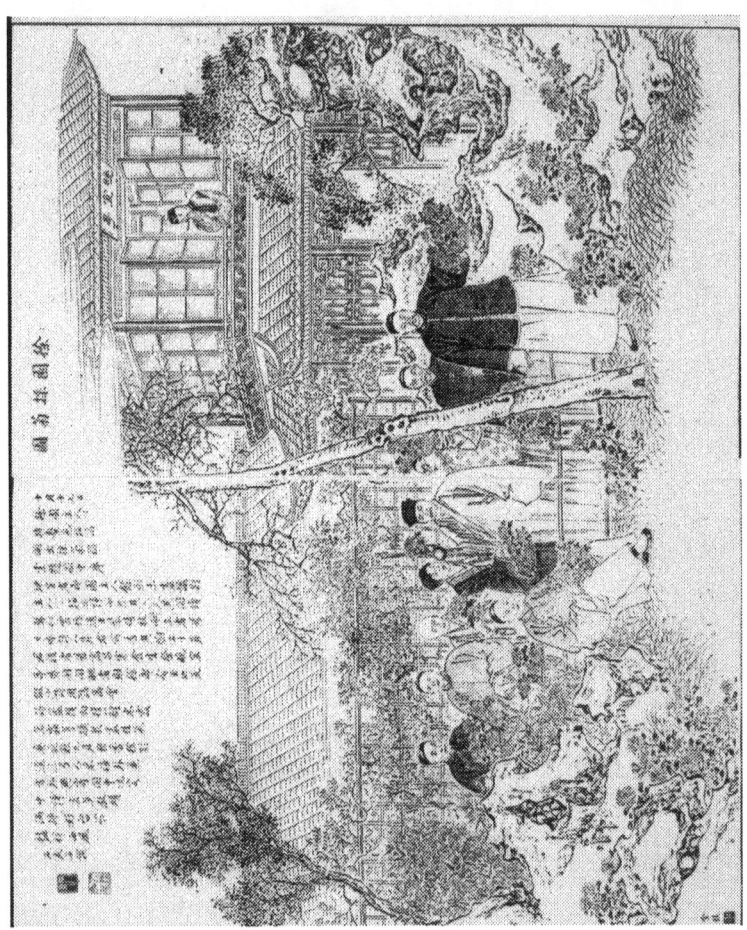

Fig. 7. Jin Gui, *Chrysanthemum-Picking in the Xu Garden. After Dianshi Zhai huabao* 15.3 (1890): 12b–13a.

portraitist might take his inspiration from the formal, hieratic aesthetic of ancestor portraits. This is the case, for example, for Gongtai's portrait of the Daotai of Anqing and his family (fig. 4).[30]

Advertising: Writing in the Street and Images on the Page

In China, as elsewhere, advertising is so fundamental to modern urban life that the origins of the twentieth century forms so familiar to us constitute a historical question of some importance. In a long-term perspective, there is no doubt that the history of advertising can be traced back hundreds of years to include, for example, the very early shop signs or publications of ink-cake designs such as the *Chengshi moyuan* around 1600. However, modern advertising also has a more recent genesis that is derived essentially from the nineteenth century, from cities where Chinese and foreigners formed a hybrid commercial culture. Cities particularly important include Guangzhou, Hong Kong, and Shanghai, although the importance of overseas "Chinatowns" in the United States, especially in San Francisco and New York, should not be underestimated. Here I deal in a very preliminary way with two aspects of late nineteenth-century-Shanghai advertising that are relevant in different ways to the larger question of the city's visual culture. The first of these is the role of written advertising in the visual environment of the street, while the second is the use of visual elements in advertisements on the printed page.[31]

A certain W. MacFarlane, in his *Sketches in the Foreign Settlement and Native City of Shanghai* (1881, reprinted from *Shanghai Mercury*) describes narrow streets near the New North Gate in the Chinese City as having "the sky almost obscured from view by the wooden and canvas signboards and ornamental tablets stretching from one side of the street to the other." Although few if any photographs of these streets in the Chinese City survive today, the many photographs of the commercial streets of the Concessions demonstrate that MacFarlane's description would have held almost as true for them (fig. 8). As in Guangzhou and Hong Kong during the same period, Shanghai's commercial streets were saturated with written characters, and nine times out of ten the writing was an advertisement. Obviously, written advertising in the street was by no means new in the nineteenth century. It is vividly recorded from the Northern Song dynasty onwards, in paintings of street scenes such as the many versions of the *Qingming shanghe tu* theme, or the court depictions of Kangxi and Qianlong's southern inspection tours. However, comparison of more modern images of Shanghai with these earlier representations quickly reveals that in the late nineteenth century writing saturated the streets to an unprecedented degree. In the most crowded streets, so little advertising space was available on the shopfronts that merchants projected their advertising outwards into the no-man's-land spanning the street, until, as MacFarlane describes it, "the sky [was] almost obscured from view."

In such streets, the basic advertising form was the shop sign, carved in wood or embroidered on canvas. Some shops used visual signs for their products. For example, tailors suspended a garment, watchmakers had signs painted to look like clockfaces, cobblers used a boot design, and paper and fan shops used the silhouette of a fan. On the whole, however, Shanghai businesses, perhaps continuing a Jiangnan regional tradition, placed their trust in the written word, whereas Beijing businesses, for example, continued to make heavy use of visual shop signs into the 1930s. Written shop signs had numerous potential locations. They could be set into the shop front itself, or be suspended just in front of it; they could project out into the street, a practice that followed the use of English-language signs by Chinese businesses; and they could be suspended across the width of the street. Written signs were visual as well as textual: great attention was paid to the style and script of calligraphy, and culture- or leisure-oriented businesses often invited reputed calligraphers to supply the initial designs for carved wooden signs. In addition to signs made of wood or cloth, there were also painted signs (calligraphic, not pictorial) used by businesses that were housed in buildings with whitewashed walls (fig. 9). Their written characters were several feet high and could be seen from a great distance, so consequently they were not restricted to most commercial areas, with their narrow streets.

The carved wooden shop sign was expensive, decorative, and made to last; the embroidered banner, though less solid, was also meant to last; and the more-strictly-functional painted shop sign, although it might fade, could be refreshed. Contrasting with these long-term advertisements were the various forms of ephemeral advertising on paper. Announcements of upcoming performances by various performers were hung outside teahouses and theaters. Certain buildings also had the names of courtesans or prostitutes living there posted outside. Least glamorous of all, and a practice still common in Shanghai today, were slips of paper—with information on the availability of products, services, or theatrical performances—pasted strategically onto those walls where they would be seen by the greatest number of people (fig. 10). These fragile and ephemeral posters inspired the authorities, or the owners of the wall, to ban the pasting of posters with the ubiquitous formula, "Posters will be torn down" (*zhaotie ji zhi*)—itself in poster form. So humble a form of advertising as the *zhaotie* might seem too insignificant to mention, but as one of the precursors of modern advertising posters the *zhaotie* is very important. Thus the

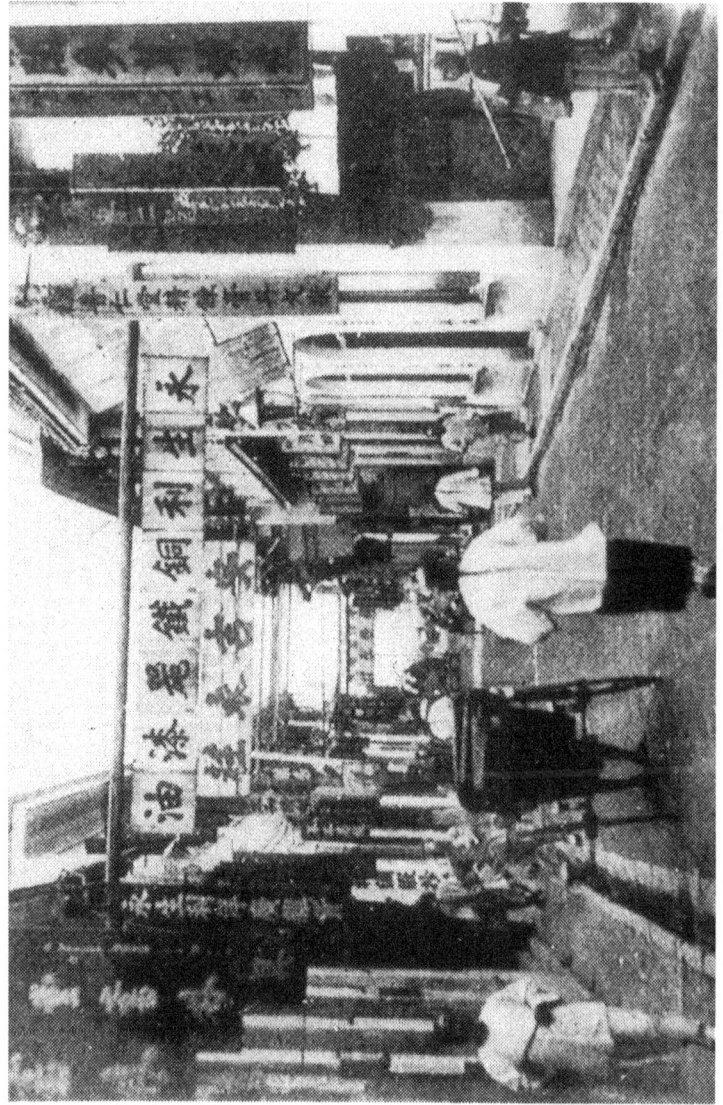

Fig. 8. Unidentified photographer, *View of Honan Road*, late Qing. After Tang Zhenchang, ed., *Jindai Shanghai fanhua lu* [Splendor of modern Shanghai] (Shanghai: Shangwu yinshuguan, 1993), fig. 28.

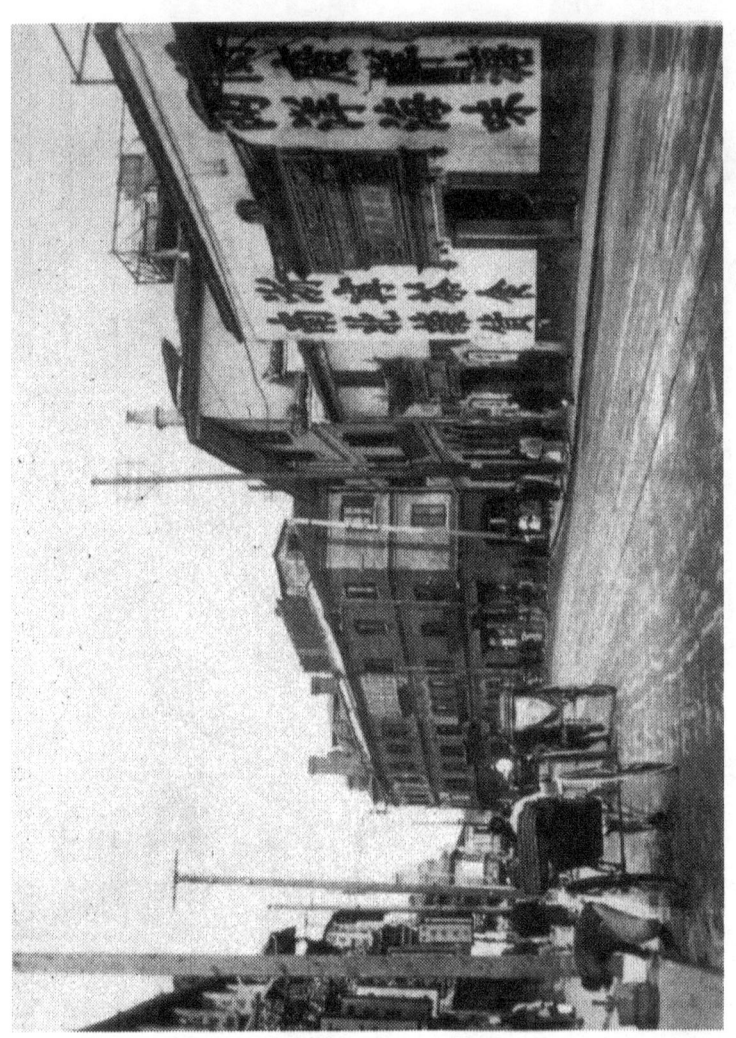

Fig. 9. Unidentified photographer, *View of Paoqiu Chang*, late Qing. After Deng Ming, ed., *Survey of Shanghai 1840s–1940s* (Shanghai: Shanghai renmin meishu chubanshe, 1996), 60.

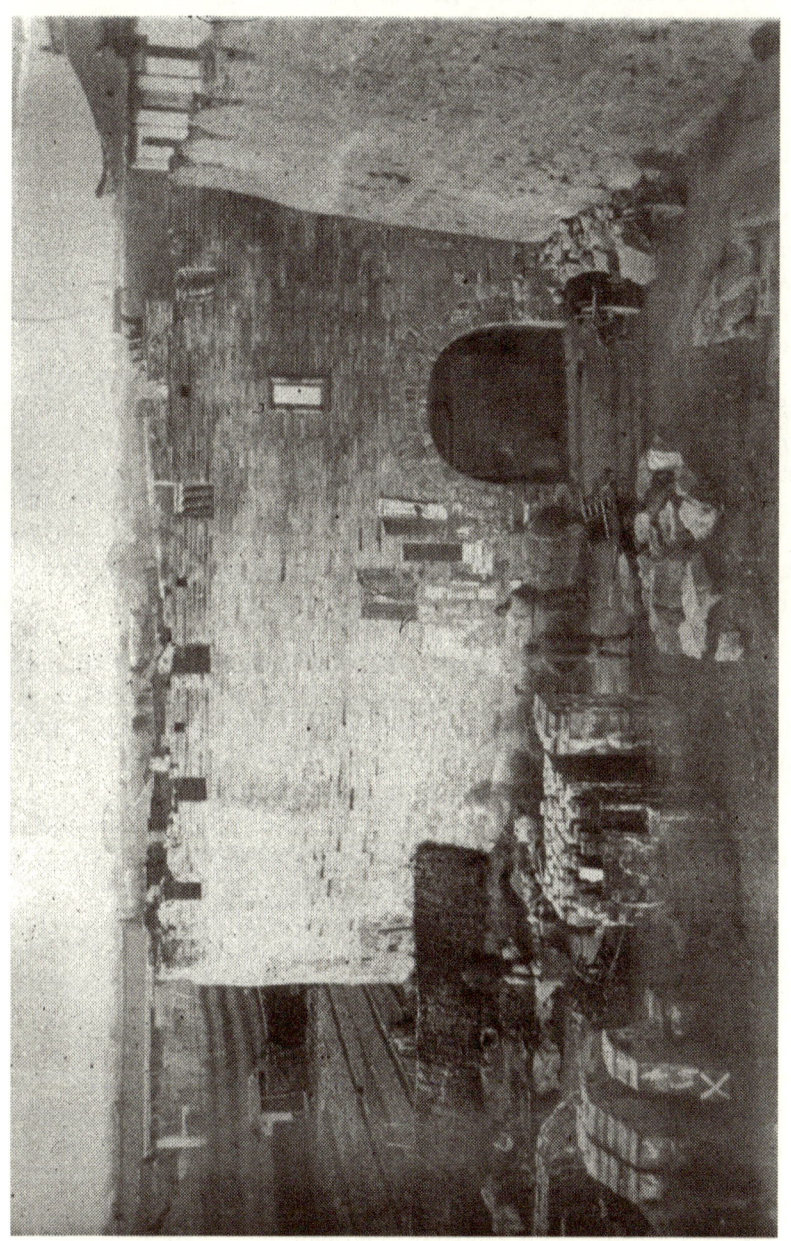

Fig. 10. Unidentified photographer, *West Gate of the Chinese City, Shanghai. After The Far East 2* (1877).

streets were saturated by advertising on several levels: the orgy of advertising in commercial areas, the large-scale painted sign meant to be seen from a distance, and the humble poster that insinuated itself onto walls all over the city.

A particularly significant aspect of street advertising is the role of calligraphy and calligraphers. The calligraphers signed their work, and their signatures were then carved into the wooden shop signs along with the texts. This has proved to be a remarkably resilient practice, enjoying a renaissance in Shanghai and Beijing in the 1990s. Since shop fronts often incorporated many signboards, a single shop could have contributions from several different calligraphers. An example is the fan shop Xihongtang, whose appearance is faithfully recorded in a pictorial advertisement that appeared repeatedly in *Dianshizhai huabao* during the late 1880s. The advertisement shows that the shop had six different calligraphic signboards, five of which were signed. I have been able to identify only two of the five calligraphers. Both were officials, whose contributions were presumably meant to give an upmarket tone to the shop. Tao Fangqi (1845–1884), 1876 *jinshi*, was a native of Shaoxing who had a reputation as both a painter and a calligrapher, until his premature death at the age of 40. Xu Fu (*zi* Songge), a native of Shanghai (Jiading) born in 1836, was the top-ranked candidate in the 1862 *jinshi* examination and later served in several high official positions. He, too, was both a painter and a calligrapher.[32]

A signed shop sign, it should be noted, must have advertised not only the shop but in some cases the calligrapher; a viewer might have wondered whether the displayed calligraphies could be obtained through the fan shop. In any event, by helping calligraphers to become known to a broad and largely anonymous public, as was also accomplished by some of the decorated letter papers sold by the same shops, shop signs indirectly contributed to the creation of a commercial public space for calligraphy. How far back in time can this phenomenon be traced? Did calligraphers sign shop signs in the eighteenth century? I am not aware of evidence that they did; on the other hand, they certainly signed titleboards and *duilian* couplets for buildings in semipublic spaces such as gardens. For one garden in eighteenth century Yangzhou, the East Garden built by the Shanxi merchant He Junzhao in 1744, for example, Li Dou in the *Yangzhou huafang lu* records that by 1746 a thousand calligraphers had written *duilian* couplets and title-board inscriptions for the various buildings of the garden, although not all of these would have been used. Li Dou's account names more than 140 calligraphers.[33] If the garden is in some sense typical of eighteenth-century Yangzhou, and the commercial street typical of late nineteenth-century Shanghai, then it may be legitimate to speak of the creation of a more democratically public space for calligraphy in Shanghai.

This process can be seen elsewhere, for example, in the expanded use of both paintings and calligraphies as decoration in restaurants, teahouses, and other easily accessible leisure spaces; and in the new phenomenon of cheap photolithographic reproductions of paintings and calligraphies (a role played earlier by copies and fakes).[34]

Print advertising for a Chinese public in late nineteenth-century Shanghai was predominantly textual.[35] However, from a very early date a certain proportion of advertisements incorporated visual images, and in some cases they were primarily visual. Although there are missionary publications that could be discussed as well, I particularly want to focus here on the newspaper *Shenbao* and the magazine *Dianshizhai huabao*. I discuss these two publications separately, because they used visual elements in advertising differently.

At its founding in 1872 *Shenbao* made a very small amount of space available for visual elements. During the 1870s the few visual advertisements that were included tended to be for foreign products. They reused advertising images from Western publications. In the course of the 1880s, the number of visual advertisements increased, and came to include Chinese examples alongside Western ones (fig. 11). Although there are exceptions, such as one repeatedly placed advertisement for a lithographic printing press, in general the visual elements are small, and tend to be signs rather than fully fledged pictures that illustrate either the product or the trademark. For illustrations of products, a simple diagrammatic drawing—for example, of a feather fan, or books—was often considered sufficient. The more numerous advertisements illustrating trademarks are sometimes pictorial, for example, a Japanese decorative design for Japanese soap, a pretty woman's face for cosmetics, or the Daoist immortal Li Tieguai for medicines. Others, however, are written shopmarks. This is particularly the case for lottery enterprises, of which there were large numbers, many of them concentrated in Qipan Jie (Chessboard Street), in the area outside the north gate of the Chinese City.

In line with its orientation to images, the *Dianshizhai huabao* (founded 1884) always constructed its advertising pages around images. Pages usually incorporate several different advertisements, but in rare cases a single one takes a full page. Because they were largely omitted from the two reprint editions of 1911 and 1983, which scholars tend to use for convenience, these advertisements are not as well known today as they should be. Although not very numerous and often repetitive, they are nonetheless historically important as some of the earliest Chinese experiments in pictorial advertising. Some are closely related to the *Shenbao*-type advertisements: they incorporate an image of a product or a trademark; the products include water pumps, medicines, matches, waterpipes, and books.

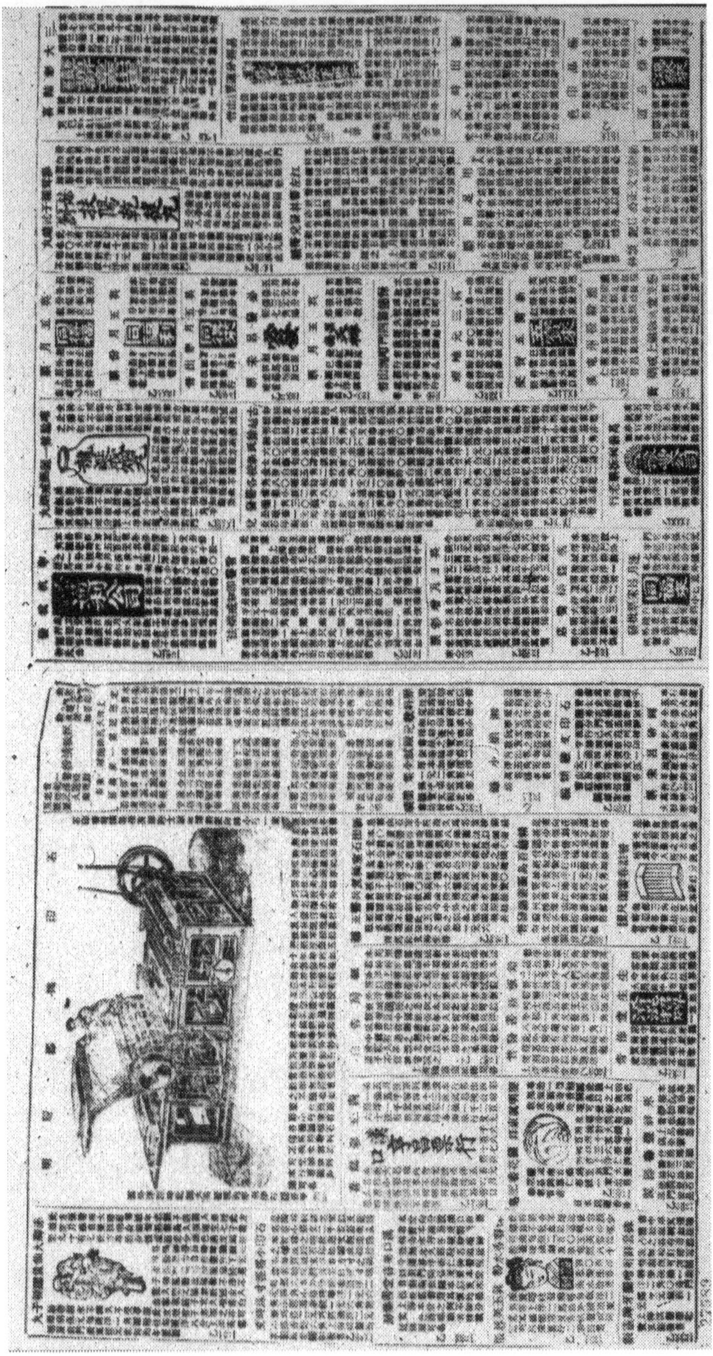

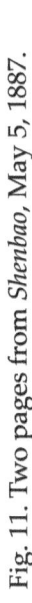

Fig. 11. Two pages from *Shenbao*, May 5, 1887.

Others depict consumers using the product or service: readers in need of books, artists in need of an outlet for their work, and the sick in need of medicine. These images of the consumer, although again few in number, are highly significant: they may be the first images ever to make the consumer alone a pictorial theme. Among the advertisements of this kind is one for a medicine sold by the Cantonese pharmaceutical company Liang Kaiti Tang, located on Qipan Jie, which had long been an active advertiser in *Shenbao*. As Sherman Cochran has shown, pharmaceutical companies were among the most active and innovative advertisers in the early twentieth century, but the case of Liang Kaiti Tang shows that they had understood the possibilities of media advertising from the beginning.[36]

A third type of advertisement is centered on the depiction of a shop, in which can be seen shop signs, products, sales staff, and consumers. Several of the shops represented, including the Dianshizhai head office, and the branch office at Paoqiu Chang (the crossroads of Nanjing and Honan Roads), were owned by the magazine's publisher, Ernest Major. The Shenchang Shuhuashe bookshop on San Malu (Hankou Road), for example, was the main outlet for Dianshizhai publications, including periodical publications, books, and art reproductions; it also served as an informal office for Major's other business concerns. And when Shenchang Shuhuashe opened a branch office on Good Fortune Street (Jixiang Jie) in the French Concession, the new building got a full-page advertisement. The Suzhou branch of Tongwen Shuju was established only after this lithographic publishing house was acquired by Ernest Major. Outside the borders of Major's commercial empire, Fuying Shuju on Qipan Jie was the Shanghai branch of a Tokyo publishing house specializing in copperplate printing; while Jiongying Ge and Jiangzou Shulin on Si Malu (Foochow Road) were bookshops selling all kinds of old and new books. Finally, the Xihongtang at Paoqiu Chang and the Jiuhua Tang just to the south of Paoqiu Chang on Er Malu (Kiukiang Road), were two of the leading fan shops specializing in the sale of paintings, fan, and decorative letter papers. These various cultural shops consistently refer to their clientele using the terms *shishang* or *shenshang*, acknowledging the mixed scholarly/mercantile character of their customer base.

Finally, although I have been emphasizing visual elements in print advertising, writing also plays an important role and reveals certain parallels and contrasts between advertising on the printed page and in the street. Unlike *Shenbao*, *Dianshizhai huabao* did not use movable type, so calligraphy, with its range of script-types and styles, plays a large role in the advertisements. The use of standardized styles is especially noteworthy, since it anticipates the twentieth-century exploitation of calligraphic typography in advertising. Among the standardized styles that are used, perhaps the most important is a form of standard script derived from the mid-nineteenth-century innovations of calligraphers such as Zhao Zhiqian (1829–1884), who made a special study of Northern Dynasties stone-carved inscriptions. This style more than any other defines the calligraphy of commercial culture in late nineteenth-century Shanghai. Such standardized styles in print advertising certainly contrast with the individualized shop signs written and signed by specific calligraphers, but they are continuous on the other hand with the similarly standardized styles that were used for the bulk of the anonymous signs incorporated into shopfronts as well as for large-scale painted signs on whitewashed walls. When such Chinese writing practices receive any art historical attention it is usually under the category of calligraphy, of which they are seen as debased forms. It may be more useful, however, to reserve the term *calligraphy* for writing that makes a claim to self-expression, and to recognize standardized writing styles as belonging to a separate history of *public writing* that from the beginning shadows that of calligraphy.[37] Within this long history, late nineteenth-century Shanghai and related cities are important. There advertising emerged as the primary motor of the modern development of public writing, a trend that would continue in mainland China until the establishment of the People's Republic in 1949.

Photography and advertising are two examples of how late nineteenth-century Shanghai functioned as an experimental laboratory for commercial mass culture in China. My discussion of advertising has brought into play two very different advertising *sites*: the street and the printed page. One of the advantages of discussing them together is that they reveal contrasting mechanisms for how advertising was transformed into its fully modern form. In the case of the street, preexisting practices are expanded and intensified to the point where the quantitative change becomes qualitative: more advertising eventually transforms its very significance. Although the same mechanism can be seen in the use of standardized styles of writing in print advertising, visual elements make the printed page the site of experimentation; as in photography, distinctively new practices emerge, stimulated by imported technologies. The more general conclusion one can draw for China's visual culture, then, is that when a fully fledged modernity crystallized in the late nineteenth century, it was as the result of the confluence of two different historical processes, one more obviously internal to China, with roots in early-modern history, and the other more obviously global and contemporary. Of course one must always bear in mind that closer analysis would quickly erode this as a hard and fast distinction.

Notes

1 "Painters and Publishing" (intro., n. 11).

2 For a daguerrotype by Lai Chong dated 1853, see Christie's London 1994/10/19, "The Lau Collection of 19th Century Chinese and Japanese Photographs," lot no. 1. On the photographer Luo Yuanyou, active in Shanghai during the late 1850s and early 1860s (?), see Huang Shaofen et al., *Shanghai sheying shi* (Shanghai: Shanghai renmin meishu chubanshe, 1992), 2–3.

3 See *Picturing Hong Kong: Photography 1855–1910* (New York: Asia Society and George Braziller, 1997), catalogue of an exhibition curated by Roberta Wue. Two of the catalogue essays, by Roberta Wue and Edwin K. Lai, include important discussions of Chinese photographers in Hong Kong. The only studies on photography in late nineteenth-century Shanghai of which I am aware are Hu Zhichuang and Ma Yunhong, eds., *Zhongguo sheying shi, 1840–1937* (Beijing: Zhongguo sheying chubanshe, 1987); Huang, *Shanghai sheying shi*, 1–18; and Hongxing Zhang, "From Slender Eyes to Round: A Study of Ren Yi's Portraiture in the Context of Contemporary Photography" (unpublished manuscript).

4 Huang, *Shanghai sheying shi*, 4–6.

5 Ibid. Note the following company names: Su Sanxing [Sanxing], Yichang, Huaxing, Gongtai, Baoji (founded 1888), and Lizhu. Zhang, "Slender Eyes," adds the company name Hengxin, and the name of the photographer Lian Shitai. To this list can be added the names of Yeh-chong, the Shanghai Photographic Enlarging Co. and, perhaps, Ah-fong (a branch of the Hong Kong company of the same name?), whose premises can be seen in a later photograph, from 1906. See *L'Illustration*, September 1, 1906.

6 *Xiazhuan* picture no. 35, accompanying commentary.

7 *Wu Youru huabao*, "Haishang baiyan tu" [One hundred Shanghai beauties], 16.

8 *Jia* 5/37.

9 *The Far East* 5 (1878): facing pp. 82 and 94.

10 Christie's London 1994/10/19, "The Lau Collection of 19th Century Chinese and Japanese Photographs," lot nos. 19, 22, 34.

11 Ibid., lot no. 22.

12 Both Roberta Wue and Edwin Lai make this point for Chinese photographers in Hong Kong in their essays in *Picturing Hong Kong*. Wue writes: "The earliest Chinese commercial photographers were almost certainly Cantonese first active in Hong Kong. They learned their trade in a variety of ways, the majority probably already being skilled artisans working in the field of export painting" (34). Lai (55) notes that "many early Chinese photographers were originally painters from Hong Kong." For the implications of this historical connection, see Wue's discussion on pp. 39–40.

13 *Shanghai Mercury*, October 2, 1890. I am grateful to Roberta Wue for this information.

14 Christie's London 1994/10/19, "Lau Collection," lot no. 34.

15 Vol. 2, facing p. 4, ("Theatrical Group"); vol. 3, facing pp. 52, 56, 60, 86 (views of the upper Yangtse), and 128 ("Pekingese Lady"); vol. 5, facing pp. 82 (portrait of the Daotai of Anqing and his family) and 94 (view of Anqing).

16 Ibid., vol. 5, facing pp. 82 and 94.

17 *Wu Youru huabao*, "The Hundred Beauties of Shanghai," no. 16. The Paris-based scholar Dr. Régine Thiriez identified as a group the portrait photographs, now in a North American collection, through similarities in the studio accoutrements. I thank Dr. Thiriez for showing me her documentation of late nineteenth-century Chinese photographs in Western collections, and for introducing me to *The Far East*.

18 *The Far East* 3 (1877): facing pp. 52, 56, 60, and 86. For the editor's comments, see p. 69.

19 *The Far East* 5 (1878): facing p. 94.

20 *The Far East* for the month of August 1876 notes that two Western photographers established in Shanghai, Saunders and Fisler, took photographs before the departure of the first train.

21 Commenting on a photograph of musicians, ca. 1870s–80s, from Hong Kong's Pun Lun photography studio, Roberta Wue writes, "Chinese genre images were an important stock-in-trade for photographers, and the clichéd, even stereotyped nature of such images did not prevent Chinese photographers from also producing them for sale" (*Picturing Hong Kong*, 118).

22 Vol. 2, facing p. 4; and vol. 3, facing p. 128.

23 *North China Herald* (March 28, 1890), 363.

24 Vol. 3, p. 10a.

25 *Wu Youru huabao*, "haishang baiyan tu," 14; "Fengsu zhi tushuo," xia 9, 14.

26 For a possible example, perhaps slightly later in date, see Tang Zhenhua ed., *Jindai Shanghai fanhua lu*, 98.

27 Xiazhuan, picture no. 35, accompanying commentary.

28 Li Mou'an, "One Hundred Poems on Different Aspects of Shanghai" [Shenjiang zayong bai shou], cited in Huang, *Shanghai sheying shi*, 6.

29 See Wue's discussion in *Picturing Hong Kong*, 38–39.

30 See also a portrait by an unidentified Chinese photographer of an actor with his concubine and another actor, published in *The Far East* 2, p. 4.

31 Other forms of advertising which deserve further study include packaging, the photographic *carte de visite*, and the decorative images given away by newspapers, magazines, and businesses.

32 The other calligraphers are: Liu ?fu, *zi* or *hao* Yabing; Wu Dayan; and Miao Siyong, whose sign, dated 1880, was already several years old when this advertisement was drawn—perhaps all the signs date from that year.

33 Vol. 13.

34 See Hay, "Painters and Publishing."

35 For a detailed study of late nineteenth-century Chinese-language newspaper advertising (principally *Shanghai xinbao* and *Shenbao*), see the earlier part of Barbara Mittler's as-yet-unpublished paper titled "'Stay Home and Shop the World'—The Cosmopolitan Nature(s) of Newspaper Advertising in Shanghai (1860s–1910s)," prepared for the conference "The Formation of a Multiethnic Urban Culture: The Shanghai Concessions 1850–1910," Heidelberg, 1998.

36 "Marketing Medicine."

37 For a study of public writing in an early-modern and political context, see Jonathan Hay, "The Kangxi Emperor's Brush-Traces: Calligraphy and Public

Writing," forthcoming in a collection of essays on body and face in Chinese visual culture, edited by Wu Hung and Katherine Tsiang Mino.

6
Artwork, Commodity, Event: Representations of the Female Body in Modern Chinese Pictorials

Yingjin Zhang

In "The Body Invisible in Chinese Art?" John Hay detects a general absence of the body, in particular the female nude, in East Asian art and poses this intriguing question: "Why does the body seem to be almost invisible in a figurative tradition that flourished for over two thousand years?"[1] After admitting that our current academic obsession with the body is a peculiarly Western enterprise, Hay nonetheless proceeds to discuss cultural differences in Chinese and Western conceptions of the body. As he argues, the human body in Chinese art is "dispersed through metaphors locating it in the natural world by transportational resonance and brushwork that embodied the cosmic-human reality of *qi*, or energy."[2]

Hay's argument regarding the ontology of a *dispersed* body rather than an "objective body"—the latter typically found in classic Western painting—seems to confirm Mark Elvin's earlier observation on the categories of *shen* (body-person) and *xin* (heart-mind) in Chinese art and literature.[3] In a comparative study of three fictional works from the late Qing, the early Republican, and the Communist period, Elvin supplies dozens of illustrations and emphatically indicates that the human body is generally absorbed into or hidden behind layers of clothing in Chinese graphic arts. Only one exception stands out from Elvin's selection. An illustration for chapter 75 of *Annals of Shanghai* [*Shanghai chunqiu*] by Bao Tianxiao (1876–1973), a popular writer specializing in the type of urban fiction known as "butterfly literature," presents a female nude model (fig. 1).[4] She is smoking a cigarette and pacing around in an art-school classroom, its walls decorated with four artworks of nudes. Somewhat surprisingly, the model appears comfortable with her complete nudity, ignoring the male artists and a crowd of curious people who have gathered at the door to witness this eye-opening modern event in Shanghai. Without specifying the nude model as a Western (presumably Russian) woman, as does Bao's novel, Elvin states the obvious in his caption: "The unclothed human body was not seen as an aesthetic object in China before Chinese taste was—in the largest cities—influenced by Western ideas on this subject."[5]

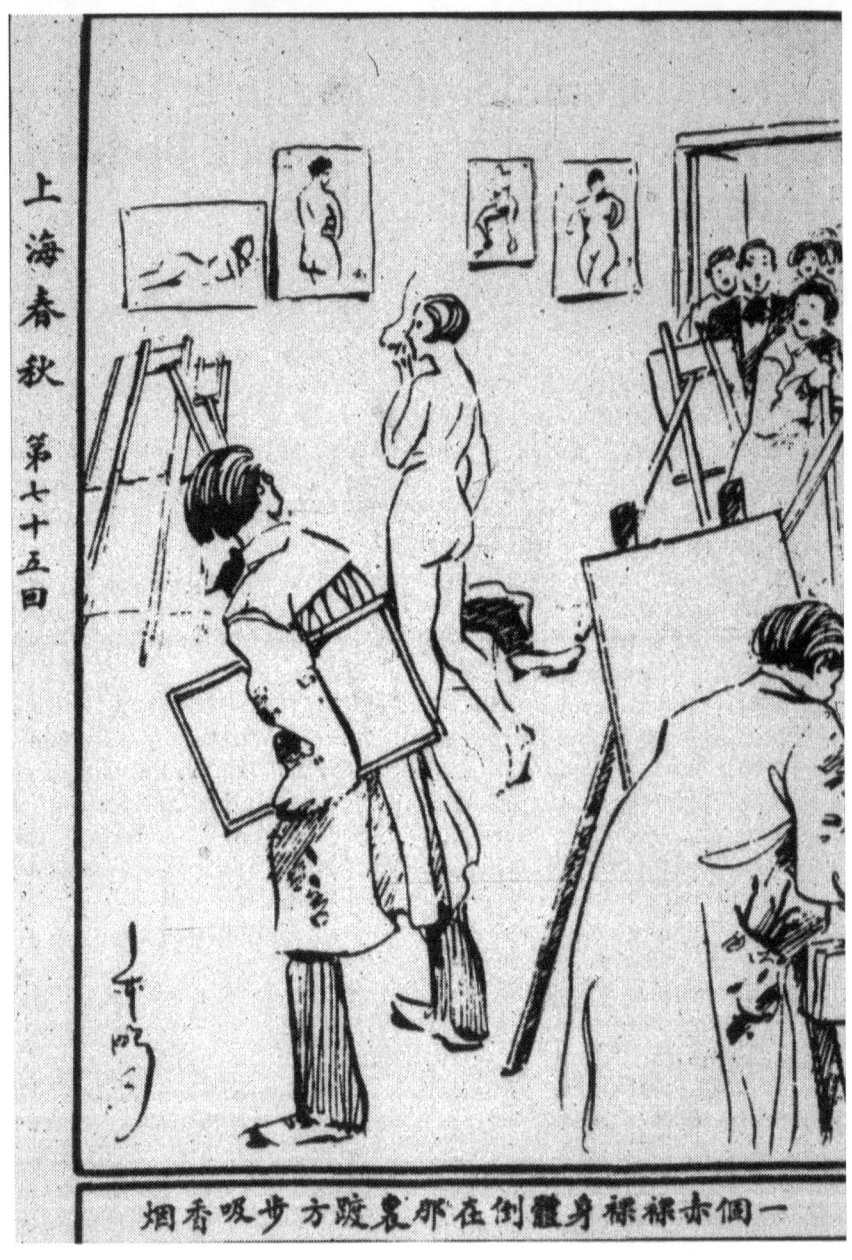

Fig. 1. Illustration for *Annals of Shanghai* [*Shanghai chunqiu*, 1924–26], chapter 75: a female nude model pacing around at ease.

Mark Elvin and John Hay would probably concur that the human body is by no means invisible in Chinese art, but that its visibility is instead controlled or obscured by conventional symbols, motifs, and techniques that convey a specific Chinese conception of the body. Acknowledging the controlled visibility of the conventionalized body in Chinese art, I investigate here a wide range of representations of the body in Chinese pictorials (*huabao*) and the complicated ways in which these representations were circulated and functioned in the late Qing and Republican periods. Specifically, I focus on images of Chinese female bodies, most of them fully clothed and only a small portion classifiable as nudes in the Western sense.[6] Most examples in this study are drawn from two principal sources. The first is *A Treasury of Wu Youru's Illustrations* [*Wu Youru huabao*], which contains many lithographs from *The Dianshizhai Pictorial* [*Dianshizhai huabao*] and *The Feiyingge Pictorial* [*Feiyingge huabao*]. The second is *The Young Companion* [*Liangyou*], a Shanghai-based pictorial that furnishes a wealth of visual and textual materials.[7] To situate my study in a broader context of modern Chinese visual culture, I also mention literary works (e.g., modernist poetry and fiction) as well as other pictorial, cartoon, and film magazines during these periods, in particular *The Pei-yang Pictorial News* [*Beiyang huabao*], *Oriental Puck* [*Duli manhua*], and *The Chin-Chin Screen* [*Qingqing dianying*].[8]

To sort out a great variety of visual materials in modern Chinese pictorials and to clear way for a future, more theoretical, study of related issues (such as vision, visuality, urban modernity, and gender experience) I approach the Chinese female body in three distinctive—albeit *not* distinct—modes of representation: artwork, commodity, and signifier of a culturally significant event. First of all, as artwork, the female body was thought to embody feminine beauty and male aesthetic tastes, even though the tastes in question had changed since the late Qing. In this first mode of representation, the female body works in both ways: on the one hand, to remind the female viewer of her prescribed domestic roles and her sexual desirability (in accordance with male idealization), and, on the other, to solicit a private aesthetic gaze from the male viewer and eventually to boost his confidence in erotic connoisseurship. Second, as commodity items, female bodies were offered in graphic form for public consumption (for men as well as women) and, frequently, to increase the circulation of the pictorials. Consistent inclusion of photographs and paintings of female nudes in *The Young Companion* from the late 1920s through the late 1930s performed this double function: to promote magazine sales (i.e., commodification) while enhancing its reputation as a vanguard in China's modern art (i.e., aestheticization). Finally, as signifier of a culturally significant event, the female body was inserted in a space of liminality, where the traditional (visually coded as female) was forced to secretly admire or openly flirt with the modern (imagined as technologically superior), while the power-less (China) fantasized outsmarting or even overcoming the powerful (the West). Inevitably, the female figure in this third mode served as a surro-gate for the absent male body and sought to provide a certain amount of comfort and security to the male viewer, who, in his discursive negotia-tion and symbolic confrontation with the West, could feel vindicated for being Chinese.[9]

The three modes of representation delineated here were shaped obvi-ously by multifarious cultural, socioeconomic, and psychological forces in China during the late Qing and Republican periods. Each mode of rep-resentation, therefore, would hardly become a self-contained, water-tight space; instead, each was open to ideological and commercial appropria-tions and was frequently penetrated and crisscrossed by the other modes. Indeed, the three modes of representation appear more like three inter-locking circles, but together they constitute a multilayered mapping of the female body in modern Chinese pictorials.

The Female Body as Artwork

Let us begin with a late Qing lithographic illustration "The Fragrant Breath" [Cuiqi rulan] (fig. 2). Two pretty young Chinese ladies are seen in the middle of their opium-smoking routine, one stooping over to fill an opium pipe, while the other stretches her arms upward in ecstasy. At-tended by a dutiful servant girl, the ladies are framed in their frontal pose by an elaborately carved circle gate, and the potted orchids on a side table by the gate metaphorically point to the ladies' "orchid-like" breath, as in-dicated in the Chinese title. In this intimate domestic scene, the ladies' soft curves are contrasted with the straight lines of the couch and the patterned wall carpet. Although their bodies are completely covered by fashionable costumes and headgear, their concealed sexuality is articulated in the im-age of a cat sitting on the lap of the ecstatic lady (*WYRHB* 3.1:6).

That "The Fragrant Breath" resembles a popular genre in Chinese art, the painting of gentle women (*shinühua*), should not surprise anyone. In fact, Wu Youru (1850–1893), the artist who drew the picture, received rigorous training in traditional genre painting under Zhang Zhiying, an established Suzhou painter. In his lifetime Wu had acquired such a reputa-tion as a master of female figures, flowers, birds, animals, and landscapes that he was compared with the noted Ming painter Qiu Shizhou.[10] Sure enough, when *A Treasury of Wu Youru's Illustrations* was published post-humously in thirteen volumes by Shanghai's Wenruilou Books in 1908, the

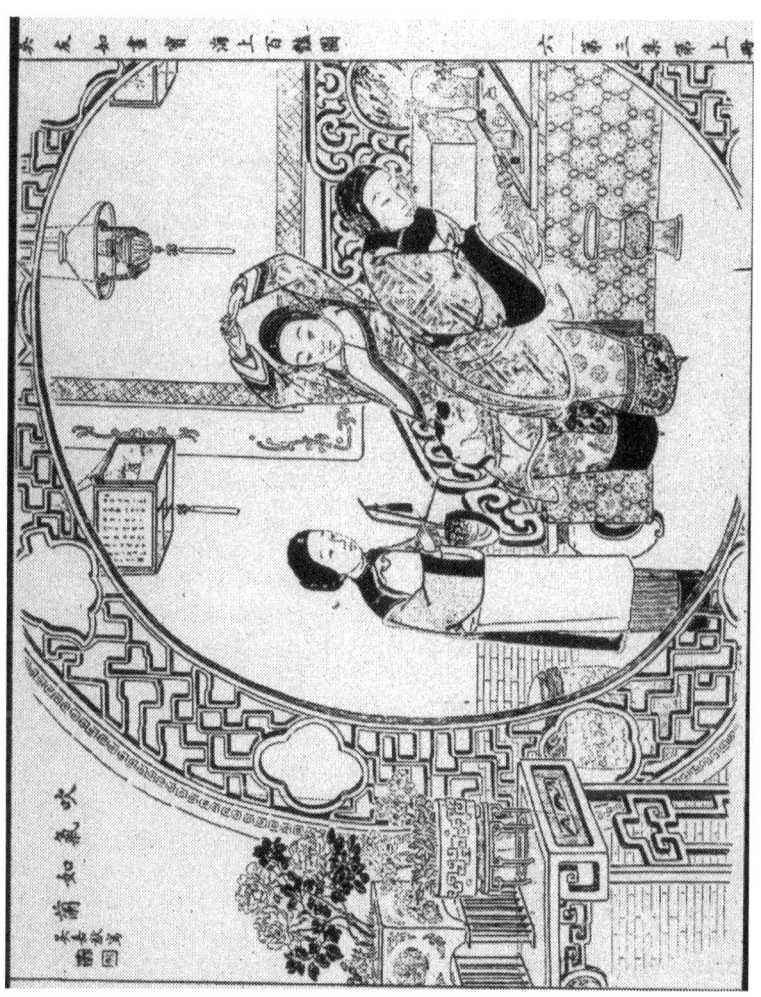

Fig. 2. Wu Youru, "The Fragrant Breath" [Cuiqi rulan]: domesticity and the ecstasy of opium-smoking. *Wu Youru huabao* (1908; repr. Shanghai: Shanghai guji shudian, 1983), 3.1:6.

publisher divided Wu's illustrations into conventional categories such as human figures, animals, birds, legends, wonders, and folk custom. By presenting Wu's illustrations in those categories, the publisher obviously expected their contemporary readers to collect Wu's lithographs as artworks in the same manner as for works of traditional Chinese painting and calligraphy. The collectors did as expected, and the influence of *A Treasury of Wu Youru's Illustrations* reached a "fantastic" scope, shaping later genre painting as well as other types of new visual arts, such as *lianhuanhua* (picture books) and *nianhua* (popular Chinese New Year's posters).[11] On the basis of Wu's positive influence, Zheng Yimei praises him as a master who made a "breakthrough in the art of Chinese painting" (Zheng's preface to *WYRHB*).

Zheng's word *breakthrough* places Wu Youru in a transitional period where artistic innovation and technological development brought new meaning and new ways of viewing to the Chinese visual arts. Two details in "The Fragrant Breath" exemplify this. First, the frontal display of the female body tactically acknowledges the presence of a viewer for whom female figures reveal their bodies.[12] The acknowledgment of the absent viewer at once enriches and complicates the textual meaning of a picture, and the act of viewing may take on new contextual meaning as a consequence. Second, the image of the couch (or sofa) appears over and over again as a stage prop on which to display the female body in a sensual and oftentimes erotic pose. In Wu Youru's "Whoring with One's Concubine" [Xiaqie tongpiao], for example, a cross-dressing woman lies drunken on a couch inside a brothel room, and a band of courtesans who have been dallying with her for weeks are shocked to find her "tiny lotus feet" upon removing her boots.[13]

Significantly, the couch and the frontal pose were recognized as crucial artistic elements and soon found their way into photography and cinema in China. Two photographs of late Qing courtesans present the female bodies in a similar reclining pose, one poetically described as "a picture of spring sleep" (*chunshui tu*).[14] If we compare these photographs to Wu's lithographs, we find a striking difference. Whereas the female figure in Wu's pictures tends to close her eyes in an ecstatic moment or demurely cast her glance sideways, in the photographs the courtesan gazes directly at the camera, thus acknowledging and communicating with the absent viewer. Although it refers to a particular interpretation of Western art, John Berger's remark on two models—one in a famous painting by Ingres (1780–1867) and the other in a modern magazine photograph—perceptively captures the silent but meaningful communication between the woman and the absent viewer: "Is not the expression remarkably similar in each case? It is the expression of a woman responding with calculated charm to the man whom she imagines looking at her—although she doesn't know him. She is offering up her femininity as the surveyed."[15]

My assumption that the viewer of the female body in modern pictorials is typically male in the Chinese context does not preclude the possibility of a female readership, for the latter would indeed be the target audience when the pictorials printed fashion drawings and photographs of the athletic, healthy women (a topic to be pursued in the next section). Theoretically speaking, however, the predominant mode of the male viewing of the female body—a mode in which a woman may imaginatively participate if she is willing to adopt dominant male values—has long been established in both art history and film studies.[16] In the Chinese case, such a mode of male viewing is made explicit in an elaborate scene of modeling in *Boatman's Daughter* [Chuanjia nü, 1935], an acclaimed "leftist" film directed by Shen Xiling (1904–1940). Three playboy artists instruct an inexperienced young woman to sit upright and then lean on a couch and stage several artistic poses so they can take photographs and paint. The poses the artists stage are based on their understanding of "what can be found in famous French paintings." This quotation has led me to speculate elsewhere that the erotic frontal pose and the direct gaze at the viewer under discussion here may have resulted from Chinese artists trying to appropriate Western painting and photography.[17] Note, for example, a pencil sketch published by *The Pei-yang Pictorial News* in 1927 that bears this English caption: "A study of pose for [a] model . . . [by] a famous artist in Paris." There, the female model is displayed in a frontal pose identical to that of the late Qing courtesan mentioned above, except that as a Parisian she poses completely nude. A question printed in the Chinese caption—"Is this pose good?" (Zheyang hao ma)—unmistakably establishes a direct relationship between the female figure in the picture and the male artist or viewer outside the frame (*BYHB*, Dec. 10, 1927).

The striking contrast between the self-confident Western nude model and the demure, fully clothed Chinese model attests to the persistence of Chinese aesthetic taste in the late Qing and early Republican periods.[18] The cultural preference for the traditional genre painting of gentle women is evident in most of Wu Youru's lithographs. In "The Model Mothers" [Ou meng yixing], two mothers busily teach their children how to write in brush and ink (*WYRHB* 3.1:17). In "Playing and Singing in Harmony" [Gengchang diehe], a group of beautiful women perform a family concert and show off their musical talents (*WYRHB* 3.1:21). On the surface, one may interpret pictures like these as visual exhortations to the female viewer that she must fulfill her prescribed family duties and cultivate artistic talents desirable in the male eye. On a deeper level, however, I would argue that these pictures appeal to a male figure strategically absent within the frame. He is the invisible master of the household who nonetheless is the omnipresent subject and for whom the women in the pictures, as the objects of his surveillance, are displaying their bodies as well as their embodied virtues. The absent master may even be the proud owner of the pictures who enjoys watching his women from outside the frame and showing off their paragon virtues to his fellow literati. Clearly, with an emphasis on the traditional domestic setting, Wu's two illustrations point to a typical fashion of male imagination, where the female body embodies the literati's ideals of feminine beauty, individual talent, and social harmony. Seen in this light, Wu's artworks boosted literati's self-confidence as masters of the house and further intensified their sense of cultural accomplishments in the form of exquisite connoisseurship of feminine beauty.

To a certain extent, what Mark Elvin says of a late Qing novel, *The Destinies of the Flowers in the Mirror* [*Jinghua yuan*, 1828] by Li Ruzhen (1763?–1830?), sheds light on the representation of the female body in Wu Youru's lithographs as well: "The ideals of female beauty . . . concentrate on the superficial (perfume, makeup and hairdo), the artificial (eyebrows and bound feet), the peripheral (fingers and feet) and the sartorial."[19] In most of Wu's pictures female figures always wear gorgeous costumes (in contrast to the plain clothes of their servant girls), and the tips of their tiny shoes—an erotic symbol of female sexuality—are visible regardless of whether these women are seated or not. John Hay's observation on the dispersed body in Chinese art is also pertinent to Wu Youru's pictures, for the sensuality of the female body is conveyed metaphorically through such images or objects as the cat, the opium pipe, the writing brush, and the musical instruments (*erhu* and *pipa*). Other than their faces, the only revealed parts of their body are their hands and wrists. According to the aesthetic rule of dispersal, the viewer of "Playing and Singing in Harmony" would thus appreciate all these specific female body parts: the mouth that sings, the eyes that smile, the earrings that dangle, the hairdo that bares the forehead, the costume that fits the body's curves, the fingers that pluck at the strings, and the bound feet that are partially visible behind the edge of the trousers.

One significant feature in modern Chinese visual arts is that the traditional concept of the dispersed body seems to have been preserved intact when photography first replaced lithography as the principal means of producing illustrations in the Republican era.[20] In 1928, *The Pei-yang Pictorial News* published a photographic display with this English title, "The 15-Beauty-Points of a Woman." The following enticing parts of a woman's body are each inscribed in a photograph and accompanied by a caption: hair, eyebrows, eyes, nose, teeth, lips, ears, neck, shoulders, arms, hands, thighs, feet, waist, and breasts. Many captions contain poetic lines—lines that also conjure a picture of the absent male body acting on the various parts of the woman's body: for the eyes, "An intense gaze yielded to a smile of profound meaning"; for the nose, "A piece of jade flanked by two autumn pools"; for the lips, "A taste of cherry, a bite of red velvet"; for the ears, "A soft whisper delivered to the depth of night"; for the hands, "Gently massage the tender heart in spring sickness"; and so on (*BYHB*, July 7, 1928). Apart from revealing the literati's ideals of feminine beauty, poetic captions like these simultaneously heightened the pleasure of the private viewing of these pictures at home and elevated such representations of the female body to the status of art in the public space.

Interestingly enough, when *The Young Companion* published "When Spring Arrives" [Dang chuntian laidao de shihou], a modernist story written by Hei Ying (b. 1915), in its April 1934 issue, the editor also used a few photographs of the female body parts as illustrations: the "slim figure" (photographed as a headless girl in a fashionable overcoat and high-heeled shoes), the "knowing eyes" (photographed as more alluring than knowing), and the "glib tongue" (photographed as two tightly closed lips with thick lipstick). The fragmented perception of the female body may enhance a modernist aesthetic in Hei Ying's story.[21] Yet, significantly, a traditional concept of the dispersed body persisted in Chinese pictorials from the late Qing through the Republican period, thereby revealing this mode of viewing to be dominant in the Chinese visual arts.

Representations of the female body as artwork are found everywhere in two popular pictorials in Republican China. Based in Tianjin, *The Pei-yang Pictorial News* was dedicated to promoting art as modern knowledge in addition to reporting current news. In its second anniversary commemoration issue, the pictorial features as center of its front cover Regnault's "Les Troi Graces" ("The Three Graces," rendered *zhen shan mei* [good, beauty, and truth] in Chinese), an oil painting of three full-bodied Western female nudes (*BYHB*, July 7, 1928). Paintings and photographs of Western female nudes appeared frequently in the pages of *The Pei-yang Pictorial News* from the late 1920s to the mid 1930s, as they did in *The Young Companion*, which was based in Shanghai.[22] In fact, the latter's March 1927 change of editorship marked a decisive turning point in the gradual transformation of tastes in Chinese pictorials, from literati connoisseurship to modern aesthetics. Immediately after he took over the pictorial from Zhou Shoujuan (1895–1968), a well-known butterfly writer, Liang Desuo proudly designated *The Young Companion* as "the most attractive and popular magazine in China"—an English designation printed in the pictorial's front cover for several consecutive issues. On the one hand, Liang justified this designation by printing select Western paintings, European saloon news, photographic studies, United States beauty pageants, as well as his own translated book, *An Introduction to Art* [*Meishu dagang*], in chapter installments. On the other hand, he started regular coverage of new art forms and art societies that were emerging in China. As a result, representative Chinese works of oil painting, watercolors, sculpture, art design, and photography were given prominent space in *The Young Companion*.[23] By the end of 1932, the pictorial reportedly printed 40,000 copies per issue and claimed to have reached 500,000 readers each month in China as well as overseas (*LY*, Dec. 1932, back cover).

Although *The Young Companion* was not the first publication to feature Chinese female nudes, its wide circulation and its status as a leading venue in China's modern art made it possible to encourage the reading public to view and accept the newly revealed Chinese female body as an embodiment of high art. Strategically, therefore, the pictorial shared the double intention Heinz von Perckhammer declared in his 1928 Berlin publication, *The Culture of the Nude in China*: "to show the Chinese woman as she really is nude" and "to enter into the spirt of the idea of beauty in different nations."[24] Not surprisingly, one of the earliest photographs of the Chinese female nudes to appear in *The Young Companion* is titled "Renti mei xiezhen" in Chinese (literally, "A true picture of the beauty of the human body") and "A Photographic Study" in English. Photographed by Zhang Jianwen (C. W. Chang), it shows a model raising her left arm and facing a mirror, thereby exposing her face and breasts in a frontal pose in the reflection (*LY*, Oct. 1929, 29). A month earlier, the pictorial had published Zhang's other photograph, "A Nude Study" [Guang yu ying, literally "light and shadows"], in which the artist contrasts the whiteness of the model's skin with her dark shadows on the wall (*LY*, Sept. 1929, 17).[25] Featuring the Chinese female nude in a strikingly new way, Zhang's photographs seek to represent—or rather refigure—it as the *objective* rather than the dispersed body.

I have chosen several modern-style artworks that further illustrate this significant change in artistic representation of the female body. These works are considered modern, not just because of their new artistic medium or form (e.g., photography or watercolors), but more because of their new conception of the female body as an aesthetic object in and of itself, even though the object in question may sometimes be enhanced by traditional Chinese motifs.

My first example is "It's Cooler Amidst Lotus Blossoms" [Qingliang de yijing], an art photograph by Zhu Lisheng (fig. 3). Published in the August 1933 issue of *The Young Companion*, which happened to be the last issue under Liang Desuo's editorship before Ma Guoliang took over the pictorial, this photograph features a completely naked Chinese woman, her muscular back and buttocks facing the viewer. In the middle of several

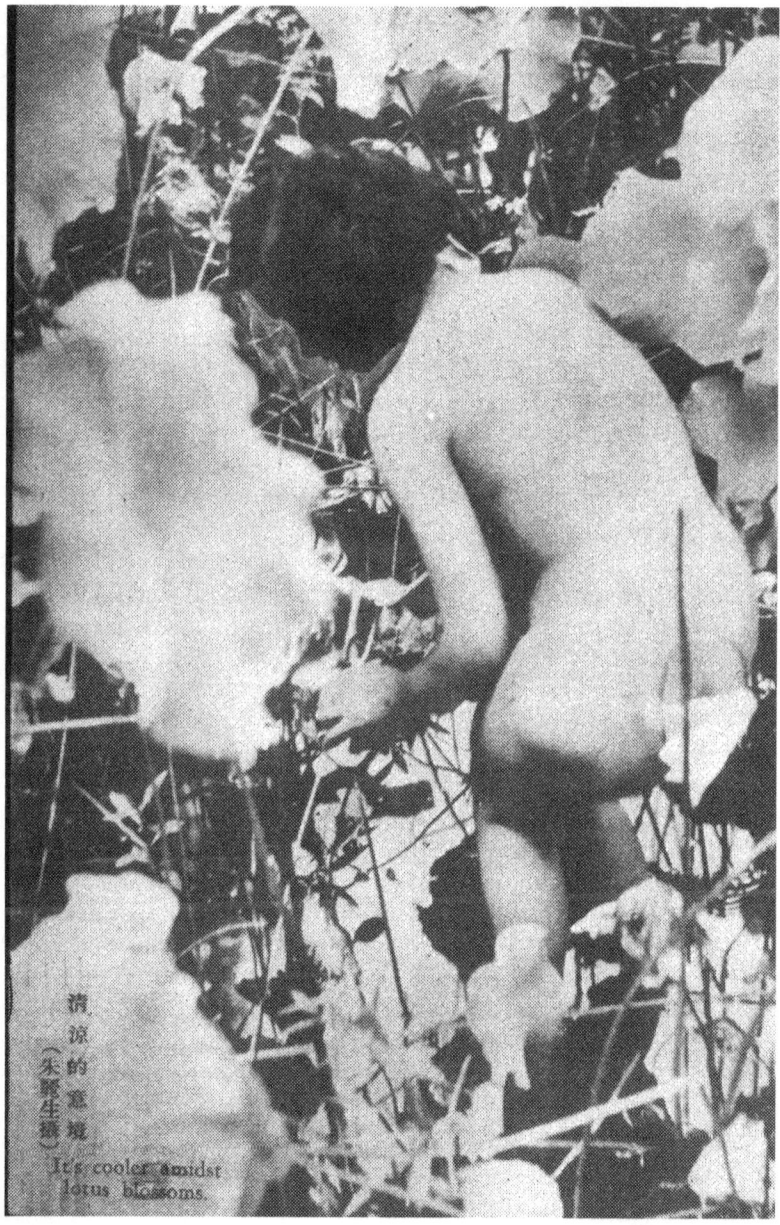

清涼的意境
（朱堅生攝）

It's cooler amidst
lotus blossoms.

Fig. 3. Zhu Lisheng, "It's Cooler Amidst Lotus Blossoms" [Qingliang de yijing, 1933]: the female body accented by nature imageries. *The Young Companion*, August 1933.

full-bloomed lotus flowers in a shallow pool, she turns her head to the left, stoops over as if to catch a dragonfly, and seems to be totally unaware of the viewer's gaze (or undisturbed by the artist's intruding camera). The composition of this photograph reveals the continued influence of Chinese aesthetics. The phrase *yijing* (poetic world) in the Chinese title not only alludes to the poetic device of comparing a young woman to a pretty flower but also highlights a Chinese preference for surrounding the female figure with imagery from nature. Such a cultural preference was evident in two earlier nude photographs, "The Girl in the Water-Lily Pond" [Lianzhao zhi nü] and "Under the Shade of a Willow Tree" [Puliu zhi zi], both by Chen Bingde (P. T. Chen). While presenting both nude models in a semi-frontal pose—one standing with her head bending down toward her right shoulder, and the other sitting on a small boat with a forced smile, Chen insisted on framing their nudity with two hackneyed images in Chinese poetry: willow branches and lotus flowers (*LY*, Nov. 1930, 36–37).

   If Zhu Lisheng's and Chen Bingde's photographs still adhered to a Chinese aesthetic taste by situating the female nude in a poetic world of natural imagery, another photographic study of the same period chose to foreground the female body as the exclusive aesthetic object. Presented by Ao Enhong (E. H. How) of the Black and White Society (Heibai She), "The Nude Pose" [Ruozi] keeps the female model seated on a stool in a typical academic-style pose in an art studio. Except for a picture frame on the upper corner of the wall, the empty studio keeps the viewer's gaze on the female body: her torso, arms, and thighs are given delicate skin tones by the lights coming from behind her back and from her upper left (*LY*, Dec. 1933, 22). The representation of the female body as an aesthetic object is also found in "Repose" [Shaonü], a color painting by Pan Sitong (Stone Pan, 1903–1970?), the founder of the White Goose Painting Society (Bai E Xihua Hui). Seated against a neutral background in a similar academic-style pose, the naked Chinese woman looks to her left, her lower body parts covered by a piece of gauzy silk, while her left hand holds a round fan—a clever substitute of the mirror typically seen in classic Western paintings (*LY*, Oct. 1931, 21). Compositionally, both Ao Enhong's and Pan Sitong's works convey Western taste, but they appeal to Chinese sensitivity by featuring female nudes who behave demurely: both women turn their face sideways and thus avoid a direct confrontation of the viewer with their nudity.

   My final example is "The Fading Youth" [Liu bu zhu de qingchun], a highly decorative work in watercolors by Fang Xuegu (fig. 4). Two female nudes are featured against the background of a large female face in profile. While one of them kneels on the ground with her hands covering her weeping face—metaphorically linked to the face that looms large above

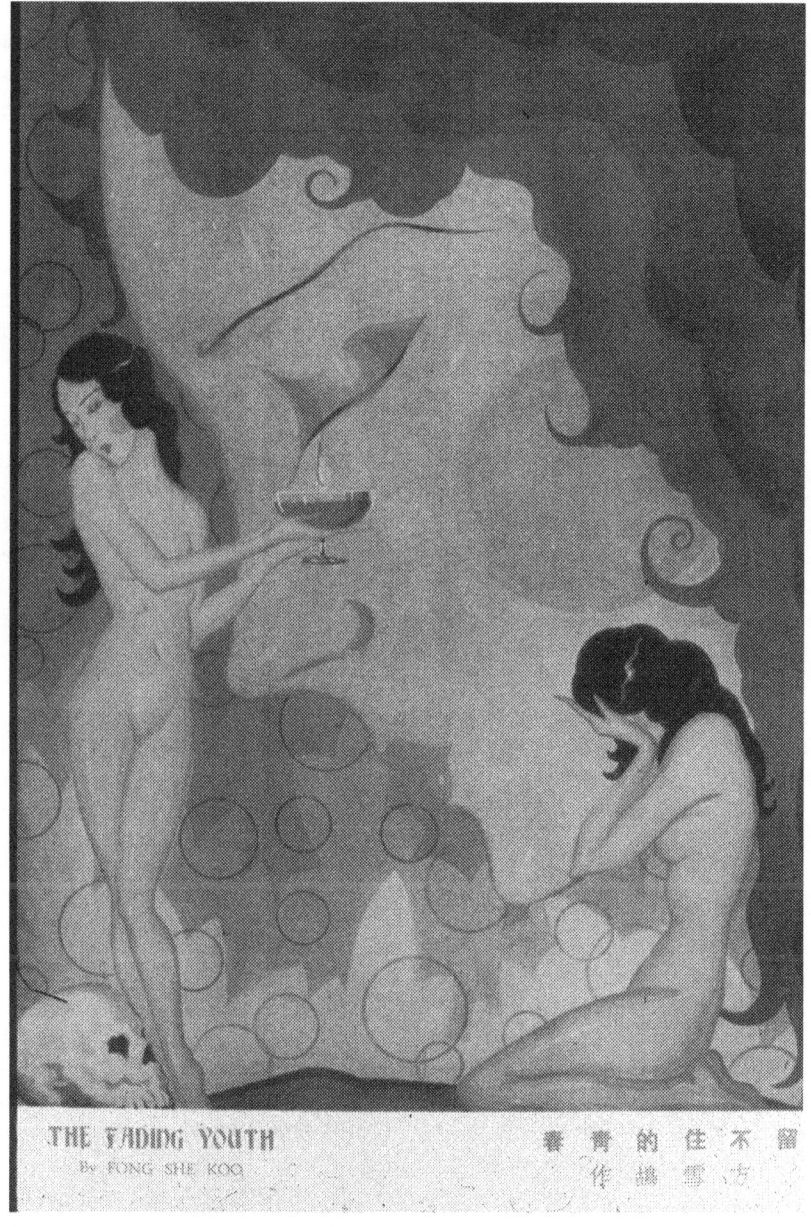

Fig. 4. Fang Xuegu, "The Fading Youth" [Liu bu zhu de qingchun, 1933]: flaunting female sexuality in the public. *The Young Companion,* August 1933.

her—in a submissive side pose that outlines her voluptuous but apparently tormented body, the other stands up in a seductive frontal pose holding
a big wine cup that catches the tear drops from the large face in the background. Slightly leaning her head to the right, the standing woman leers
at the viewer, seemingly delighted at her companion's tears while defiant
at the threat of fading youth, allegorically evoked by the skull by her feet
(*LY*, Aug. 1933).

Dramatizing an allegory within the frame and explicitly acknowledging the viewer outside the frame, Fang Xuegu's picture succeeds not only
in representing the female body as artwork but also—and more important—in revealing the power structure embodied in such artistic representation. Despite her triumphant airs, the standing nude is denied the
position of subject and is framed as an aesthetic object to be looked at.
The aestheticization of this object, the female body in nudity, projects and
glorifies the male ideals of feminine beauty and, simultaneously, contains
any threat mysterious female sexuality might pose to the subjectivity of
the male viewer. In other words, although she is allowed to flaunt her un-
concealed sexuality in front of the absent male viewer, the standing nude's
defeat as a seductress (a gender-specific type of agency assigned by male
representation) is already assured by the image of her alter ego, the weeping, self-tormenting female figure kneeling by her side. In many ways, the
female figures in Fang's picture, along with those in other artworks discussed in this section, invite an interpretation suggested by John Berger:
"Her body is arranged in the way it is, to display it to the man looking at
the picture. This picture is made to appeal to *his* sexuality. It has nothing
to do with her sexuality. . . . Women are there to feed an appetite, not to
have any of their own."[26]

The Female Body as Commodity

John Berger's insightful remark reminds us that we must go beyond the
sheer fact of art and expose a market mechanism in modern Chinese visual culture. Since the turn of the twentieth century, this mechanism transformed artistic creation into commodity production by capitalizing on the
male appetite for the female body, an appetite mirroring the desire for
an ideal form of art in Western painting.[27] Thus, the publication of paintings and photographs of female nudes in Republican China was never intended for aesthetics alone. Apart from reproducing images of the female
body in large quantities in its pictorial pages, *The Young Companion* regularly printed advertisements for books issued by its publisher, Liangyou
Books. In 1933, for instance, collections of artwork by Fang Xuegu and Pan

Sitong were advertised alongside promotions for two books of art photography. Other advertised titles published by Liangyou Books include *Famous Nude Paintings* [*Ruoti minghua xiezhen ji*], *The Beauty of the Female Body* [*Nüxing renti mei xiezhen ji*], and *The Beauty of the Male Body* [*Naxing renti mei xiezhen ji*].[28] As if appreciation of the female body as artwork was too academic or passive an activity for the modern reader, Liangyou Books published a title that glorified nudity as actual event. An advertisement for Yu Daozhen's *On the Nude Movement* [*Ruoti yundong lun*] promised one hundred thirty photographs and an examination of this real-life movement in Hong Kong "from the perspectives of philosophy, education, art, economy, politics, race, and hygiene." Among the book's chapter titles are "Back to Nature," "Appreciation of the Human Body," "The True Equality of Man and Woman," "Sports and the Nude," and "The Integration of Social Classes" (*LY*, March 1933, inside back cover). From such advertised books, it is obvious that images of the human body were produced and reproduced as commodities but were marketed (or masqueraded) as artworks or essential items of "modern" knowledge.

The advertising of *The Young Companion* in the early 1930s thus reveals another dimension in modern Chinese visual culture, namely, the female body represented as commodity.[29] This mode of representation reached its peak in the 1930s, but it is traceable to the late Qing period, when Wu Youru's illustrations aimed to increase not only the circulation of his pictorials but also the sales of his other paintings. After all, the late Qing saw a rapid rise of the periodical press and a blooming popular culture.[30] When *The Dianshizhai Pictorial* was launched in May 1884 to supplement *Shenbao* [Shanghai news], its two British owners, Ernest and Frederick Major, believed in the great financial promise of the rotary lithographic press. Issued every ten days and consisting of eight illustrations each issue, the pictorial was delivered free of charge to *Shenbao* subscribers and was sold separately for five *yuan* (Chinese dollars). Modeled after Western journals such as *The Illustrated London News* and *The Graphic*, *The Dianshizhai Pictorial* was an immense commercial success in the late Qing and greatly influenced popular culture in modern China.[31] By the time it was closed in December 1898, the pictorial had "played the role of *Life* magazine in China before the age of photography, recording in pictures and words the fin de siècle consciousness of the Chinese urban gentry one hundred years ago."[32]

Reexamining Wu Youru's illustrations as a commodity production, we see that fashion was a major attraction. Chinese ladies were always dressed fashionably, and from time to time Wu was attracted to even Western-style fashion. In "Gorgeous Dresses" [*Cancan yifu*], two Chinese ladies in fashionable, Victorian-style dresses and hats enjoy themselves

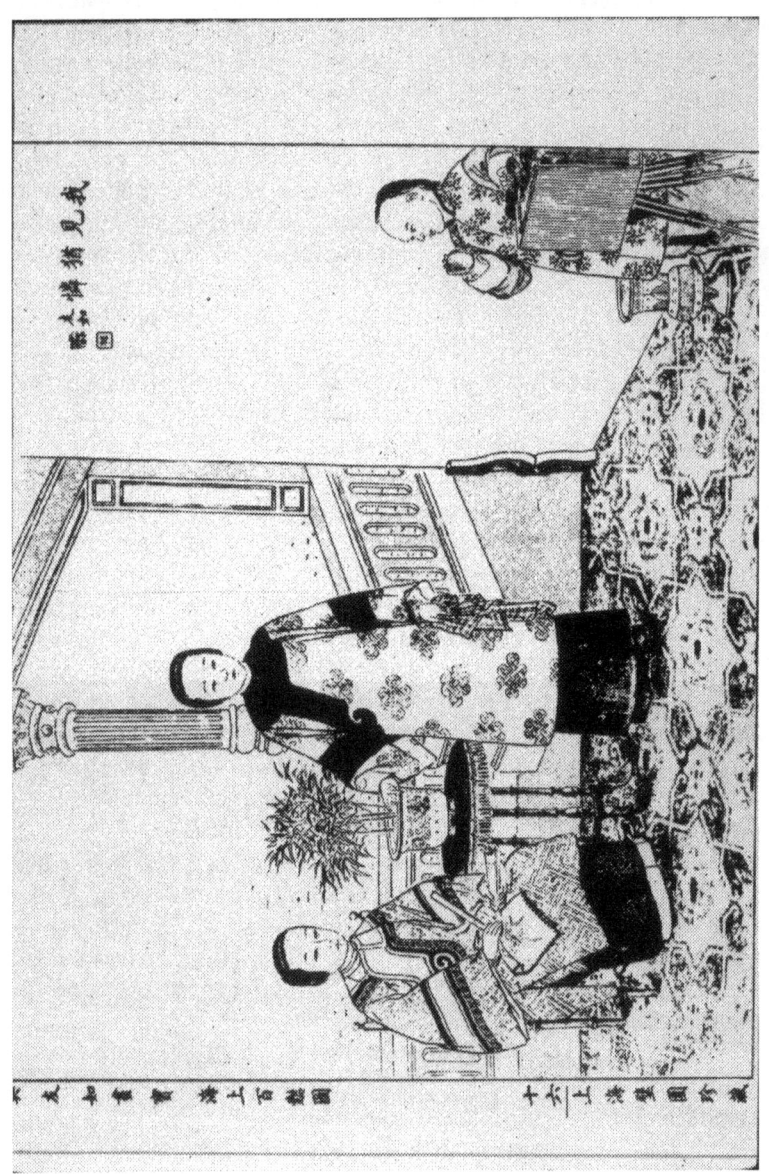

Fig. 5. Wu Youru, "Pitiable Self-Perception" [Wojian youlian]: an uneasy pose before the camera. *Wu Youru huabao* (1908; repr. Shanghai: Shanghai guji shudian, 1983), 3.1:16.

in a customary Chinese courtyard, attended by a servant girl wearing traditional Chinese clothing (*WYRHB* 3.1:24).[33] In "Pitiable Self-Perception" [Wojian youlian], another pair of Chinese ladies wearing colorful dresses pose before a camera, apparently to have their picture taken in one of the newly opened photography studios (fig. 5). In contrast to the unfeeling or flirtatious nude models in Fang Xuegu's and Pan Sitong's works of the 1930s, Wu's ladies appear rather uneasy and sometimes "pitiable" when confronted with new technology from the West (*WYRHB* 3.1:16).

Wu's illustration of the photography studio in the late Qing anticipated a promotional device employed by several popular magazines in the early Republican period. For instance, fashion photographs of famous courtesans and society ladies were regularly featured in the front illustration pages of *The Grand Magazine* [*Xiaoshuo daguan*, 1915–21] and *The Half-Moon Journal* [*Banyue*, 1921–25]. According to Bao Tianxiao, who edited *The Grand Magazine* and other urban publications, his boss Di Pingzi (Di Baoxian, 1872–1940), the owner of the influential newspaper *Shibao* (Eastern times, 1904–39), invested in a photography studio in Shanghai and invited the city's demimondes to have their pictures taken there free of charge, so that his line of publications would have a reliable source of pretty faces and bodies to attract their readers. Di's plan worked instantly, because many courtesans were fond of the publicity derived from having their photographs printed in the mass-circulated magazines. As a result, Di had a surplus of such photographs. Being a shrewd businessman, he quickly published an album of photographs, *Gorgeous Beauties* [*Jinghong yanying*], and profited from the album's brisk sale.[34]

Fashion drawings and photographs continued to appear in pictorials during the 1920s and 1930s. Apart from showcasing Western styles in titles such as "Summer Fashions in Europe and America" (*LY*, Aug. 1931, 18–19), *The Young Companion* would print stylish drawings of seasonal fashions by Chinese artists like Ye Qianyu (1907–95) (*LY*, March 1927, 34; April 1928, 31; Oct. 1928, 28–29; Nov. 1928, 23), Wan Laiming (1900–?) (*LY*, March 1928, 31; Aug. 1928, 21; Sept. 1928, 32), and Fang Xuegu (*LY*, July 1930, 23; Sept.–Oct. 1930, 23; Jan. 1931, 23; May 1931, 23; fig. 6). A more attractive way to glamorize the female body in fashion was to present photographs of movie stars wearing the latest fashions. From its first publication in February 1926, *The Young Companion* featured many Chinese movie stars as its gorgeous-looking "cover girls"—Huang Liushuang (Anna May Wong, 1907–1961), Li Minghui (b. 1906), Ruan Lingyu (1910–1935), Tan Ying (b. 1915), Wang Hanlun (1903–1978), Yang Aili, and numerous others.[35] In addition, female stars appeared regularly in the pictorial's special photographic pages, such as the "Portraits of Femininity" [Renxiang zitai] with Hu Die (1908–1989), Ruan Lingyu, Yang Aili, and Xu Qinfang

(1909–1985) (*LY*, July 1928), and "Fashion Show" [Shizhuang biaoyan] with Hu Die, Tan Ying, and others (*LY*, Nov. 1933, 24). Distinguished by their heavy makeup and attractive frontal poses, these movie stars displayed their charming bodies and faces as their courtesan predecessors had done for popular magazines of the early Republican period. Although the ideas of fashion and feminine beauty had changed over time, the commodification of the female body for mass consumption remained a fundamental commercial interest.

The visual and conceptual links of the female body to commodity were further evident during the Republican period in the publication of commercial calenders as well as in ubiquitous advertisements for cigarettes, soaps, fragrance, medicine, and other domestic products.[36] What connected these commercial practices to the art photographs mentioned above was their concentration on the body of a female who appeared always eager to exhibit herself in the latest fashion. This was one of the driving forces behind the mass circulation of images of the female body in print culture in general and in pictorials in particular.[37] After all, images of female consumption were best used to sell commodities to the female audience, to solicit their self-identification as passionate modern consumers of high fashions.

In urban literature of the time, the impact of commercialization was visible in many new magazines, especially those established in Shanghai.[38] Openly flirting with modernist—and at times decadent—aesthetics, avant-garde writers started to depict an urban landscape adorned with delicate and sensual images of the female body. For Ye Lingfeng (1904–1975), lights from Shanghai's skyscrapers blink like the alluring eyes of a mysterious woman.[39] For Shi Zhecun (b. 1905), a silver fish in a grocery shop is magically transformed into a virgin girl who offers to bare her heart to her first lover.[40] In their commodification of the female body and geographic space, some writers eventually entered the realm of the erotic or even the pornographic.[41] A self-proclaimed decadent poet in Shanghai, Shao Xunmei (1906–1968), piles flowery imagery on specific female body parts and enriches his romantic poems with references to the virgin girl and the seductress as well as to their profuse tears, sweats, fragrance, and so on.[42] In his story "Craven A," Mu Shiying (1912–1940) has his narrator relish in every detail of an imaginary trip through an exotic nation that turns out to be an extended metaphor for a voluptuous female body. The trip starts from top down, traversing a dense forest (hair), a plain (forehead), and prairies (eyebrows), bypassing two lakes (eyes) and a volcano (mouth) that contains a flaming fire (tongue), climbing on top of the purple peaks (nipples) of the twin mountains (breasts), and finally penetrating into a busy trading port (genitalia) protected by two banks (thighs), with a

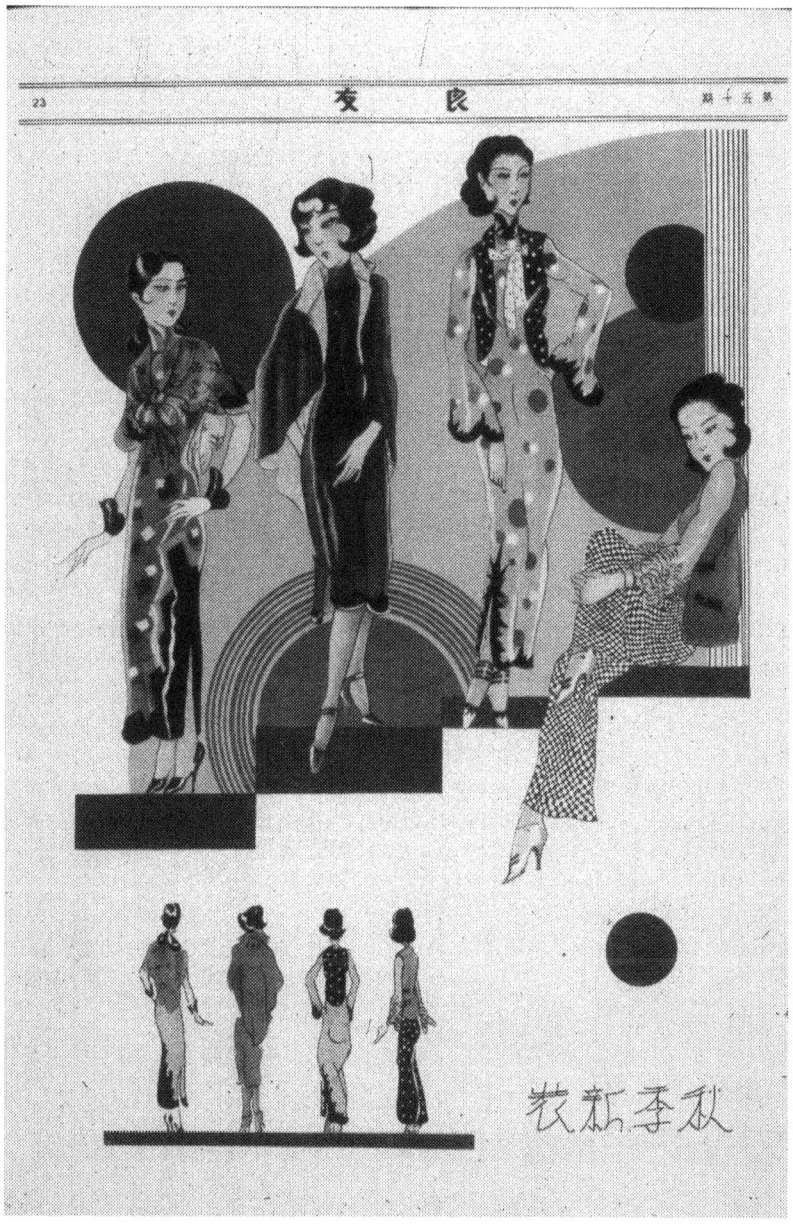

Fig. 6. Fan Xuegu, "Autumn Fashions" [Qiuji xinzhuang, 1930]: an artistic rendering of fashion ideas. *The Young Companion*, September–October 1930.

pair of white sea gulls (shoes) flying in a near distance.[43] Mu Shiying's reference to an annual ceremony in which men are "sacrificed" to the erupting volcano (the female desire) is echoed by another poet, Wang Mingzhu. Presumably inspired by a poem on the female breasts by Horiguchi Daigaku, a Japanese modernist admired by many young Shanghai writers of the time, Wang thus integrates Chinese literati's connoisseurship with the modernist aesthetic in his "Eulogy to the Breasts" [Ru di zhanli]:

At the start of a serenade, on top of
The twin peaks of Mt. Fuji, someone held a sacrifice.
His hands blessed with the luck of plenitude; at a sumptuous
Feast, it melts like the snow in southern China. . . .[44]

The pornographic nature of Wang Mingzhu's poem is best illustrated by a nude photograph found in a special issue of *The Young Companion* on art photography. Titled simply "Nude" [Ruonü], Chen Bingde's picture is a close-up of a nude model in her "ecstatic" frontal pose: her eyes closed, her chin raised, her mouth wide open as if in complete satisfaction, and, most important, her two hands lifting her breasts upward so as to highlight their fullness (*LY*, Dec. 1933). The titillating, unmediated exhibitionism in Chen's photograph is especially prominent when it is contrasted with another nude photograph from the same issue. Shot by Chen Chuanlin (C. L. Chen), "Paper Ribbons" [Zhitiao] features a nude model leaning against a draped object, her right arm half-concealing her breast, and her right hand reaching over to a bamboo-basket of paper ribbons. Whereas Chen Chuanlin's "Paper Ribbons" allows for multiple interpretations due to the juxtaposition of a basket of paper ribbons and the model's direct gaze at the viewer (as if she was questioning his erotic intention), Chen Bingde's "Nude" does nothing but exhibit the naked female body, thereby projecting a world of male fantasy in which the model appears ecstatic simply because her nakedness is appreciated in a double act of exhibitionism and voyeurism.

Like its literary and photographic counterparts, the "erotic cartoon" (*seqing manhua*) flourished in China during the 1930s. Publishers and artists alike were eager to cash in on "the city dwellers' growing appetite for entertainment and pleasure."[45] The commodification of the female body became a lucrative business, and low-cost cartoon magazines and collections, such as *Modern Sketch* [Shidai manhua, 1934–37], *Modern Puck* [Manhua jie, April–Dec. 1936], *Oriental Puck*, Xiao Jianqing's *Shanghai in Cartoons* [Manhua Shanghai, 1936] and *Society in Cartoons* [Shehui manhua, 1936], and *Selected Cartoon Masterpieces* [Manhua mingzuo xuan, 1937] edited by Zhang Zhengyu (1904–1976), soon flooded the market.[46] Even veteran artists like

Ye Qianyu and Lu Shaofei (b. 1903) were tempted by such erotic imagination in their early years. Ye's "Snake and Woman" [She yu Furen], for
instance, "showed a naked, voluptuous woman caressing a python" and
was featured on the front cover of *Shanghai Cartoons* [*Shanghai Manhua*,
1928–30].[47]

As I have explained elsewhere, two recurring subjects in erotic cartoons in the 1930s were folk love and the nude modeling.[48] The first theme
is best exemplified by "Folk Love Songs" [Minjian qingge] (fig. 7), a series of soft-porn illustrations for erotic folk songs. As its editor, Zhang
Guangyu (1900–1965) collected and serialized them in *Oriental Puck* (e.g.,
DLMH, Dec. 10, 1935; Jan. 15, 1936). Zhang reissued his illustrations of
rural courtship and lovemaking in book form and repeatedly advertised
the book in his magazine. The second theme, nude modeling, quickly appeared in cartoon books that supposedly lashed out at widespread de-
bauchery and decadence in Shanghai.[49] In this new genre, the artist could
achieve a humorous effect by sometimes involving familiar cartoon characters, such as the bookish nobody Niu Bizi (literally "Buffalo Nose") created by Huang Miaozi (b. 1913) (*DLMH*, Sept. 25, 1935) and the orphan
boy San Mao (literally "Three Hairs") created by Zhang Leping (b. 1910)
(*DLMH*, Dec. 25, 1935).[50] Humorous or not, erotic cartoons like these commodified the female body (i.e., the price and appeal of the publication
increased in proportion to the degree of nudity) and promoted the sales of
the books and magazines that carried them.

Not surprisingly, erotic cartoons became "an alarming sign" for many
critics who "denounced them as a decadent art and began to call loudly
for an end to pornography" by the mid-1930s.[51] Typical for literary or art
criticism in China, the attack was launched from high moral ground, and
defenders of eroticism and pornography were hard to find.[52] Nevertheless, erotic cartoons did not disappear overnight, nor did the lucrative
business of commodifying the female body. The ambivalent attitude toward the so-called "nudity movement" (*ruoti yundong*) illustrates a skillful
combination of moral condemnation and visual indulgence in cartoons of
the time. In a picture by Qian Dunzhi, a newly hired nanny is stunned to
find that she has entered a "nude" apartment, where two ladies wearing
nothing but high-heel shoes greet her. With their backs toward the viewer,
the naked ladies smoke cigarettes; their modern lifestyle is hinted at by
three large frames of provocative nude poses hung on the walls.[53]

Other than the cartoons and the advertised book in *The Young Companion* mentioned at the beginning of this section, I found very little reliable
evidence for the alleged "nudity movement" in China during the 1930s.
Regardless of whatever form such a movement might assume, I surmise
that it might have drawn its inspiration, at least in part, from the West. As

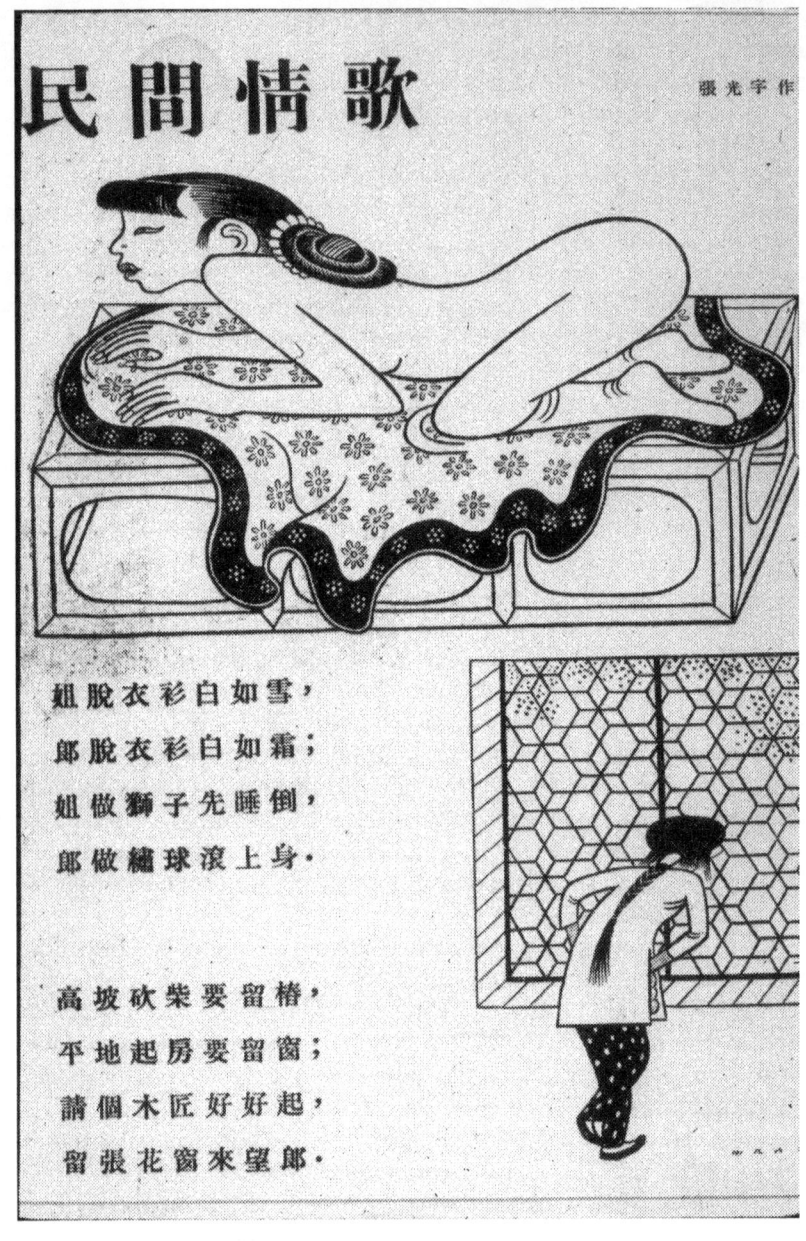

Fig. 7. Zhang Guangyu, "Folk Love Songs" [Minjian qingge, 1936]: a stylist visualization of folk love. *Oriental Puck*, December 10–January 15, 1936.

Karl Toepfer demonstrates, Weimar Germany witnessed a nudity movement in the forms of *Nackttanz* (nude dance) and *Nacktballett* (nude ballet).[54] Nudity aside, Western-style dancing was extremely popular in treaty ports like Shanghai and Tianjin, and it was only natural that Chinese pictorials, just like film and literature, found the rise of commercial dance a subject of great interest in the Republican period.[55] In its early years, for instance, *The Pei-yang Pictorial News* regularly carried photographs of the naked or seminaked dancers from Europe, published news of the leading dance halls, like Café Riche (Dahua) in Tianjin, and ran articles debating moral issues related to social dance (e.g., *BYHB*, May 26, 1928, 8).

The commodification of the female body was perfectly expressed in commercial or social dance, which in turn engendered considerable publicity for Chinese pictorials. *The Pei-yang Pictorial News* coverage of Ming Yue Gewutuan (the Bright Moon Song and Dance Troupe) in 1930 is one example. Organized in 1928 and managed by Li Jinhui (1891–1967), a controversial pioneer in Chinese popular music, the Ming Yue Troupe—identified as "Ming Yue Mulsikverein" in the pictorial—specialized in a new form of urban entertainment. It offered an ensemble of short songs and dances featuring romantic lyrics and fresh images of adolescent girls.[56] As captured in the pictorial's photographs, these cheerful, energetic teenage girls appeared on stage in sleeveless shirts and short skirts or pants (a new, startling public sight in China around 1930). Wearing their trademark innocent smiles, they waved their thin arms, kicked their bare legs, bent, twisted, thrust their underdeveloped bodies, and formed different kinds of aesthetic, visually enticing patterns with their bodies (*BYHB*, Aug. 19, 1930, 2; Sept. 4, 1930, 2; Oct. 28, 1930, 3; Oct. 30, 1930, 2).[57]

As in the case of erotic cartoons, this commodification of the female bodies—in particular the bodies of adolescent girls—provoked angry criticism from many moralists in China. They charged that Li Minhui had exploited his young students by forcing them to endure a rigorous regimen of physical training, to sing frivolous songs, and to exhibit their bodies in licentious poses in the public. Li's defender, on the other hand, praised him as a pioneer who drew inspirations from classical Chinese poetry and folk literature (*minjian wenxue*) as well as from Western art and music (*BYHB*, Aug. 19, 1930, 2). Li's impact on modern Chinese entertainment life was substantial, since several of his favorite protégées, such as Li Lili (b. 1915) and Wang Renmei (1914–1987), had become successful leading movie stars by the mid-1930s. Through his musical compositions and choreography, not only did Li Jinhui transform the female body into a "moving" embodiment of art and commodity, but he also revealed another dimension of visual representation: he constructed the female body as signifier of a culturally significant event.

The Female Body as Signifier of a Culturally Significant Event

Let us look closely at how Ming Yue Troupe's 1930 tour in Tianjin led to the construction of the female body as a signifier of a culturally significant event. The tour of the adolescent dancing girls was much anticipated by the press and welcomed in Tianjin, a large coastal city that included an area of foreign settlements. A local photography studio, Tongsheng, seized the Ming Yue's visit as a rare opportunity to publicize itself. On the one hand, the studio invited the young artists to have their picture taken free; the studio issued these pictures as postcards, thereby making reproductions of the attractive female faces and bodies available as a commodity. On the other hand, the studio dispatched its photographers to shoot pictures of live stage performances and published them in *The Pei-yang Pictorial News*, where the studio was credited. The Ming Yue's tour occasioned another event, the writing of classical-style poetry. This typical literati practice expressed personal feelings by eulogizing the ideal of feminine beauty embodied by the adolescent dancers. Four poems in the form of *qijue* (septenary quatrain) were printed in the pictorial; each was devoted to a dancer: Li Minghui, Li Lili, Xue Lingxian, and Wang Renmei. Marked heavily by white circles of emphasis on the right margin of the characters (the outmoded Chinese equivalent to the use of italic or bold face in Western typesetting), these poems were followed by endnotes, set in smaller print, that further explained the ideas expressed in the poems. Originally planned as a profit-oriented cultural program, the Ming Yue's tour in Tianjin was indeed eventful, engendering both a secondary commodity production (i.e., postcards of the female bodies and faces) and a replay of age-old artistic tradition (i.e., aestheticizing the female figure as the embodiment of art).

Li Jinhui's construction of the female body was connected to other culturally significant events that cut across the boundaries of space and time. On the basis of the Tongsheng Studio's photographs reprinted in *The Pei-yang Pictorial News*, one could detect that Li's choreography relied heavily on various Western dance genres, especially musicals from the United States, that featured beautiful formations of female bodies on stage.[58] In turn, Li's dances helped shape the production of emerging Chinese film musicals. A film still of *The Worldly Immortals* (Renjian xianzi, 1934), a musical from the Yihua Film Studio, shows a female dancer who faces the backstage but turns her head to the right so that her smiling face is half visible to the viewer (fig. 8). This pose is similar to many in Li's stage productions, but the dancer here wears much less, merely a swimsuit-like gauzy dress. And she appears more artistic by balancing a cello (arguably a phallic symbol) on her hip with the help of her right hand, and using her left hand to play the instrument behind her back with the bow.[59] Not surprisingly, the film is about a group of five poverty-stricken girls who aspire to become professional dancers in a song and dance troupe (hence, a tribute to Li Jinhui's achievement). Dan Duyu (1897–1972), the film's director, used to be a Shanghai painter noted for his traditional-style collection, *Paintings of a Hundred Beauties* (Baimei tu). Unlike Wu Youru, who had likewise specialized in female figures, Dan managed to graduate from the Shanghai College of Fine Arts (Shanghai Meishu Zhuanke Xuexiao), which had been established by Liu Haisu (1896–1994) and was famous—or rather, infamous—for its studies of the human figure, especially female nudes, in the 1920s.[60]

Sports was another area in which the construction of the female body as signifier of a culturally significant event was fully operational.[61] The visual and conceptual links between modern dance and sports are easy to perceive, for both emphasize movement and promote images of the healthy body. As typical of visual representations in general, it is the female body rather than the male that received the most attention in Chinese pictorials. Apart from a few photographs of the muscular male athletes in *The Young Companion* (*LY*, May 1926, 2; Jan. 1929, 22; April 1931, 29; Aug. 1931, 33; Oct. 1931, 34), pictorial pages devoted to physical culture or sports (*tiyu*) were full of athletic-looking women wearing swimsuits or sports shorts. An enlarged photograph of Miss Yang Xiuqiong (1920–1982), smiling with her bare arms and thighs in a self-confident frontal pose, was featured as the front cover of *The Young Companion* (*LY*, June 1933; see fig. 9). In contrast to demure late Qing courtesans and oftentimes flirtatious contemporary movie stars, Yang Xiuqiong, a Hong Kong swimmer who won five national titles and broke five national records in 1933, proudly displayed her athletic figure as a perfect embodiment of the new ideals of feminine beauty: energetic, youthful, and healthy.[62] Indeed, "Healthy and Pretty Swimmers" was used as the equivalent of a Chinese section title "Jiankang mei" (literally, "beauty of being healthy"). The photographs in that section feature a girl student (as another representative of the new women) sitting by the swimming pool, a second female swimmer playing a mandolin, and the third standing by a rail and posing as "The Modern Venus" [Weinisi zaishi] (*LY*, Sept. 1931).

One could hardly fail to notice that, always wearing the latest fashions—and swimsuits appeared to be one of the most fashionable items of apparel at that time—nearly all these healthy, athletic-looking women smile to the viewer. For the pictorial, the theme "Youth and Pleasure" [Qingchun di huanxiao] presented well the new ideal of feminine beauty. Accented with English captions such as "Is She Charming?" and "Pleased in Her Swimming Suit," photographs of smiling young women direct

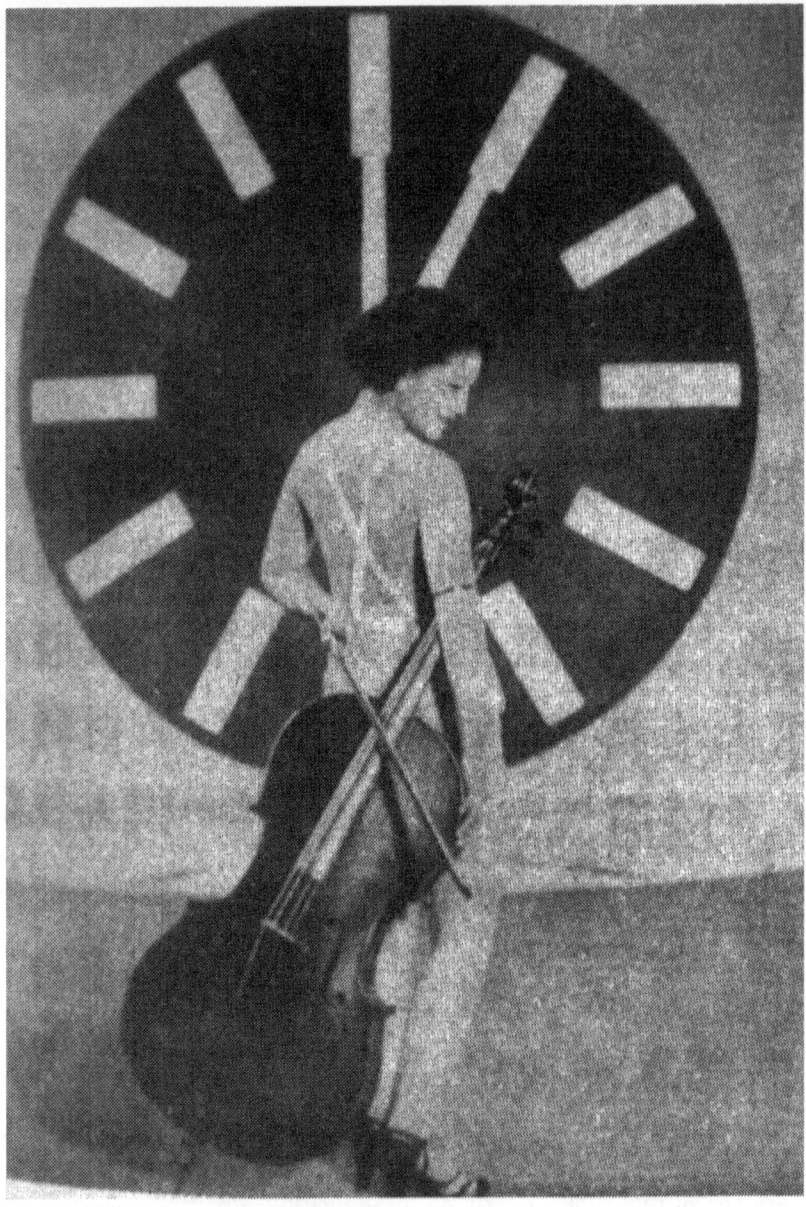

Fig. 8. A scene from of *The Worldly Immortals* [Renjian xianzi, 1934], di-
rected by Dan Duyu: an enticing pose with a cello in the silver screen.
Zhang Junxiang and Cheng Jihua, eds., *Zhongguo dianying dacidian*
(Shanghai: Shanghai cishu chubanshe, 1995), 793.

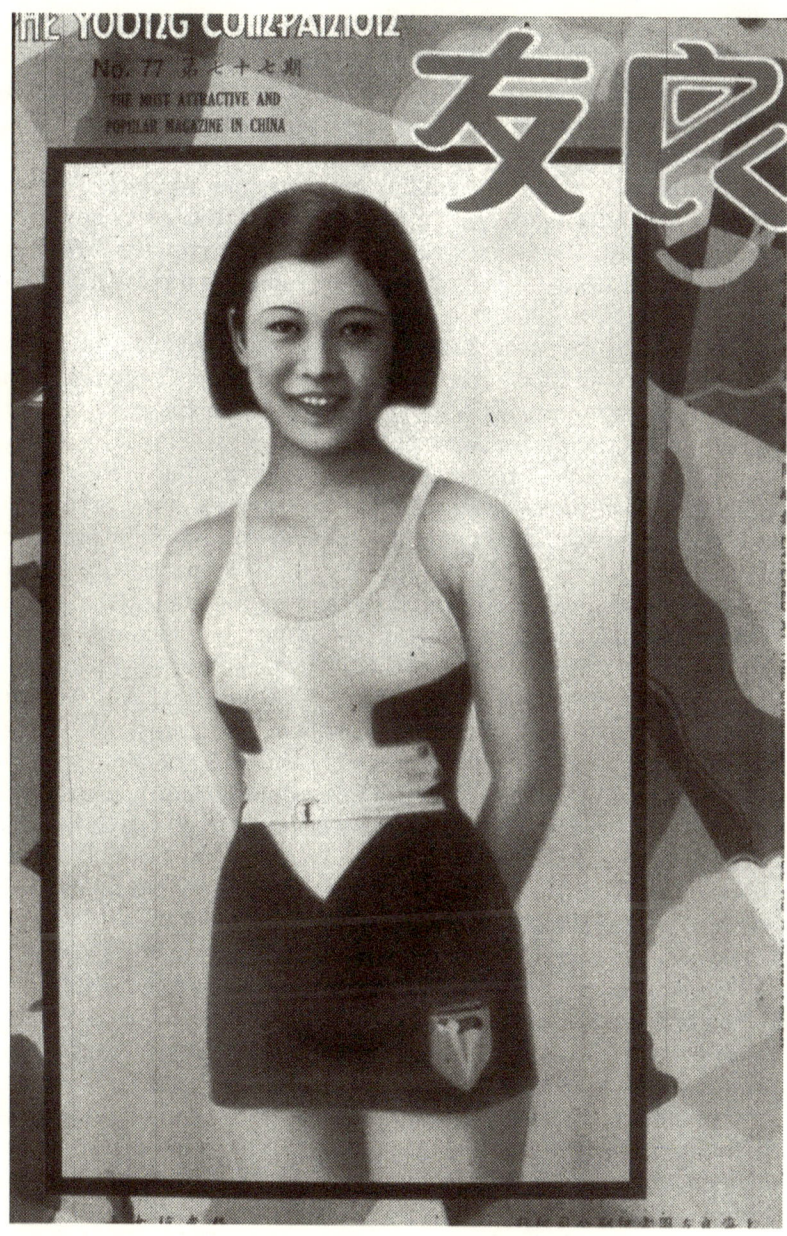

Fig. 9. "Miss Yang Xiuqiong" (1933): a national champion turned cover girl of *The Young Companion*, June 1933.

the viewer's gaze at their "pleasurable" (*kuaihuo*) exhibitionist poses (*LY*, July 1933, 29)—poses that link them intertextually to traditional ladies in Wu Youru's illustrations, although Wu's ladies rarely smiled as happily as these modern women. In "Let's All Smile and [Be] Happy" (Xiao de zong dongyuan), another photographic page devoted to new images of the youthful body and the smiling face, we find a young woman in sports shorts displaying herself "upside down" with her legs holding on to a horizontal bar. The Chinese caption consists of a couplet: "Who cares about the world turned upside down, / I'd rather be a pleasurable wild woman" (*LY*, Sept. 1933, 29).[63]

Ostensibly, by featuring these new images—or new ways of perceiving female bodies and their symbolic values, *The Young Companion*, rather than reproducing mere artwork, reconstructed the female body as signifier of a culturally significant event. No longer intended only for a connoisseur's private viewing at home, these pictures were issued in a "general mobilization" (*zong dongyuan*, as used in one of the Chinese section title quoted above) to urge China's young women to *look modern* by exercising, smiling, and acquiring an athletic, healthy body.[64] By participating in this new discursive and visual construction, the pictorial managed to capture in vivid detail new tastes and new ideals of the Chinese female body in the 1930s.

A similar change in tastes and ideals is documented half a century earlier in Wu Youru's lithographic illustrations. For instance, the Chinese fascination with Western civilization is recorded in "Sightseeing with Binoculars" (Shiyuan weiming), in which three Chinese ladies in traditional costumes stand on the veranda on the second floor and take turns using binoculars to admire the steeple of a Western church in a distance.[65] The demarcation between China and the West is symbolized by its spatial division (China as the interior, the near, versus the West as the exterior, the faraway—or *yuan* in the Chinese title), architectural styles (the Chinese houses decorated with carved phoenixes), and gender difference (the feminine icons, such as costumes and phoenixes, versus the masculine—or even phallic—icons of the steeple and the cross). But the act of watching with binoculars—itself a significant event—inevitably bridges the sets of binary terms from across the demarcation line (*WYRHB* 3.1:14). Of particular import in this illustration is that Chinese ladies, not Chinese gentlemen, are given agency in admiring West civilization in a period of historical transition.

The deliberate choice in assigning agency to Chinese ladies in an imaginary encounter with the West is evident in Wu's other illustrations as well. "With a Female Companion" [Younü tongche] conveys the pleasure of riding in a Western-style horse carriage: two Chinese ladies wear traditional costume but carry a Western-style parasol; even the Chinese driver looks professional with his Western-style hat (*WYRHB* 3.1:19). While the location is not specified in this illustration, in "Riding at Twilight" (Yibian canzhao), three Chinese ladies with their hair tied in a traditional fashion are shown riding in their Western-style horse carriage against the background of a Western-style house with iron-bar railings (*WYRHB* 3.1:25). Unlike their counterparts in "Sightseeing with Binoculars," the Chinese ladies in these two illustrations are physically—if not emotionally or psychologically—moved by the product of Western civilization.[66]

Even within domestic settings, the presence of the West is easy to see. In "A Special Taste" (Bierao fengwei), Wu Youru depicts a group of Chinese ladies, again in beautiful costume, gathering at a long, oval dining table, trying out wineglasses and silverware (knives, forks, and spoons), as well as Western sauces and dressings. The dinning room is complete with a fireplace and a chandelier (*WYRHB* 3.1:10). In "Hitting at the Billiards" [Mingmou haowan], Wu has the Chinese ladies, still wearing their costumes, gather around a billiard table, one of them bending over to hit a billiard ball. In accordance with traditional aesthetic, Wu emphasizes not so much Western-style entertainment as female body parts—"bright eyes and white wrists," as indicated in the Chinese title (*WYRHB* 3.1:9).

The poetic language used in this and other titles, however, did not prevent Wu Youru either from constructing the female body as signifier of an urgent cultural event (i.e., an encounter with the West) or from taking extra precaution to ensure that such an event would *safely* take place. I emphasize *safely* to convey irony, because the "guinea pigs" used in this test were innocent Chinese women. If anything went wrong, they would be the ones to take responsibility; if the test worked out well, then the "masters" of these women could safely proceed to enjoy various forms of Western styles, from riding horse carriages in public to appreciating Western cuisines and recreational activities at home. Make no mistake, Chinese gentlemen were just as much fascinated with the West as their women were; this is self-evident in Wu Youru's familiarity with Western styles in his illustrations. Yet, by assigning agency—at least on a symbolic level—to Chinese women in an imaginary encounter with the West, male artists and viewers in late Qing China learned to construct the female body for an urgent purpose. Apart from being an artwork and a commodity, the reproduction of the female body could be a test ground for an imaginary event, and its outcome would prove ultimately beneficial to Chinese men.

Ambivalences of the Visible Body

To reconsider John Hay's question on the "invisible body" in Chinese art, we can now state with confidence that the female body is highly visible not only in modern Chinese art, but in pictorials and other forms of commercial products (e.g., calendars, advertisements, and film posters). What deserves our further attention are the ambivalences and contingencies of meaning that inevitably arise from the multifarious and complex ways of perceiving, conceiving, representing, circulating, commodifying, and consuming the female body in modern China.

In its October 1933 issue, *The Young Companion* carried "The Heroine" [Fankang], a full-page color painting by an anonymous artist (fig. 10).[67] The titular heroine is a Western-looking female nude featured in a vulnerable frontal pose—vulnerable not only because of her somewhat saddened, almost scared, look but because of her body's motion, suggesting that she is about to step back from some immediate physical danger. She leans her head to the right, thrusts her hips to the left, and seems to rest on a Chinese sword (*dadao*) she carries in her right hand (*LY*, Oct. 1933). Presented in this dynamic but sexually exposed fashion, the model enters a problematic relationship with her sword. On the one hand, the sword as a phallic symbol is expected to protect her completely naked body; on the other hand, by pointing the tip of the sword to the ground, the model appears to have been disappointed by the sword's impotence or lost power. Without further recourse to "masculine" protection, the female nude is left alone to defend herself—her full-bodied self as well as the ideas embodied by her nudity (e.g., beauty, truth, youth, etc.)—and thus allegedly becomes a "heroine" (as indicated in the English title).

But who is the enemy she is supposed to "fight against" (*fankang* in the Chinese title)? For the historical context, note two events reported in *The Young Companion*. In the same issue that featured Pan Sitong's nude painting, "Repose" (discussed earlier), the pictorial reported the Japanese invasion of Northeastern China (or Manchuria) in September 1931 and the Nationalist army's anti-Communist campaign in Southern China (*LY*, Oct. 1931, 14–15). In January 1932, the battle against the Japanese troops in Shanghai inflicted heavy damage to the city's cultural establishments, including film studios, publishing houses, and bookstores. When the pictorial resumed publication in May 1932, it apologized to its readers, attributing the four-month delay to Japanese bombings that had destroyed their January issue, sent to print at the Commercial Press (Shangwu Yinshu Guan). Apart from numerous photos informing the readers of the battle and damage to the city, the resumed issue featured "The Model Rests" (Renti), a full-page color nude photograph by Bertram Park, a British

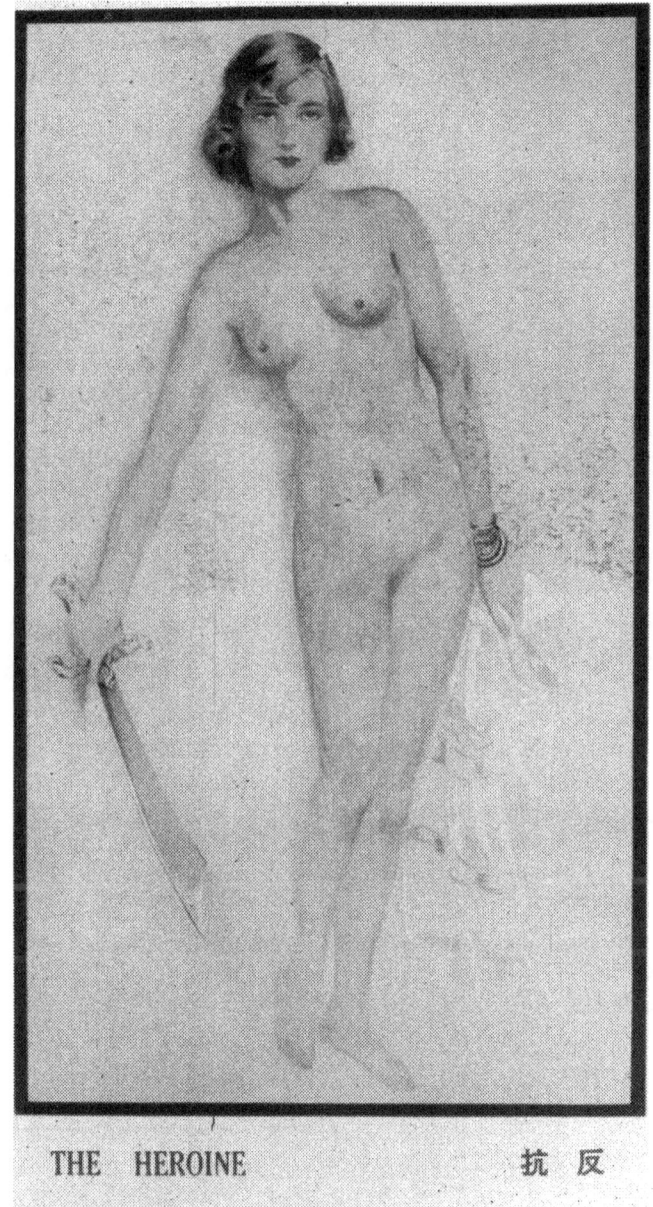

THE HEROINE   抗 反

Fig. 10. Anonymous artist, "The Heroine" [Fankang, 1933]: ambivalences of the female nude and contingencies of meaning. *The Young Companion*, October 1933.

artist, and two nude paintings by the students from the Shanghai College of Fine Arts (*LY*, May 1932, 32, 46–47). Aesthetic taste embodied in the female nude, therefore, did not contradict the news of the war; rather, their coexistence in the same issues was considered normal. This deserves further scrutiny.

To return to "The Heroine," we are now faced with what John Hay has found absent in traditional Chinese art: the "image of a body as a whole object . . . a solid and well-shaped entity whose shapeliness is supported by the structure of a skeleton and defined in the exteriority of swelling muscle and enclosing flesh."[68] In other words, we have here an equivalent of the "objective body"—if there ever is one—that was found missing in traditional Chinese visual representation. Upon closer examination, however, the female body in "The Heroine" is by no means entirely objective; its meaning is contingent on a number of textual, intertextual, and contextual factors. Contextually, the naked heroine was intended in part to stage a symbolic fight against the Japanese aggression. But her very nakedness (i.e., being stripped of protective clothing) casts her fight in an ambivalent light. Marked by her vulnerability as a prime sexual target (and hence a potential victim of sexual violence), how could she ever stand for a nation that would heroically defend herself?[69]

The question of vulnerability is further complicated by the racial features of the female nude in "The Heroine": with her bobbed blond hair and a body shaped like an ancient Greek statue, how could she possibly replace the Chinese female nude to symbolize the nation? And, if she is meant to represent a Western image of heroism, why does she carry a Chinese sword? Despite her stature, in Western pose, the way she carries the Chinese sword may remind the viewer of traditional Chinese opera performances, in which an actress, fully wrapped in layers of costumes and sword in hand, often strikes a similar martial pose. In this comparison, the theatricality embodied in the pose of the female nude in "The Heroine" tends to bracket off the contextual reading suggested above and, instead, to highlight the naked body itself as an exclusive source of meaning, a symbol of pure art that is nonetheless threatened by forces of commodification.

Reading the ambivalences of "The Heroine" intertextually, we discover that the painting is connected to other contemporary nude pictures that presented the female body as artwork, commodity, or both. "The White Chrysanthemum" (Baiju), another full-page color painting by an anonymous artist, features a female nude with her bobbed, permed blond hair. Like the figure in "The Heroine," she is fully aware of her nakedness. But instead of being sad or scared, she feels totally at home in the garden (a conventional symbol of nature), smiling to a bouquet of flowers she holds in front of her breasts, moving her right leg forward so as to partially cover her private parts, and flaunting her adolescent sexuality in a titillating manner (*LY*, Sept. 1933). The similarity in color, brushwork, and facial features between "The Heroine" and "The White Chrysanthemum" is too striking to be ignored. Such intertextual resonance reduces the fighting potential of the female nude in "The Heroine" and fixes the viewer's gaze on her fair skin, delicate features, and gentle nature—a perfect embodiment of the male ideal of feminine beauty.

Considering the textual, intertextual, and contextual factors in visual representation, we have located in "The Heroine" a complex process of signification through which the viewer can negotiate multifaceted, multilayered—and sometimes conflicting—meanings: the innocence of the female nude, the visual beauty of femininity, the power of sexual titillation, the ideas of health and modernity, the complicity of art in commodity production, the possibility of art resisting commodification, the threat of physical or moral violation, the interracial, intercultural tension in visual representation, and so on. The *contingency* of meaning in the viewing of the female nude thus brings us to this insightful comment: "the body is a site of multiple discourses, a veritable fleshly tower of Babel."[70] As I have demonstrated in this study, the female body is precisely such a site of multiple discourses and practices, a site where the male artist displays his unusual talent, the male viewer practices his exquisite connoisseurship, the male entrepreneur invests for financial gains, and the male adventurer tests his imaginary encounter with the West. Represented as artwork, commodity, and signifier of a cultural significant event, or any combination thereof, the female body in modern Chinese pictorials simultaneously constitutes a sight for visual pleasure, a site for cultural consumption and discursive formation, and a space for articulating private fantasies, public anxieties, and unresolved tensions and ambivalences.

My conclusion does not preclude other inevitable questions about representations of the female body in modern China. The repeated emphasis on the male-centered positioning in the preceding paragraph, for instance, raises a crucial question: How could we imagine or define a female viewership of the female body in modern pictorials in particular and in visual cultural in general? To be sure, the three modes of representation I identify in this study are structured around—and in turn compel the viewer to structure—a dominant male, whose viewing, among other things, denies or suppresses feminine desire and female subjectivity. But in the case of pictorial representations of social dance and modern sports, could we entertain the possibility that urban Chinese women, like their Western counterparts in the early twentieth century, imaginatively assumed a subject position in public activities and articulated "a feminine desire to escape bourgeois domesticity's constraints and to create other, transformative identities that were convergent with those qualities of the New Woman that disturbed social conservatives"?[71] Similarly, in the case of high fashions, could we entertain another possibility that, with their consumeristic passion for acquisition, Chinese women actively participated in defining their own aesthetic, and ultimately contributed their share to fashioning the kind of popular culture that would take shape in Republican China? Examined from such a gender-specific perspective, modern Chinese pictorials seem to provide space—however liminal in form—for feminine desire and female subjectivity. I look forward to further research to explore such possibilities, so we might better comprehend the nature of a female viewership of the female body.

Notes

An earlier version of this essay was presented at a conference on the body and face in Chinese visual culture at the University of Chicago in April 1998. The author thanks Wu Hung for his invitation, to the audience for their questions, and to Sarah E. Stevens for her research assistance and comments.

1 In *Body, Subject and Power in China,* ed. Angela Zito and Tani E. Barlow (Chicago: University of Chicago Press, 1994), 42–43. Compare Hay's question to this comment by a famous scholar of Western art: "The idea of offering the body for its own sake, as a serious subject of contemplation, simply did not occur to the Chinese or Japanese mind"—not, I would like to qualify, at least until the modern era; see Kenneth Clark, *The Nude: A Study in Ideal Form* (Princeton: Princeton University Press, 1956), 11.

2 Hay, "Body Invisible," 44.

3 For examples of objective bodies in Western painting, see Jean-Louis Vaudoyer, *The Female Nude in European Painting from Pre-history to the Present Day* (New York: Harry N. Abrams, 1957).

4 For a study of butterfly literature, see Perry Link, *Mandarin Ducks and Butterflies: Popular Fiction in Early Twentieth-Century Chinese Cities* (Berkeley: University of California Press, 1981).

5 Mark Elvin, "Tales of *Shen* and *Xin:* Body-Person and Heart-Mind in China during the Last 150 Years," in *Fragments for a History of the Human Body,* ed. Michel Feher (New York: Zone Books, 1989), pt. 2, 312. See also Bao Tianxiao, *Shanghai chunqiu* [Annals of Shanghai] (1924–26, repr. Shanghai: Shanghai guji chubanshe, 1991), 736.

6 Attempts have been made to distinguish between "nakedness" and "nudity" in Western art. Kenneth Clark clearly favors nudity as an "ideal form" of art over nakedness: "To be naked is to be deprived of our clothes, and the word implies some of the embarrassment most of us feel in that condition. The word 'nude,' on the other hand, carries, in educated usage, no uncomfortable overtone," for it projects an image of "a balanced, prosperous, and confident body: the body re-formed" (*Nude,* 3). In his radical revision of Clark's theory, John Berger prefers

the self-aware, natural state of nakedness to the deceptive, calculated appearance of nudity: "To be naked is to be oneself. To be nude is to be seen naked by others and yet not recognized for oneself. . . . Nakedness reveals itself. Nudity is placed on display. To be naked is to be without disguise. . . . Nudity is a form of dress." *Ways of Seeing* (Harmondsworth, England: Penguin, 1972), 54. For a feminist critique of male conceptions such as Clark's and Berger's, see Lynda Nead, *The Female Nude: Art, Obscenity and Sexuality* (London: Routledge, 1992). In general, my study of the Chinese female body does not follow a clear-cut distinction between nakedness and nudity, for the Chinese word *ruo* covers both meanings in Western art. By the way, complete male nudity was rarely displayed in Chinese pictorials. I came across two such photographs: "Back to Nature" [Huidao ziran qu], which features a group of naked Chinese men playing by a waterfall (see *Liangyou* [May 1930]: 24), and "Ruby, Gold, and Malachite" [Xiatian] by H. S. Tuke of England, which features three naked Western men posing with two other men and a small boat (*Liangyou* [July 1931]).

7 See Wu Youru, *Wu Youru huabao* [A treasury of Wu Youru's illustrations] (1908, repr. Shanghai: Shanghai guji shudian, 1983), hereafter abbreviated **WYRHB** and cited with volume and page numbers. *Dianshizhai huabao* [The Dianshizhai pictorial] was drawn by Wu Youru and his team of artists and issued by Dianshizhai Company of Shanghai from May 8, 1884 to December 1898, 473 issues in all. *Feiyingge huabao* [The Feiyingge pictorial] was edited by Wu Youru and published by his Feiyingge Studio in Shanghai from August 1890 to March 1894, 132 issues in all. For a recent edition of Wu's works, see Zhang Qiming, ed., *Diansh zhai huabao: Daketang ban* [The Dianshizhai pictorial: Daketang edition] (Shanghai: Shanghai huabao chubanshe, 2001), 44 vols. *Liangyou* [The young companion] was edited in succession by Wu Liande, Zhou Shoujuan, Liang Desuo, and Ma Guoliang, and published in Shanghai by Liangyou Chuban Gongsi [Liangyou Books] from February 1926 through October 1945; hereafter the title is abbreviated **LY** and cited with dates and page numbers (when available).

8 *Beiyang huabao* [The Pei-yang pictorial news] was edited by Wu Qiuchen and published in Tianjin from July 7, 1926 to July 29, 1937, 1,587 issues in all. The edition of *Beiyang huabao* used here is a reprint issued by Beijing's Shumu wenxian chubanshe in 1985; hereafter the title is abbreviated **BYHB** and cited with dates and page numbers (when available). *Duli manhua* [Oriental puck] was edited by Zhang Guangyu and published in Shanghai by Duli chubanshe from September 1935 to February 1936, 9 issues in all; the title is abbreviated **DLMH** and cited with dates and page numbers (when available). *Qingqing dianying* [The Chin-Chin screen] was edited by Yan Ciping and published in Shanghai by Qingqing Dianying She [The Chin-Chin Screen Society] from April 15, 1934 to April 30, 1949.

9 As Laikwan Pang argues, "*Dianshizhai* characterized a look that was entertaining and fun, through which . . . anxieties of modernity were partially defused"; see her "The Pictorial Turn: Realism, Modernity and China's Print Culture in the Late Nineteenth Century," *Visual Studies* 20.1 (April 2005): 30.

10 See Don J. Cohen, ed. and trans., *Vignettes from the Chinese: Lithographs from Shanghai in the Late Nineteenth Century* (Hong Kong: Chinese University of Hong Kong, Renditions Paperback, 1987), iii.

11 "Fantastic" is taken from Lu Xun (Lu Hsun), *Selected Works*, trans. Yang

Xianyi and Gladys Yang (Peking: Foreign Languages Press, 1980), 3:129.

12 The frontal pose, however, is not an invention of modern times. In Tang dynasty portraiture, for instance, sensual ladies often assume a frontal pose, and "though standing alone they are always fully aware of an onlooker's eyes"; see Wu Hung, *The Double Screen: Medium and Representation in Chinese Art* (Chicago: University of Chicago Press, 1996), 99.

13 Cohen, *Vignettes*, 100–101; Yingjin Zhang, "The Corporeality of Erotic Imagination: A Study of Pictorials and Cartoons in Republican China," in *Illustrating Asia* (intro., n. 6).

14 *Xiaoshuo Daguan* [The grand magazine], June 1916: illustration pages; Tang Zhenchang, ed., *Jindai Shanghai fanhua lu* [Splendors and glamors of modern Shanghai] (Hong Kong: Shangwu yinshuguan, 1993), 232.

15 Berger, *Ways of Seeing*, 55 (n. 6 above).

16 In art history, see Berger, *Ways of Seeing*; Clark, *Nude*. In film studies, see Laura Mulvey, *Visual and Other Pleasures* (Bloomington: Indiana University Press, 1989).

17 "Prostitution and Urban Imagination: Negotiating the Public and the Private in Chinese Film of the 1930s," in *Cinema and Urban Culture in Shanghai, 1922–1943*, ed. Yingjin Zhang (Stanford: Stanford University Press, 1999), 160–80.

18 One exception to this "fully clothed" Chinese model is found in a color photo, "Repose" (Shui, literally "sleep"), by Lang Jingshan. Set against a gauzy mosquito net, Lang's model poses nude in a reclining sleep posture (*LY*, Sept. 1932, 14). This posture is reminiscent not only of the French sketch but of the photographs of late Qing courtesans discussed above. Intertextually, Lang's Chinese title is thus linked to the courtesan's "spring sleep" (*chunshui*), which, in turn, may have derived from such Western paintings as "Sleeping Venus" by Giorgione (1478–1510). The ubiquity of a similar posture in Western nude paintings is evident in "The Venus of Urbino" by Titian (ca. 1477–1567), "Reclining Bacchanete" by Trutat (1824–1848), and "Olympia" by Manet (1832–1883). For sources of these Western paintings, see Vaudoyer, *Female Nude*, 51–54, 116 (n. 3 above).

19 "Tales," 285 (n. 5 above).

20 Huang Tianpeng, "Wushinian lai huanbao zhi bianqian" [Transformation of pictorials over the past fifty years] *LY* 49 (July 1930): 36–37; Zhang Zhongli, ed., *Jindai Shanghai chengshi yanjiu* [Urban studies on modern Shanghai] (Shanghai: Shanghai renmin chubanshe, 1990), 1067–72.

21 Yingjin Zhang, "The Texture of the Metropolis: Modernist Inscription of Shanghai in the 1930s" *Modern Chinese Literature* 9.1 (Spring 1995): 11–30.

22 See, for instance, these two European nude photos: "The Beyond" by B. Leedham from Paris and "The Birch of Eve" by Yvonne Gregory from London (*LY*, May 1931, 23).

23 For sample artworks, see the exhibits of the Disai Designing Society and a photographic page titled the "Beauty of Columns" (*LY* July 1931, 23–24); a two-page spread of modernist designs, "Symbolic Pictures" (*LY*, Sept. 1931); and another two-page spread, "Sculptural Exhibits," that contains three nude statues of Chinese women (*LY*, Oct. 1931, 24–25).

24 Pp. 5–6. The book features 32 original photographs in addition to one on the cover. The cover photograph carries a frame design with these three Chinese

characters on the top margin: *baimei ying* (photographs—or rather "shadows"—of a hundred beauties), a phrase evoking *baimei tu* (paintings of a hundred beauties) that were popular in China during the same period. Perckhammer's photographs feature Chinese female nudes in sitting, meditating, praying, standing, leaning, kneeling, reclining, and sleeping positions. Almost all photographs are set in an art studio with adequate lighting control, and all female nudes are accompanied or framed by such chinoiseries as a lotus throne (a Buddhist meditation seat), an iron incense burner, a Bodhisattva statuette, a scroll of religious painting, traditional landscape, or flowers and birds, a flower vase, a bronze plate, a set of floral-patterned panel screens, a paper lantern, a pair of candles, an oval-shaped mirror, or a large chest with carved decorations. Perckhammer's rationale for his nude photographs runs, "Pictures of nude women, setting aside the ugly caricatures of the 'Sprig pictures' of erotic scenes, simply do not exist in China. Therefore, I believe, I have created something entirely new and of value" (7).

25 Zhang Jianwen's two photographs closely resemble those of the female nudes in Heinz von Perckhammer's book, especially in their use of the mirror and the contrasting motifs of light and shadows.

26 The omitted part in Berger's quotation applies to Fan Xuegu's picture as well: "the convention of not painting the hair on a woman's body helps towards the same end. Hair is associated with sexual power, with passion. The woman's sexual passion needs to be minimized so that the spectator may feel that he has the monopoly of such passion" (*Ways of Seeing*, 55).

27 See Clark, *Nude* (n. 1 above).

28 To consolidate its reputation as a leading Chinese publisher in art and literature, Liangyou Books issued series of world literature in translation as well as the famous 10-volume *Compendium of Modern Chinese Literature* [*Zhongguo xiandai wenxue daxi*] in 1935–36; see a discussion in Lydia H. Liu, *Translingual Practice: Literature, National Culture, and Translated Modernity—China, 1900–1937* (Stanford: Stanford University Press, 1995), 214–38. Liangyou Books, in other words, cannot be dismissed as a commercial enterprise publishing for profits only.

29 This commercial practice was not limited to the pictorial alone. For instance, *The Chin-Chin Screen*, a popular film fan magazine in Shanghai, advertised in its inaugural issue a three-volume work, *Selected Nude Photographs* [*Ruoti sheying xuanji*], produced by its editor Yan Ciping and his associates Lang Jingshan and Chen Bide (*Qingqing dianying*, April 15, 1934, inside back cover).

30 Leo Ou-fan Lee and Andrew F. Nathan, "The Beginning of Mass Culture: Journalism and Fiction in the Late Ch'ing and Beyond," in *Popular Culture in Late Imperial China*, ed. David Johnson, Andrew J. Nathan, and Evelyn Rawski (Berkeley: University of California Press, 1985), 360–95.

31 Michael Sullivan, *Twentieth-Century China*, 27 (intro., n. 2); Wu Xiangzhu, ed., *Dianshizhai huabao de shishi fengsuhua* [Folk pictures about current events in the *Dianshizhai Pictorial*] (Beijing: Renmin meishu chubanshe, 1958), 1–3; Ye Xiaoqing, *The Dianshizhai Huabao Pictorial: Shanghai Urban Life, 1884–1898* (Ann Arbor, Mich.: University of Michigan, Center for Chinese Studies, 2003).

32 Cohen, *Vignettes*, iv (n. 9 above).

33 Wu provided a counterpart to the Western fashion in his "Fashion from the North" [Beidi yanzhi], which features two Chinese ladies wearing colorful

Manchu costumes, headgear, and high-heel clog shoes (*WYRHB* 3.1:23).

34 Bao Tianxiao, *Chuanyingou huiyi lu* [Reminiscences of the Bracelet Shadow Chamber] (Hong Kong: Dahua chubanshe, 1971), 359–61.

35 On the cover photograph of her typically "oriental" image—with her tiny lips and a colorful Chinese costume, Anna May Wong thus penned her autograph: "Orientally yours" (*LY*, Jan. 1929, front cover). By contrast, male stars rarely if ever appeared in the covers of this pictorial.

36 See Ellen Johnston Laing, *Selling Happiness: Calendar Posters and Visual Culture in Early-Twentieth-Century Shanghai* (Honolulu: University of Hawaii Press, 2004); Shi Shumei, "1939 nian de Shanghai nüxing: cong houzhimin lunshu de jiaodu kan Zhongguo xiandai nüxing de 'xiandaixing'" [Shanghai women in 1939: Modern Chinese women's "modernity" from the perspective of postcolonial discourse], *Lianhe wenxue* 115 (May 1994); for an English version, see chap. 8 of this book.

37 See Stephen R. MacKinnen, "Toward a History of the Chinese Press in the Republican Period" *Modern China* 23.1 (Jan. 1997): 7–11.

38 Wu Fuhui, "Zuowei wenxue (shangpin) shengchang de haipai qikan" [Shanghai-style literary magazines as products of literature (*qua* commodity) production], *Zhongguo xiandai wenxue yanjiu congkan* 1 (1994): 1–15.

39 Yingjin Zhang, *The City in Modern Chinese Literature and Film: Configurations of Space, Time, and Gender* (Stanford: Stanford University Press, 1996), 219.

40 Zhang Tongdao, "Dushi fengjing yu tianyuan xiangchou" [Urban landscape and rural nostalgia], *Wenyi yanjiu* 2 (1997): 97.

41 Heinrich Freuhauf, "Urban Exoticism in Modern and Contemporary Chinese Literature," in *From May Fourth to June Fourth: Fiction and Film in Twentieth-Century China*, ed. Ellen Widmer and David Der-wei Wang (Cambridge, MA: Harvard University Press, 1993), 134–52.

42 Li Oufan (Leo Ou-fan Lee), "Zhongguo xiandai wenxue de 'tuifei' ji zuojia" [The decadent and the decadent writers in modern Chinese literature], *Dangdai* (Taiwan) 93 (Jan. 1994): 37–9. See also Lee, *Shanghai Modern*, 215–17, 241–57 (intro., n. 2).

43 Mu Shiying, *Gongmu* [The cemetery] (Shanghai: Xiandai shuju, 1933), 108–10.

44 Zhang Tongdao, "Dushi fengjing," 98, 104.

45 Chang-tai Hung, *War and Popular Culture: Resistance in Modern China, 1937–1945* (Berkeley: University of California Press, 1993), 34.

46 Xiao's works were published by Jingwei shuju; Zhang's, by Zhongyan shudian.

47 Hung, *War and Popular Culture*, 34.

48 Zhang, "Corporeality" (n. 13 above).

49 Xiao Jianqing, *Shehui manhua*, 10; Zhang, *Manhua mingzuo xuan*, 94. All models in these cartoons are female. I found only one photograph showing a male model posing for students at the Shanghai College of Fine Arts; significantly, one of the students shown at the center of the photograph was a female (*LY* [April 1931]: 14).

50 Except for occasional humorous twists such as this, San Mao is generally regarded as a symbol of class oppression and social injustice in Republican China.

See Hung, *War and Popular Culture*, 32; Mary Ann Farquahar, "*Sanmao*: Classic Cartoons and Chinese Popular Culture," in *Asian Popular Culture*, ed. John A. Lent (Boulder: Westview Press, 1995), 139–58.

51 Hung, *War and Popular Culture*, 34. As late as 1979, nudity in art was still considered a problem in China. "Water Splashing Festival" (Poshui jie), a mural in the Beijing Capital International Airport painted by Yuan Yunsheng (b. 1937), provoked criticism for its portrayal of partial nudity and had to be covered up by the government authorities. See J. L. Cohen, *The New Chinese Painting, 1949–1986* (New York: H. N. Abrams, 1987), 41; Julia F. Andrews, *Painters and Politics*, 390–92 (chap. 4., n. 28).

52 I found only three articles by Zeng Die that defended pornography, sensuality, and feminine beauty in *Oriental Puck* (*DLMH* Oct. 10, 1935; Dec. 10, 1935; Jan. 15, 1936). In sharp contrast to China, where the female nude is associated with pornography and generally treated as a sensitive moral or political issue, in the West pornography—both as a literary and visual practice and as a category of understanding—has been linked to the emergence of Western modernity. See Lynn Hunt, ed., *The Invention of Pornography: Obscenity and the Origins of Modernity, 1500–1800* (New York: Zone Books, 1993), 9–45. Terms related to pornography, such as *obscenity* and *sexuality*, have been subject to critical scrutiny in the fields of art and cinema over the past decade; see Nead, *Female Nude* (n. 6 above); Linda Williams, *Hard Core: Power, Pleasure, and the Frenzy of the Visible* (Berkeley: University of California Press, 1989).

53 Zhang, *Manhua mingzuo xuan*, 85.

54 See *Empire of Ecstasy: Nudity and Movement in German Body Culture, 1910–1935* (Berkeley: University of California Press, 1997).

55 For a study of Chinese dancers, see Andrew Field, "Selling Souls in Sin City: Shanghai Singing and Dancing Hostesses in Print, Film, and Politics, 1920–1949," in *Cinema and Urban Culture*, 99–127 (n. 17 above).

56 The German word *Mulsikverein* (music club) used in the pictorial's English caption betrays the influence of the body culture in Weimar Germany, as I speculate above. The Ming Yue Troupe grew out of the China Song and Dance School (Zhonghua Gewu Xuexiao) Li Jinhui established in 1927; it was formally known as the China Song and Dance Troupe (Zhonghua Gewutuan).

57 Among pieces performed during the Ming Yue's tour in Tianjin were "Little Thrush" (Xiaoxiao huamei niao), with Wang Renmei; "The Night of Moon Light" (Yueming zhiye), with Xue Lingxian; "Misty Rain" (Maomao yu), sung by Li Lili; "Delight of Spring" (Chuntian de kuaile); "The Fairy of Hundred Flowers" (Baihua xianzi); "Three Butterflies" (San hudie); and "Triumph" (Zuihou zhi shengli). Their popularity in Tianjin was evident in the four-page coverage *The Bei-yang Pictorial News* devoted to their performances from mid-August to late October in 1930. Two photographs of the Ming Yue dancers, one featuring Xue Lingxian, and the other Wang Renmei and Li Lili, were reprinted in the children's section of *The Young Companion* (*LY*, July 1930, 38).

58 Western dances and Hollywood movies were regularly featured in *The Bei-yang Pictorial News* and *The Young Companion*, as well as in numerous other Chinese film magazines throughout the Republican period. The public interest in the aesthetic of dance movement and the athletic female body was reflected in a

two-page spread, "Callisthenic Patterns" [Renti xuehua tu], which contained six photographs—each set in a circle frame—featuring seven Western female athletes/dancers forming exquisite patterns by coordinating and joining their heads, arms, waists, thighs, and legs. An English caption commented, "These pictures present the beautiful star formations which resemble closely the snow flake crystals" (*LY*, May 1933). The modern sport calisthenics did not seem to have developed much in Republican China. As late as 1987, the Hollywood type of calisthenics, with its display of female bodies in varieties of beautiful twists and turns, was still viewed in China as politically suspect and was largely excluded from the opening ceremony of the National Games in that year. See Susan Brownell, *Training the Body for China: Sports in the Moral Order of the People's Republic* (Chicago: University of Chicago, 1995), 115–17.

59 Zhang Junxiang and Cheng Jihua, eds., *Zhongguo dianying dacidian* [China cinema encyclopedia] (Shanghai: Shanghai cishu chubanshe, 1995), 793.

60 Andrews, *Painters and Politics*, 15; Sullivan, *Twentieth-Century China*, 44–46.

61 Susan Brownell thus elaborates the connection between sports and body culture in modern China: first, "sports should be analyzed as part of the entire culture of the body"; second, "the culture of the body is strongly shaped by power relations"; and third, "sports events are one of the main arenas in which the body as a cultural artifact is publicly displayed" (*Training the Body*, 8).

62 Yang Xiuqiong, nicknamed "Mermaid" (Meirenyu), instantly became a media celebrity and went on to compete in the 1934 Far East Games in Manila, the Sixth National Games in Shanghai, and the 1936 Olympic in Germany. For more on her see Wei Shaochang, *Dongfang yetan* [Evening talks of the East] (Fuzhou: Haixia wenyi chubanshe, 1981), 142–52.

63 English captions to other photographs in this page include "Look This Way, Please," "Feeling Elated," and "Sunshine and the Smile"—all directly appealing to the viewer.

64 As if publishing *The Young Companion* alone was not enough to drive home to its readers the new ideas of health and beauty, starting in November 1932, Liangyou Books issued another pictorial, *Health and Beauty* [Jianmei huakan], devoted exclusively to promoting "world-class knowledge" of the "athletic body" while explicitly avoiding "vulgarness" (*chu*) and "pornography" (*yin*; *LY*, Oct. 1932, back cover). Two cover photographs from *Health and Beauty* were reprinted in *The Young Companion*, one of them, "Back to Nature" [Fanyu ziran], featuring the back view of a nude dancer (*LY*, Dec. 1932).

65 Admittedly, the use of the Western perspective was not done perfectly here, as is typical of the majority of Wu's illustrations. One may argue that the ladies are looking at some faraway objects other than the steeple, but this does not affect my reading of the picture.

66 Compare these two illustrations of a peaceful ride by Chinese ladies with another illustration by Wu Youru, "A Horse Carriage Accident" [Chuangma huo]. Two Chinese silk merchants are riding in a horse carriage to the Yu Garden in Shanghai. It is a fair day but the traffic is terrible. When they are blocked by a rickshaw with a courtesan, their horse suddenly runs wild and throws them to the ground. One of them dies later that night and the other is hospitalized (*WYRHB* 11.1:12). The gender contrast in Wu's pictorial representation—the female as

elegant and peaceful versus the male as vulnerable and violent—unravels a hidden anxiety or phobia in China's encounter with Western technology in the late Qing period. The Chinese fascination with Western technology continued throughout the Republican periods. As late as 1931, *The Young Companion* presented a folded two-page spread of photographs showing "Vehicles of Every Description Now in Use in Shanghai," including the rickshaw and the coach (*LY*, Jan. 1931, 26–27).

67 My guess is that the artist chose to remain anonymous because he did not want his name to be associated with the female nude, which was still very controversial in the 1930s. The style of this picture resembles Fang Xuegu's "The Fading Youth," discussed earlier.

68 "Body Invisible," 51 (n. 1 above).

69 By contrast, a photograph on the first page of the issue resumed after the Shanghai battle, which shows a male "boxer" naked waist up, may better serve as a symbol of national defense, as the caption clearly emphasizes his fighting spirit (*LY*, May 1932, 1). However, such fighting spirit was again cast in an ambivalent light as the pictorial reprinted in the same issue a traditional landscape painting by Lin Qinnan (Lin Shu, 1852–1924), titled "The Peach Blossom Spring" [Taohua yuan]. In his inscribed poem, Lin lamented the fallen kingdom (*wangguo*) and found no utopia to call his home (*LY*, May 1932, 45).

70 Hay, "Body Invisible," 46 (n. 1 above).

71 Gaylyn Studlar, "'Out-Salomeing Salome': Dance, the New Woman, and Fan Magazine Orientalism," in *Visions of the East: Orientalism in Film*, ed. Matthew Bernstein and Gaylyn Studlar (New Brunswick, NJ: Rutgers University Press, 1997), 105–6.

7

The Bare Truth: Nudes, Sex, and the Modernization Project in Shanghai Pictorials

Carrie Waara

The rise of the pictorial press in Republican Shanghai demonstrates a belief among Chinese artists and entrepreneurs in the power of visual representation to construct a vivid, new culture. Striking images of the human body, clothed and unclothed, endowed these periodicals with a modernist prestige and made them a vehicle for projecting sexual messages about Chinese cultural modernity. Some members of the pictorial press, particularly the prominent art magazines *Zhenxiang huabao, Liangyou,* and *Meishu shenghuo,* advocated a Chinese-style cultural modernism as the key to strengthening China in the Republican-era political, military, social, economic, and cultural crisis. They promoted periodical publishing to develop a commodity-oriented, modernist culture that united the power of advanced printing technology with an ideology of nation building. Examples from the Shanghai art press's "modernization project," particularly the fine art nude, raise questions about the social, political, and historical functions of representation and reception, and about the interstices of nationalism, internationalism, individualism, and sexuality in early twentieth-century China.[1]

The growing literature of feminist art history has debated seriously the question of women and men as spectators or consumers of art—particularly of art that takes the female form as its subject/object. One view holds that all representations of the female body have to be seen through the male heterosexual gaze, given the sociohistorical dominance of patriarchy. The female fine-art nude embodies this paradigm of spectatorship, with the male artist and audience having free, uncensored access to the female as passive object. This view argues that despite the elevation of the nude to the status of high art—presumably ennobling and desexing the body—male-female power relations that are essential to the creation and viewing of the nude cannot be made invisible.[2] Thus each female nude image reproduces the gendered social hierarchy.

However, there is another view. The modern Chinese fine-art nude, and other representations of women in the Republican art press, intimated that sexuality had the power to transform society. As I argue below, the controversy behind the nude's introduction to the Chinese art scene showed its *destabilizing* potential. That potential was even commodified in later art magazines engaged in the modernization project. In addition, the concern with truth, authenticity, and beauty that marked this modernization project offered other, gendered interpretations of the human form. Thus, the symbolic economy of sexuality in Chinese art periodicals of the Republican era demonstrates that Chinese attempts to construct a modernist culture both constituted and confronted a dynamic configuration of cultural forms, social relations, and historical processes.

The Artist–Publisher–Audience Relationship and Cultural Construction

Before I elaborate on the symbolic economy of sexuality in Chinese art periodicals, however, certain theoretical assumptions about the dynamic interrelationships among the cultural producers, agents, and audiences for these periodicals must be clarified.

Until recently, in the West the artist was widely conceived as the independent (often alienated) genius of personal vision, aloof from political and social concerns. In China, too, the amateur ideal of the eremitic scholar-painter has long been juxtaposed with low-status professional artists who sell their work and are thus more dependent on social and political patronage.[3] In the last two decades art historians and cultural theorists concerned with the sociology and cultural politics of art have made great strides to correct that conception of the artist and to promote research on the institutional, organizational, and ideological contexts of artistic production.[4]

Pierre Bourdieu explains the ideological function of culture in terms of its consecration of the social order. When a particular definition of culture predominates in a given society, it divides society into two groups, barbarians and civilized people, thereby justifying certain persons' possession of culture and its lack among other persons. The appropriation of cultural wealth, Bourdieu notes, depends to a great extent on education and social class, both of which provide a familiarity with cultural works and with the categories of perception used by the dominant cultural authorities. The possession of cultural knowledge or artifacts adds another layer of privilege to otherwise strictly economic differences, thus reinforcing existing social distinctions.[5]

Furthermore, as demonstrated by Foucault and others, the production of meaning is inseparable from the production of power. I define culture as social practice embedded in power relations—alternating exchanges between authority and subversion, affirmation and critique, appropriation and resistance. Republican China experienced multiple struggles for control over its politics, economy, and society, and over the creation and representation of new cultures. Art publishing provides an extraordinary case study of this larger struggle for cultural authority and cultural subversion within the modern industrialization of culture—that is, the application of machine production to cultural commodities like periodicals, prints, graphic designs, and so on.

Chinese art publishing exemplifies the power of representation, the power of appropriation, and the possibility of resisting authority. On the one hand, we have the authorizing function of publishing: it legitimizes and sanctions whatever cultural elements it reproduces for mass consumption. Merely by appearing in print, cultural images convey authority and universalized value. Publication makes a work of art appear to be an authorized part of the canon of culture, part of the cultural code that supports the social order. Publishing constitutes and reinforces the hierarchy of cultural wealth. This interpretation directly challenges Walter Benjamin's notion that mechanical reproduction jeopardizes and destroys the authority of the art object.

On the other hand, Benjamin's argument has merit, in that publishing's power of appropriation also democratizes. Making art and literature accessible to larger audiences allows more people to familiarize themselves with what otherwise would be objects of only the elite. Through print the audience penetrates the distance between themselves and the original work of art, demystifying its features and its claims to uniqueness. Essentially, this corresponds to Benjamin's notion that the mechanical reproduction of art destroys the aura of the thing reproduced and increases the perception of the "universal equality of things." This encourages the audience to become experts themselves, opening up the social and cultural order.[6] This was the stated goal of many of the cultural modernizers who promoted art magazines in Republican China.

Both of these contradictory functions of publishing, one authorizing and one subverting, clearly coexisted in Republican China; they paralleled the coexistence of cultural affirmation and cultural critique, of appropriation and resistance, in the modernist movement. Their tensions echo in the shifting modern relationship between high art and mass culture. The predominance of one over the other at any given time is due partly to structural factors like the socioeconomic order and partly to the roles and relationships within that order assumed by the audiences, artists, and publishers.

Patronage, a crucial socioeconomic element in artistic production, connects editors, publishers, artists, and their audience in intertwined relationships. As Chu-tsing Li notes, "the artist is always dependent on either an institution or an individual for his livelihood."[7] Yet Li's emphasis of the power of the individual artist is too conventional. Li further notes that artists since at least the Song have been viewed popularly in China as influential arbiters of taste and styles, "with a tremendously important role in the transmission of Chinese cultural values."[8] The development of mass media, particularly the Republican-era periodical press, enhanced this power of artists (and publishers) to influence opinion. Imbued with a sense of their own cultural responsibility, artists and editors in the pictorial press reached ever-larger audiences.

The power of publishers to shape modern Chinese culture depended on the circulation both of cultural and material capital. The latter, in the form of adequate financing and printing capacity, particularly of photographic-plate and printing-press technology, was fundamental. The former was more complex. Publishers who successfully engaged in art publishing possessed different kinds of cultural capital. For example, cultural capital could come from editors' and publishers' relationships to other people. In the case of *Zhenxiang huabao*, the publishers had belonged to Sun Yatsen's revolutionary alliances very early on in Japan, and thus were able to access cultural capital in the form of photographs and first-person stories about the 1911 revolution—which had overthrown the Manchus just before *Zhenxiang huabao* began publishing. Their prestige as revolutionary elders was also a form of cultural capital. And because they were located in Shanghai, *Zhenxiang huabao*'s, *Liangyou*'s, and *Meishu shenghuo*'s publishers had access to images of and information about the latest Western and Chinese news, technology, and styles. Such access amounted to power in the form of cultural capital.

As for artistic content, publishers' cultural capital generally consisted of access both to modern, Western-style art and artists and to distinguished traditional-style Chinese art and artists.[9] The new art was often presented as the height of progressivism, embodying modernistic content and methodology to construct a superior culture that would put China back on the world's cultural map. Promising publishers had access to salons or studios where the cultural elite, both traditionally minded and modern, met and mingled. They could borrow good reproductions of Western art from artists and others who had studied and traveled abroad. Publishers with connections to the Chinese elite cultural tradition had access to private collections, which could be photographed and reproduced in the magazines.

Both kinds of artistic capital were essential—especially for modernizers promoting the cultural reform. Art magazines followed a formula of printing traditional Chinese art, Euro-American-inspired art, as well as art that combined elements of each. This was more than a businessman's attempt to supply "something for everybody," but was a demonstration, circulation, and creation of cultural capital in Shanghai's uniquely cosmopolitan site.[10] Rather than condemn the hybrid qualities of these treaty-port periodicals (I object strenuously to those who see *hybrid* and *treaty-port* as derisively describing some kind of "unnatural" and disfiguring mix of cultures), we should view them as creative attempts to define the Chinese position in a new world civilization. Magazines like *Meishu shenghuo*, which championed contemporary Chinese artists who worked solely in Western painting styles, also included paintings from the Yuan, Ming, and Qing dynasties in every issue, thereby partaking of centuries of Chinese cultural prestige.[11] Likewise, the inclusion of art and articles from Western sources endowed a publication with the prestige of Western civilization. In fact, Republican Shanghai was a battleground of cultures, where nationalism and imperialism influenced everyday attitudes toward art.

The reading audience for Republican-era Chinese art periodicals most likely resembled the audience for popular fiction in late Qing and early Republican times: those who could afford to buy—well-to-do businessmen, landlords, bankers, industrialists and their families; some intellectuals and government officials; and rural gentry who ordered magazines by mail—and those much larger numbers who shared periodicals and books: students, shop clerks, and office workers.[12] Economic growth in urban commercial and industrial centers and the consolidation of the Nanjing regime in the 1930s meant that the numbers of potential readers swelled in this period. Advanced printing technologies and advertising also made periodicals affordable to many more people.

Magazine circulation is a complex topic fraught with problems for the historian and the marketing specialist alike. First of all, as is the case today, publishers used circulation statistics to secure advertising; thus, official figures cannot be taken to be reliable. Moreover, in the age of advertising, which China entered with the rest of the world nearly simultaneously, a magazine's success or failure was not determined solely by a large circulation. Often advertisers want to reach specific audiences, and publishers attract and please advertisers as well as readers. More useful than circulation figures for this study, perhaps, are the factors in the rapid expansion of the magazine audience in the Republican period.[13]

The expansion of the urban middle class, less educated and less wealthy than the traditional elite, meant an audience more concerned with the issues of everyday life. One must distinguish most of this audience in general from the educated youth who were the audience for May Fourth literature, although undoubtedly there was some overlap, especially as the new culture reform movement consolidated itself in the late 1920s and 1930s. Particularly in the constant gloom of the Depression years, just as in the West, comfort and entertainment was needed. The development of color printing—and, of course, the movie industry—illustrates how technology shaped this market. As exciting, well-illustrated magazines appeared, they met certain needs for amusement and stimulation.

Art magazines both stimulated and were stimulated by a rising desire for culture. A desire for self-improvement paralleled the desire for an improved nation. Chinese audiences had had very narrow exposure to Western art, technology, and lifestyles, and this limited supply created demand, at least among the urban middle and elite classes, who looked increasingly to magazines to supply visual information about the world outside China. Likewise, they also expected magazines to supply them with reproductions and insights from the traditional aesthetic of the privileged classes of China.

The reading, viewing, and consuming audience may have affirmed, criticized, or ignored works of art or literature and their place in the cultural hierarchy, but it would be a mistake to assume that the audience response was generated on its own. The artist's role in shaping taste and style and in transmitting cultural values was fundamental to the strategies and effects of Republican-era artists and publishers in the modernization project. Nonetheless, as Martin Powers notes, "whatever his bias, the author [or artist] had to maintain credibility with his readers. . . . [He] could not stray too far from contemporary practice."[14] Thus, especially considering the commodified culture of the periodical press, one must continually acknowledge that artists, publishers, and audiences exerted mutual influence on one another.

Representations, Gender Ideologies, and the Modernization Project in Republican Art Pictorials

The prototypical Republican art magazine, *Zhenxiang huabao*, was established right after the 1911 revolution, when the Lingnanpai (Canton School) artists and brothers Gao Jianfu and Gao Qifeng, allegedly funded by Sun Yatsen, opened a bookstore and publishing house in Shanghai, and began to publish their own pictorial magazine.[15] It ran only from 1912 to 1913, but its unique appearance in that dramatic first year of the republic left an impression in the art and publishing worlds. Not only did its use of advanced photographic printing technology create a new form of publication in China, the photographic art pictorial, but its combination of art, culture, society, politics, military, technology, commerce, and history set a tone for the fascinating hybrid magazines that followed.

The rise of the pictorial press points to photography as a quintessentially modern art form that illustrates important aspects of the power of representation and its relation to the modernization project as defined above. Susan Sontag notes, "To photograph is to appropriate the thing photographed. It means putting oneself into a certain relation to the world that feels like knowledge—and, therefore, like power. . . . [There is] the presumption of veracity that gives all photographs authority, interest, [and] seductiveness."[16]

Photography's ability to appropriate images that seem to be "miniatures of reality" justified the truth claims of China's first photographic magazine, *Zhenxiang huabao*, whose name translates literally as "The Truth (or True Face) Pictorial."[17] It based its claims on the accuracy of photographic illustration. It portrayed itself as uniquely capable of communicating objective reality to the viewing audience.

Zhenxiang huabao, devoted to "using art for national salvation," assumed the role of promoting an "authentic" new Republic (as opposed to a false one). Cover illustrations and editorial statements modeled the magazine's self-representation as an authoritative source for "true republican government" and for truth in general. Portrayals of male figures, particularly self-representations of the artist, were integral to that message, and centered on an awareness of audience that provided gendered roles for artist and spectator.

The editor's opening statement in the inaugural issue of *Zhenxiang huabao* (June 5, 1912) began with an anecdote from the life of Oliver Cromwell. When a portrait painter eliminated a blemish on Cromwell's face to improve his portrait, Cromwell shouted angrily, "Paint me as I am!" The *Zhenxiang huabao* editor reasoned,

> Now that's courage! Only a hero can know his own true face, and only a hero can preserve his own true face. Random enthronement is at an end. The Republic is established. The false face of the constitutional government established by our vile enemies is broken, and the true face of a republic appears.[18]

In this opening statement *Zhenxiang huabao* condemned the recent machinations of the Manchu court, its intrigues over the last emperors, and the last-gasp contrivance of the Qing constitution. Its ardent concern for authenticity marks it as a member of the modernization project in China. Moreover, its strong, masculine model of Cromwell—a painter's subject who dares to talk back—sharply contrasts with the few portrayals of women in *Zhenxiang huabao*, whose females either modeled the latest clothing fashions, or represented the claims of medicinal tonics to strengthen the enervated.

The most telling example of the magazine's claim to deliver truth is the cover illustration on the third issue, published in July of 1912 (fig. 1). Not a photograph, but a painting, it shows a man dressed in a Western suit, top hat in one hand, drawing back a heavy curtain with the other to reveal in bold calligraphy the words THE TRUTH [*zhenxiang*].[19] Like a magician, the magazine means to expose hitherto-unknown realities. This is one of several self-portraits on *Zhenxiang huabao* covers painted by Gao Qifeng, the artist-editor. The inaugural cover, published in June of 1912 (fig. 2), raises the same theme, only slightly more subtly: A bohemian artist in long jacket, floppy hat, and bow tie sits outdoors on his folding stool before an easel that resembles a signboard, to which he is applying the finishing touches from his oil palette. A Western-style jug and painter's supply case are on the ground by his feet, while tree branches and leaves and background shapes suggest a natural setting. But the easel does not contain a landscape painting; instead, it displays the title of the magazine—*Zhenxiang huabao*—in stylized *lishu* calligraphy. Here again the artist presents himself as a chief delineator of reality, or at least of the true image of reality. He appears as the spokesman or bearer of the universal, as the master of truth.[20] Locating himself and his tools among tree leaves and branches shows the artist literally in the field as opposed to in the ivory tower, and thus able to capture reality as it truly is. This setting also naturalizes his authority as an accepted element of how things are in the actual scheme of things.

Illustrations like these raise the complicated issue surrounding artistic self-representation, its meaning, and its relationship to public culture. Both pictures are essentially *representations of representation*. The man with the top hat presents to the viewer what is behind the curtain, and the bohemian artist is making a representation of truth. On the surface these portrayals take what Svetlana Alpers has called a "commanding attitude toward the world" (or truth). Both men seem to control what the viewer sees. But in addition, the artists within the pictures, their backs to us, join the viewer to observe the preexisting image of the world (or of truth) before them. This identifies them *with* the viewer even as they take the commanding role of representing the world (truth) *to* the viewer. The artist claims not only "I see the world" but also that "the world is 'being seen' [by *us*.]"[21]

This complex mode of double representation centers on an awareness of audience in several ways. First, it shows the viewer how to think about art and artists: the artist gazes at the world like (and with) the viewer, so his vision is a shared one. Since the artist is in the world that he and the viewer are observing, the illusion is that he and the viewer see the same world, which encourages the viewer to accept the artist's representation of that world. Again, this naturalizes the artist's commanding role through his location within the gaze. Moreover, in utilizing his special talent for representation, the artist serves the cause of truth and beauty, an ennobling pursuit. The artist is "a mediator of the world's truth, . . . bringing it forth into public view—and providing a role for the viewer as spectator, centered before a stage, poised for both entertainment and instruction."[22] These roles for artist and spectator objectify and reiterate the gendered cultural practice of the authoritative, commanding male gaze of the artist-author and the passive, receiving female gaze of the reader-audience.

Zhenxiang huabao gave the artist an active role in shaping public culture. In its stated rationale for using illustrations it cautioned against the ambiguous effects of *words*, and asserted the directness of the visual *image*: "Using words to move people can have a contrary effect; the use of pictures to move people has a *direct* influence"[23] *Zhenxiang huabao*'s presumption of the unmediated power of visual representation was not completely naïve. It buttressed the conviction that artist-intellectuals were the cultural critics needed to make China a strong nation. *Zhenxiang huabao* consistently printed articles and illustrations intended to cultivate a critical eye among its readers. That eye could distinguish between truth and falsehood, between quality and inferiority, and see subtleties that the uneducated eye might miss. A translation by the Lingnanpai artist Chen Shuren of a Japanese book on painting methods, serialized over nearly the entire run of *Zhenxiang huabao*, included a section on the importance of "the education of the eye."[24] To that end, a wide variety of paintings were reproduced in the magazine. The scholar-painter-revolutionary Huang Binhong and others contributed illustrated articles on Chinese art and artists to raise the level of readers' knowledge.[25] The editor's brother, Gao Jianfu, contributed sketches, photographs, and designs for a special section to serve as a serialized model copybook for elementary and middle schools.[26] And nearly every issue contained allegorical cartoons intended to provide "the sudden realization of an alarm clock."[27] Artists were to advance China intellectually, materially, and politically through their visually compelling work in *Zhenxiang huabao*.

Interestingly, in the mid-1920s, *Liangyou* magazine spoke of its printing authority with a contrasting humility. "We have no wild hopes," the opening statement concludes coyly, "and dare not say we have some grand contribution worthy of appreciation."[28] Rather than representing mastery, the magazine is modestly coquettish, youthfully emotional. On its covers are photographic portraits of young women, not male masters of

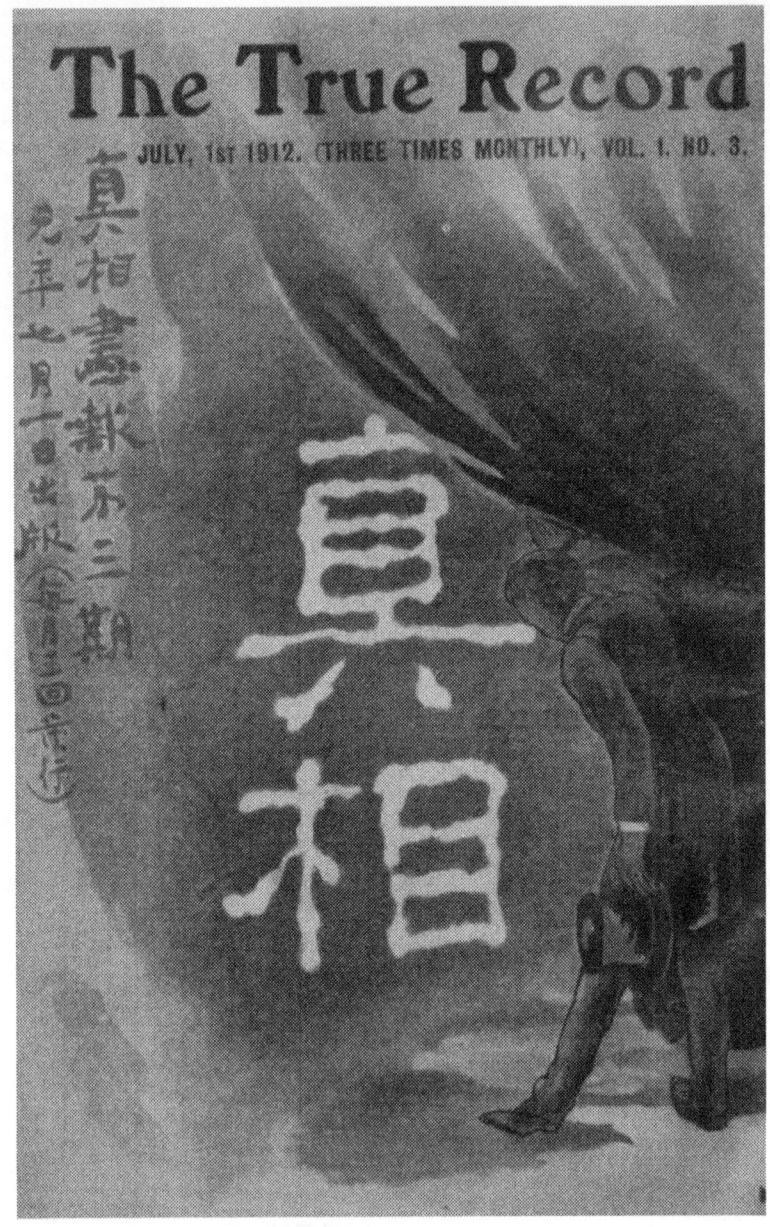

Fig. 1. Gao Qifeng, Untitled [self portrayal] Cover, *Zhenxiang hua-bao* 3 (July 1, 1912).

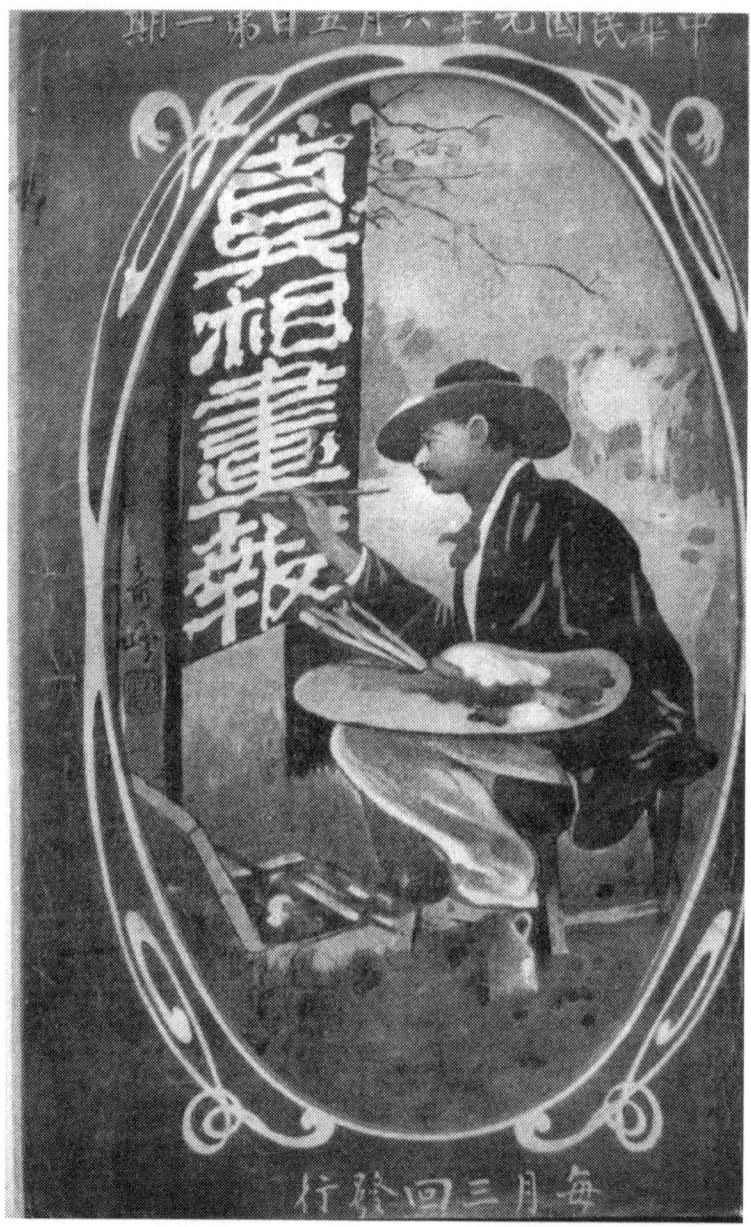

Fig. 2. Gao Qifeng, Untitled [self portrayal] Cover, *Zhenxiang huabao* 1 (June 5, 1912).

ceremony or artistic experts. Appearing a decade after the disappointing failure of the first Republic and its descent into warlordism, *Liangyou* offered comfort, entertainment, and loyal friendship; and loyalty was what the magazine wished from its readers. Probably reflecting the impact of the mass market on the Shanghai culture industry by the 1920s, *Liangyou*'s "little sister," "feel-good" approach was more entertaining and less didactic on the whole than *Zhenxiang huabao*. Nevertheless, like *Zhenxiang huabao*, the magazine voiced serious concerns about China's place in the world and asserted art's positive effect on citizenship.

Published from 1926 to 1941, *Liangyou* was founded and managed by Wu Liande, a nationalistic entrepreneur with broad overseas connections, ably assisted for the magazine's first decade by his chief editor, Liang Desuo, a Western-trained artist and writer. One of the most popular and successful pictorials of the 1920s and 1930s, *Liangyou* developed the diverse format introduced by *Zhenxiang huabao*, used high-quality copper-plate printing, and continued to make technical improvements over the life of its publication. *Liangyou* solicited—and printed—complaints and kudos from readers, thereby reinforcing its unpretentious, eager-to-please image. Many issues contain almost gratuitous apologies from the editor. For example, after reorganizing the format following the twelfth issue, the editor still maintained four issues later that "The current *Liangyou* is still very far from the point of perfection that we hope."

Its name, "Liangyou," connotes warm, trusting companionship and means literally "Good Friend"; *Liangyou* used the English title *The Young Companion Pictorial Magazine*.[29] The name is explained in its introductory issue by the social function of art:

> When beautiful, grand works of art are presented before us, we feel limitless joy and . . . empathy. When people express empathy toward others, they become good companions—friends. This is the world's happiest thing.[30]

Liangyou's notion of the social function of art was a popularized version of Cai Yuanpei's aesthetic theory. Cai held that beauty moves people emotionally, enabling them to overcome distinctions between self and other because their feelings are drawn to the object of their contemplation. Cai asserted that the appreciation of beauty cultivates an individual's ability to transcend selfishness and petty interests. Therefore, one's noble, cooperative, and sympathetic impulses toward humanity and the nation are strengthened.[31] In *Liangyou*'s third issue, an article not only referred directly to Cai's theory of aesthetics, but also asserted art's positive effect on citizenship:

For a nation's people, the deeper their level of art appreciation, the more progressive their culture. Therefore, we hope Chinese people take more responsibility to promote the fine arts in order to make China's hitherto weakened national spirit develop to a position of equality in the world.[32]

This belief in the power of art to correct China's international subordination lay in the assumption that art could bring people together in sympathetic coalitions. From an essentialist perspective, this might appear to be an almost feminized contrast to the masculine *Zhenxiang huabao*.

In fact, *Liangyou* covers almost exclusively pictured beautiful women (fig. 3). Usually they were glamour portraits taken at commercial photographic studios. Color was applied by artists to the black-and-white photos.[33] Unlike the mostly idealized, anonymous beauties on contemporary Chinese calendar posters, each of these covergirls was identified by name, and sometimes also by school or vocation.[34] Most were movie stars or students, who wore their hair fashionably bobbed and dressed in the latest Shanghai styles. As photography and color printing developed, photos of beautiful women were presented in many magazines as superior examples of photographic and color printing techniques—ostensibly appealing to public interest in modern technological progress—and also to advertise the quality of the commercial photographic studios that supplied the photos.[35] By the mid-1920s, popular magazines, with little artistic or technological rationalization, printed large-scale, colorful photos and paintings of beautiful women.

These pictures indicate an important change in the representation of women in Chinese periodicals. They are not merely a borrowed convention from the West; they have Chinese antecedents. In the late Qing dynasty there was a popular commercial tradition of reproducing paintings of beautiful women [*shinü*], often dressed in the latest fashions. Traditionally, Chinese figure painting of women took for its subjects popular deities, courtesans, elegant court ladies, and noble wives and daughters, usually famous women of literature, legend, or history. Like the modern Chinese covergirls, figure paintings of court ladies were drawn with meticulous attention paid to the details of attire and accessories.[36] Each of the *Liangyou* covergirls had her own distinctive look. Nevertheless, just like the court ladies in traditional paintings, "their faces were sweet and expressionless, conforming to ancient standards that emphasized elegantly arched eyebrows . . . and pursed lips."[37]

In one way, these female portraits can be seen as functioning like the popular Edo woodblock prints [*ukiyo-e*] in Tokugawa Japan, which spread news about the latest styles and supplied a bit of cheesecake for popular

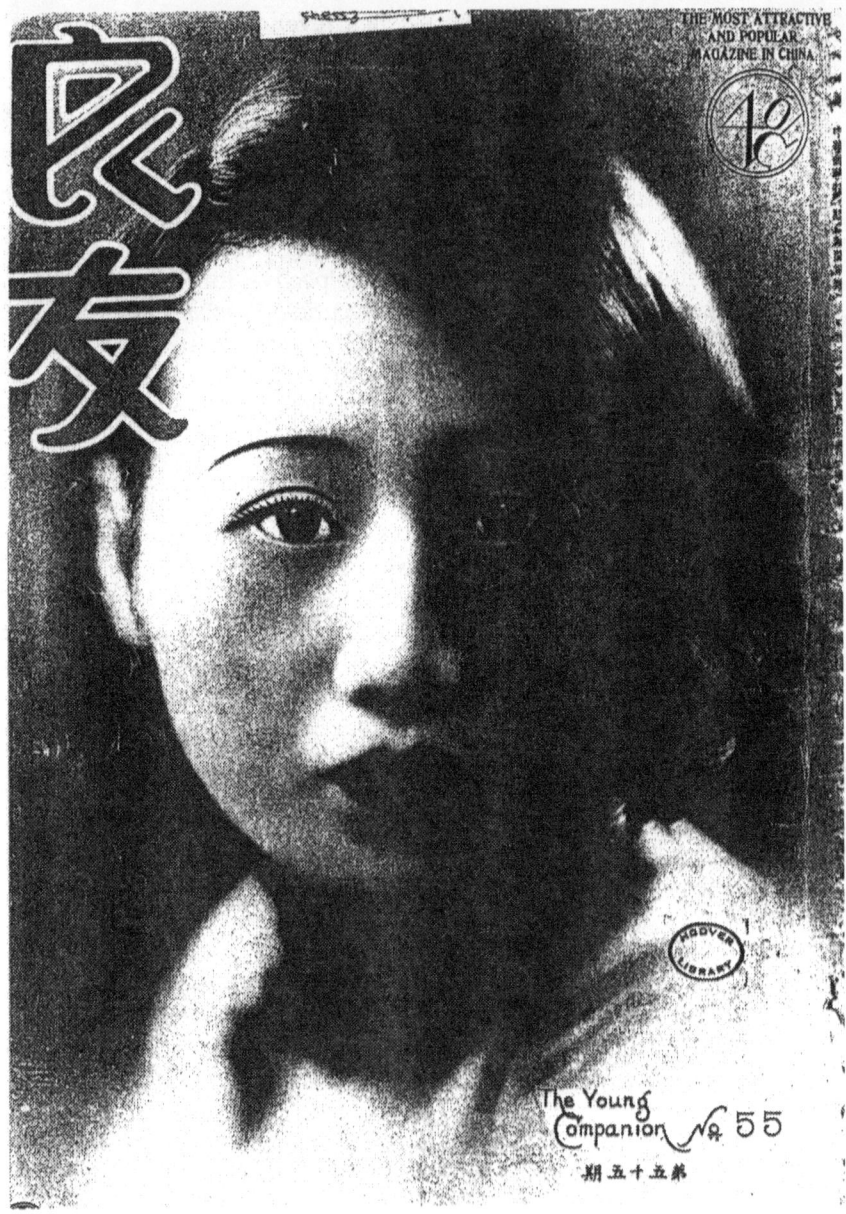

Fig. 3. Portrait of Ms. Ma Shuzhen, photographed by Shanghai [Hujiang] Photo Studio, colored by Liang Desuo. Cover illustration, *Liangyou* 55 (March 1931).

consumption. But the *Liangyou* covergirls are not posed in intimate scenes as the *ukiyo-e* females are; they are not caught unaware by the male artist's gaze. Rather, they seem to hold out merely a promise of intimacy: most look directly at the camera, returning its gaze, fully aware of being seen, of being on display. Departing from traditional figural representations of Chinese women, each individual covergirl plays her charms to the camera. The predominance of head or upper-body shots emphasizes close conversation with the camera lens (and cameraman). There is present an immediacy lacking in traditional Chinese painted portraits. This suggests that the covers were describing new, interactive public roles for women in China, even though the "conversation" was based on women serving as objects of the audience's gaze.

The covergirls' direct gazes also conveyed to viewers erotic undertones. The fetching portraits intimated to the magazine's audience the fulfillment of their fantasies. Yet the women's seductive beauty was clothed in a certain wholesomeness, a covergirl respectability. The convention in Chinese figure painting was for women to illustrate moral stories, where well-bred, virtuous women represented paragons of filial piety.[38] In a similar manner these cover portraits represented *Liangyou*'s standard for modern Chinese womanhood: poised and confident, exquisitely coifed and attired, the model of contemporary, urban propriety. The covergirls represented both *Liangyou*'s physical and its social ideal of the modern woman: the beautiful prospective wife.

In Western art history, John Berger's well-known essay on the female nude broke new ground by suggesting the correspondence between Western representations of women in oil painting and in contemporary mass media. Some of his ideas about the social presence of women seem relevant here. A woman's looks, her appearance to others, has been critical to her success in life—a success conventionally predicated on marriage—both in the West and in China. The artistic representation of women often has abstracted socially-constructed standards of ideal beauty intended for the heterosexual male and female gazes. Female *Liangyou* readers would have been attracted by the covers, in a "way of seeing" by which, Berger explains, glamour was a function of social envy. The covergirls highlighted the gap between what the spectator feels herself to be and what she would like to be.[39] The readers of *Liangyou* were encouraged to imagine themselves as the "little sisters" of the covergirls. Given the lack of role models for the dawning modern world, readers sought them "on the screen and glossy page."[40]

Female readers wanted to look like the covergirls.[41] The fantasy of being beautiful supported the daydream of modern love and romance preceding marriage. The revolution in marriage customs, particularly the modern opposition to the tradition of arranged marriages by extended families, was promoted in the Republican periodical press. In the context of changing Chinese social mores, the *Liangyou* covergirls represented a new and sexually empowered female role, even as it shaped its modern-style domestic subjection. The *Liangyou* woman challenged traditional female social roles.[42] At the same time, she contributed to the modern social construction of the docile female body, self-regulated through fashion, advertising, and her duty to be beautiful.

According to Berger, painting has traditionally celebrated material property and status in the West, and this may also be evident both in traditional Chinese court figure painting and in modern magazine covers.[43] Many of the covergirls were movie stars—celebrity glamour incarnate. One of the most famous international stars to grace the cover of *Liangyou* was Anna Mae Wong [Huang Liushuang], the Chinese American actress who signed her publicity portraits, "Orientally yours." Wong capitalized on exoticism in American society and at the same time afforded modern Chinese the prospect of an Asian woman successfully competing in a business dominated, like Western culture in general, by notions of white supremacy. The gazes of the *Liangyou* covergirls must have distinguished the magazine from others, fulfilling the primary purpose of the magazine cover: to make a publication stand out at the newsstand or bookstall. No wonder *Liangyou* touted itself as "the most attractive and popular magazine in China."

Another remarkable instance of the Chinese publishing boom was *Meishu shenghuo* [*Arts & Life*], which first appeared in April of 1934. The showcase publication of a small but technically advanced printing company, *Meishu shenghuo* paraded its capacity for fine-color reproduction in a monthly spectacle of art, cinema, news, and feature photographs, until August 1937, when the Japanese bombing of its printing presses ended its run. Its union of technical and aesthetic expertise under a theme of national salvation and populism captured and amplified the middle-class modernization project of which it was a part.

The cover illustration of *Meishu shenghuo's* inaugural issue was a shocking representation of a mostly nude woman fending off the fierce attack of a huge bird of prey in the midst of smoke, flames, and destruction (fig. 4). The focal point of the painting is the woman's bare torso and powerful, outstretched arm, which forces back the bird's head. At the base of her arm the bird's claws dig into her bloodied breast. Her other hand grasps a sword, drawing back to deliver the blow. Her bulging eyes and flamelike hair express raw resistance.[44] The image bears the Chinese title *Minzu yingxiong* [National hero], leaving little doubt that it was meant by the publishers to dramatize the climate of national crisis and to evoke the idea of Chinese resistance.

Interestingly, it is one of many nineteenth-century European portraits symbolizing the French Revolution and the continuing French struggle for Republican values. The French Republic is commonly symbolized by a woman, whose character historically has ranged between two polar opposite types, the wild, erotic libertine ("Liberté") and the calm, nurturing matron ("République"). Marianne is the name pejoratively first given to the French Republic by its aristocratic opponents, since it was a common woman's name. The inference was that the Republic had a weak base in the feminized popular rabble and could not be allowed to succeed. However, by the time this portrait of France in the throes of revolution had been painted in the late nineteenth century, the Republic was victorious, and portraits of Marianne captured the vehemence, vitality, valor, and democratic force of the revolution. An 1830s poem describes her as a strong woman with thrusting breasts, a harsh voice, and a hard charm, bronzed hair and flashing eyes, and as one who "takes her lovers only from among the people."[45] Victor Hugo spoke in a poem of "the goddess, the terrible, weird, avenging goddess who killed the old world and created the new."[46] This is the Marianne represented on the cover of *Meishu shenghuo*'s inaugural issue.

This shockingly sensational image was more likely to offend than attract readers, and it risked government censorship. Thus it is important to try to understand why *Meishu shenghuo*'s editors published this feminized spectacle, this eroticized China-as-woman, transforming a European female image into a representation of their own culture. China is portrayed as the threatened victim who must be saved by her own efforts—and by the spectator-artist-hero.[47] Essentially, this cover illustration functions like those *Zhenxiang huabao* covers that convey heroic authority. As a bold, multi-hued reproduction, it also demonstrates an unusual degree of technical expertise for the Chinese pictorial press, adding to the prestige of the magazine.

The background setting of the painting on the magazine's cover further reveals a subtext asserting *Meishu shenghuo*'s claim of authority and expertise. A thin, light-colored border around the painting emphasizes its object status. This is clearly meant to be a photoreproduction of a painted image. This framing may be thought of as a visual form of "reflexivity," which conventionally refers to moments in fiction and film when the work suddenly calls attention to itself as a fictional construct. Moreover, a three-dimensional effect is achieved by making it look like the photo of the painting is placed on top of depictions of the various tools and artifacts of artists. One discerns a palette and brushes, a camera, a saw, a bellows,

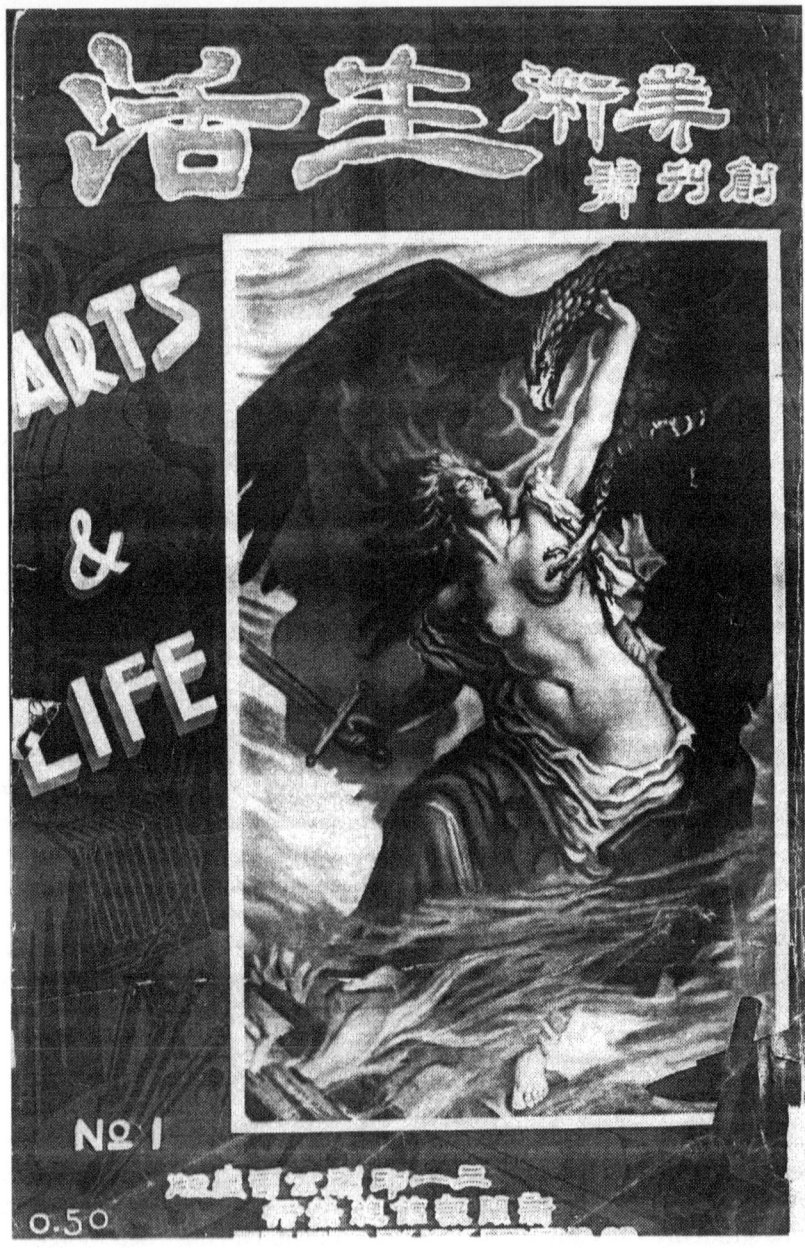

Fig. 4. Jean Delville (1867–1953), *Meishu shenghuo* 1 (April 1934) cover illustration titled *Minzu yingxiong* [National Hero].

hammer, and anvil—which even protrude over a corner of the painting itself, confirming the imposture of representation and the importance of the "tools of the trade." The background thus draws attention to the making of art and to artists themselves. Just as in *Zhenxiang huabao*, we see an awareness of audience and the role of the artist in mediating truth.

This manipulation of image and form is clever and worldly, a sophisticated appeal to China's modernizing cultural elite. By claiming expertise, it entices middle-class autodidacts to the art periodical. In addition to artists' tools, the background design also contains hints of cultural artifacts, Venus de Milo (ironically armless) framed by a Roman arch and columns, above which a painted "ceiling" of trompe l'oeil clouds and sky repeats the play of artifice and art. The combination of images implies a kind of agency and empowerment in art—the knowledge and power to move emotionally and manipulate materially—qualifying and legitimating *Meishu shenghuo's* cultural modernization project, and echoing *Zhenxiang huabao's* claim to universal expertise and conscience.

Thus *Meishu shenghuo* seems to share with *Zhenxiang huabao* and *Liangyou* their confidence in the power of art and visual representation. Moreover, with *Meishu shenghuo*, advanced color printing technology intensified the power of images to inspire, to incite, and to promote a new national and social consciousness. The inaugural (April 1934) issue's "Opening Statement" proclaimed, "Now art's power to move people deepens to wipe out the lethargic, corrupt, and degenerate, and to arouse the strong and vigorous elements." The essay ends with an appeal reminiscent of, yet distinct from, that found in *Liangyou* magazine. *Liangyou's* coyness is replaced by urgency in entreating readers' guidance and advice, for, *Meishu shenghuo* asserts, "the future welfare of the Chinese people depends on [your help]."[48] *Meishu shenghuo* is not a friendly companion, but a leading comrade in the crisis. It is ready to do battle.

To whom did *Meishu shenghuo* direct its national salvation message? What audience did the editors expect to be attracted to this colorful hybrid of art and current events? Ascertaining the potential audience of a publication is difficult without marketing or subscription and sales documentation, but some conjectures may be made based on its contents and advertising, particularly the presentation and contents of the advertisements. This imperfect method is sometimes validated by reappearing iconographies. For instance, the conventionalized treatment of human figures in ads may strongly indicate the target audiences. Indeed, this is the case with *Meishu shenghuo*. Taking into account the glamour built into modern advertising iconography, we find that both the economic class and gender of its reading audience seem modeled consistently in its advertisements.

They picture well-dressed and stylishly coifed young women at leisure, often relaxing outdoors in parklike settings, engaged in recreational activity like swimming, or else relaxing in nicely decorated and furnished homes.[49] The archetype for most of the female images in *Meishu shenghuo* advertising wears her hair in a stylish wave and is clothed in a short-sleeved, not-too-loose, not-too-tight *qipao* in a modern fabric design (fig. 5). The conformity of these images is quite remarkable, given that the ads cross a spectrum of products, including cigarettes, fabric, cosmetics, and pharmaceuticals.

By including a wide variety of contents, *Meishu shenghuo* certainly was marketed to appeal to a broad readership. But its foundation was most likely female subscribers who sought, both to polish their cultural proficiency through exposure to *Meishu shenghuo*'s colorful reproductions of Chinese and Western art, and to learn about news and trends while preparing to raise families under the radically new circumstances of 1930s urban China. As Wen-hsin Yeh has noted,

> Already in Republican cities a new breed of cultured women was being brought forth through . . . [new-style] schools. Compared with old-fashioned ladies, these women saw the importance of speaking softly and conducting themselves with style. Those who had attended missionary schools had even acquired a love for Western visual arts and music for the elevation of the spiritual state of everyone in their future families.[50]

Combining entertainment and instruction on the themes of beauty, health, home, and nation, *Meishu shenghuo* helped Chinese women of means understand that they could play an important role in reconstructing the nation as homemakers, mothers, and consumers of art and household goods.[51] There are obvious parallels with the Victorian cult of domesticity, which, like *Meishu shenghuo*, emphasized the cultivation of taste and style among the middle class.[52] Many articles are geared toward presenting new lifestyles for modern families, such as one devoted to "the practice of artful living."[53] The article describes a Chinese version of the garden-city movement, and is illustrated with photos of upper-class children, some artfully posed and others at play and study, a Western-type (Sears bungalow-style) model home, and bird's-eye view of "Rose Garden New Village." The article outlines the benefits and responsibilities of suburban versus city living. It even includes ideas about how women's businesses, like silkworm and honeybee raising, embroidery, weaving, and sewing enterprises, could be established to give women "opportunities for

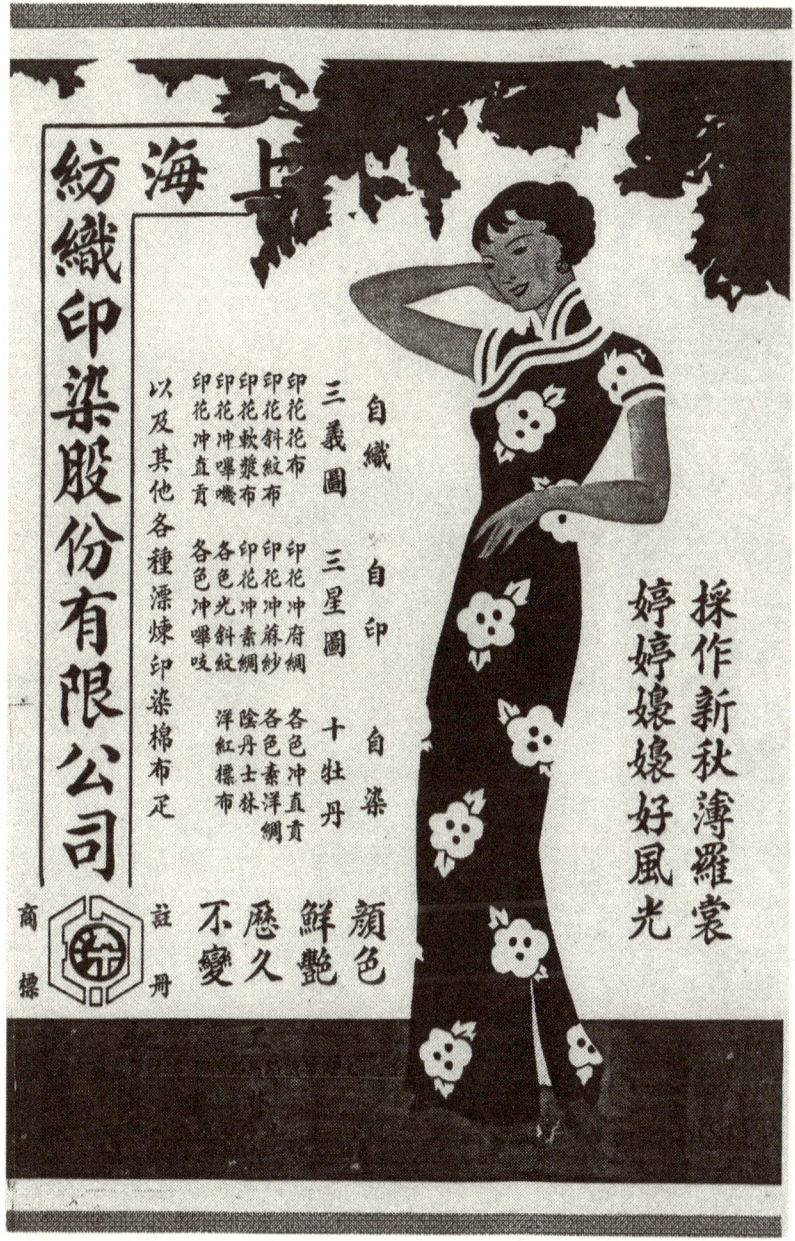

Fig. 5. Advertisement for fabric in *Meishu shenghuo* 6 (September 1934).

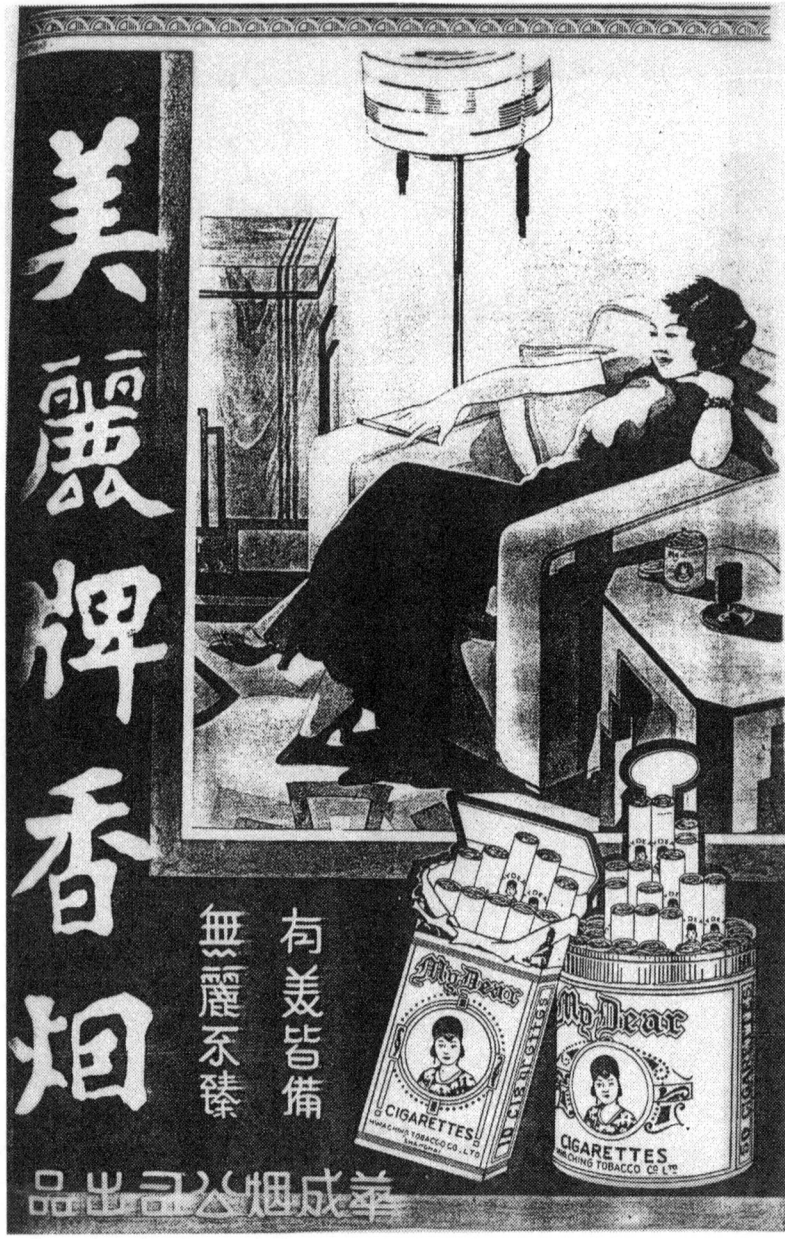

Fig. 6. Advertisements for cigarettes in *Meishu shenghuo* 29 (August 1936).

service." This describes a new, nationally contributive role for women, as well as new kinds of urban-rural relations.

Another source of information about *Meishu shenghuo*'s audience is to be found in its cover illustrations. Several *Meishu shenghuo* covers seem to exemplify its ideal audience, showing stylish Chinese women relaxing, reading, embroidering, or knitting in pleasant domestic settings.[54] Those comfortably decorated homes clinch the identity of the main audience of *Meishu shenghuo*: urban, female, educated, and middle-to-upper class (fig. 6).

The Female Nude and Sexuality in Meishu shenghuo

Meishu shenghuo's frequent representation of female nudes, a new conven-tion for portraying women in China seems to contradict the ideology of domesticity and consumerism that the magazine fostered, and may have presented problems of spectatorship for the target audience of middle-class women readers. Moreover, when the body is arranged by the art-ist for the viewer then the female art nude signifies passive submission. What, then, do all of these nudes have to do with *Meishu shenghuo*'s activ-ist modernizing mission? And how is the middle-class female audience expected to receive these images of nude female bodies?

The Chinese spectator's way of seeing is shaped necessarily by the ex-perience of national and cultural loss in the modern age. "'Western things' to a Chinese person are never merely dispensable embellishments; their presence has for the past century represented the necessity of fundamen-tal adaptation and acceptance."[55] All the Western art in *Meishu shenghuo*, including the nudes, allowed the reader to learn about and accept the cul-tures behind the dominant world powers. The nude of antiquity had long represented civilization to the West.[56] Knowledge like this, and adaptation to its structures, was seen as necessary for the Chinese people to join the world community on an equal footing. Thus, *Meishu shenghuo*'s publica-tion of female nudes must be understood as another element in its mod-ernization project.

Moreover, in the 1920s and 30s the globalization of a major trans-formation in gender relations had begun, specifically via modern West-ern images of feminine strength and independence (exemplified by the flapper). Second, the same period saw in Northern Europe and in North America the beginnings of a middle-class obsession with physical fitness. Both cultivation of the Greek ideal of physique and fascination with the naked human form found adherents in cosmopolitan Shanghai as well as in Berlin, Paris, and New York. Thus sophisticated Chinese may have seen the *Meishu shenghuo* covers, including the sensational first cover, as progressive models of female power.[57] Both of these trends also contributed to the embrace of the nude as an advanced subject matter for art by modern Chinese artists and the modern art audience, which looked to classical and modern European art for fresh models outside the so-called "stagnant" stream of traditional Chinese art. After all, the female nude had been an icon of Western culture since the Renaissance.

One *Meishu shenghuo* cartoon caricatures the eagerness of artists to utilize nude models in their quest to be seen as progressive. It pictures a giant (literally "statuesque") nude in a provocative pose, surrounded by a painter, photographer, and filmmaker capturing her image—but these men are only about one-quarter her size, and the title of the piece is "Tool for Fame and Wealth" (fig. 7). This was not the only cartoonist who found laughable the popularity of the female nude among ambitious artists. In another cartoon, we see a nude female artist sketching her own image, reflected in a large mirror in her studio. This work is titled "The Convenience [or Expedience] of Female Painters" (fig. 8). Obviously, access to nude models—a cachet in the Shanghai art world—was a good target for lampooning.[58]

Not all of the nudes in *Meishu shenghuo* were women; many of the sculptures were of males, including Rodin's *The Thinker*. Probably the most striking male nude is a Chinese full-length portrait painting by Qian Ding of Xu Langxi, an artist (and for a short time, president) at Xinhua Art College. It shows a balding Xu outdoors, seated modestly but not prudishly on a rock (fig. 9). An impressionistic landscape forms the background. He stares openly and unselfconsciously at the viewer. The painter, who was quite taken with the "beauty" of Xu's progressive thinking, wrote that Xu "didn't cover up a thing, and [revealed] the *real truth, not appearance.*"[59] This recapitulation of *Zhenxiang huabao*'s concern for truth over appearance, carried perhaps to extremes here, is nonetheless instructive with regard to the Republican audience's modern obsession with "real life." Qian enthuses, "Now in art is reflected his true human nature." Qian's praise of Xu's "naked healthy body" and "brave spirit" makes great sense in light of the modernist approach in representing the human body. The modernist nude was no longer "veiled in mythology or history" as in Renaissance painting, but "as she is."[60] This demystification was congruent with the Republican China demand for truth.

One article in *Meishu shenghuo* discusses the significant role of physical education and art education in creating a strong nation. Using ancient Greece as a model, it notes that Greek art took the human body as its foundation. Greeks used art to beautify life, and Greek education paid special attention to physical and spiritual health. The author contrasts contemporary trends in German education with those of Chinese education, which

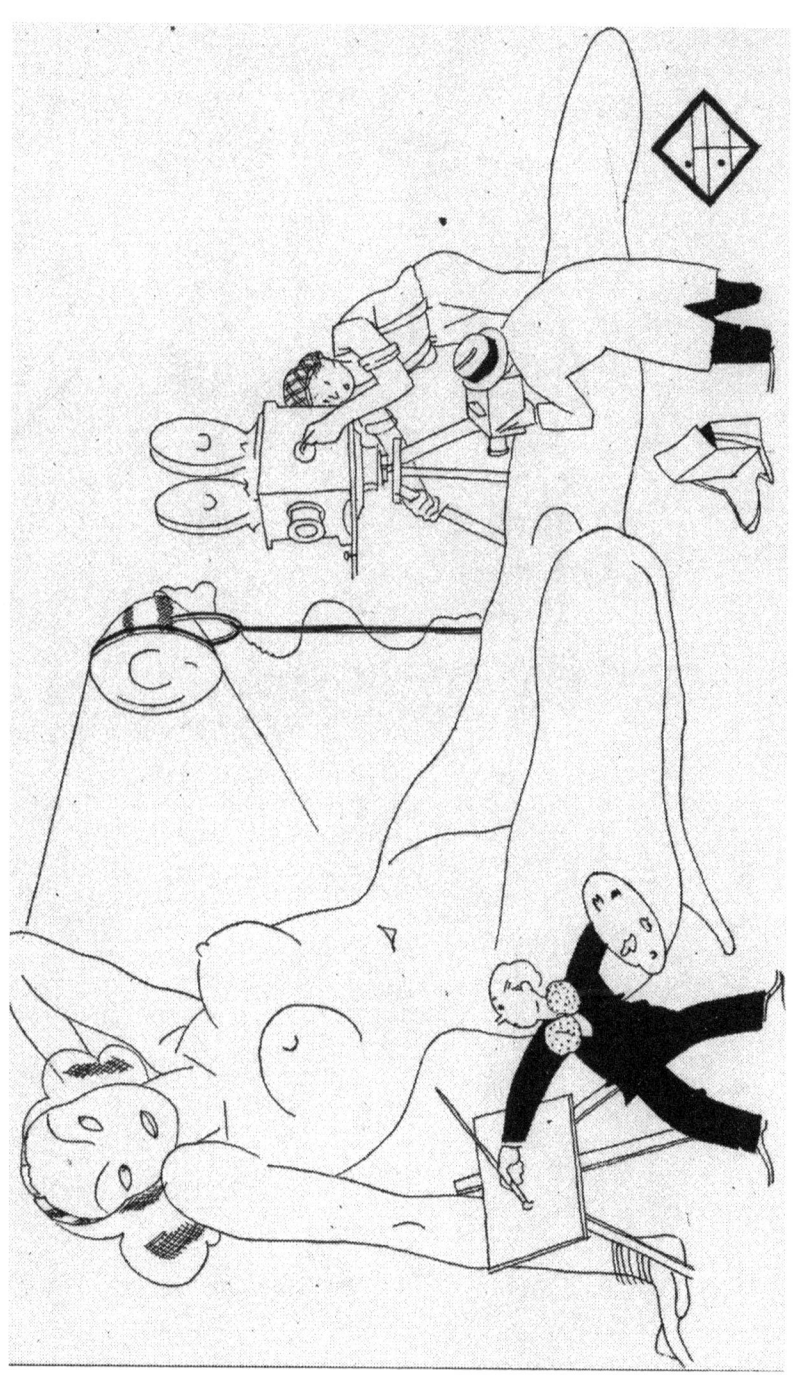

Fig. 7. Kang Nian, "Mingli di gongju" [Tool for fame and wealth], *Meishu shenghuo* 9 (December 1934).

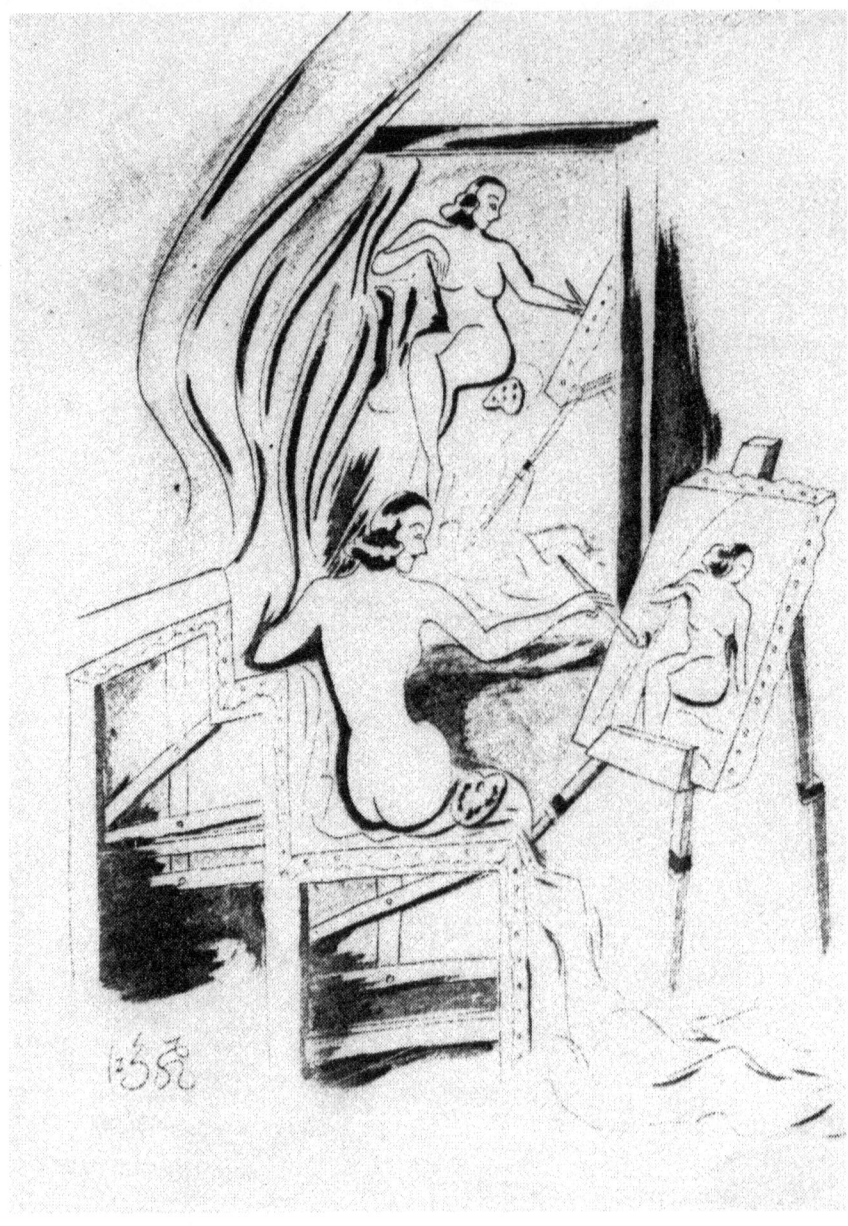

Fig. 8. Zhang Hongfei, "Nü huajia di bianli" [The convenience of female painters], *Meishu shenghuo* 5 (August 1934).

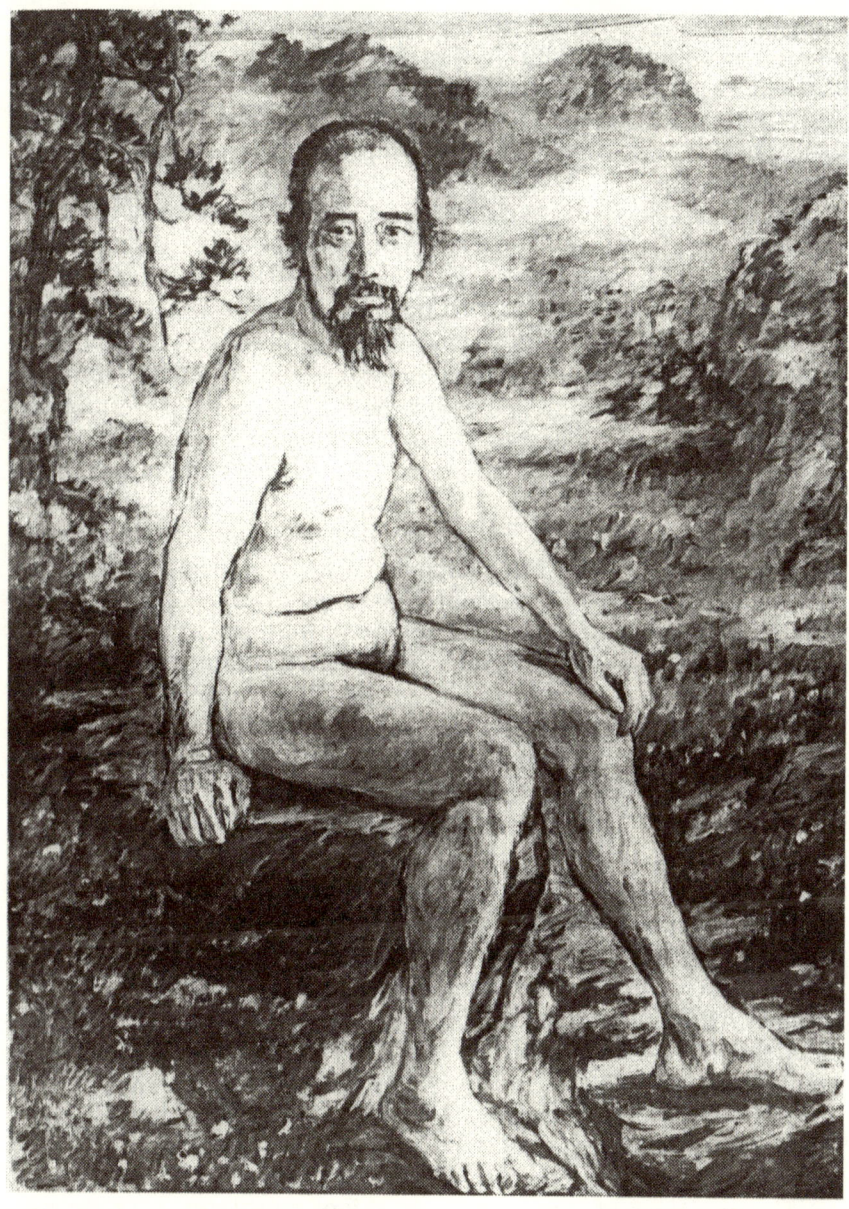

Fig. 9. Qian Ding, "Xu Langxi xiaoxiang" [Portrait of Xu Langxi], *Meishu shenghuo* 4 (July 1934).

"only promotes knowledge and morality, but is not as good at nourishing physical and spiritual health. . . . Not only are art and physical education the basis for healthy bodies and spirits, they also foster the development of social consciousness and the appreciation of order."[61] In the emerging Republican bourgeois definition of civilization, the body is a key social and political site.

Meishu shenghuo favored the new world trend toward physical culture and athleticism, printing all kinds of photos and articles featuring athletic meets, from local swim meets and college games to China's Far Eastern Olympic trials, to the 1936 Berlin Olympics.[62] *Meishu shenghuo* modernizers valued and promoted China's strong participation in the Olympics, no doubt in part because the Olympics exemplified the atmosphere of international competition that pervaded the modernization project. *Meishu shenghuo* also printed pieces on the healthful benefits of nudity for children, such as a two-page photo spread on a progressive nursery school in Paris.

All this stress on cultivating healthy bodies of course is central to the bourgeois modernization project's goal of a strong nation. A little boy on the cover of issue 6 of 1934 (fig. 10), whose caption defiantly declares that he is not the sick man of Asia, was emblematic of the healthful child rearing that *Meishu shenghuo* promoted. His educated parents were congratulated in an editorial postscript for their child having won a third place trophy in a Nanjing Child Health Contest. The editorial expresses "the hope that from now on Chinese children can all be as healthy as he."[63] Thus women readers were supposed to be reminded by representations of nude bodies of their responsibility to their family's bodies, and of the progressivism of appreciating the beauty of the human form.

Nevertheless, it is the sexuality of the female nude that supplies insights into the positioning of women in Republican society. The late nineteenth-century European nude, many examples of which appeared in *Meishu shenghuo*'s art section, embodied the "realism of the prostitute," which becomes the quintessential nude of early twentieth-century avant-garde painting.[64] Desire in the male photographer's and painter's gaze is likewise intimated in the *Liangyou* covergirls, the "good companions" whose undertones indicated sexual desire as well as desirability. At the extreme, the female nude is associated with uncontrolled sexuality, prostitution, and the "spiritual pollution" of urban entertainment districts.[65]

The profligacy of men in the company of prostitutes was a frequent object of critique in *Meishu shenghuo* cartoons, which expressed a fear of contamination and wholesale social degeneration. Cartoons featured sketches of nude or tightly or scantily clad females who represented dangerous exhibitionism and corrupting influences in modern Shanghai. The

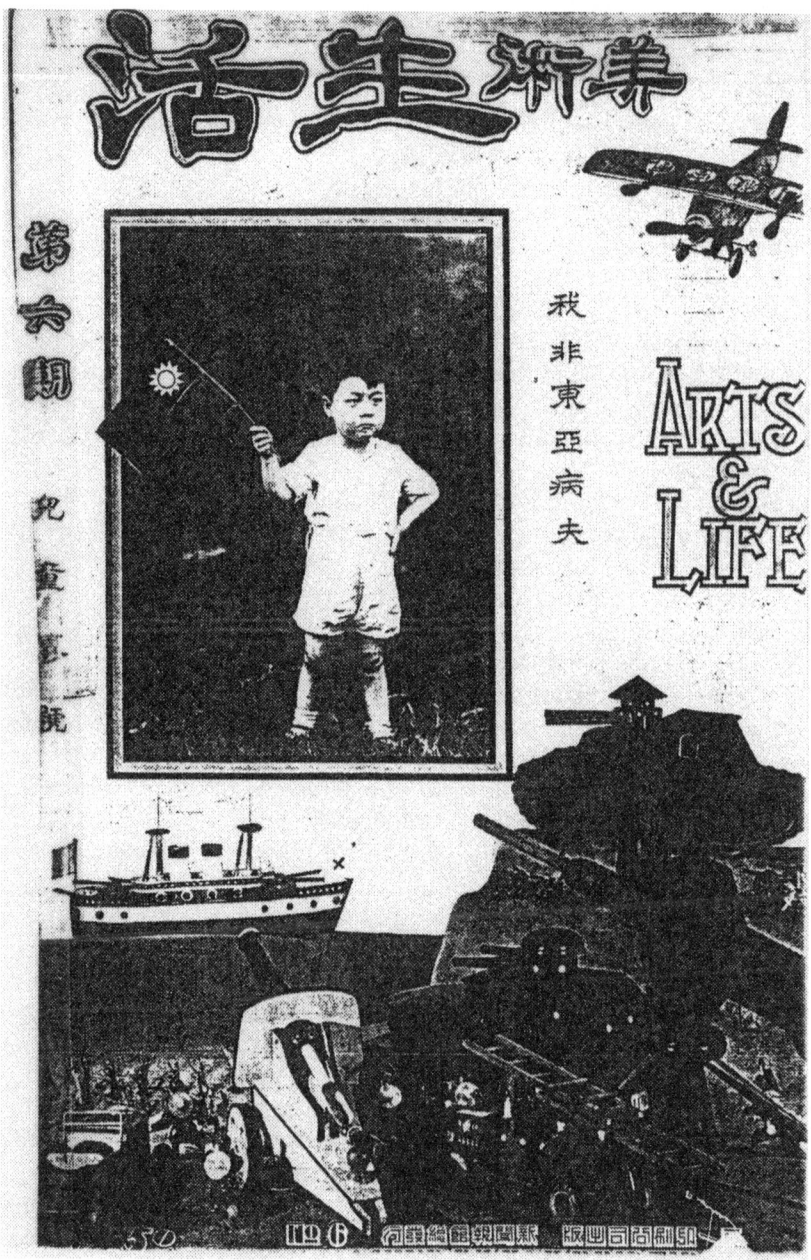

Fig. 10. Cover illustration *Wo fei dong Ya bingfu!* [I am not the sick man of east Asia!] *Meishu shenghuo* 6 (September 1934).

threat was that society's already weakened vitality would be dissipated by such unwholesome behavior, and China's survival as a nation would be compromised even further.[66] This peril of *degeneration* was diametrically opposed to the periodical's mission to *regenerate* Chinese culture. The depravity of female sexuality outside the bounds of marriage thus jeopardized the whole modernization project.

On the other hand, I would contend that the artistic representations of the female nude as well as the smutty cartoons in *Meishu shenghuo* function on another level that views human sexuality as a sign of vitality—of virility—and life. Like *Meishu shenghuo* photographs of common people and everyday life, this material reflects the editorial belief that attention to this-worldly themes would revivify Chinese art and culture. Reproducing images of the earthy and indecent, the meretricious and unrefined, held a kind of atavistic hope in *Meishu shenghuo* that primitive desire could foster an identity with the "living, public, and practical."

Some feminist theorists have contributed theories of spectatorship that distinguish between men's and women's ways of seeing, particularly in regard to representations of nudes. Rosemary Betterton notes that in Western culture (from which the fine art nude arises), the dominant iconographic code for the female nude is: nudity = sexual availability = heterosexual male pleasure.[67] This is the ideology embedded in the imagery when it is transported to China. Patriarchal Chinese culture also fetishized the female body and, as in the West, presumed the dominant spectatorship of men, which is associated with sexuality, voyeurism and power. The power of the male gaze here derives in part from the fact that the subjects of nude representations are passively arranged specifically for the viewer's pleasure. The female nude is exhibited, while the viewer—the voyeur—is hidden from view, protected from surveillance, and free to investigate the image at will. This kind of commanding gaze is illustrated most artfully in photographs of female nudes by Lang Jingshan.

Meishu shenghuo published significant numbers of photographs of nudes, most by Lang, a pioneer in Chinese art photography. In fact, *Meishu shenghuo's* photography section was initiated by a nearly full-page photo by Lang of a very young, nude woman kneeling on a lace-draped platform (possibly a bed), leaning forward with her arms forming two sides of a triangle that is completed by her folded legs. Soft light and shadow make it, by contemporary standards, a tasteful photo. In the three photos of nudes by Lang in the same issue, all the women's faces are obscured, their heads either downcast or thrown back, as in the one titled *Regret*, which shows only the woman's torso in full light (figs. 11 to 13).[68] One of Lang's early photographs of a nude female won an award from *Liangyou* magazine.[69] With his subject posed semireclining on a draped chaise, it

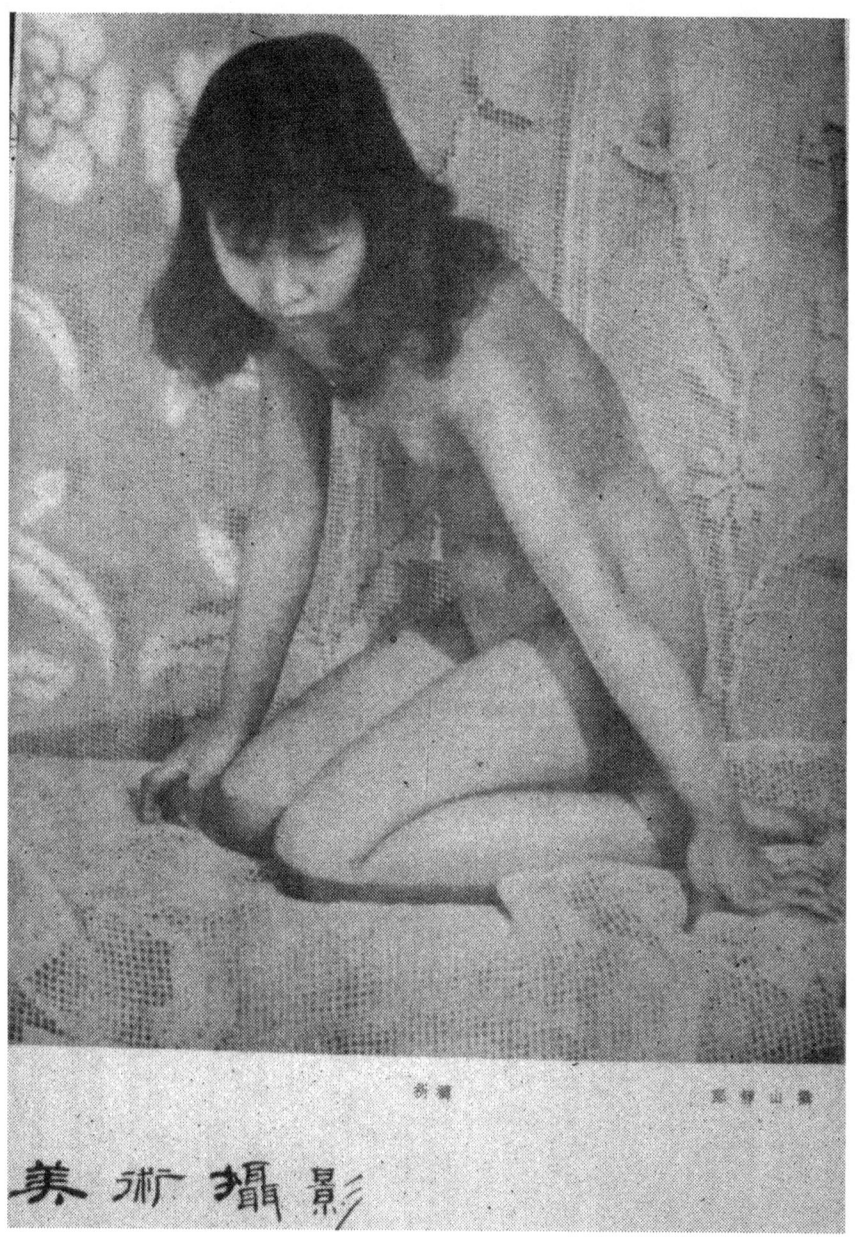

Fig. 11. Lang Jingshan, *Qidao* [Prayer], *Meishu shenghuo* 2 (May 1934).

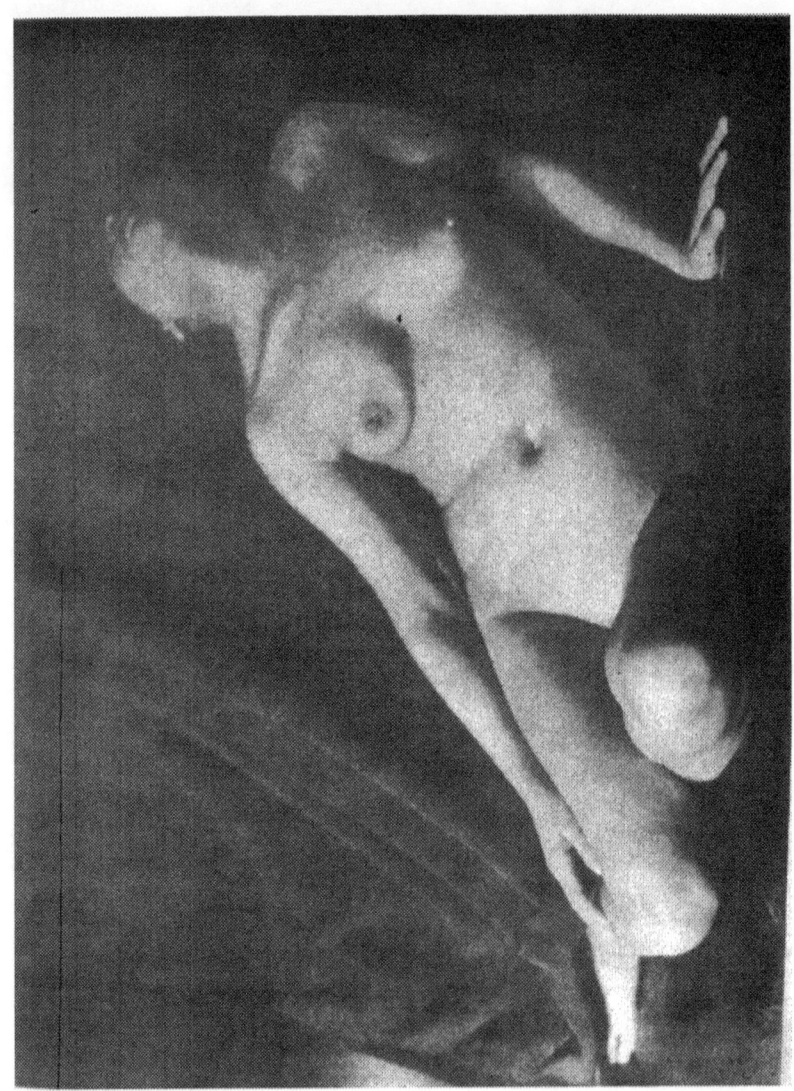

Fig. 12. Lang Jingshan, *Yuanwang* [Regret], *Meishu shenghuo* 2 (May 1934).

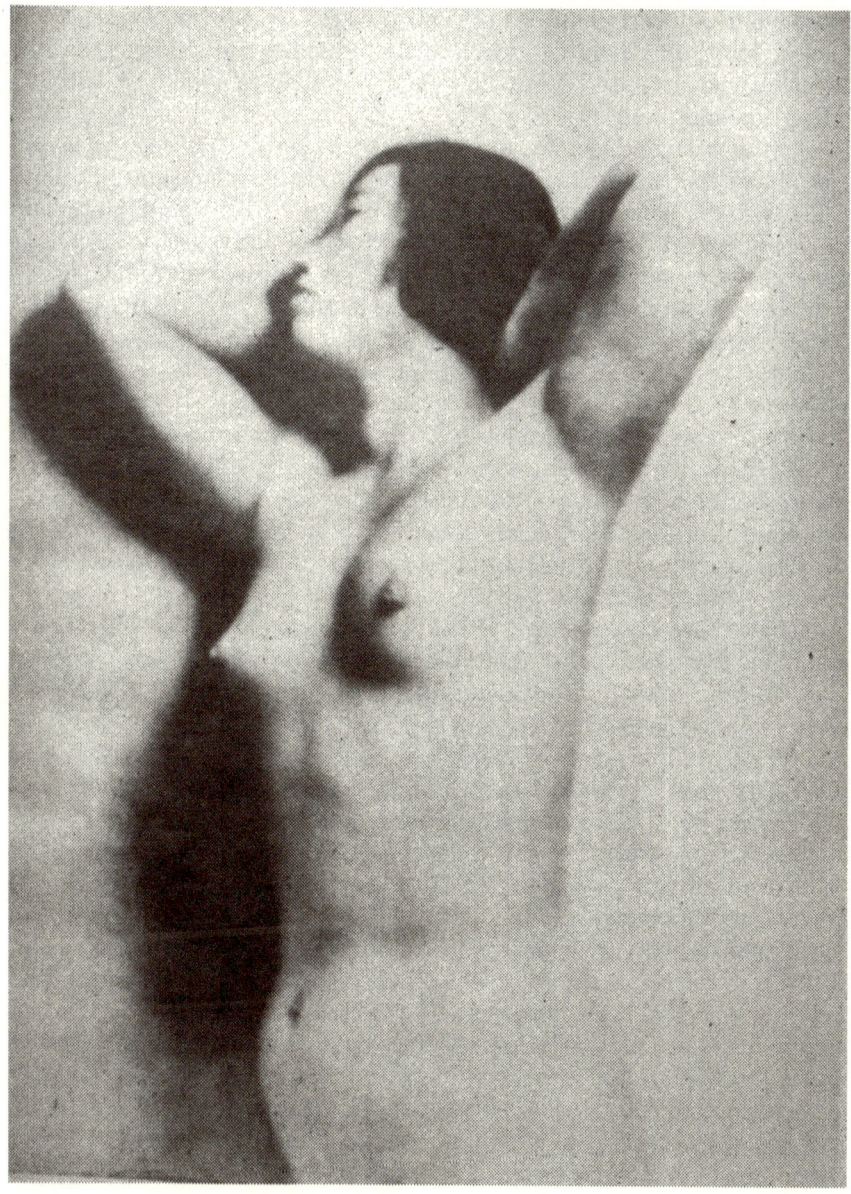

Fig. 13. Lang Jingshan, *Siyouyou* [Thinking afar], *Meishu shenghuo* 9 (December 1934).

emulates European paintings of female nudes. According to Lang, the "rules" for photographing nudes differed among some countries, but the focus was not supposed to be on a woman's crotch, nor should the subject's attitude be libidinous.[70]

The woman as spectator-reader of the images in *Meishu shenghuo*, according to this argument, "is offered the dubious satisfaction of identifying with the heterosexual masculine gaze, voyeuristic, penetrating and powerful." But it would be a mistake to interpret this as only a lascivious gaze. This way of looking, with the power and control of the male gaze, is related to the aesthetic detachment that is taught for looking at art.[71] Thus *Meishu shenghuo* readers could cultivate their artistic connoisseurship— their own "commanding view of the world"—via the nudes printed in the periodical.

A woman spectator also has another major way of looking at female nudes: identifying with the female body as desirable. Women love their own desirability because desirability has been elevated to being the crucial reason for sexual relations; it sometimes appears to women that the whole possibility of being loved and comforted hangs on how their appearance will be received.[72]

This connection between female appearance and desirability corresponds to my point earlier about the social importance of female appearance and the role of early Chinese pictorials in upholding it. In *Meishu shenghuo* and *Liangyou*, covergirls represented the glamorous, desirable goal for modern Chinese womanhood. But the fine art nude represented desirability, an element in *Meishu shenghuo*'s definition of femininity.

Hence, the *Meishu shenghuo* representation of female nudes is not simple. It has historical, social, and psychological functions that are sometimes contradictory, yet all are part of the magazine's overall project to create a new, modern cultural identity and to define Chinese middle-class femininity. *Meishu shenghuo*'s treatment of the human subject, clothed and unclothed, carries important messages about men's and women's identity in Republican China. Although it is often represented in contradictory and competing ways, the images of homemakers and desirable nudes, athletes and entertainers, all give form to the periodical's modernization project.

The objectification and display of the human body helped to produce and circulate the ideology of modernization and consumerism that drove the editors of these Republican art periodicals. "The attitude toward women in this art—towards the central image of the nude in particular—is part and parcel of a commanding attitude taken toward the possession of the world."[73] A Foucauldian analysis conveys how, in history, spectatorship of the female nude is produced within the context of the ideology of science and technology:

The dominant modes of looking in capitalist and patriarchal culture have been linked to surveillance and control over those perceived as inferior: children, servants, workers and women. It is possible to point to historical connections between the development of the female nude as a new genre in art and the development of perspective, with its new capacity for ordering, regulating and controlling the visible world.[74]

Likewise, photography illustrates important aspects of the power of representation and its relation to the modernization project. The magazines' pictorial programs seem to embody Susan Sontag's point that "to photograph . . . means putting oneself into a certain relation to the world that feels like knowledge—and, therefore, like power."[75] *Meishu shenghuo's* photographic reproductions, like those in *Zhenxiang huabao*, are the necessary bridge between art and science. The concurrent shift in the public representation of women to include the fine-art nude thus can be seen to be connected to the changing economic structures, social formations, and ideologies of the modernization project.

Ultimately, the hierarchies of gender are reinforced by the imagery in *Liangyou* and *Meishu shenghuo*. They present images of women as fashion plates and as objects of the male gaze. These images symbolize prescribed female behavior. Nonetheless, in another sense, the women pictured also represent the new "modern woman" who was challenging traditional female social roles worldwide and reordering the social hierarchy. But they contributed to the *modern* social construction of the docile female body, self-regulated through fashion, through advertising, and through her beauty. The idealization of female beauty and domesticity, with an almost-exclusive focus on appearance, contains a consumer imperative essential to the development of industrial society, within which *Zhenxiang huabao's* mode of presenting the artist as "a mediator of the world's truth" again reinforced the social and intellectual hierarchy.[76]

Notes

1 In using the term *modernization project*, I follow Jürgen Habermas and Max Weber: this was a self-conscious program to develop the human ability to control things, including the organization of everyday life, by rational calculation, "in terms of truth, normative correctness, authenticity or beauty" (Habermas as quoted in Peter Bürger, *The Decline of Modernism*, trans. Nicholas Walker [University Park: The Pennsylvania State University Press, 1992], 3–4). This definition clearly invites the postmodern and feminist critiques of claims to truth and objectivity, and those critiques inform the analysis that follows.

2 For a thoughtful analysis of this problem, see Linda Nochlin, "Women, Art, and Power," in *Women, Art, and Power and Other Essays* (New York: Harper & Row, 1988), 1–36. See also work by Lynda Nead, Laura Mulvey, and Lisa Tickner.

3 On the historical construction of these two views, see Janet Wolff, *The Social Production of Art* (New York: St. Martin's Press, 1981) and Li, *Artists and Patrons* (intro., n. 8).

4 See, for example, Martin Powers's *Art and Political Expression in Early China* (New Haven: Yale University Press, 1991). Powers offers a powerful, multi-level analysis of Han dynasty visual-art practices that expresses competition between different social groups for cultural hegemony. Li, *Artists and Patrons*, contributes important studies of a key socioeconomic element in artistic production from Song times to the early twentieth century. See also Wolff, *Social Production of Art* and Howard Becker, *Art Worlds* (Berkeley and Los Angeles: University of California Press, 1982) for good introductions to the ideological and institutional approaches to the sociology of art. Exemplary works on the newer social history of European art include John Barrell, *The Political Theory of Painting from Reynolds to Hazlitt: "The Body of the Public"* (New Haven: Yale University Press, 1986); T. J. Clark, *Image of the People: Gustave Courbet and the Second French Republic, 1848–1851* (Greenwich, Conn.: New York Graphic Society, Ltd., 1973); and Thomas Crow, *Painters and Public Life in Eighteenth-Century Paris* (New Haven: Yale University Press, 1986). Serge Guilbaut, *How New York Stole the Idea of Modern Art: Abstract Expressionism, Freedom, and the Cold War* (Chicago: University of Chicago Press, 1983), directly addresses the relationship between successful art movements and the ideological needs of societies.

5 Pierre Bourdieu, "Artistic Taste and Cultural Capital," in *Culture and Society: Contemporary Debates*, ed. Jeffrey C. Alexander and Steven Seidman (Cambridge: Cambridge University Press, 1990), especially 206–8 and 212–13. The main thrust of Bourdieu's argument here is that the acquisition of art competence legitimizes a social privilege by pretending that it is a gift of nature. Likewise, Tom Gretton states, "The material or symbolic appropriation of works of art functions to reproduce social superiority: knowledge or possession of works of art is a mark of distinction. . . . Learning to understand [art] . . . involves accepting authority, and in particular reinforces the notion that cultural authorities articulate . . . eternal values": "New Lamps for Old," in *The New Art History*, ed. A. L. Rees and Frances Borzello (Atlantic Highlands, NJ: Humanities Press International, 1988), 67. Both Bourdieu and Gretton agree that formal education tends to maintain the hierarchy of cultural wealth in a given society at a given time.

6 Walter Benjamin, "The Work of Art in the Age of Mechanical Reproduction," repr. in *Illuminations*, ed. Hannah Arendt (New York: Schocken Books,1969), 217–51.

7 *Artists and Patrons*, 5 (intro., n. 8).

8 Ibid.; see also 45–48.

9 I use the shorthand term *Western* of modern European and American art rather recklessly, especially since "modern art"—and "Western art," too—contained many "Eastern" elements and exemplified well how modernism and modern culture is multinational at heart. Likewise, my use of the term *traditional* blurs myriad distinctions in China's premodern culture.

10 Our understanding of the significant mix of sovereign Chinese authority and hegemonic Western influence in Republican Shanghai would benefit from important recent theorizing on the problem of semicolonialism, postcolonialism, cultural self-representation, and multiculturalism in the non-West. See for example Tani Barlow, ed., *Formations of Colonial Modernity in East Asia* (Durham, NC: Duke University Press, 1997) and Gayatri Chakravorty Spivak, *The Post-Colonial Critic: Interviews, Strategies, Dialogues*, ed. Sarah Harasym (New York: Routledge, 1990).

11 For an important discussion of evolving tastes and their relationship to politics and consumption trends in the Han dynasty, see Powers, *Art and Political Expression* (n. 4 above).

12 Link, *Mandarin Ducks*, 190 (chap. 6, n. 4).

13 For an interesting comparison, see John Tebbel and Mary Ellen Zuckerman, *The Magazine in America, 1741–1990* (New York and Oxford: Oxford University Press, 1991).

14 *Art and Political Expression*, 15.

15 Wang Bomin, *Zhongguo meishu tongshi* (Jinan: Shangdong jiaoyu chubanshe, 1987–88), 7:113.

16 *On Photography* (New York: Farrar, Straus, and Giroux, 1978), 4, 6.

17 The English title "The True Record" appeared on its covers. For the phrase "miniatures of reality" see Sontag, *On Photography*, 4, 91.

18 Gao Qifeng, "Fakanci" [Opening Statement], 4. I am grateful to Chris Waters for helping to confirm this story about Cromwell.

19 July 1, 1912.

20 This self-portrait of the painter-intellectual epitomizes Foucault's "universal intellectual"; see "Truth and Power," in *Power/Knowledge: Selected Interviews and other Writings, 1972–1977*, ed. Colin Gordon (New York: Pantheon, 1980), 109–33.

21 Svetlana Alpers, "Interpretation without Representation, or, The Viewing of *Las Meninas*," *Representations* 1.1 (February 1983): 37. *Las Meninas* by Velàsquez is another painting that is a representation of pictorial representation, and Alpers criticizes previous interpretations of it by suggesting ways that representation, as an aesthetic order, also engages a social order. I disagree with her finding that the two modes of pictorial representation identified here are incompatible (they seem complementary to me) and that the world "being seen" mode does not acknowledge "that interplay between sender and receiver." (I think it does.) Ibid., 41 and n. 9.

22 Alpers. There is a remarkable correspondence between the *Zhenxiang huabao* cover of the man opening the curtain and a self-portrait by the American artist, Charles Willson Peale, which is reproduced and discussed in Alan Trachtenberg, *Reading American Photographs: Images as History: Mathew Brady to Walker Evans* (New York: Hill and Wang, 1989), 6–9.

23 Anonymous, "Benbao tuhua zhi tese" [The special character of this publication's illustrations], *Zhenxiang huabao* 1 (June 5, 1912): 1. This view is consistent with Cai Yuanpei's views on aesthetic education, and probably shares some of the same European sources, most likely Schiller. Since this piece was published several years before Cai began lecturing and publishing on this subject in China, mostly likely the author read Schiller in Japanese translation.

24 Chen Shuren, trans., "Xin huafa: Yiming huihua duxishu" [New painting

methods: An independent study book] serialized in *Zhenxiang huabao* 1–16; section on the "education of the eye" appears in issue 3 (July 1, 1912): 15–16.

25 See, for example, Huang Binhong's articles on ancient seals of the Three Dynasties period (issues 11–12) and the flourishing of Northern Song painting scholarship (issue 14) in the "Wenyuan" [Literary garden] and "Lunshuo" [Essays] sections of the magazine.

26 See "Qianbihua fanben" [Pencil drawing copybook] in *Zhenxiang huabao* issues 12, 13, and 14.

27 "Benbao tuhua zhi tese," 1.

28 "Juantou yu" [Preface to the beginning of the volume], *Liangyou* 1 (February/March 1926): 1.

29 *Liangyou tuhua zazhi* literally translates as "Good friend illustrated magazine."

30 Li Zuoren, "*Liangyou* zhu" [*Liangyou* congratulations], February/March 1926, n.p.

31 See my article "Ts'ai Yuan-p'ei's Theory of Aesthetic Education," *Spring-Autumn Papers* 1.1 (Spring 1979): 13–30.

32 Zhuo Xuehan, "'Mei' suo ju zhi diwei" [The status occupied by "beauty"], April 15, 1926, 11.

33 For example, Liang Dingming tinted the *Liangyou* 6 (July 15, 1926) cover portrait of Ms. Zhuo Peifang, and Wan Laiming colored the *Liangyou* 32 (November 1928) cover portrait of Ms. Ze Luolan.

34 Cheuk Pak Tong, "A History of Calendar Posters" in *Chinese Woman and Modernity: Calendar Posters of the 1910s–1930s* compiled by Ng Chun Bong, Cheuk Pak Tong, Wong Ying, and Yvonne Lo (Hong Kong: Joint Publishing, 1996), 11.

35 See, for example, *Liangyou* 55 (March 1931), which advertises prominently on the last page with the masthead, "Introducing the photographer of this issue's cover: Qiaersheng [Carson?] Photo Studio Skilled at photographic portraits of beautiful women." An interesting comparison may be made with the much later Rita Hayworth film, *Covergirl*, which, as the first Technicolor© movie, was advertised at least as much for its technological advance as for its (remarkably similar) subject. I am grateful to Siobhan Somerville for alerting me to this film.

36 Alice R. M. Hyland, *Deities, Emperors, Ladies and Literati: Figure Painting of the Ming and Qing Dynasties* (Birmingham, Ala.: Birmingham Museum of Art, 1987), 71.

37 Ibid., 70–71.

38 Thomas Lawton, *Chinese Figure Painting* (Washington, DC: Freer Gallery of Art, 1973), 9–12.

39 Berger, *Ways of Seeing*, 131–35, 146–49 (chap. 6, n. 6), and Naomi Wolf, *The Beauty Myth: How Images of Beauty are used against Women* (New York: William Morrow, 1991), 58 and passim.

40 Wolf, *Beauty Myth*, 58.

41 At least two of *Liangyou*'s readers objected to the glamorous covergirls, demanding reforms to place "real people" [*zhen ren*] on the magazine covers. The editor promised reforms, publishing a photo of a decidedly plain-looking young student reading the next issue, which sported a cover portrait of a less-colorful, more austerely elegant woman; "Bianzhe yu duzhe," *Liangyou* 28 (July 1928): 38.

However, subsequent covers were richly glamorous, as before.

42 The *xiao jiating* [nuclear family] movement in Republican China is treated briefly in Wen-hsin Yeh, "Progressive Journalism," 205–14, and is a central theme in Susan Glosser, "A Contest for Family and Nation in Republican and Early Communist China, 1919–1952" (PhD diss., University of California, Berkeley, 1995).

43 *Ways of Seeing*, 45–64, 108–10, and 139.

44 The painting is by Jean Delville (1867–1953), the principal exponent of Symbolist painting in Belgium.

45 1830 poem by August Barbier quoted in Maurice Agulhon, *Marianne into Battle: Republican Imagery and Symbolism in France, 1789–1880*, trans. Janet Lloyd (Cambridge: Cambridge University Press; Paris: Maison des Sciences de l'Homme, 1981), 40.

46 Quoted in ibid., 72.

47 The eroticized China-as-woman recalls Rey Chow's arguments about "how another culture can be 'produced' as a feminized spectacle"; "Seeing Modern China: Toward a Theory of Ethnic Spectatorship," chap. 1 in *Woman and Chinese Modernity: The Politics of Reading between West and East*, Theory and History of Literature 75 (Minneapolis: University of Minnesota Press, 1991), 3–33. Chow's Althusserian understanding of ideology as "the experience of consumption and reception . . . that . . . enable[s] people to buy, accept, and enjoy what is available in their culture" (p. 22) has resonances here.

48 "Opening Statement," in the inaugural issue of *Meishu shenghuo* (1934).

49 For example, a frequent ad for *Meishu shenghuo* subscriptions shows a fashionably dressed young woman seated on a park bench casually reading a magazine, as seen in *Meishu shenghuo* 29 (August 1936). An ad in *Meishu shenghuo* 6 (September 1934) for Bai Jin Long [Golden Dragon] cigarettes shows two young women on a park bench under a tree engaged in conversation. Significantly, the outdoor settings are not rural, but are landscaped parks. Wen-hsin Yeh points out that urban middle-class residents saw the city "as a mindfully constructed space of tree-lined boulevards, public parks and gardens" that contrasted vividly with the danger and depression of China's rural hinterlands. See her "Progressive Journalism," 213–14. *Meishu shenghuo* also enthusiastically promoted urban reform. See Hua Lin's article "Xin shenghuozhong ruhe gailiang chengshi" [How to reform cities for a new life], an essay in praise of European public parks. Another explicitly urban cue comes in an ad for Qi Xing Pai [Seven Stars] cigarettes, which features the night sky in a cityscape of densely packed, tall, lighted buildings. Both are in *Meishu shenghuo* 2 (May 1934). Ads for the Shanghai Telephone Company show a man and woman sitting in a modern-style living room, as in *Meishu shenghuo* 36 (March 1937). Men undoubtedly were counted among *Meishu shenghuo* readers, but certain products, such as fingernail polish and fabrics, indicate that *Meishu shenghuo*'s female audience was significant. Nongendered imported art supplies are also advertised in *Meishu shenghuo*, and given the magazine's strong emphasis on art and art history in the first half of every issue, it must have attracted at the least an educated, well-to-do readership. See the frequent ads for Reeves Colours, for example, in issue 9 (December 1934).

50 Yeh Wen-hsin, "Progressive Journalism," 210.

51 See for example "Shizhuang" [Fashion] (which includes directions for

making a stylish child's coat), "Qiutian di jiyang dianxin" [Several kinds of autumn snacks] (which includes recipes for mooncakes and dumplings), and an untitled photo-article on women's fall fashions, featuring glamorous evening wear, in *Meishu shenghuo* 7 (October 1934); Yu Zaixue, "Jiating yiyao weisheng jiangzuo" [Lectureship on family medicine and hygiene], "Chi xie di yishu" [The art of eating crab], and "Maoxian bianwu zhi jiben jishu ji qi yingyongfa" [Basic techniques and applications of hand knitting] (including diagrams and step-by-step instructions) in issue 8 (November 1934); and a serialized article for pregnant women, "Renfu xuzhi" [What women with child should know], *Meishu shenghuo* 11–12 (February-March 1935). *Meishu shenghuo's* sixth issue was devoted to children, and the seventh issue was devoted to family life.

52 Among the many works on this subject, one with direct relevance to *Meishu shenghuo's* focus on homemaking is Clifford E. Clark, Jr.'s excellent *The American Family Home 1800–1960* (Chapel Hill: University of North Carolina Press, 1986). Both *Meishu shenghuo* and the Victorian cult of domesticity fostered bourgeois attempts to distinguish oneself through lifestyle. Given the difficult conditions that the Chinese majority lived in, the middle class no doubt did seek a different, materially improved lifestyle. Nevertheless, in 1930s Shanghai, much of the rhetoric was directed at improving the lives of *all* classes; in *Meishu shenghuo* this rhetoric was represented in some interesting juxtapositions. See below.

53 "Ertong yu xincun: Meishu shenghuo zhi shijian—Xincun shenghuo di jia-zhi yu renwu" [Children and New Village: The practice of artful living—The value and responsibilities of New Village life], *Meishu shenghuo* 7 (October 1934). One ideological assumption shaping this Republican discourse is the antinomious stereotype of corrupt city vs. pure countryside. See Susan Mann's valuable analysis of Republican Chinese paradigms of urbanization, "Urbanization and Historical Change in China," *Modern China* 10:1 (January 1984): esp. 87–113.

54 See the covers for issues 4 (July 1934), 9 (December 1934), and 41 (August 1937).

55 Chow, *Woman and Chinese Modernity*, 27 (n. 47 above).

56 Nead, *Female Nude*, 1–2 (chap. 6, n. 6).

57 See, for example, Fruehof, "Urban Exoticism," 138 (n. 40 above). Remember also that *Meishu shenghuo* readers were likely to have been beneficiaries of the May Fourth espousal of women's rights as well as of the emergence of the modern woman in the Western imagination in this period. However, Frank Dikötter has suggested that new attitudes to the human body in Republican China may have had autonomous roots in the late Ming or even earlier; "Body, Discipline and Modernity in Late Imperial China," paper prepared for the Annual Conference of the Association for Asian Studies, Boston, 1994.

58 See Kang Nian, "Mingli di gongju" [Tool for fame and wealth], *Meishu shenghuo* 9 (December 1934) and Zhang Hongfei, "Nü huajia di bianli" [The convenience of female painters], *Meishu shenghuo* 5 (August 1934).

59 Qian Ding, "Xu Langxi xiaoxiang" [Portrait of Xu Langxi], *Meishu shenghuo* 4 (July 1934), my emphasis.

60 Rosemary Betterton, ed., *Looking On: Images of Femininity in the Visual Arts and Mass Media*, (London: Pandora Press, 1987), 227.

61 Hua Lin, "Yishu chuangzao mei di shenghuo" [The arts create beautiful

life], *Meishu shenghuo* 2 (May 1934).

62 See, for example, photos of track and field athletes trying out for China's team in *Meishu shenghuo* 2 (May 1934) and the Fourth Zhejiang Province Athletic Meet, pictured in issue 15 (June 1935). Issue 20 (November 1935) was specially devoted to China's sixth national athletic meet, and China's Olympic team (characterized as *jianer* [healthy, strong boys]) were featured in every issue from 27 (June 1936) up to the Olympics, which was covered in a nine-page photo spread that included Nazi propaganda shots. China's modernizers' obsession with health and sickness, which I treat in some detail in my dissertation, "Arts and Life: Public and Private Culture in Chinese Art Periodicals, 1912–1937" (University of Michigan, 1995), had already been manifested in a fairly popular fascination for eugenics. See Frank Dikötter, *The Discourse of Race in Modern China* (Stanford: Stanford University Press, 1992), esp. chaps. 5 and 6. *Meishu shenghuo* provides apt illustrations for Dikötter's text. See "Shengming zhi jingyi" [Wonders of Life], a translation of Nazi eugenics propaganda in *Meishu shenghuo* 16 (July 1935).

63 "Bianhou" (September 1934).

64 Berger, *Ways of Seeing*, 63 (chap. 6, n. 6).

65 See Paul Pickowics's discussion of the theme of the "fallen woman" in his article "The Theme of Spiritual Pollution in Chinese Films of the 1930s," *Modern China* 17.1 (January 1991): 38–75.

66 See Gail Hershatter, "Regulating Sex in Shanghai: The Reform of Prostitution in 1920 and 1951," in *Shanghai Sojourners*, ed. Frederic Wakeman and Wen-hsin Yeh (Berkeley: Institute of East Asian Studies, 1992), 153.

67 *Looking On*, 232.

68 See Lang Jingshan, *Qidao* [Prayer] and *Yuanwang* [Regret], *Meishu shenghuo* 2 (May 1934); *Si youyou* [Thinking Afar] and *Huidao ziran* [Back to nature], *Meishu shenghuo* 10 (January 1935).

69 See reproduction of *Meditation* in Mindich, "A Composite Life," 59.

70 See Lang Jingshan, "Sheying yishushi hua" [Talk on the history of photographic art], *Zhongwai zazhi* 179, v. 31.1 (January 1982): 20.

71 Betterton, *Looking On*, 219–20.

72 Rosalind Coward, *Female Desire: Women's Sexuality Today* (London: Paladin, 1984), 78; quoted in Betterton, *Looking On*, 220.

73 Svetlana Alpers, "Art History and its Exclusions," in *Feminism and Art History*, ed. Norma Broude and Mary D. Garrard (New York: Harper & Row, 1982), 187.

74 Betterton, *Looking On*, 12.

75 Sontag, *On Photography*, 4 (n. 17 above).

76 Wolf, *Beauty Myth*, 18 (n. 40 above). See also Janet Wolff, "Reinstating Corporeality: Feminism and Body Politics," in *Feminine Sentences: Essays on Women and Culture* (Berkeley: University of California Press, 1990), esp. 124–25.

8
Shanghai Women of 1939: Visuality and the Limits of Feminine Modernity

Shu-mei Shih

Visual representations of women in modern China invariably invoke questions of modernity. In illustrations, magazine advertisements, photographs, paintings, and cinema, they form a complex semiotic field. Visuality, one may even say, particularly the commercial kind, constitutes one of the most fertile grounds for examining imaginations and embodiments of modernity in popular culture. Although the dictates of form necessitate that the details of commercial visual work be laid out in a striking, effective spatial design for immediate reception, the dictates of the market make persuasion the immediate goal for commercial visual work, leaving relatively little room for representational ambiguity. As a consequence, visual representations of Chinese women in advertisements provide a distinct view on the popular imaginary of modernity.

Unlike both the May Fourth enlightenment discourse and the *Jingpai* discourse that I examine elsewhere,[1] representation of women in advertisements, by virtue of its explicit connection to commercialism, exceeds the usual cultural-political nexus of most high-cultural discourses. But advertisement in 1930s Shanghai was more than a commercial form. During the height of the *Haipai* culture in the early 1930s, the so-called boundary between high and popular cultures was largely permeable.[2] The *Haipai* writer/artist Ye Lingfeng, for instance, wrote stories and designed illustrations both for literary and popular magazines with equal felicity and did not feel the need to bolster high-literary purpose with a disdain for commercialism. Given its natural position at the intersection of culture, politics, and economics, advertisements may therefore be considered a more immediate and socially embedded form of modern discourse, in contrast to some of the abstract cultural debates that often elided economic issues.

Gender is one of the ways modernity ineluctably works itself through, and out. Not only is the deployment of women a trope of modernity, but gender constitutes modernity. This can be illustrated in at least two, related ways. First, theories of colonialism and imperialism have shown in extensive detail how the conquest of colonized peoples was frequently presented as a heterosexual mastery of the feminine by the masculine, and how within this metaphor, colonized women become variously encoded as withholders or harbingers of modernity.[3] Native patriarchy being thus feminized, women either became doubly feminized in a binary, heterosexual logic of power, or risked being cast as a traitor to the national cause as defined by native patriarchy. In most cases, women were subjected to the discursive and social management of both the native and colonial patriarchies.

Second, given the dominant trope in colonial discourse of the masculine subjugation of the feminine, the colonizer's modernity thus imposed is necessarily constructed as masculine. This can be profusely illustrated by the ways in which modernity was often equated with Western armaments and hard science in Chinese reform discourses of the late Qing. We may call this the masculine modernity. But in the quotidian manifestation of modernity as Westernization in lifestyle—such as dress, furniture, behavior, and so on—the female body was very often the locus of inscription. Late Qing as well as twentieth-century stories and novels are profuse with the figure of the New Woman (*xin nuxing*), who has a very long and complex genealogy. We may call what these women embody the feminine modernity. These two modernities are constructed on two different scales—the masculine on the national scale (of colonizers or of native patriarchy), the feminine on the private scale; the latter is often manipulated in the service of the former. If women's claim to modernity can be effectively limited to the private realm, the public, national realm can be adequately safeguarded for men. According to this logic, the New Woman who wanted to be a social activist to advance women's causes was never to have an easy life, since she impinged upon the domain of masculine modernity; but the New Woman who flaunted the latest fashions and Western, liberal sexual morality could be the new object of desire for male urban elites. Better still, in patriarchal imagination, she could be conflated with the prostitutes who wore Western clothes to mark their sexual availability. She could provide simulated, fantastic access to Western women to compensate for the woundedness of native men.

Representation of women in advertisements in popular journals, particularly ones such as *Shanghai Guide* (*Shanghai shenghuo*, fig. 1) aimed mostly at urban housewives, workers, and other young female readers, sometimes reads like a how-to manual: how to look beautiful, how to exercise feminine seductiveness, how to be a good wife and mother, and above all, how to be "modern" within the feminine realm. It illustrates in profuse detail the requirements for middle-class feminine modernity, the limits of that modernity, and the circumscribed modes of participation in national modernity allowed for women. Reading these advertisements from a critical feminist perspective, with an awareness of the politics, culture, and economy of late 1930s Shanghai, alerts us to the always-existent patriarchal manipulation of modernity in the local context, even as that same patriarchy was involved in a larger cultural revolt against Japan or against Western-imposed modernity, or else busy constructing a modernity more attuned to local, national needs. Within the intersecting hegemonic spheres of imperialist authority (Japanese and Western) and native patriarchy, much collusion between them can be detected in their containment of gender issues.

Shanghai in 1939 was a peculiar urban space. Two years into the Sino-Japanese War and the Japanese occupation of the city, the most frenzied and ostentatious examples of *Haipai* culture had generally receded. A few years earlier, one could glimpse the flourish of Shanghai culture, by its hundred or so literary journals; by the felicity with which slogans such as *modernism, decadentism, new hooliganism,* and *urbanism* were circulated in fashionable literary circles (not to mention the fauvist and cubist works in the realm of art); by the hustle and bustle of the theaters, dance halls, bars, coffee shops, and restaurants; and by the streets, illuminated by dazzling neon lights and crowded with pedestrians and the latest automobiles. These scenes are vividly described in the stories of Liu Na'ou, Mu Shiying, and Ye Lingfeng. This Shanghai cultural fever generally subsided by 1939, and although the enjoyment of material culture did not necessarily diminish, pursuits in the cultural realm were largely suppressed. Intellectuals and artists who were unwilling to become cultural collaborators either left or went underground. Those who chose to remain completely disengaged themselves from politics, and many had changed political positions or were about to do so (such as Liu Na'ou and Mu Shiying). Shanghai culture seemed to have suddenly lost its center and, along with it, its leadership in the Chinese cultural scene at large. But Japanese censorship was constrictive less of commercial than of literary culture. Capitalism in Shanghai was not only encouraged by the Japanese but also fervently practiced by Japanese merchants, who had done so for several decades already. Yokomitsu Riichi's famous *Shanghai* (*shanhai*, serialized 1928–32) illustrates, for instance, the stake of Japanese capitalists in Shanghai's commercial life. The irony of the Japanese imperialist ideology of *dōben-dōshu* ("common culture, common race") in its cultural containment of China is that the Japanese knew well the old Chinese method of domination, which had always prioritized the control of literary over commercial culture.[4]

Given the above context as well as my theorization of the gendering of modernities, an interpretation of the representation of women in advertisements in 1939 issues of *Shanghai Guide* provides us particular in

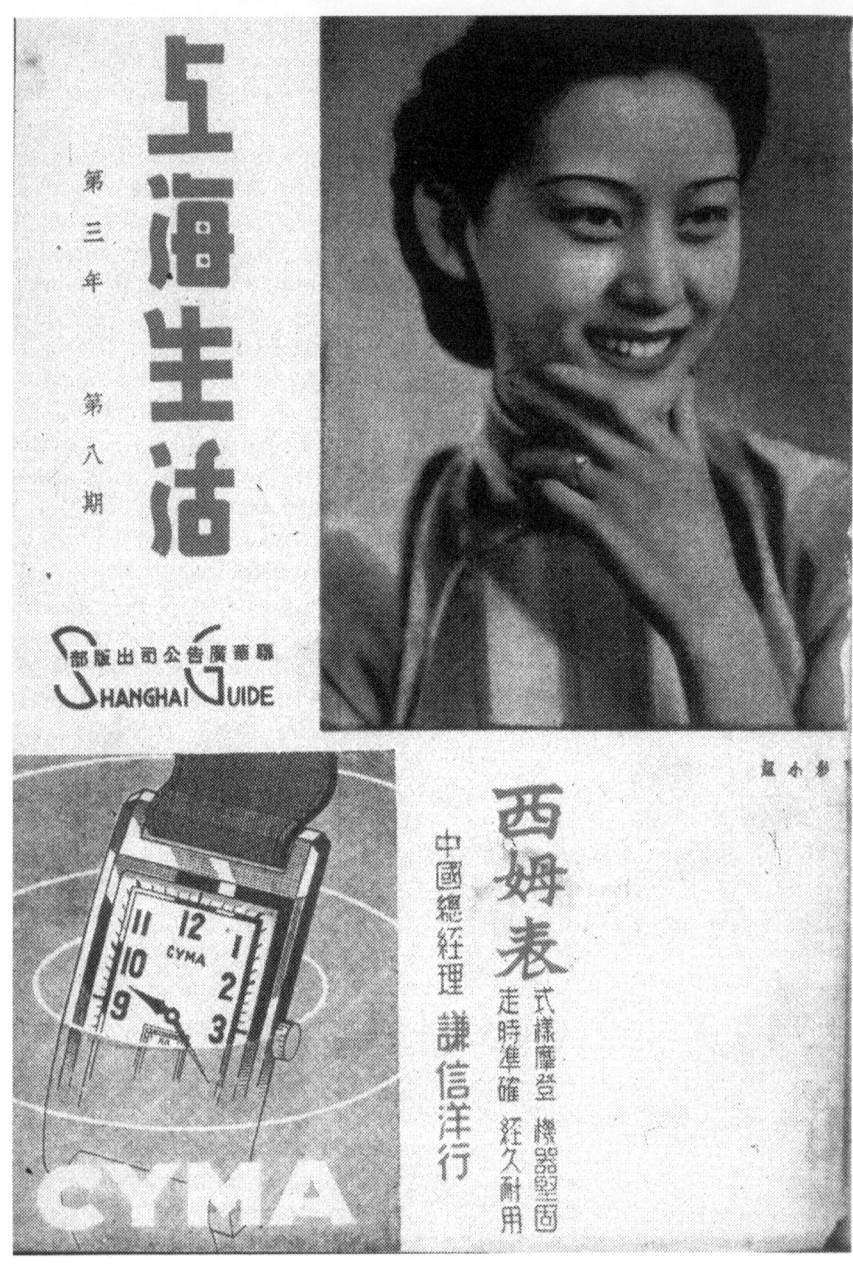

Fig. 1. *Shanghai Guide* (*Shanghai shenghuo*) 3.8 (August 1939): front cover.

sights. Specifically, they reveal how gender was deployed for commercial purposes, and how these purposes depended on the skillful triggering of consumer desire. This, in turn, suggests for us the role of women relative to modernity. I first examine cigarette advertisements, for they encourage a rather coherent reading of the relationship between the cigarette as a symbol of modernity and Chinese womanhood. The most frequently published cigarette advertisements in *Shanghai Guide* usually show a beautiful modern woman as their main signifier. Of these advertisements, Meili-brand cigarettes in particular present cigarettes as a necessary condition for "beauty" (*meili*) and modernity. In figure 2, the woman who buys Meili brand cigarettes is shown to be "elegant" (*gaoshang*) and modern. Clad in elegant dress, stylish white gloves, and fashionable, dainty high heels, the woman has apparently just returned from the store with Meili-brand cigarettes. Carrying the four tins of cigarettes in her left hand and a classy purse in her right, she walks gracefully through a hallway ornamented with a potted plant on a long-legged table and into a living room. She has a broad smile on a beautifully made-up face, framed by hair permed à la mode. As the caption tells us, her beauty is made all the more exquisite by the cigarettes she carries in her hand. The caption on the lower left hand corner skillfully puts the characters of the brand name *mei* and *li* into a well-phrased couplet—"Those who have *mei* have it all, and there is no *li* they cannot attain"—deliberately constructing Meili-brand cigarettes as indispensable for beauty. Hence the two elegantly inscribed characters *meili* on the upper right in elegant calligraphy describe the cigarettes as much as the woman, who reinforce each other. She stands there as the long-legged table does, the designs on her dress and jacket subtly echoing the designs on the door to her right and the decorative ceramic pot behind her; she is as integral to the material world of the upper-middle-class household as these objects.

In figure 3, the caption, "Beautiful people all like smoking Meili brand," further equates the brand with the beauty of the woman. The spatial arrangement of the two figures in the advertisement, with the dapper young man standing against a railing looking lovingly down at the woman, implies a power hierarchy of the to-be-pleased and the pleaser. Offering a cigarette to him, she not only recognizes his to-be-pleased-ness, but happily endorses it by providing pleasure in the form of the cigarette, and by metonymy, herself. Not only an instrument of pleasure, the cigarette is also a metaphor for her own ability to please, that is, her own role as a pleasure provider. The English name of the Meili brand, "My Dear," of course, suggests the equation woman = cigarettes = instrument of men's pleasure.

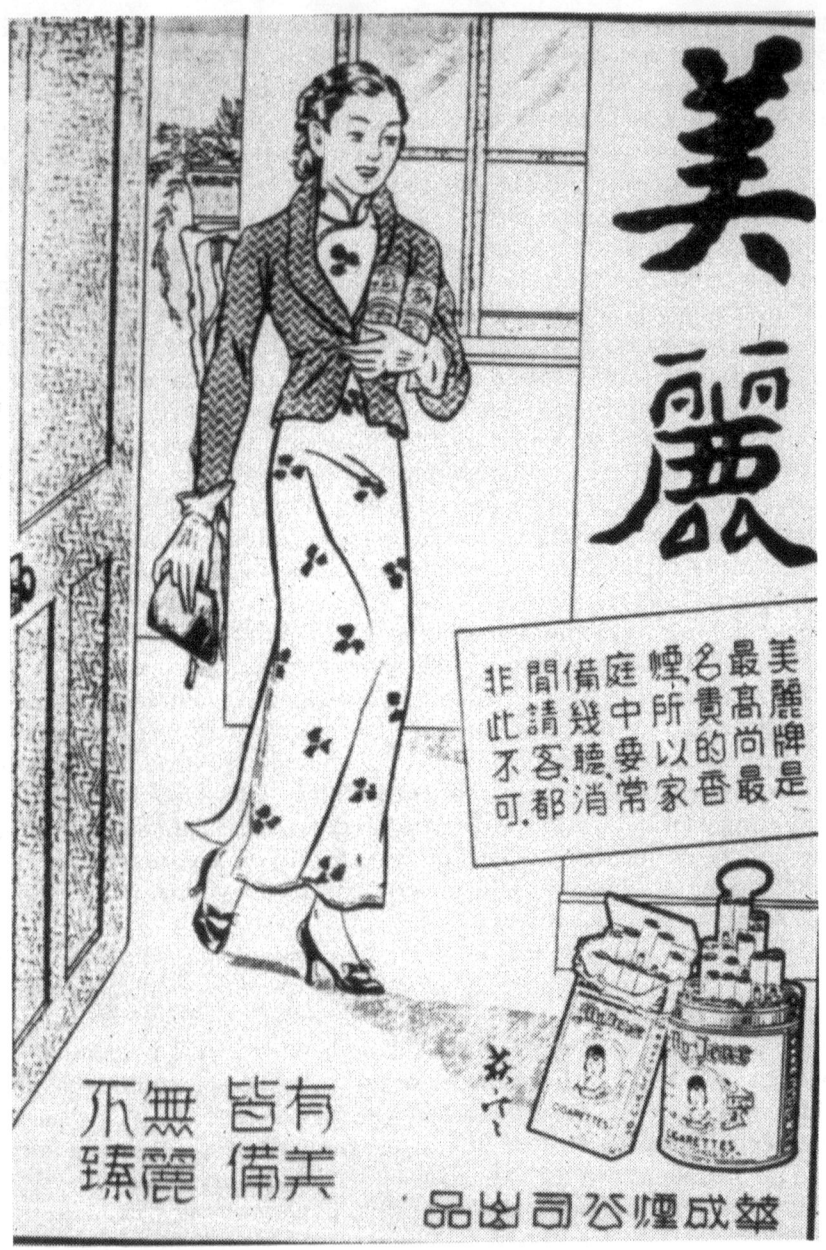

Fig. 2. *Shanghai Guide* (*Shanghai shenghuo*) 3.3 (March 1939): 1.

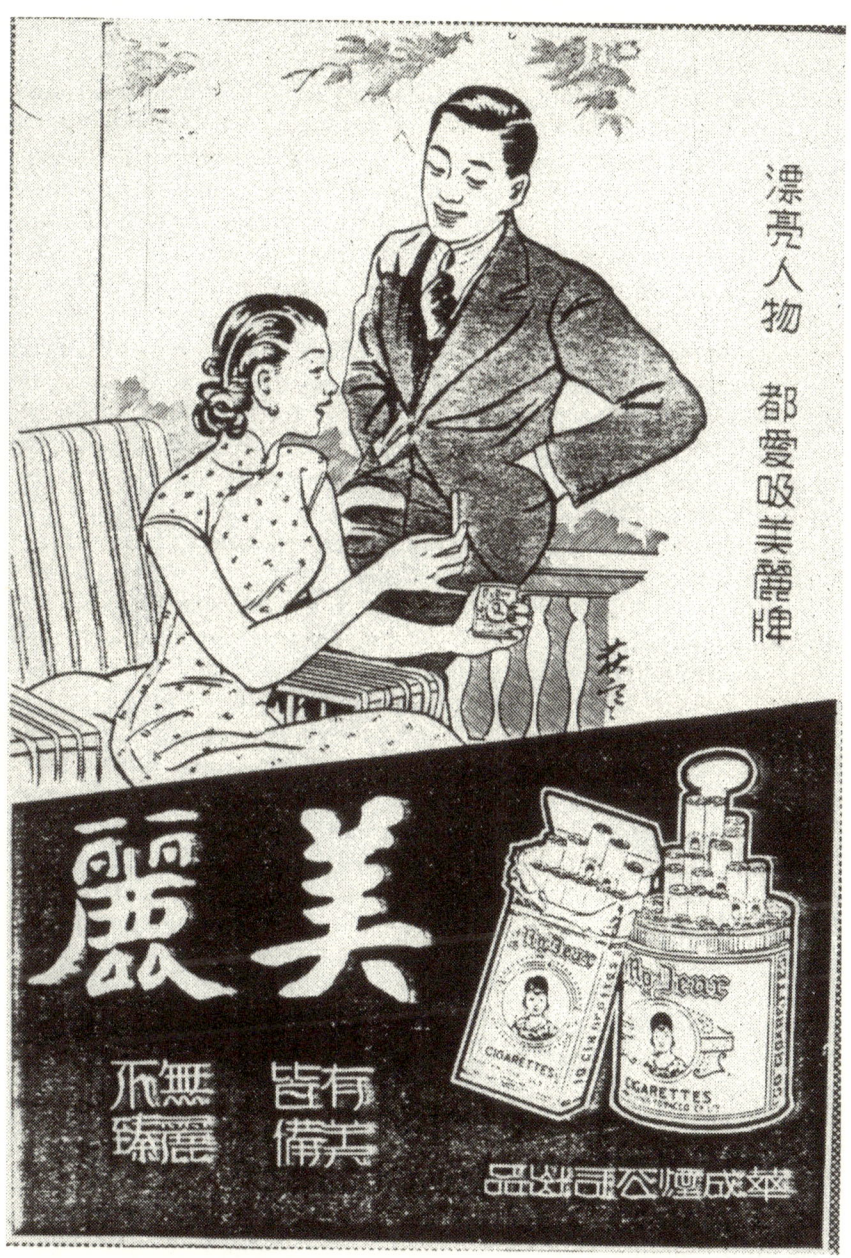

Fig. 3. *Shanghai Guide* (*Shanghai shenghuo*) 3.11 (Nov. 1939): 2.

In figure 4, cigarette smoke is presented as "fresh smoke" (*qingyan*), which provides the hazy, romantic atmosphere in which the woman and the man gaze at each other. Holding the cigarette between her fingers, she rests languidly against a pillow on the sofa, accentuating the seductive form of her body. What catches one's attention in this advertisement is her body, which, under the male gaze, becomes all the more captivating with the accessory of the cigarette. Her smoking cigarettes signifies her modernness, that she is unfettered by the shackles of tradition, and therefore is an ideal object of erotic desire. In the early 1930s, Mu Shiying in his short story "Platinum Statue of a Female Nude" (baijin de nuti suxiang) linked the modern and the erotic by praising a female nude: "Ah, the new 1933 object of erotic desire!"[5] Perhaps the viewers of this advertisement were meant to repeat Mu Shiying's words: Ah, the new 1939 object of erotic desire! In full visual display for the erotic consumption of the viewers, she/the cigarette promises an imagined access to modern eroticism and romance available only to the social elite.

An added twist occurs in figure 5. The advertisement caption—"A Meili brand cigarette after a meal makes one mentally alert and fills one's face with smiles"—suggests the possibility that the modern woman is not always mentally alert and so alludes to her overly active sexual drive and her resultant tiredness. If the name *My Dear* is taken from the male perspective, the reason why women need cigarettes perhaps can be explained from a simple psychoanalytic point of view. We may see the cigarette as a necessary adornment to the modern woman's modernity and sexuality, and, at the same time, as a phallic symbol. This advertisement is important in another way. Unlike the previous ones, this one shows through the position of the men and women on the same level that women are on an equal plane with men. It skillfully deploys the promise of gender equality for commercial ends. This suggests to us how women's desire for equality, otherwise a serious social issue, is trivialized into choosing what cigarette to smoke, or whether to smoke or not, and is thus effectively contained within the commercialized realm of feminine modernity.

Other cigarette advertisements, such as Bo'erma'er (Pall Mall), Lanmaisigan (Maskee), Jinshu (The Rat), Jinzita (Pyramid), Yinhang (Banker), Fada (Federal), Fu'erhaousi (Full House), Sanqian (Three Cash), Paike (Parkard), and so on, all adopt sales strategies similar to that of the Meili brand. They continually feed upon women's desire to be seductive, sensual, and engaged with modernity and high society. All these desires, furthermore, are linked to Westernization. For example, in the intimate pose between the man and woman in the advertisement for Parkard cigarettes, the contact of the two cigarettes is more alluring than an actual kiss because it is only suggested (fig. 6). The advertising blurb is even

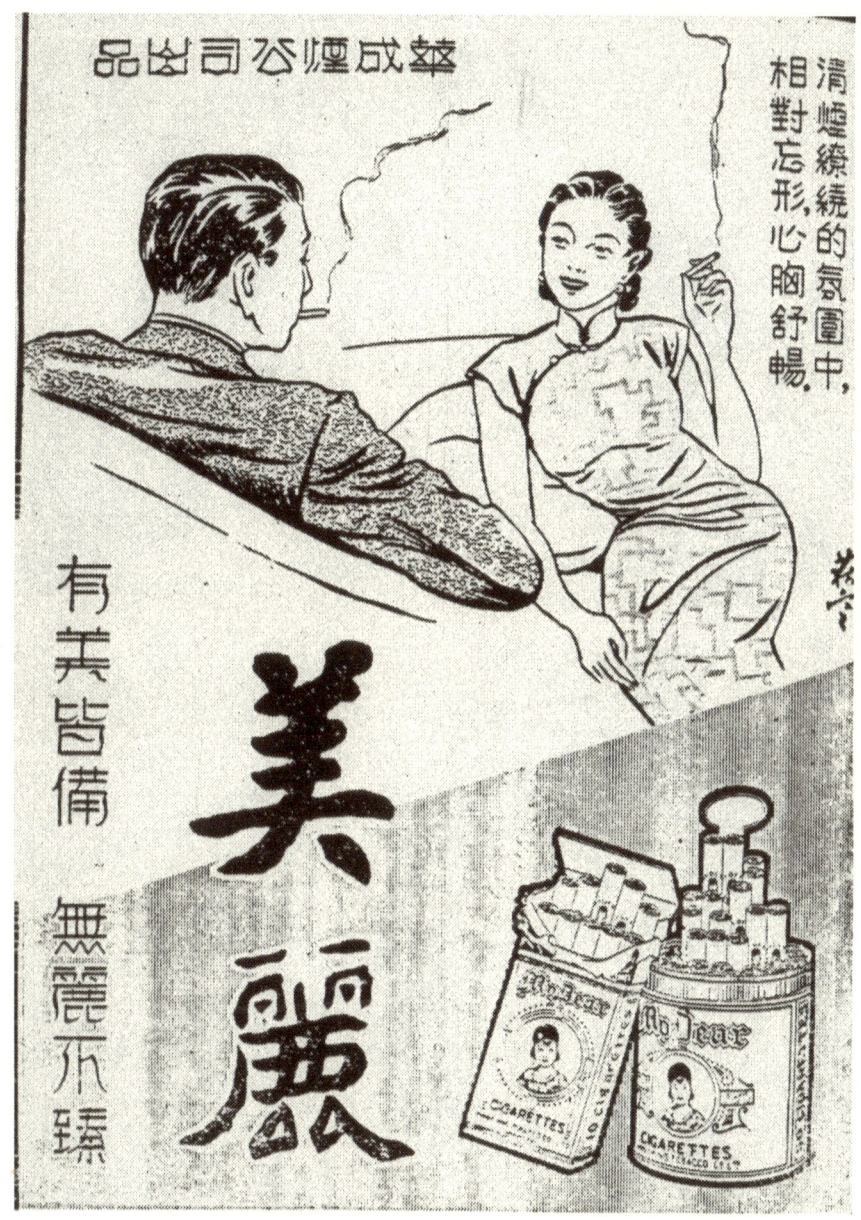

Fig. 4. *Shanghai Guide (Shanghai shenghuo)* 3.5 (May 1939): 53.

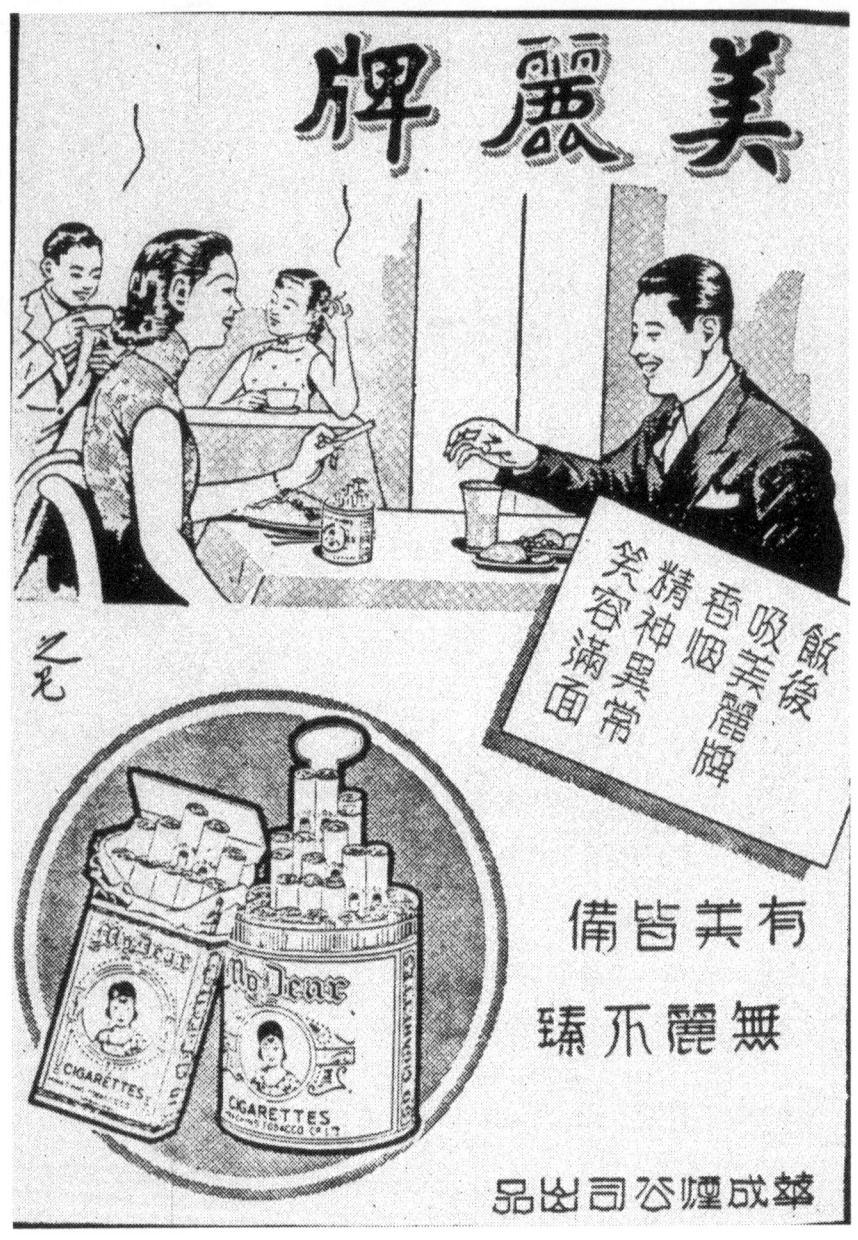

Fig. 5. *Shanghai Guide (Shanghai shenghuo)* 3.1 (Jan. 1939): 1.

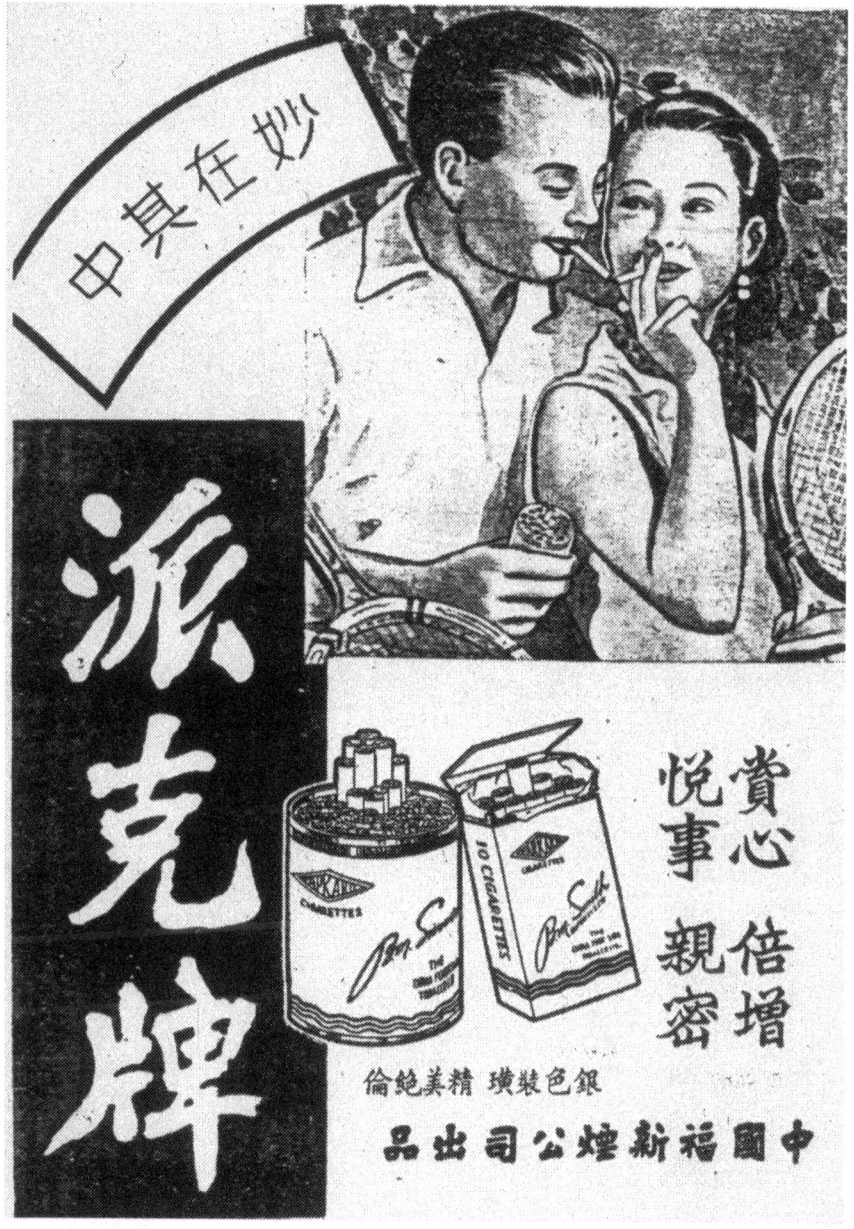

Fig. 6. *Shanghai Guide* (*Shanghai shenghuo*) 3.8 (Aug. 1939): back of front cover.

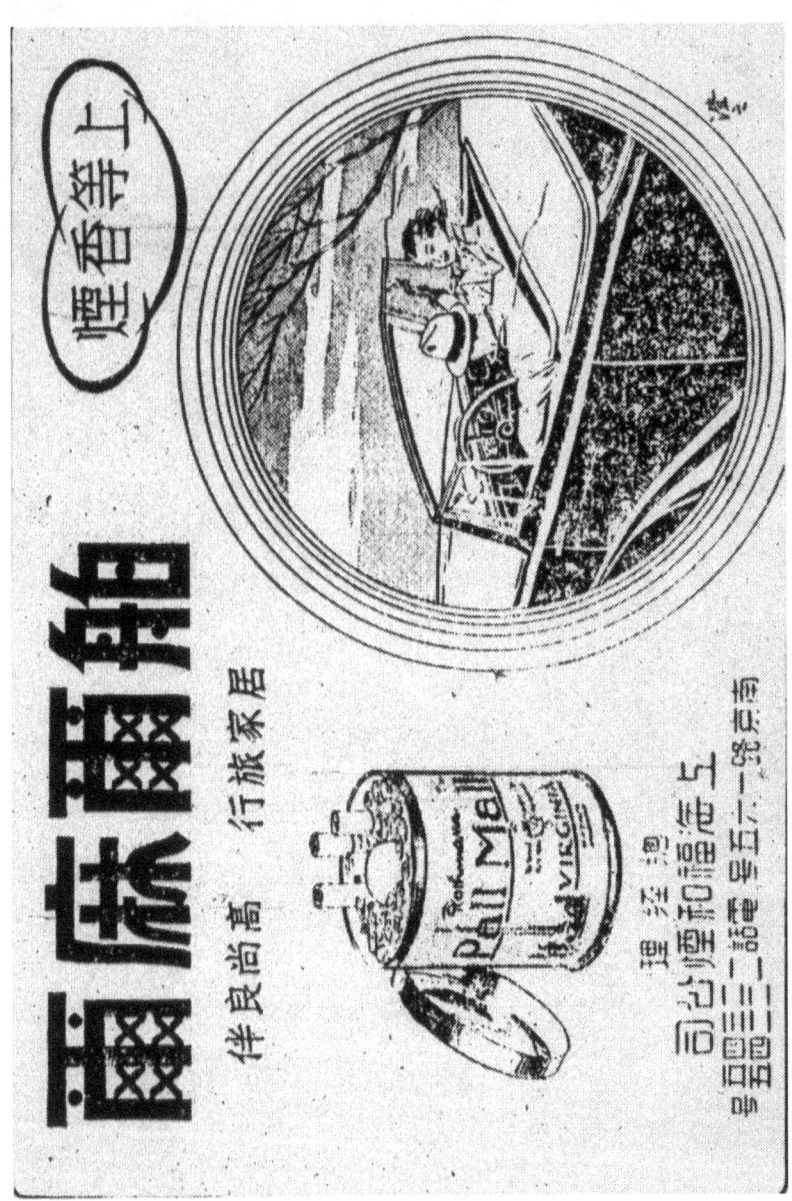

Fig. 7. *Shanghai Guide (Shanghai shenghuo)* 3.3 (March 1939): 3.

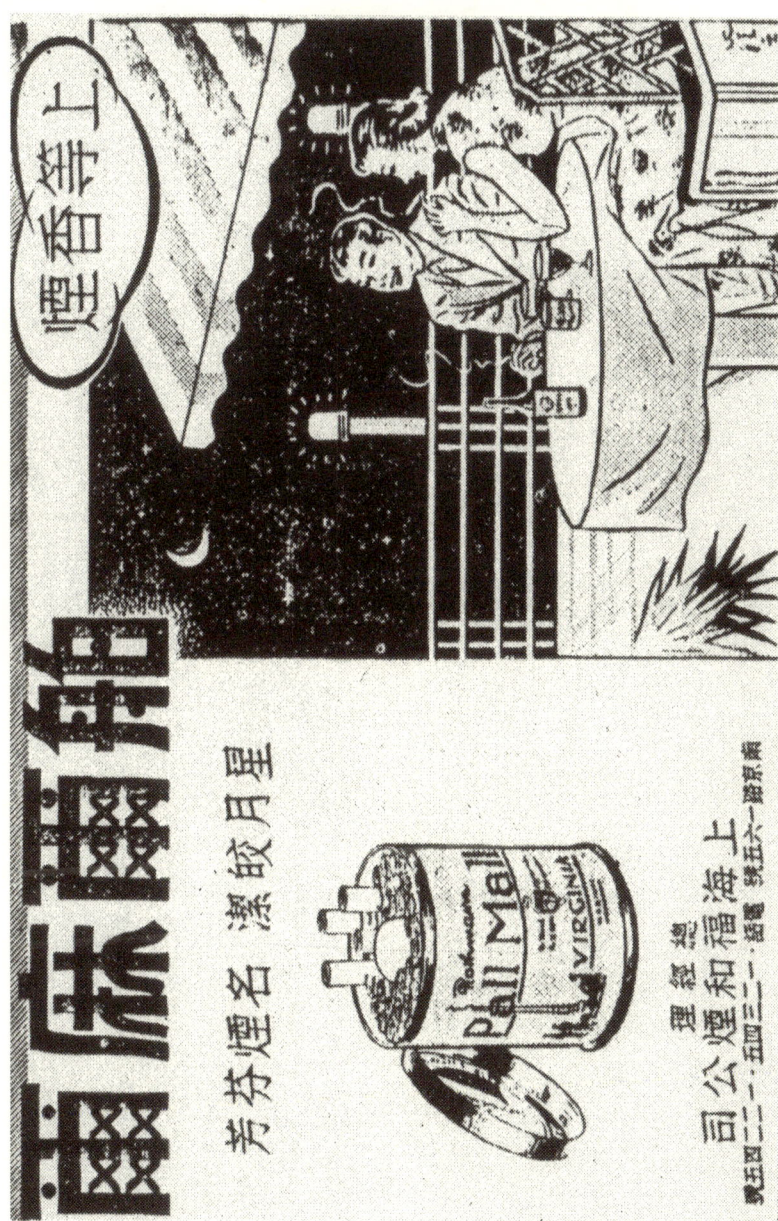

Fig. 8. *Shanghai Guide (Shanghai shenghuo)* 3.8 (Aug. 1939): 68.

218   *Shu-mei Shih*

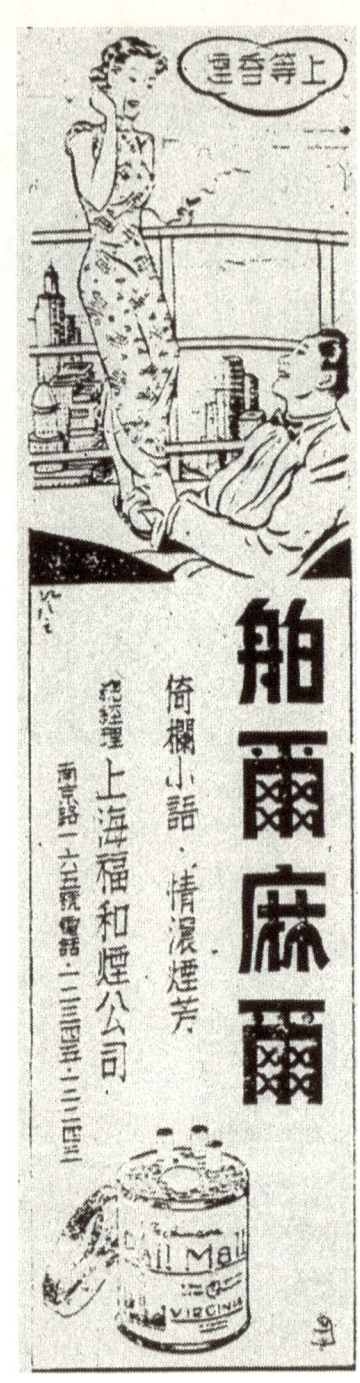

Fig. 9. *Shanghai Guide* (*Shanghai shenghuo*) 3.10 (Oct. 1939): 5.

more revealing: smoking the cigarettes will "doubly increase intimacy" between the couple. If an actual kiss is not yet realized in the ad, its ful- fillment is all but promised. And this promise has much to do with the modern woman's Westernization. Aside from her Chinese face, she could be a direct transplant of the images of Hollywood movie stars: sleeve- less tennis shirt, fashionable hairstyle, long earrings, painted nails, tennis racket, and so on. The picture in the advertisement for Pall Mall in figure 7 looks even more like a transplant from the West, as it does not have any images or signifiers that are identifiable as Chinese. One wonders how many convertibles were available in Shanghai then, and how it must be the promise, not the actual experience, of an upscale Western lifestyle that the advertisement appeals to. In figures 8 and 9, the only Chinese element is the woman's dress, a very revealing *qipao*. If Western culture brought the concept of sexual liberation for Chinese women, it is manifested, either by donning the modern *qipao* that best accentuates the curves of a woman's body for the male gaze, as in figure 4, or by the women's availability for the loving gaze and kiss of men. We can now adjust the equation make earlier into: women = cigarettes = modernity = Westernization.

The obsession with the female body only suggestively rendered in the cigarette advertisements is more fully disclosed in advertisements for body-care products in *Shanghai Guide*. If the cigarette invites men to eroti- cize the female body, the female body must be prepared for the invitee's gaze. There is Gongzhu (Princess) soap, which "makes one's skin tender and lovely," or the four-in-one perfumed soap, advertised with daring images of half nudes (figs. 10 to 12). Others, such as Wolaisi (Odorless) deodorant, all-purpose Leyi (Willingness) Oil, film star perfume, and the gonorrhea-curing medication Shande'er Midi (Santal Midy), all use the scent, feel, vitality, and cleanliness of the female body to measure beauty (figs. 13 to 16). All these products are intended to prepare a woman's body for the grace of men (hence the "willingness" oil, fragrance, deodorant, medication, and so on), all the while parading women's half- or totally nude bodies. The short articles on gonorrhea and other venereal diseases that often appear in *Shanghai Guide* (*Shanghai shenghuo*) further describe these diseases as modern illnesses, and, when read together with these advertisements, suggest that Shanghai's modern women in 1939 must have been quite sexually unrestrained. The socially explosive potential of sexual liberation though, becomes but word bites in advertisements that advance women's desirability by sanitizing, deodorizing, and perfuming them.

The advertisements discussed above indicate the expectations of a modern woman. She must have not only outward beauty (which consists of the piling of Western adornments and a Westernized look) but

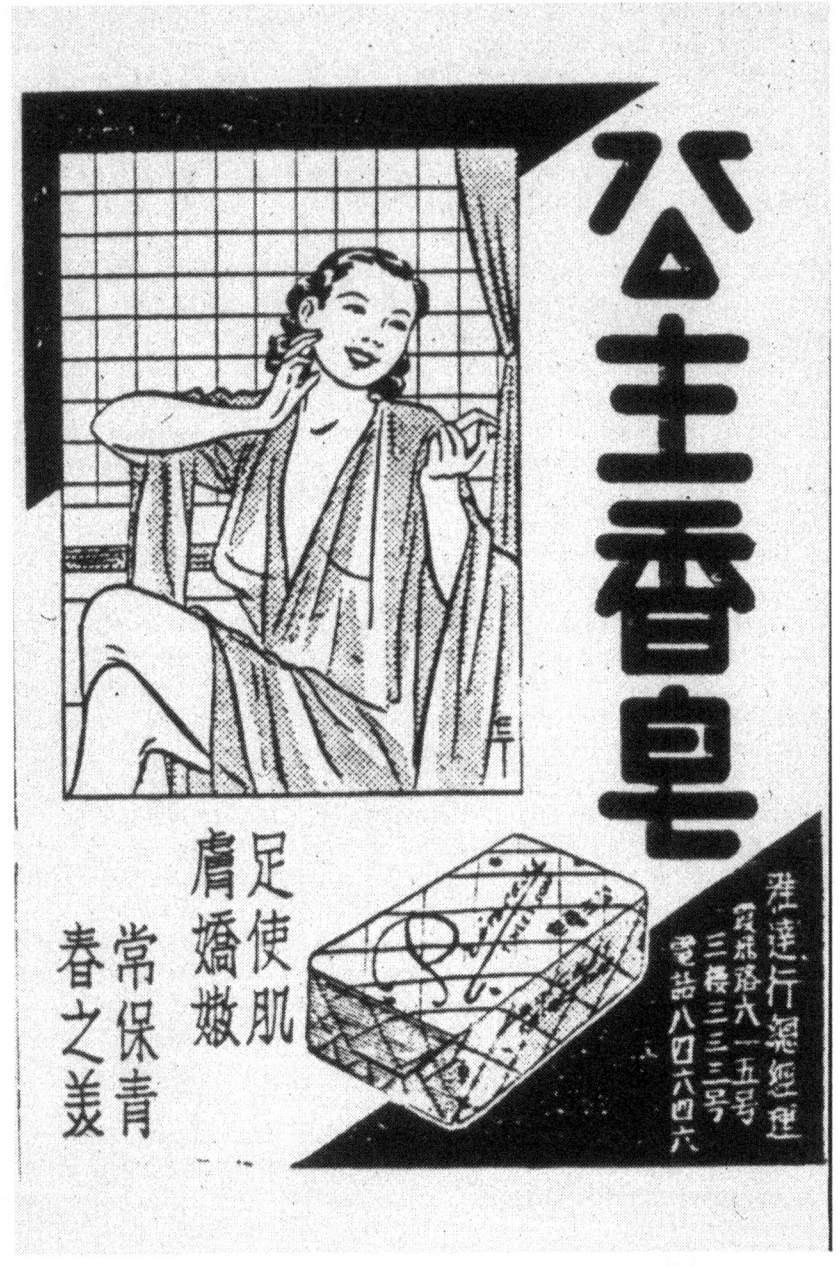

Fig. 10. *Shanghai Guide (Shanghai shenghuo)* 3.9 (Sep. 1939): 68.

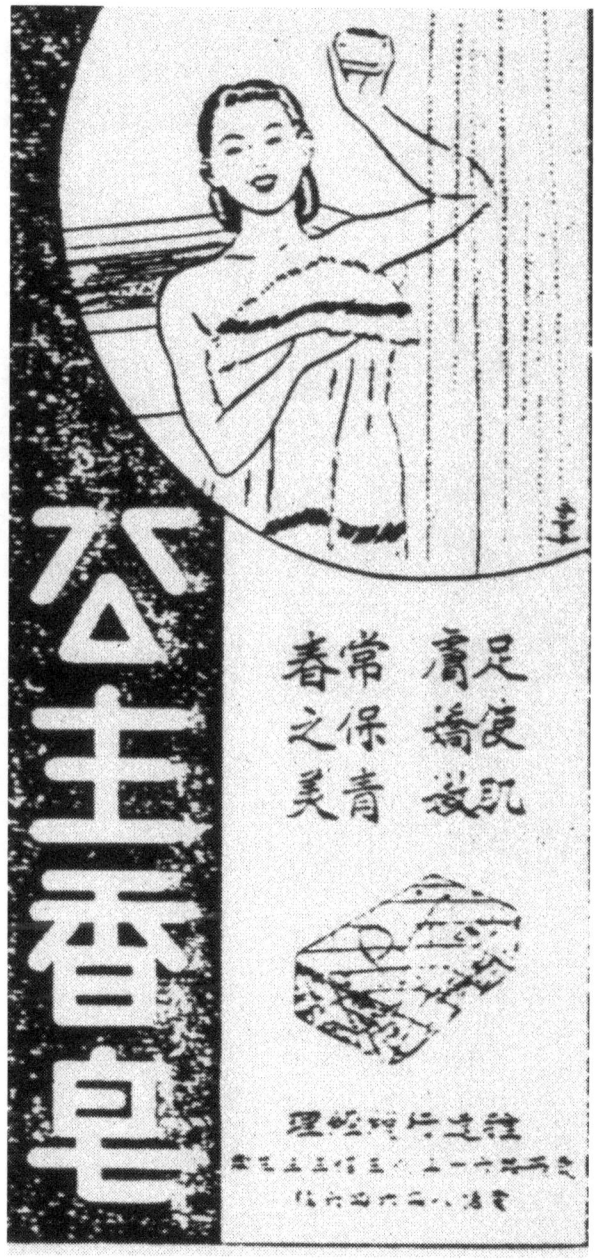

Fig. 11. *Shanghai Guide (Shanghai shenghuo)* 3.10 (Oct. 1939): 11.

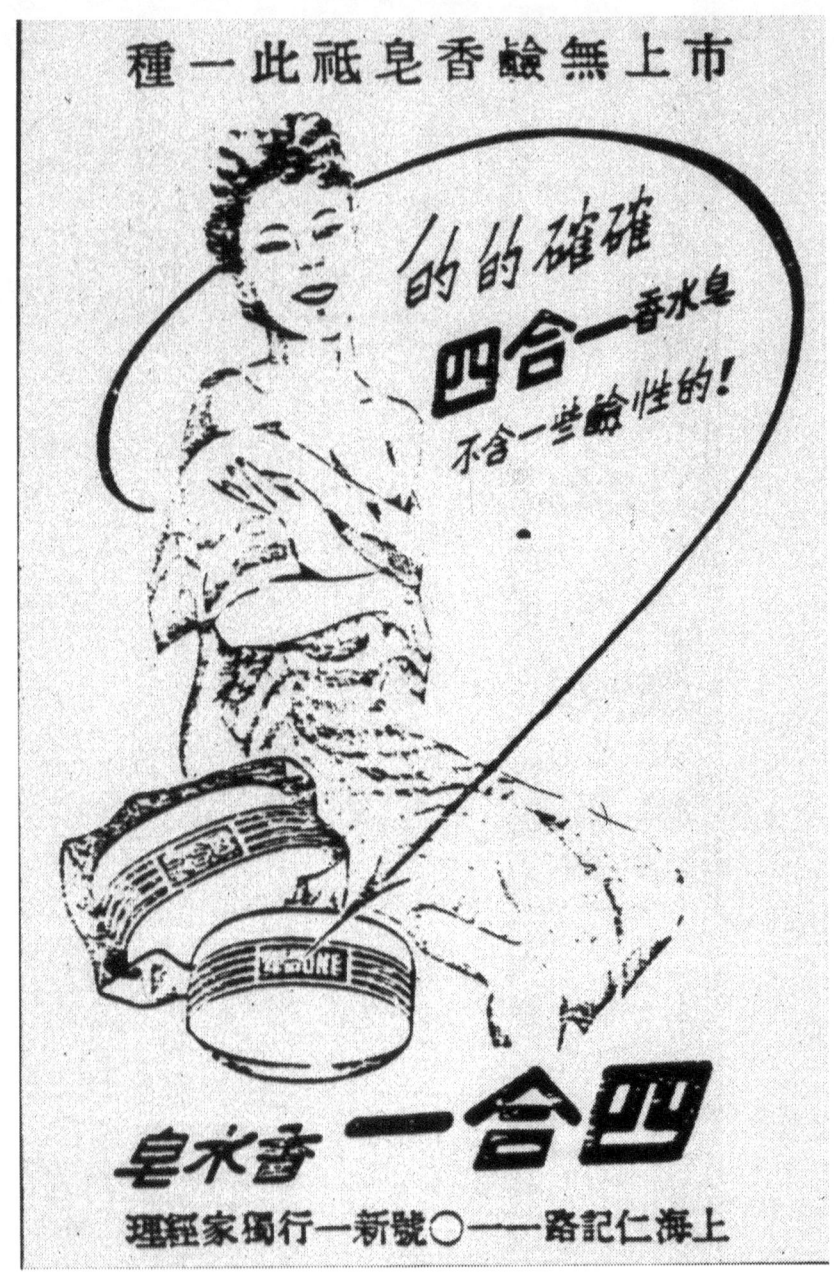

Fig. 12. *Shanghai Guide (Shanghai shenghuo)* 3.8 (Aug. 1939): 63.

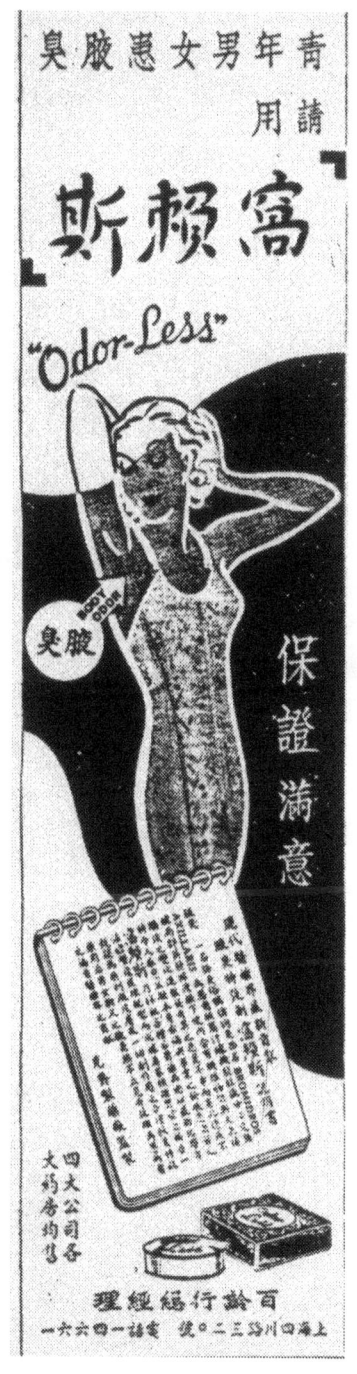

Fig. 13. *Shanghai Guide* (*Shanghai shenghuo*) 3.10 (Oct. 1939): 40.

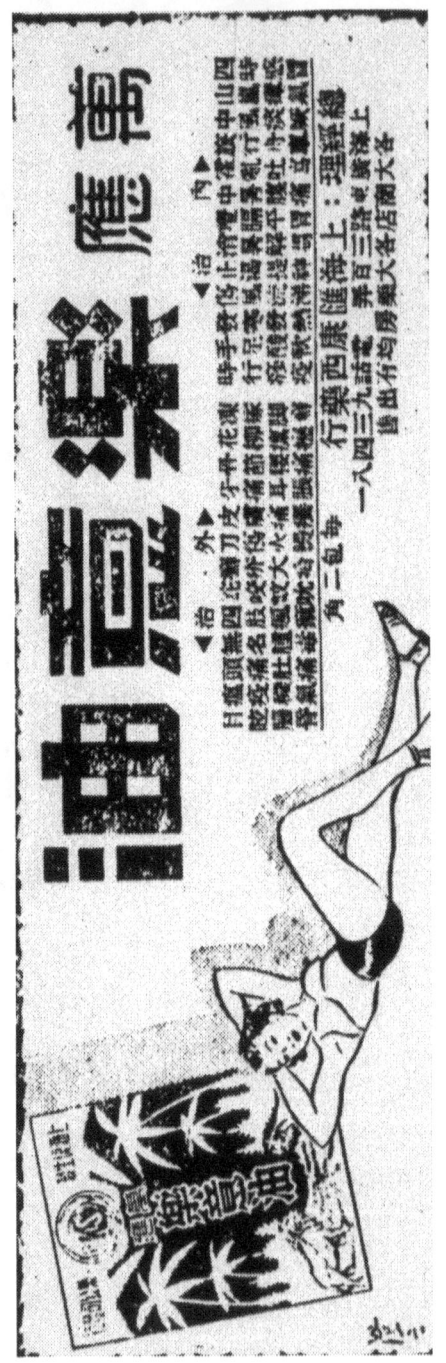

Fig. 14. *Shanghai Guide (Shanghai shenghuo)* 3.7 (Jul. 1939): 65.

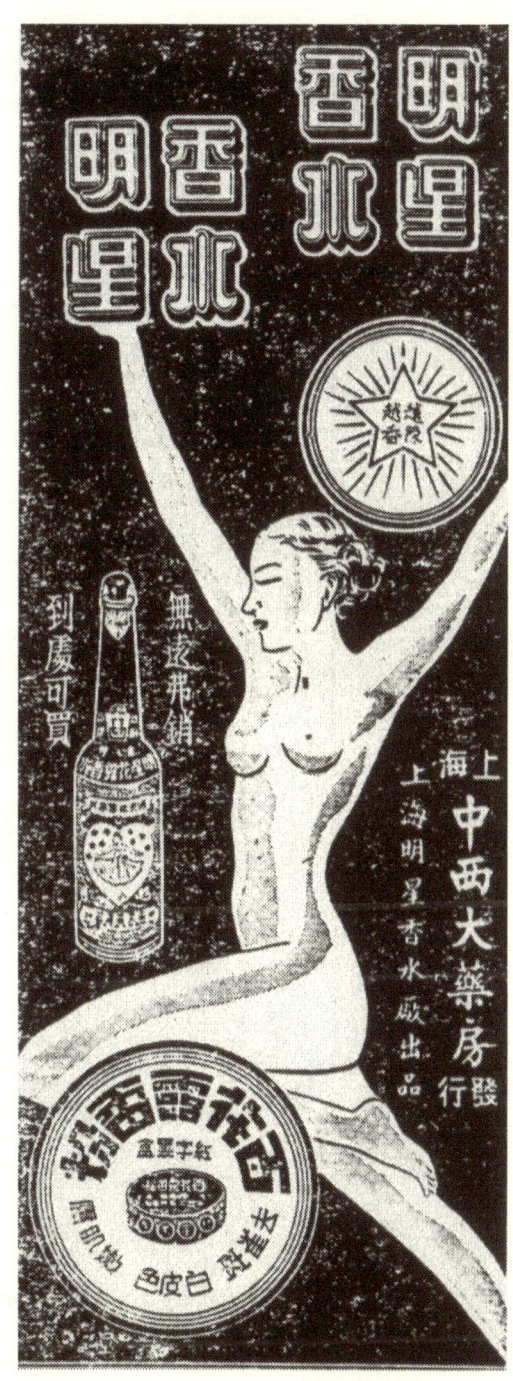

Fig. 15. *Shanghai Guide*
(*Shanghai shenghuo*) 3.4 (Apr.
1939): 32.

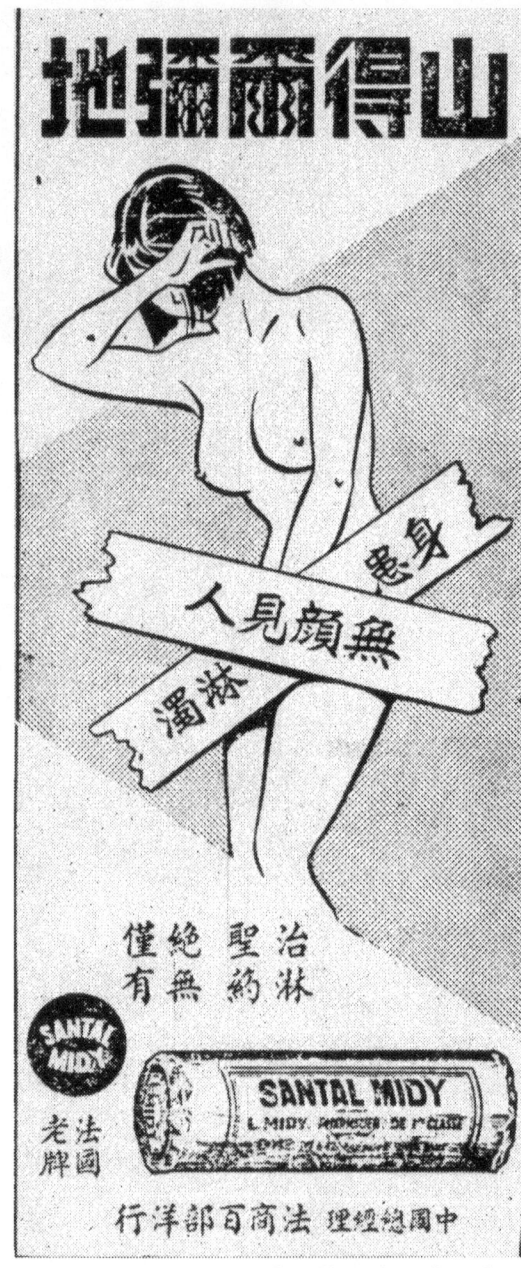

Fig. 16. *Shanghai Guide* (*Shanghai shenghuo*) 3.1 (Jan. 1939): 19.

also "inward beauty" (the body must also be clean, tender, and white; diseaseless and odorless; and full of sexual vitality). If we see the prime function of advertisements as the *kindling* of its viewers' already existing desires (erotic desire, translated into the consumer desire to buy, which in turn promises the fulfillment of erotic desire), then we can get a glimpse of the content of the feminine modernity allotted to women. But if we see their prime function to be the *production* of new forms of desire, which simultaneously sanctions certain forms and polices others, then we can see how this feminine modernity circumscribes a bounded arena within which a non-national form of commercial culture is circulated and women are characterized predominantly as objects of desire like other material objects. Here they may also be promised gender equality, access to the high society, and sexual liberation, but these promises are equated with consumption, not with a politically or socially based struggle for gender equity.

Moreover, we can sketch the physical appearance of the modern woman of 1939, at least an ideal version, from these advertisements. She is Westernized, beautiful, and liberal, and her ultimate goal in life seems to be to please men. For that goal, she does not hide her sexuality; on the contrary, she shows it off. She is the New Woman hollowed out of her social consciousness, reduced to an object of desire for male urban elites, and constricted to her roles in the male playground. She eloquently illustrates how potentially socially disruptive concepts such as sexual emancipation can be skillfully displaced into obsessions of what to wear and how to accentuate one's erotic allure. Recalling her genealogy, we are reminded of the New Woman figure from the wenti xiaoshuo (problem fiction) by such feminist writers as Lu Yin and Feng Yuanjun during the May Fourth period, when the New Woman did engage in a battle with patriarchy and pondered the heavy social questions of class inequality, heterosexual hegemony, and gendered division of labor. By the time we come to Shanghai xinganjuepai fiction (new sensationism) in the late 1920s and early 1930s, the May Fourth New Woman is more or less bifurcated into the masculine, socially conscious Marxist Girl, who was to become an ancestor to the desexualized female communist cadre after 1949, and the materialistic, urban femme fatale, the Modern Girl, who was able to challenge patriarchy to a certain extent. Although the image of the Marxist Girl who works to bring forth China's liberation from foreign imperialism was predictably censored and therefore understandably disappeared from 1939 Shanghai, the Modern Girl seems to have become completely subsumed by an even more materialistic version of the modern woman.

One characteristic common to all these versions of modern womanhood is that they are all Westernized. In the late 1920s, the fiction of Liu

Na'ou and others was criticized as direct transplants from Japan. Liu's Shanghai appeared to be a copy or transplant of Westernized Tokyo. Liu's Modern Girl clearly also has genealogical links with the Japanese *modan gaaru* (Modern Girl), as I have examined elsewhere.[6] The Westernized modern Chinese woman is therefore genealogically linked to images of modern Western women both in history and in Hollywood cinema, just as the Japanese Modern Girl is. Baptized in the stream of Shanghai's various foreign cultures, she was also in many ways a product of its semicolonial condition. She can be called alternately *xinnuxing* (the New Woman), *shidai nuxing* (the woman of the times), *xiandai nuxing* (the modern women), or *modeng nulang* (the Modern Girl). Her modernness, her sexual desire, and so on, are all inextricably tied to the influence and transplants of, or even colonization by, the sign systems of the West and Japan (the honorary West). And the factor that led to her being thus colonized is the desire of yet another colonizer (the patriarchal society) for whom she has to be Westernized in the economy of his desire. In order to please, the modern woman must assimilate the various Japanese and Western cultural signs, which simultaneously establish and limit her value and status within modern society. Without a doubt, her modernity is not necessarily one that is completely passive, and includes her liberation from some of the shackles of tradition; but the main concern of this essay is to show how, despite this liberation, the domain of feminine modernity circumscribed by patriarchal imagination rechannels any potential challenge of modern womanhood to commercial purposes. Under the control of modern consumer culture, this feminine modernity has typologized women into sexual object and beautiful adornment. Thus her sexuality and beauty—that is, her feminine modernity—becomes a product of multiple colonizations.

Opposing the colonization by Western culture was once a topic of heated debate among certain Shanghai intellectuals. The League of Leftwing Writers of the 1930s had an obvious anti-Western inclination. As early as 1931, Hu Qiuyuan of the Cultural Criticism (wenhua piping) group called Shanghai a semicolonial city. What is interesting are not the cultural values controlled by the Leftist ideology, but how this anxiety towards Westernization was manifested in popular culture. Some of the advertisements in *Shanghai Guide*, while reconfiguring the Westernized modern woman into a commercial icon, also counteract the image of the overly Westernized woman by depicting a modern housewife who supposedly loves to use Chinese products (guohuo). Preferring Chinese products over foreign products, she in a way participates in nationalism by being a patriotic consumer; she therefore potentially exceeds the limits of a feminine modernity.

But her mode of participation is so strictly prescribed that any potential challenge to masculine, national modernity is suppressed from the start. The advertisements in which the modern housewife appears are almost always captioned by: "old brand native product," "natively made in China," "completely Chinese capital and Chinese labor," "natively produced yarn," "completely native product," "all native materials," and so on. She is a good wife, uses native seasonings to cook delicious-smelling food for her husband and his friends. She willingly plays the role of cook, serving her man with a happy smile; hence she always stands rather than sits (figs. 17 to 19). The thermos she uses is a native product, she eats mid-autumn-festival moon cakes, and she wears clothing made of Chinese wool, such as a wool sweater made of the Chinese Hero-brand yarn (yingxiongpai). She uses the natively produced threads to mend clothes, since these threads "are far superior to imported ones." And most importantly, she is often a mother whose priorities are her children and her family, and thus she especially knows how to pick economical and reliable native products to save on the family budget (figs. 20 to 24). And if she does not have children, she uses tenderness and care to knit sweaters for her man. The advertisement for Hero-brand yarn in figure 25 alludes to the man in the picture as her hero, whom she looks up to as she holds in her hands the wool sweater she has just knit for him. The huge characters "natively produced yarn" links heroism with nationalism. The woman's role here enforces this link. Her participation in nationalism is thus reduced to buying Hero-brand yarn and knitting a sweater for the master of the nation.

Here, her mode of participation in the nation is restricted strictly to consumption of native products and servitude to men. She differs from the Westernized modern woman only in her choice to consume native rather than foreign products; she is, like the Westernized woman, equally defined by her role as pleasure giver. Both roles are strictly defined: the former within the private space of home, the latter also within home, although she may venture into coffee shops, cinemas, or even an outdoor tennis court. Either they are consumers or they are men-serving socialites or wives. The seeming distinction between the two thus breaks down since both are confined to feminine modernity. The old, extreme bifurcation of women into seductresses/prostitutes and housewives, is reincarnated into modern forms with minor variations.

The seemingly liberated seductress (the Westernized woman), furthermore, is so in appearance only. She was liberated from some of the restrictions of the traditional woman, but she has slipped into a new set of protocols—her dress must be in good taste, her actions liberal, she must follow trends and fashions, and must rely on the haven of consumer culture. The meaning of her sexual liberalness thus deserves further consideration.

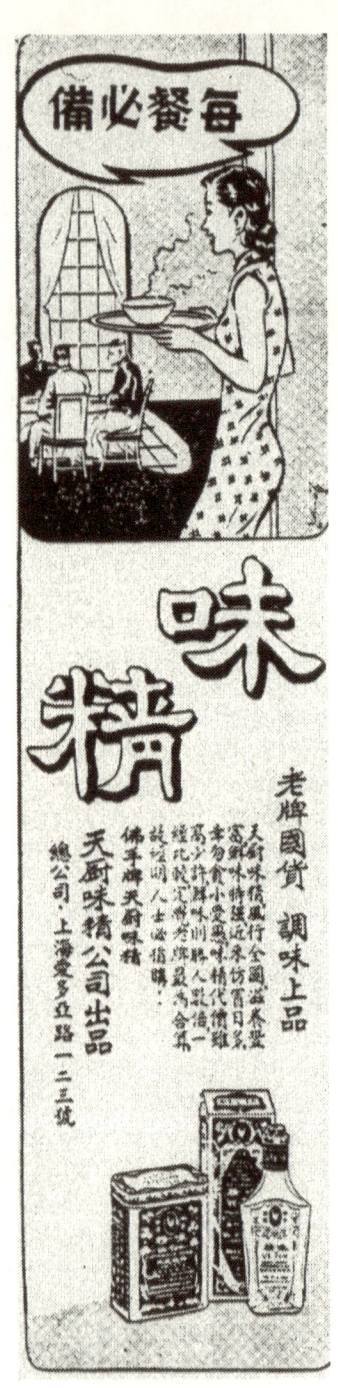

Fig. 17. *Shanghai Guide (Shanghai shenghuo)*
3.11 (Nov. 1939): 7.

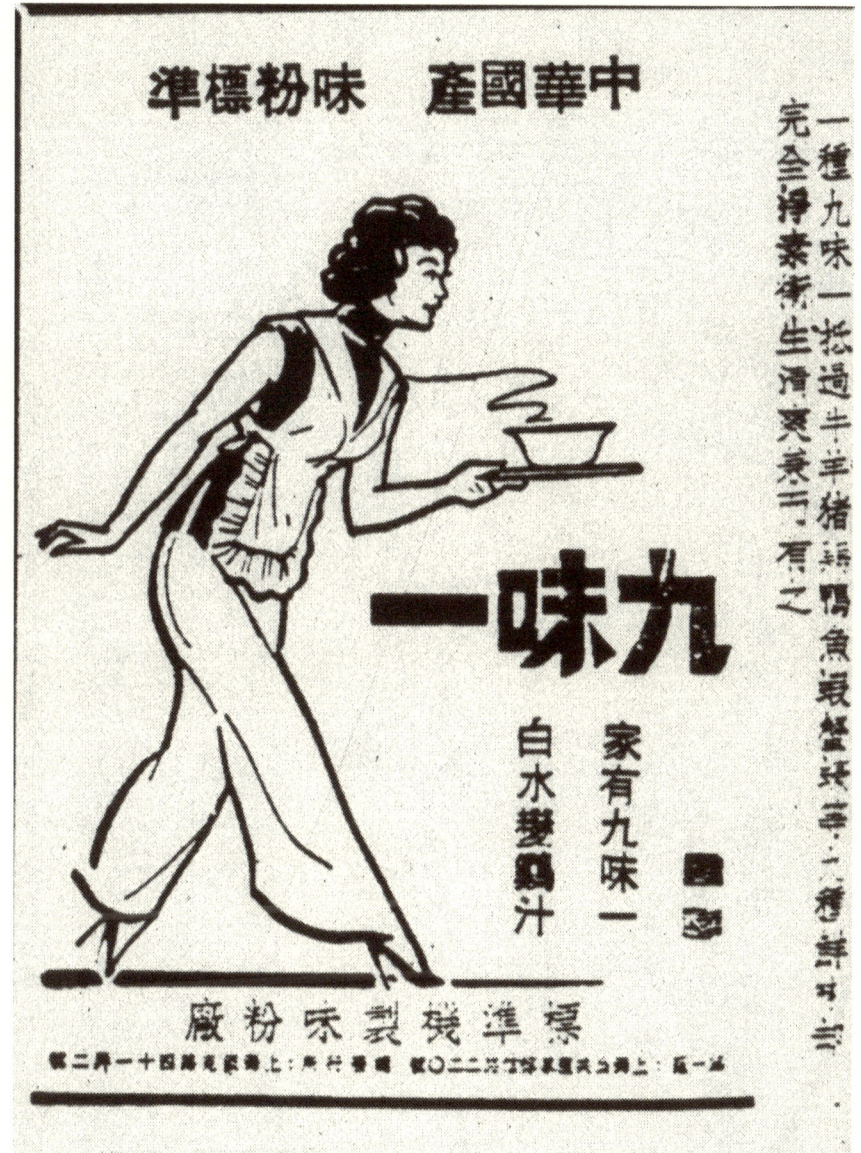

Fig. 18. *Shanghai Guide (Shanghai shenghuo)* 3.8 (Aug. 1939): 45.

232　　*Shu-mei Shih*

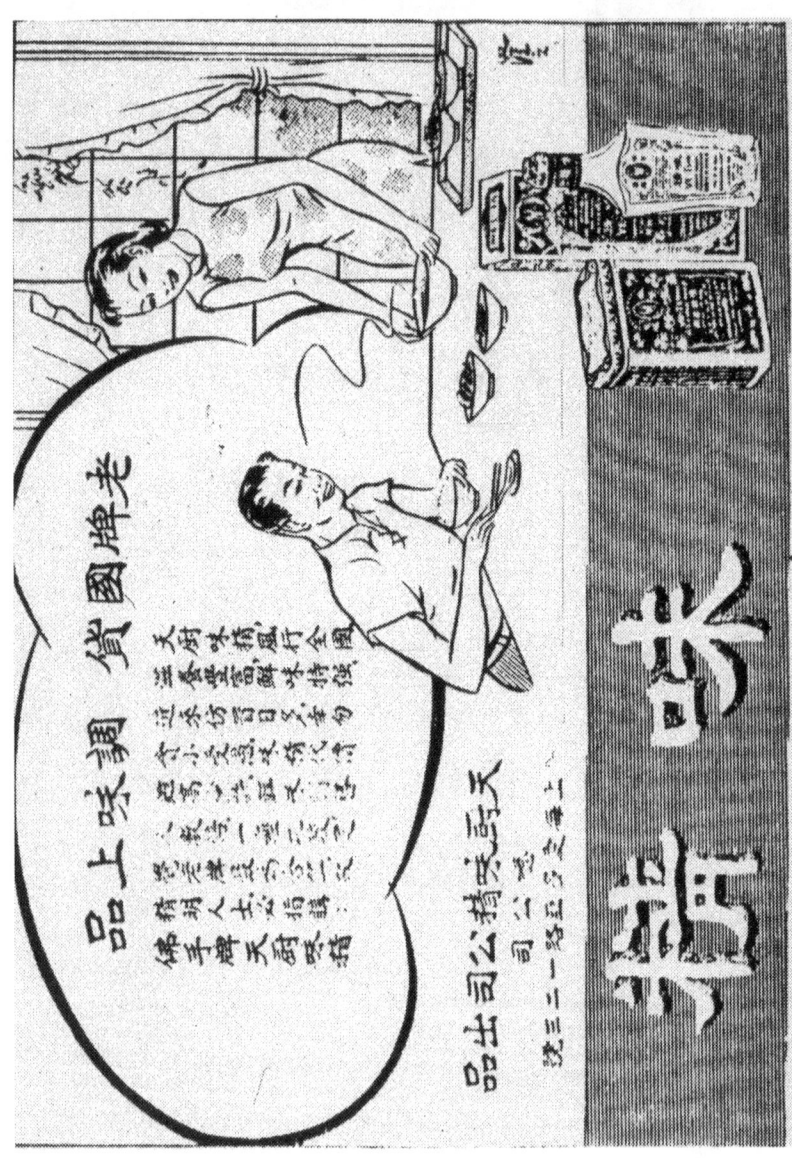

Fig. 19. *Shanghai Guide* (*Shanghai shenghuo*) 3.7 (July 1939): 79.

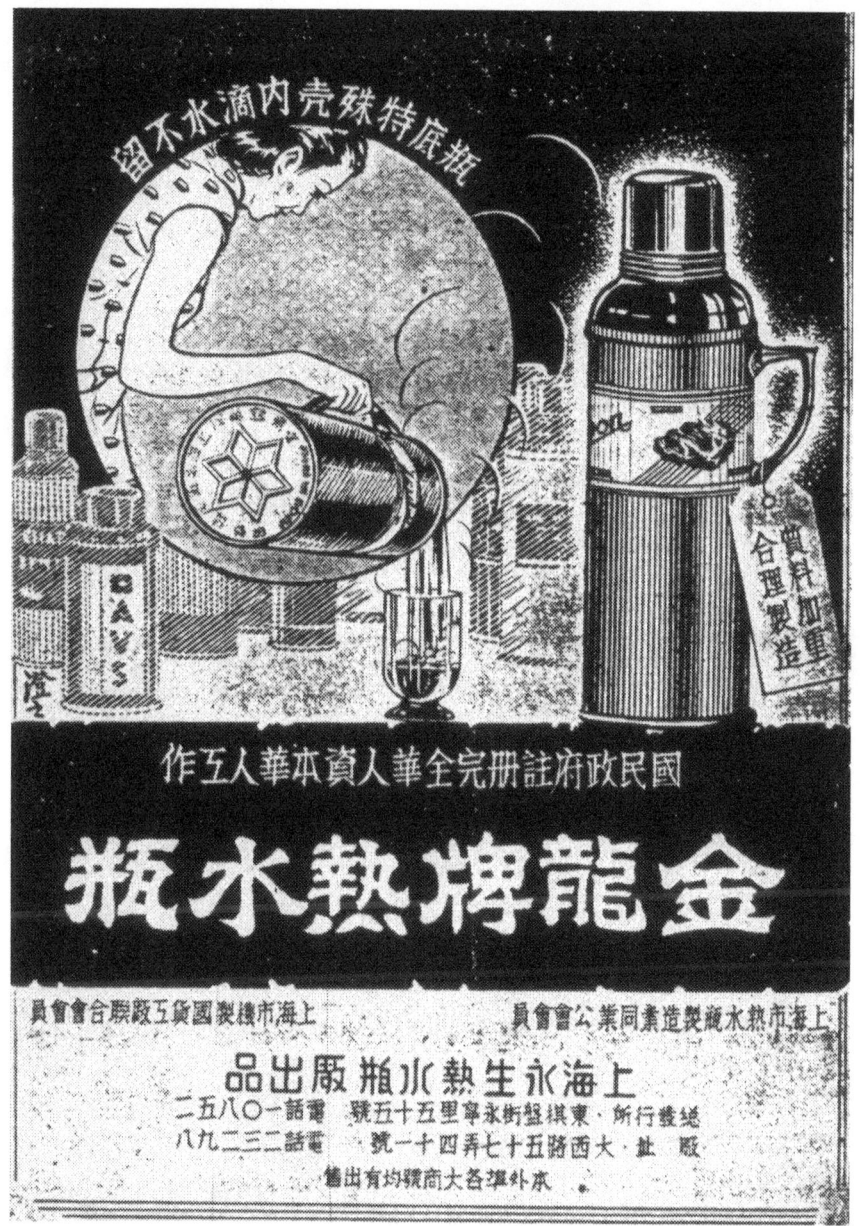

Fig. 20. *Shanghai Guide (Shanghai shenghuo)* 3.5 (May 1939): 11.

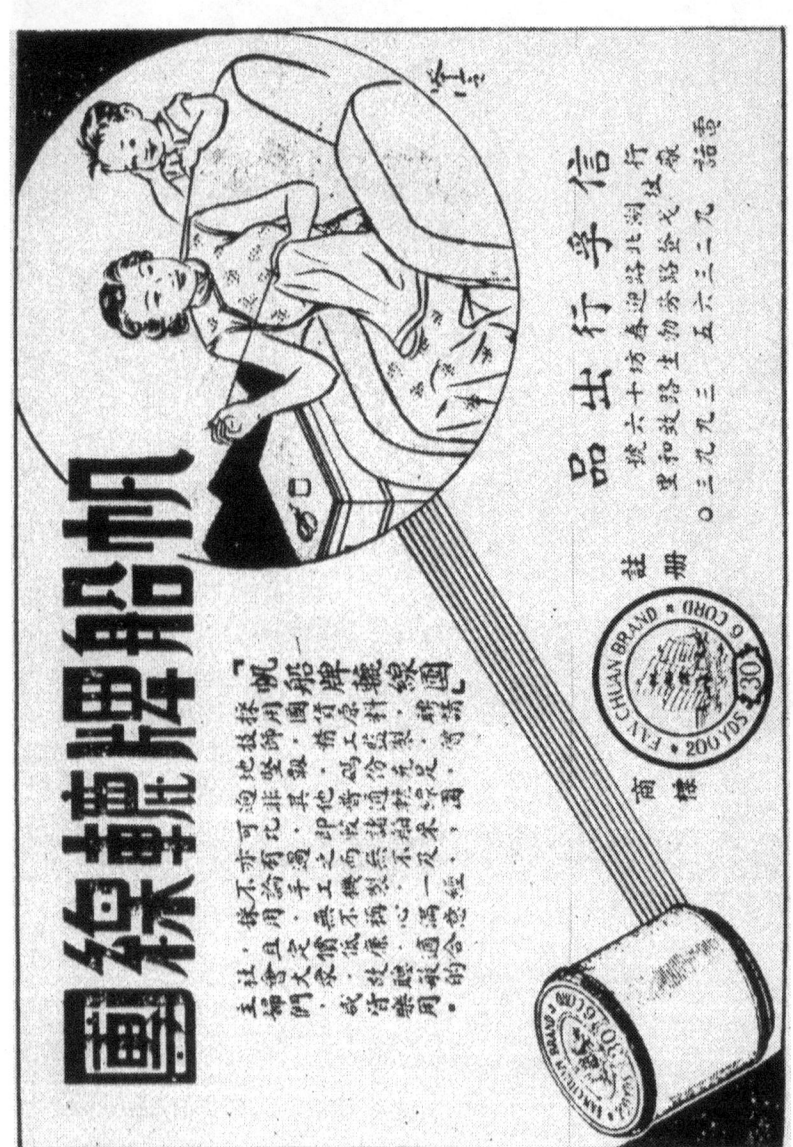

Fig. 21. *Shanghai Guide (Shanghai shenghuo)* 3.9 (Sep. 1939): 16.

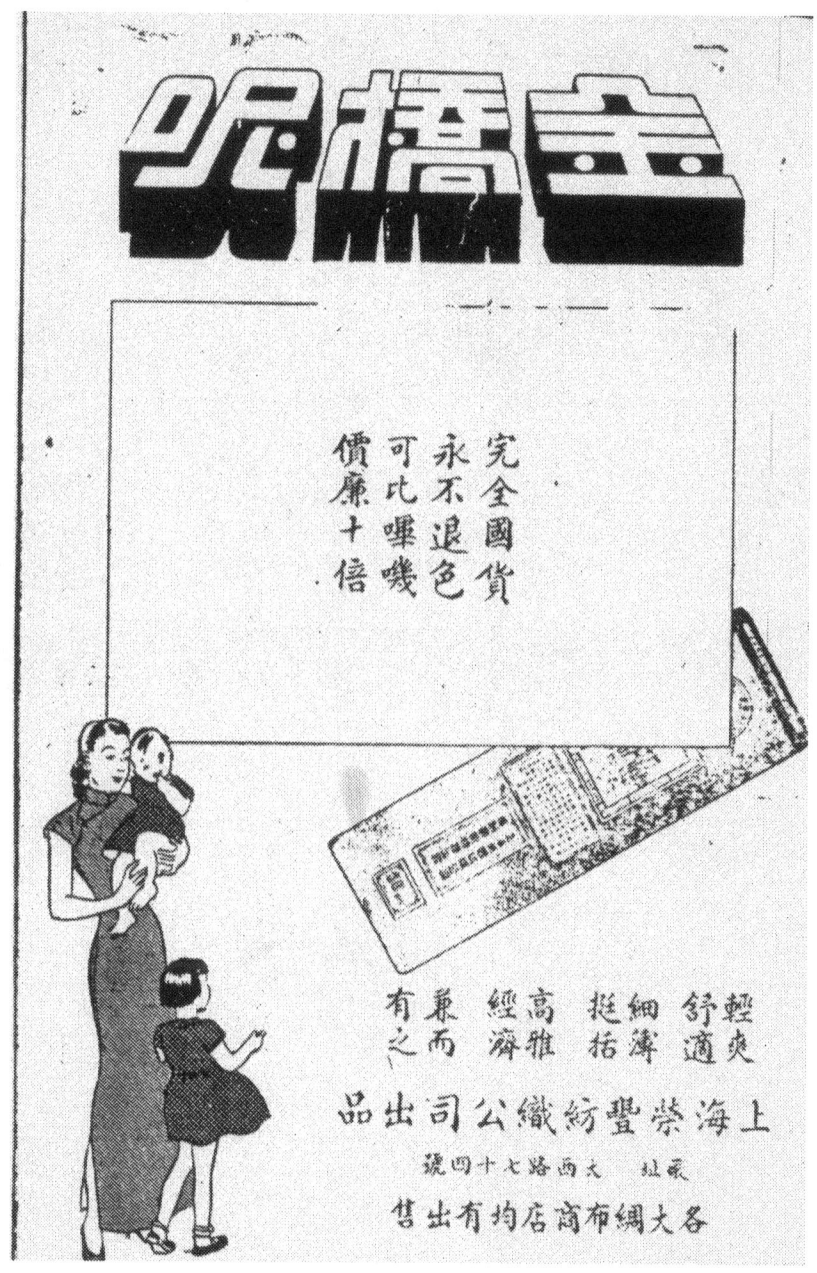

Fig. 22. *Shanghai Guide* (*Shanghai shenghuo*) 3.5 (May 1939): 33.

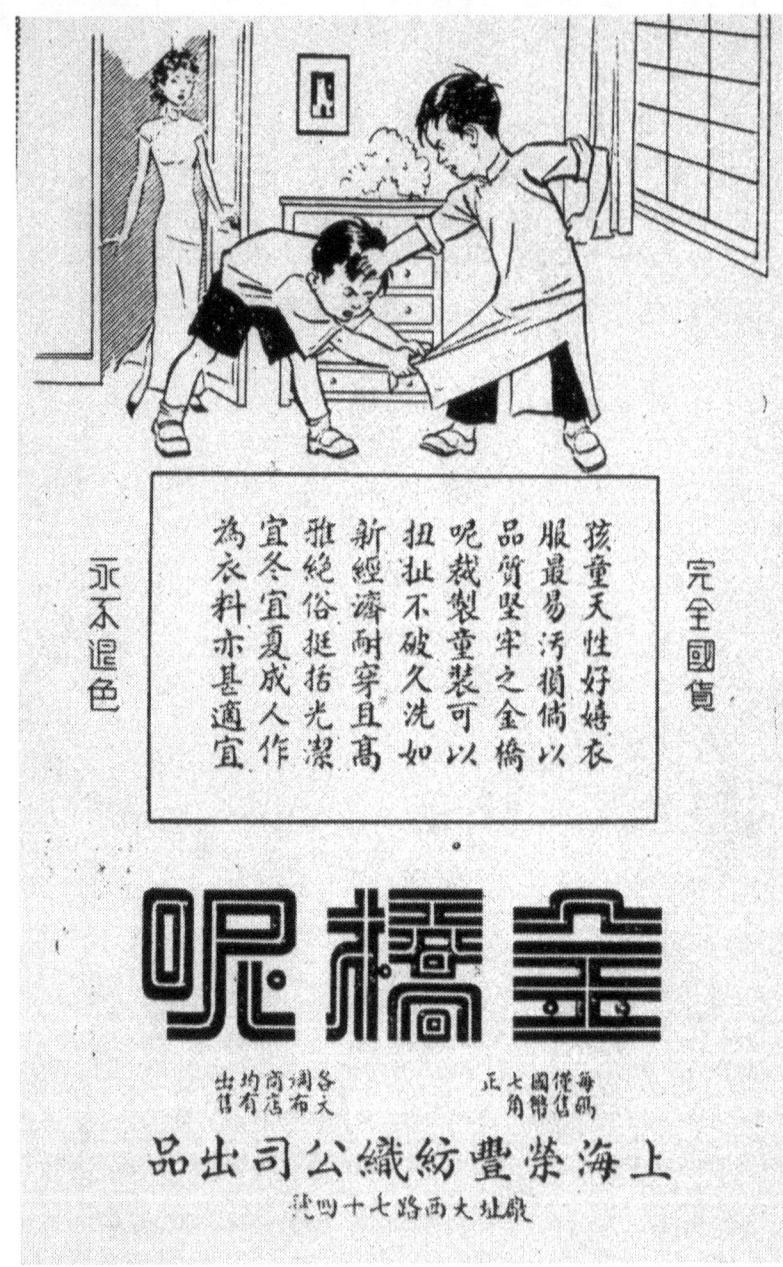

Fig. 23. *Shanghai Guide (Shanghai shenghuo)* 3.9 (Sep. 1939): 49.

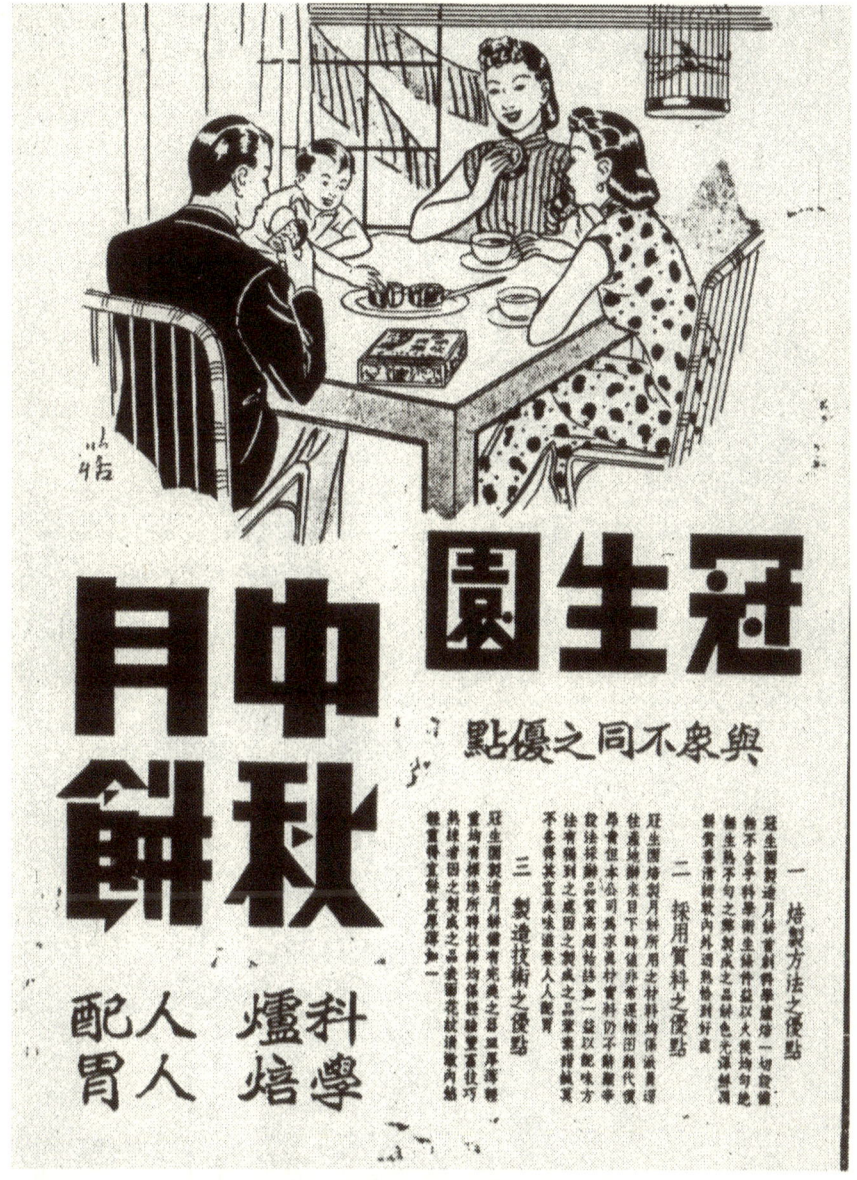

Fig. 24. *Shanghai Guide (Shanghai shenghuo)* 3.9 (Sep. 1939): 2.

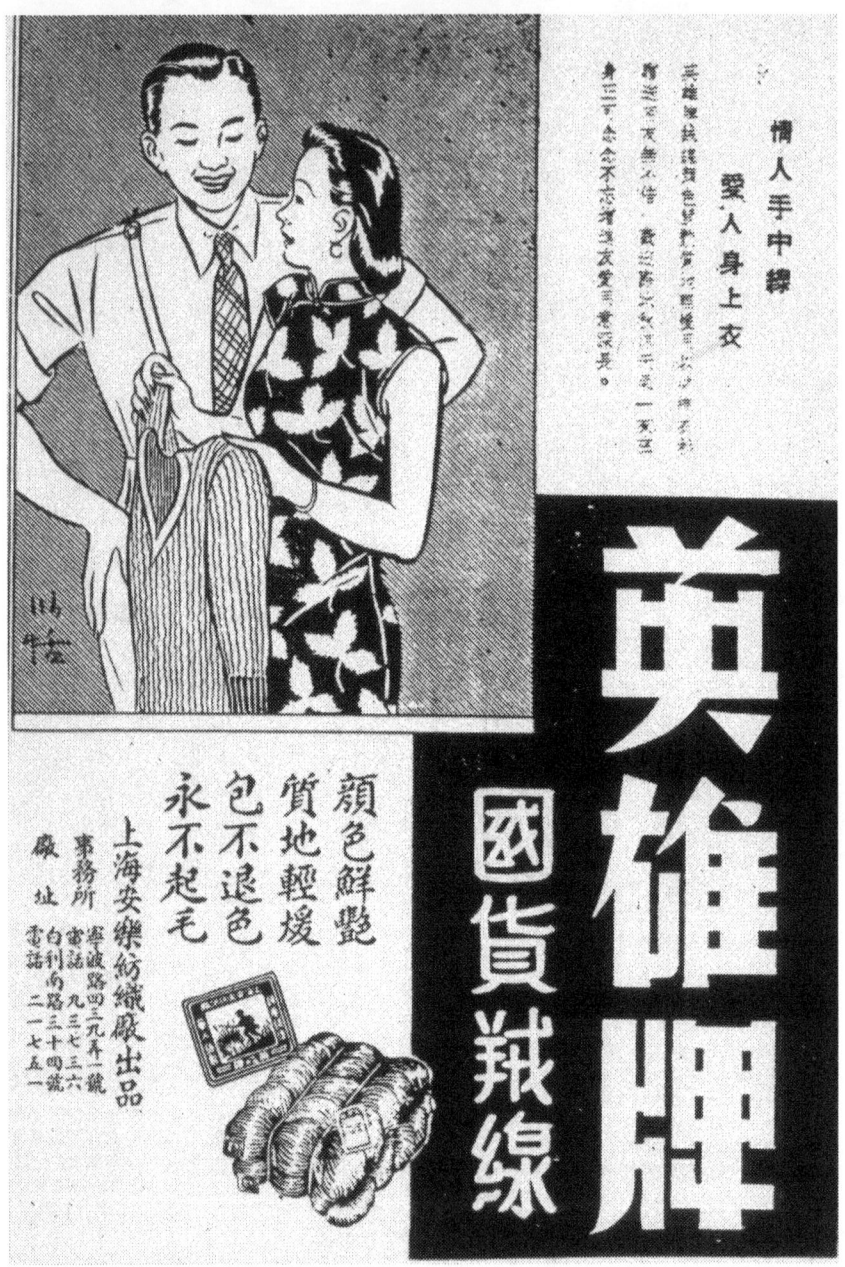

Fig. 25. *Shanghai Guide (Shanghai shenghuo)* 3.9 (Sep. 1939): 34.

For whom is she sexually liberal? What are the consequences? Many works of the male and female writers in the 1920s, and even up to Su Qing's early 1940s' *Jiehun shinian* (Ten years of marriage), look dismally upon the fate of women like her. Lu Xun's famous words, that the Nora (the woman who rebelled against patriarchy and walked out of her home in Ibsen's *A Doll's House*) who walked out would either become degraded or return home, to a certain extent addresses the predicament of this New Woman. The sexually liberal woman in her youth and beauty could be the object of pursuit of men, thus she appears to be without a care in the world and enjoys her life to the fullest. But once her youth and beauty have waned, her fate may be quite tragic. The suicide of the famous (and once sensational) actress Ruan Lingyu was also directly related to the gap between her liberalness and society's conservatism. The 1920s writer Lu Yin repeatedly used tragic endings to tell the story of the New Woman, as did Mu Shiying in the 1930s.

In summary, although there appears to be a discrepancy between the image of the Westernized modern woman and that of the housewife in the advertisements of *Shanghai Guide*, both sets of advertisements taken together constitute a book of warning to women. As a woman, you can choose between being a New Woman or a housewife. The former is exciting but dangerous, the latter is safe but requires adherence to traditional gender values. Using the language of Eileen Chang, one can say that the former is a red rose, the ideal male object of desire, and the latter a white rose, the proper wife and good mother who remains in the home. Men want but cannot have both, thus their distinction is but a reflection and manifestation of men's desires. Neither the New Woman nor the housewife can escape this kind of phallocentric typology, and in the end must abide by the guidelines prescribed by male desire.

David Fraser has pointed out that the advertisements for cigarettes and medicine originated with nineteenth century missionaries.[7] Not only were these advertisements created exclusively to sell Western products, but some of the foreign merchants selling Western products also had direct connections with the opium trade. The same connection applies to the relationship between advertisement and the colonization of consciousness or desire. Most of the products advertised in *Shanghai Guide* that presented themselves as modern had packages printed with English words, implying the equivalence between modernity and things Western. While kindling the readers' desire for modernity, they also imply that the West is the object of this desire, and the Westernized modern woman thus becomes the simulated West that may fulfill this desire. Neither making a totalistic argument about the West or Japan's colonization of China (or other imperialist invasion) as the sole criterion for considering Chinese woman's modernity, nor stripping Chinese men or women of their subjectivity or agency, I hope to have demonstrated here simply the intimate relationship between the modernity of the modern Chinese woman and the colonizing foreign cultures, something of how this kind of cultural colonization in turn influenced and restricted gender relations in modern China. Semicolonial, capitalist, and patriarchal controls converged in the construction of feminine modernity, so as to persistently and effectively contain modern Chinese womanhood.

Notes

This article is partly based on my earlier essay, "Shanghai Women of 1939: Investigating Chinese Women's Modernity from a Postcolonial Perspective" [1939 nian de shanghai nuxing: cong houzhimin lunshu de jiaodu kan zhongguo xiandai nuxing zhi xiandaixing], *Lianho wenxue* 115 (May 1994): 139–48. The bulk of the original essay was translated into English by Eileen Cheng, whose help I gratefully acknowledge. My gratitude also goes to Jason Kuo for encouraging me to revise this essay for the current anthology.

   1 *The Lure of the Modern: Writing Modernism in Semicolonial China, 1917–1937* (Berkeley: University of California Press, 2001).

   2 The term *Haipai*, used of the more popular and Westernized orientation of Shanghai writers and artists, is usually distinguished from *jingpai*, used of the classicism and traditionalism of the Beijing writers. Originally *Haipai* was used as a derogatory term by the more conservatively oriented critics, but over time, it became a neutral, if not positive, and helped emphasize the uniqueness and openness of Shanghai's cosmopolitan culture.

   3 See my "Gender, Race, and Semicolonialism: Liu Na'ou's Urban Shanghai Landscape," *The Journal of Asian Studies* 55.4 (November 1996): 934–56, for a summary of gender politics in colonial and semicolonial contexts.

   4 For a discussion of the *dōben-dōshu* ideology, see Peter Duus, "Introduction," in *The Japanese Informal Empire in China, 1895–1937*, ed. Peter Duus, Raymond Myers, and Mark R. Peattie (Princeton: Princeton University Press, 1989), xxvi.

   5 The story is the title story in his collection *Platinum Statue of a Female Nude* (Shanghai: Xiandai shuju, 1934), 17.

   6 See n. 1 above.

   7 "Fumigating the Body Politic: The Advertising of Nationalism in Republican China," unpublished material.

9
Art Deco and Modernist Art in Chinese Calendar Posters

Ellen Johnston Laing

In Europe during the first decades of the twentieth century, painters and sculptors shifted their subjects and motifs from the representational to the abstract. At the same time, craftsmen who made fine furniture and interior appointments rejected the prevalent notion of recycling established styles in favor of new ideas more compatible with the world of modern machinery. New decorative design elements and styles, eventually to be known as Art Deco, were subsequently seen everywhere as ornaments on public and utilitarian art, ranging from fashions to teapots to posters. Ultimately, the principles of Art Deco spread from Europe to the United States and to China. This paper first introduces several salient characteristics of Art Deco traditions. It then identifies and discusses the influence of Art Deco on the popular Chinese calendar posters (*yuefenpai*) of the 1920s and 1930s, focusing on the decorative borders, on the domestic interiors rendered as backgrounds for depictions of modern women, and on typography.[1]

The term *Art Deco* came into common usage in English in the late 1960s and is used primarily to refer to the decorative arts and to certain types of architecture and architectural decoration. Art Deco is not a unified movement, it has no founder, no written manifesto, and no philosophy. It is difficult to pin down because it is a meld of disparate artistic tendencies.

Some critics assert that the time period encompassed by Art Deco covers the years between the two world wars; others push its origins back to around 1900; others extend its influence to include the Art Deco revival of the 1970s. All agree, however, that 1925 was a pivotal year, for in that year a grand exhibition titled the "Exposition Internationale des Arts Décoratifs et Industriels Modernes" opened in Paris. It was originally scheduled a decade earlier, but the First World War forced its postponement. The 1925 exhibition displayed the latest in architectural designs and interior decoration, including unique furniture and decorative pieces carefully handcrafted for affluent patrons from rare and luxurious material like ebony, ivory, and shagreen (fish skin). The artists freely borrowed ideas from ethnic cultures and from modernist schools. From ancient Persian and Egyptian traditions came the sunburst motif and the new color schemes of blues and greens, along with orange and scarlet. From cubism came geometric motifs and sharp color contrasts. In the 1920s and 30s glassware, metalwork, wallpaper, carpets, and pottery were ornamented with abstract designs or stylized motifs of deer, gazelles, antelope, women with dogs, and felines, fountains, and sunbursts.[2]

After 1925, as museums began to hold special exhibitions of contemporary decorative arts and department stores began to make them available to the general public, these onetime-luxury goods came "within the reach of the ordinary purse."[3] Quickly, Art Deco became international, transcending social class, and uniting architecture, fine decorative art, and the cheapest consumer goods. In the United States, the skyscraper and the cinema would be recognized as icons of Art Deco architecture. Art Deco impacted fashion and accessories, furniture and interior decoration, posters and typography, package and industrial design, and automobile design.[4]

In the late 1920s, the strong simple shapes; geometric designs; intersecting squares, circles, and triangles; angular chevrons and zigzags; smooth curves; and stylized representations of modernist art began to dominate the Art Deco decorative language.[5]

After the initial spurt of rich luxury materials seen in the 1925 exhibition, furniture and interior decoration began especially to feature clean lines. By the 1930s, plastics, chrome, and glass, esteemed because of their bright surfaces and their convenience for machine mass production, began to replace wood as the preferred materials for chairs and tables.[6] Electric light fixtures of abstract form replaced the imitation candlesticks and replicas of gaslight globes, both holdovers from earlier eras when candles and gas provided illumination. The old-style lighting emphasized the ornament of the fixture, but the new style depended upon the light itself for decorative effect; thus greater emphasis was placed on the structure of the fixture, rather than on its decoration.[7] By the 1920s in the West, small mirrors had been moved out of the ladies' private boudoir and into the public living room, where their reflections of light made a small room look larger. Secondary furnishings included bookends shaped like miniature skyscrapers and ashtrays made of shiny steel with brightly colored, shiny, enamel linings.

Posters and advertisements were strongly influenced by Art Deco principles, which affected the layout of the advertisements, the appearance and rendition of the figures and landscapes, and the typography. Art Deco layout tended toward the diagonal and unexpected irregular organization. It included "dynamic designs, powerful symbols, simple designs, images reduced to the essentials of product and brand name, sharp linear compositions floating in flat areas of background color, aerial or diagonal perspective and sans serif typefaces."[8] The brand name, slogan, or other text could be placed on the diagonal or otherwise tilted to be more eye-catching. In the images, figures were elongated, facial features defined by thin lines, without shadows, or with sharp contrasts of light and dark. The new style of typography featured sans-serif letters. Each letter was custom designed. Some were formed with ruler and compass for crisp, straight lines and arcs of circles. Some letter forms were split into large and small elements, others were shadowed. Dramatic visual effects were achieved by eccentrically arranging parts of a single letter. Visual tension might be created by juxtaposing dots or circles and rectilinear shapes (figs. 1 and 2).

Chinese students and travelers who studied in or visited Paris or London or other European or American cities in the 1920s and 1930s returned home with at least a basic exposure to these decorative trends. Western women's magazines and books entering China, along with Chinese magazines and newspapers, also spread throughout China visions of the latest styles. There was little time lag. A selection of illustrations from a book of modern domestic interiors printed in London in 1933 was published the very next year in *Meishu shenghuo*.[9] During the 1930s, inside Shanghai cinemas like the Paramount, the Majestic, the Cathay, and the Grand, all designed along Art Deco lines, the moviegoer could see Chinese actresses dressed in Art Deco–style clothing acting on Art Deco–designed sets (figs. 3 and 4). Dance halls like Ciro's and the Great East were constructed in Art Deco style (figs. 5 and 6).

In China, the calendar poster is an accurate gauge of popular acceptance of cultural developments, especially since these calendars reached all levels of Chinese society. They first appeared in the early twentieth century and continued to be printed throughout the 1940s. Some were given away by commercial firms, others were displayed in street stalls and sold to ordinary citizens from all walks of life. One of the subjects most depicted in the calendar poster was the modern woman. To be successful, calendars depicting modern women had to reflect the latest fashions in dress and lifestyle. Art Deco quickly showed up in these pictures. Rarely, however, did calendar posters employ a full range of Art Deco ideas consistently blended into a harmonious whole. Rather, Chinese use of Art Deco modes for calendar posters was mostly selective and piecemeal, combining scattered Art Deco motifs with traditional Chinese ones. In addition, entire categories of Art Deco media rarely if ever entered the Chinese calendar poster: glassware, ceramics, metalwork, wallpaper, book bindings, small sculptures, and carpets. Instead, Art Deco and modernistic art in the calendar posters are primarily limited to borders, interior furnishings, and

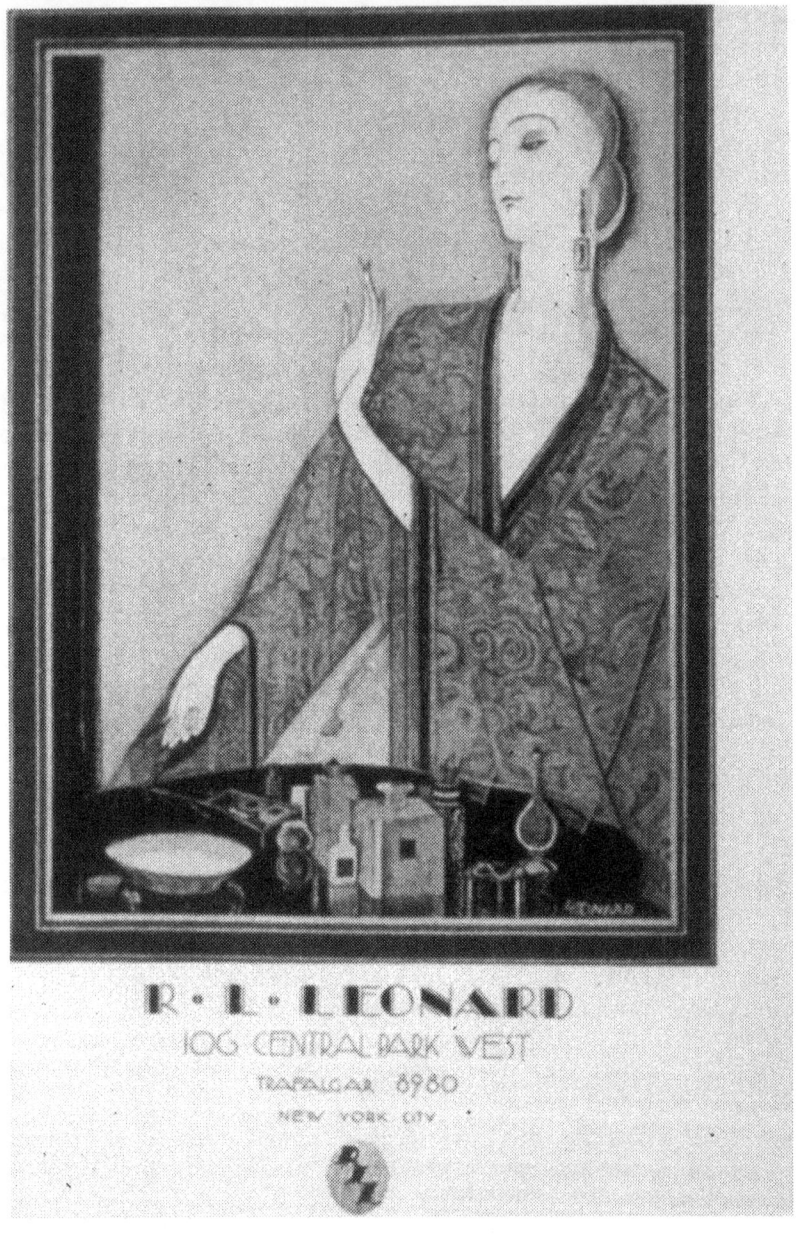

Fig. 1. R. L. Leonard, *Advertisement*, 1926. After Theodore Menten, *Advertising Art in the Art Deco Style* (New York: Dover Publications, 1975), pl. 26.

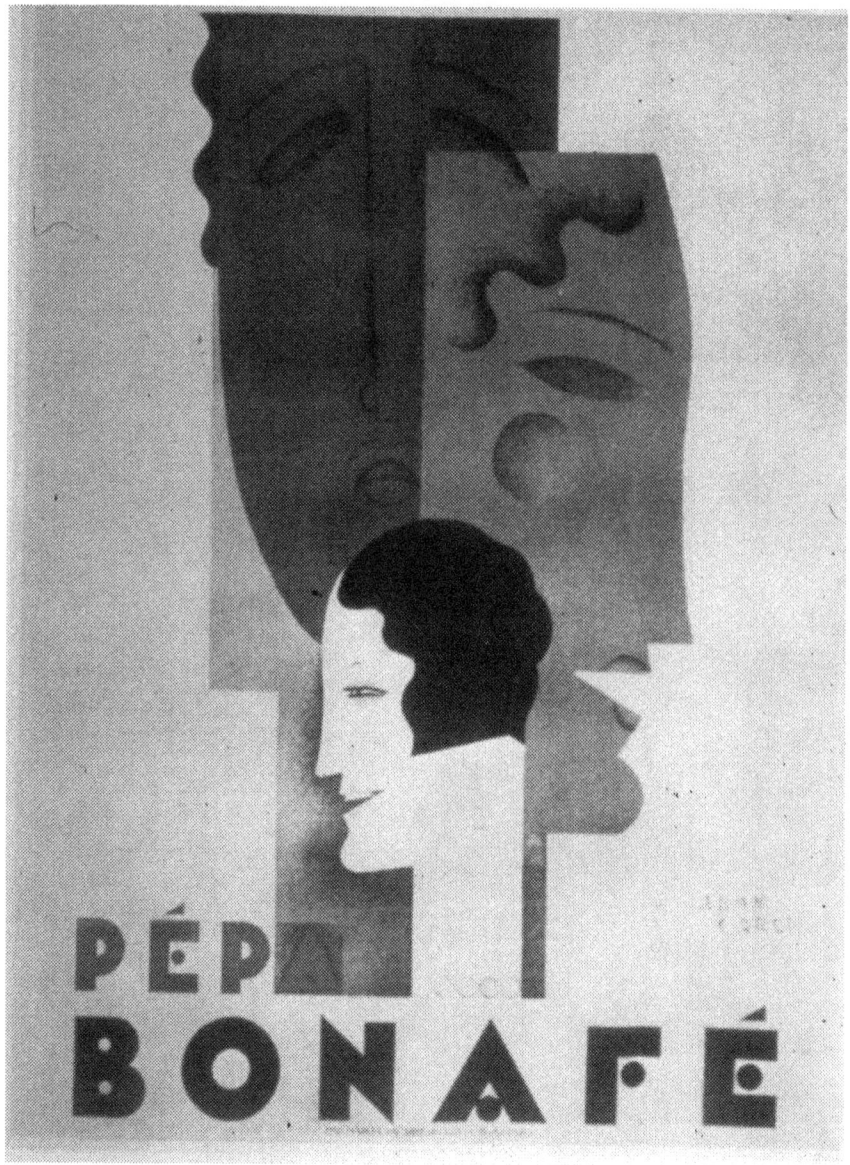

Fig. 2.   Jean Carlu, *Advertisement for a Performer*, 1929. After Menten, *Advertising Art*, pl. 27.

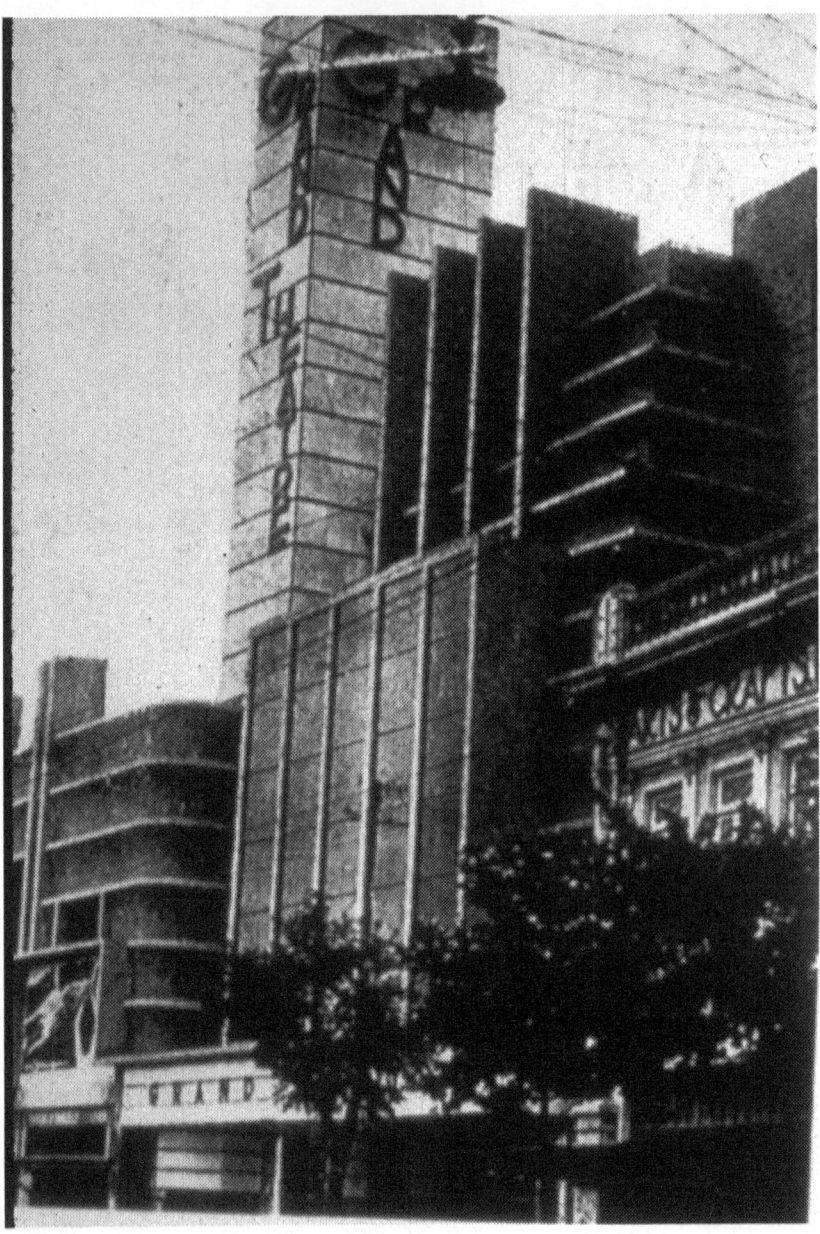

Fig. 3. The Grand Theater, Shanghai, 1930s. After Tang Zhenchang, ed., *Shanghai's Journey to Prosperity 1842–1949* (Hong Kong: The Commercial Press, 1996), p. 221, fig. 48.

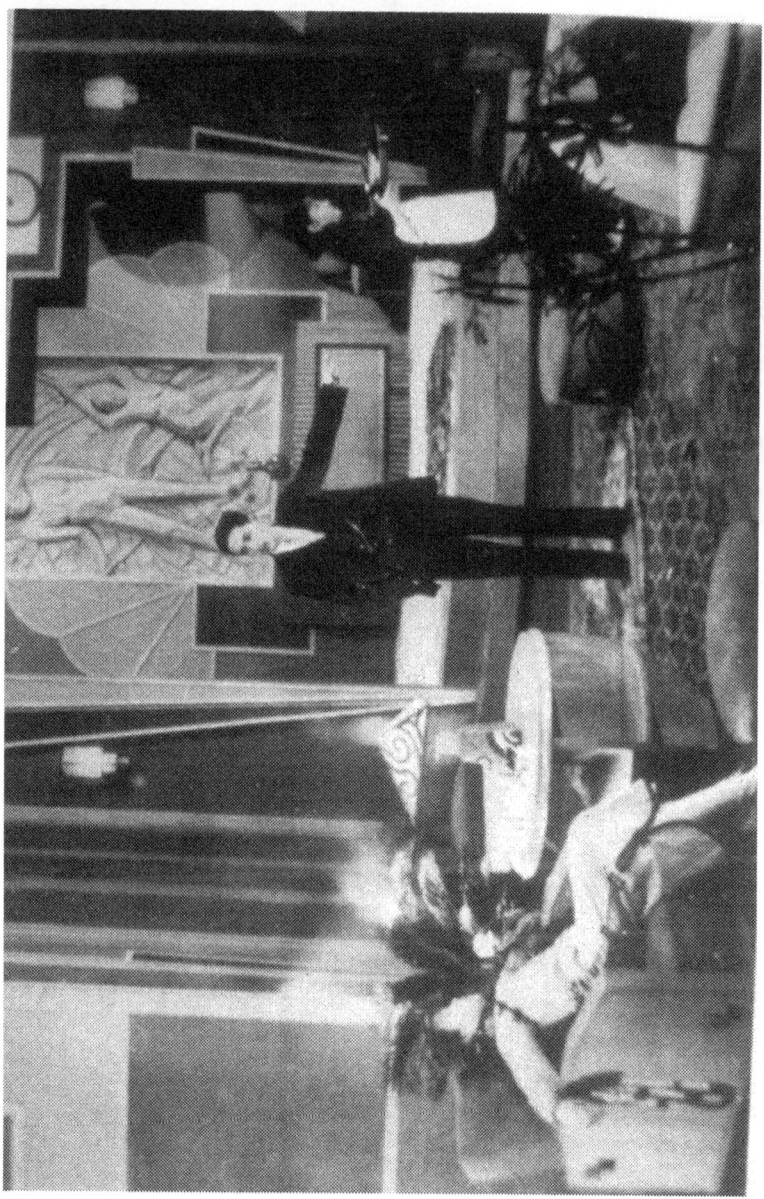

Fig. 4. Scene from the film *Hengniang*, 1931. After *Zhongguo dianying tuzhi* (Guangzhou: Zhuihai chubanshe, 1995), p. 59.

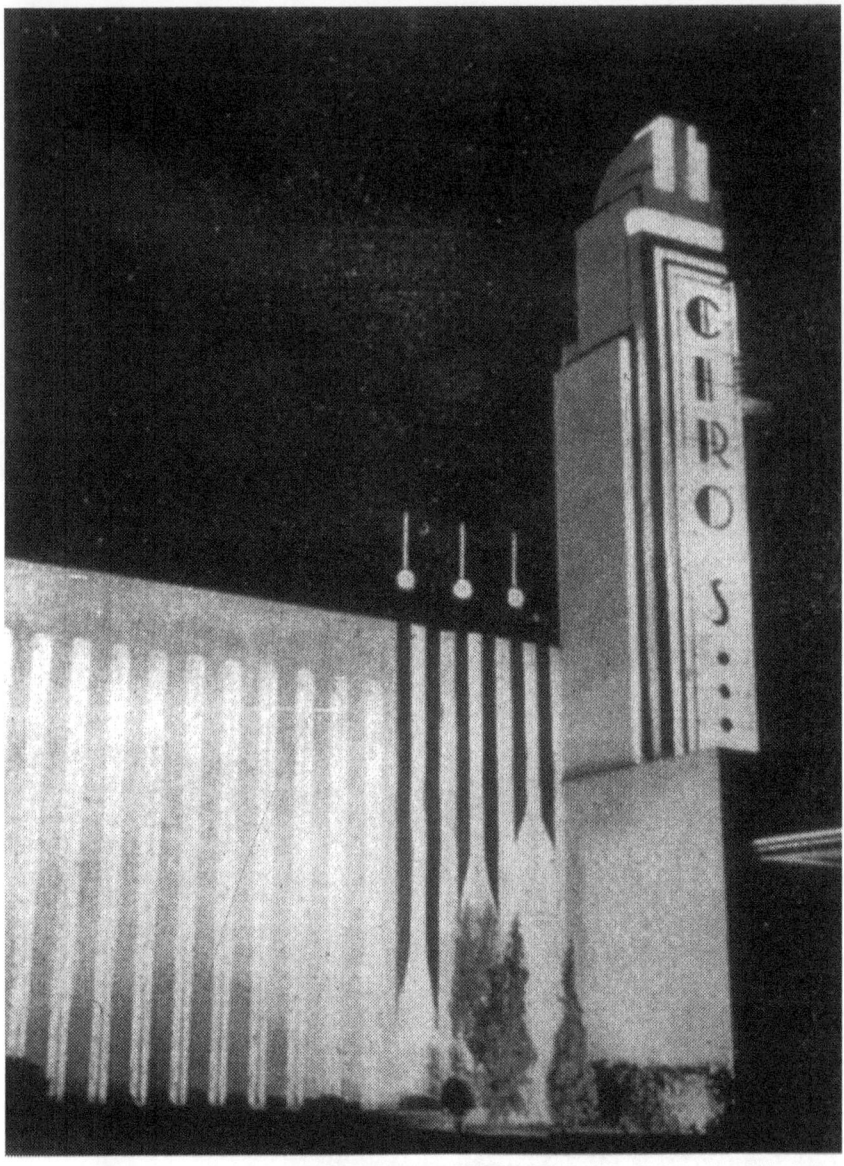

Fig. 5. Ciro's [Dance Hall], 1933. After Deng Ming, ed., *Shanghai bainian lueying* (Shanghai: Renmin chubanshe, 1996) p. 201.

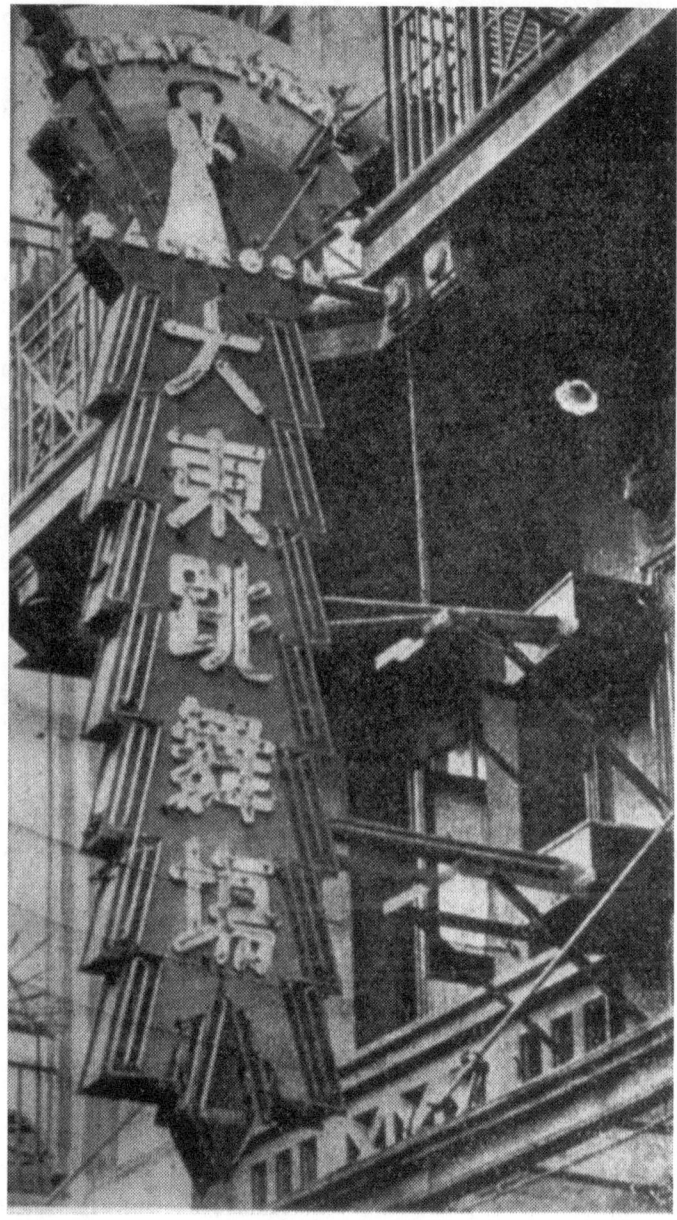

Fig. 6. Dadong Dance Hall, 1930s. After Deng Ming, ed., *Shanghai bainian lueying*, p. 201.

typography. Since examples of more than one category might appear in a single poster, it is impossible to treat each category separately.

A particularly striking Art Deco border surrounds the main image in Xie Zhiguang's (1900–1976) undated poster for an English thread company (fig. 7). The border is a complex arrangement of geometric forms in chevrons, rectangles, and concentric semicircles. Part of the design cleverly repeats the circular shape of the ends of the thread spools, of which four are connected by chains (the chain being the trademark of the thread company). The color scheme is black, blue, and rose, a favorite Art Deco palette. Both the Roman letters of the English text and the characters of the Chinese text are designed along the lines of Art Deco typography. The juxtaposition of angular and rounded forms creates a visual tension and also suggests the pistons of modern machinery, perhaps those used to manufacture the thread.

In the late 1930s Wang Yiman painted the calendar poster advertising Scott's Cod Liver Oil (fig. 8). The abstract design bordering the main image is rendered in brilliant yellow, red, magenta, white, blue, and black. Its distinctly modernistic patterns are distantly related to the stark design on the facade of a 1927 Parisian shop front (fig. 9).

Especially effective is the border on an advertisement for Pirate-brand cigarettes by the Zhiying studio in the late 1930s (fig. 10). Although initially reminiscent of painted ornament on the beams of Chinese palace buildings, this design is different in the following respects. The colors are black, white, acid green, and brown, suggesting worked metals, iron, bronze, and gilded bronze. It was a color scheme never seen in Chinese architectural decoration. The stepped repeats of the ends of the lozenge that fades from black to grey to white is also characteristic of Art Deco design, not Chinese decoration. A comparative example from Western Art Deco advertisement is seen in figure 11. The main design in the lozenge is composed of overlaid or interwoven diamond shapes; this shape is also seen in the lower panel.

The diamond shape was exceedingly popular in China of the 1920s and 30s. It is frequently seen in buttons closing a lady's *qipao*, and is a major motif in the truly elegant white and Nile-green silk ensemble of dress, short jacket, and shoes worn by the woman smoking a Hatamen cigarette in a poster designed by Ni Gengye (fig. 12). Even one of the large soft pillows behind her is covered with an abstract design of diamond shapes in green and gold, like the pillows by a Paris designer (fig. 13), and recalling the low, upholstered sofas and soft pillows associated with the craze in Europe for a Persian atmosphere.

Other, more lasting, innovations in interior decoration are reflected in the Chinese calendar posters. One, an advertisement by the Zhiying

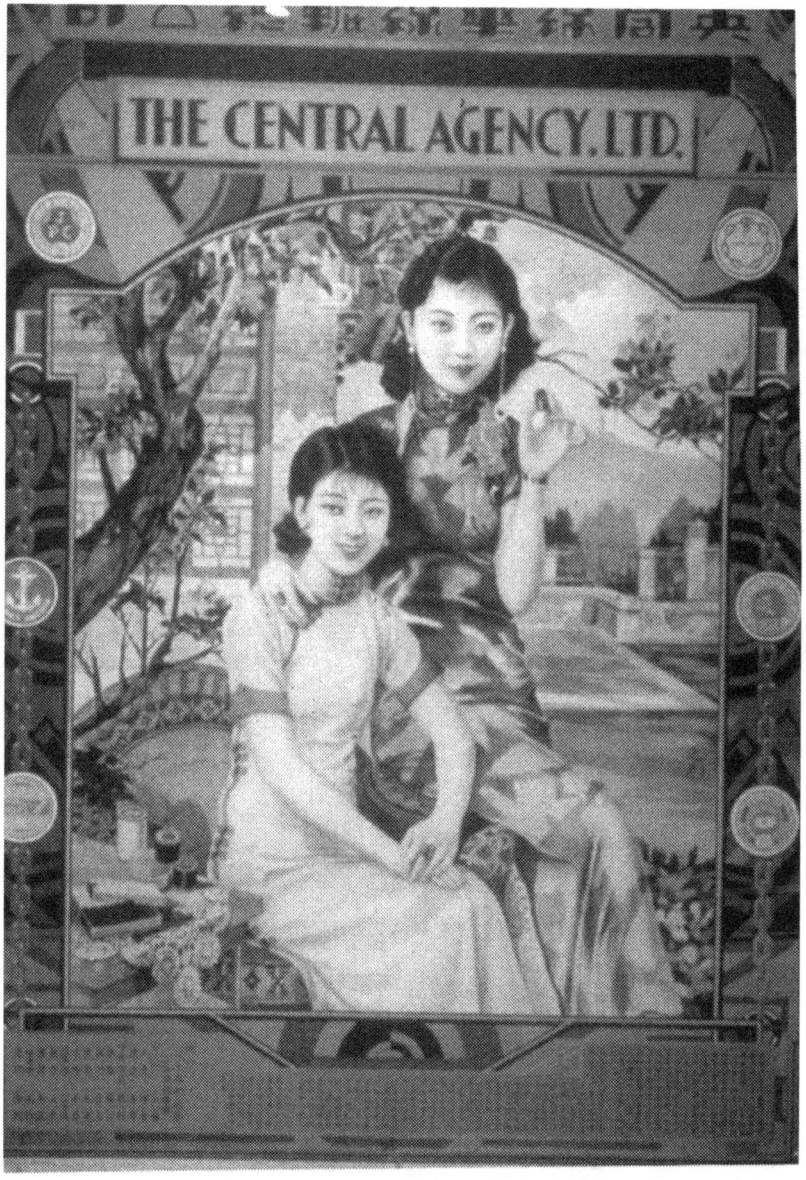

Fig. 7. Xie Zhiguang, advertisement, undated. After Zhang Yanfeng, *Lao yuefenpai guanggaohua* (Taipei: Hansheng, 1996), vol. 1, 43.

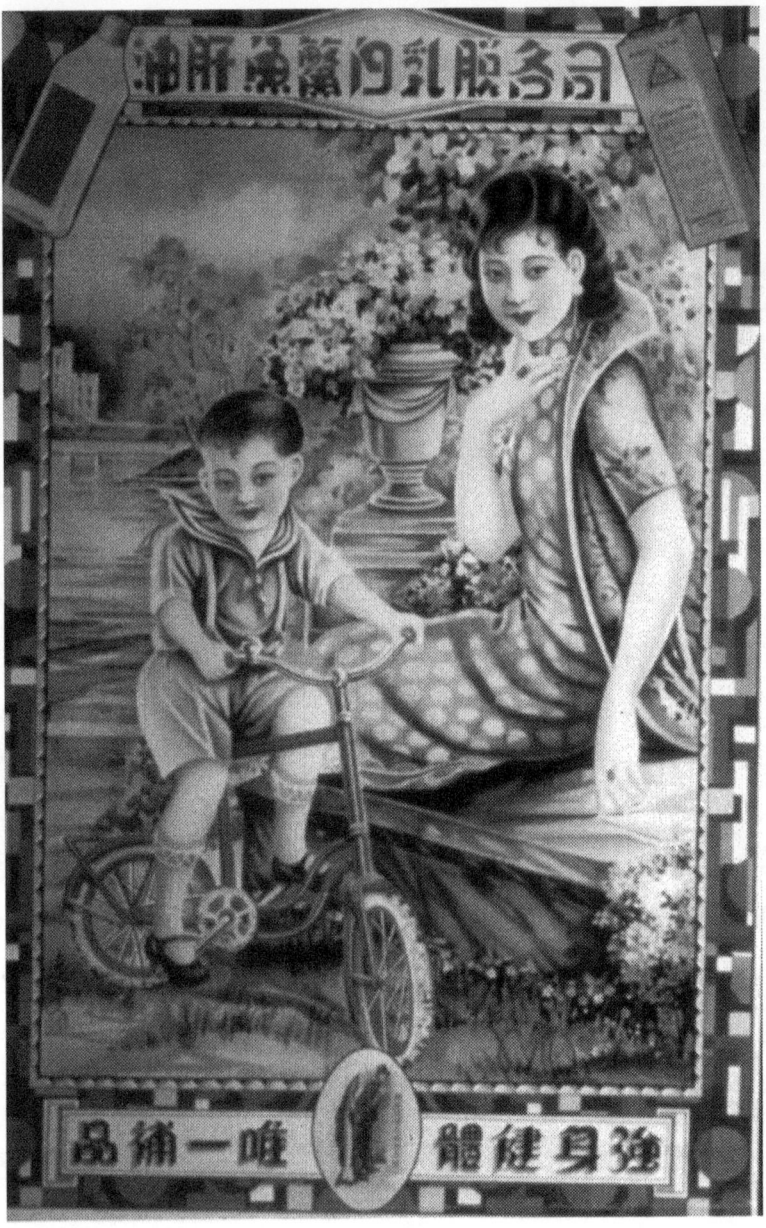

Fig. 8. Wang Yiman, advertisement, undated. After Ng Chun Bong and others, *Chinese Woman and Modernity: Calendar Posters of the 1910s–1930s* (Hong Kong: Joint Publishing, 1996), 54.

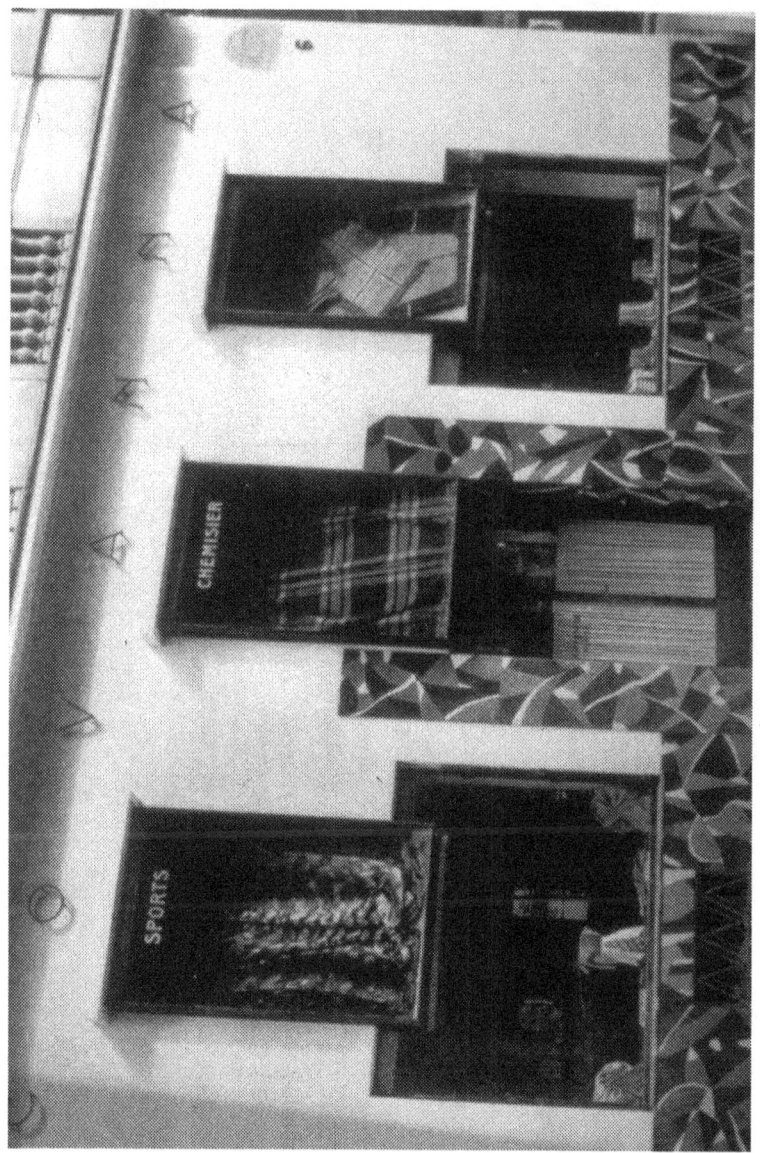

Fig. 9. Pierre Patout, Shop front for Covanna, Paris, 1927. After Bevis Hillier and Stephen Escritt, *Art Deco Style* (London: Phaidon, 1997), p. 43.

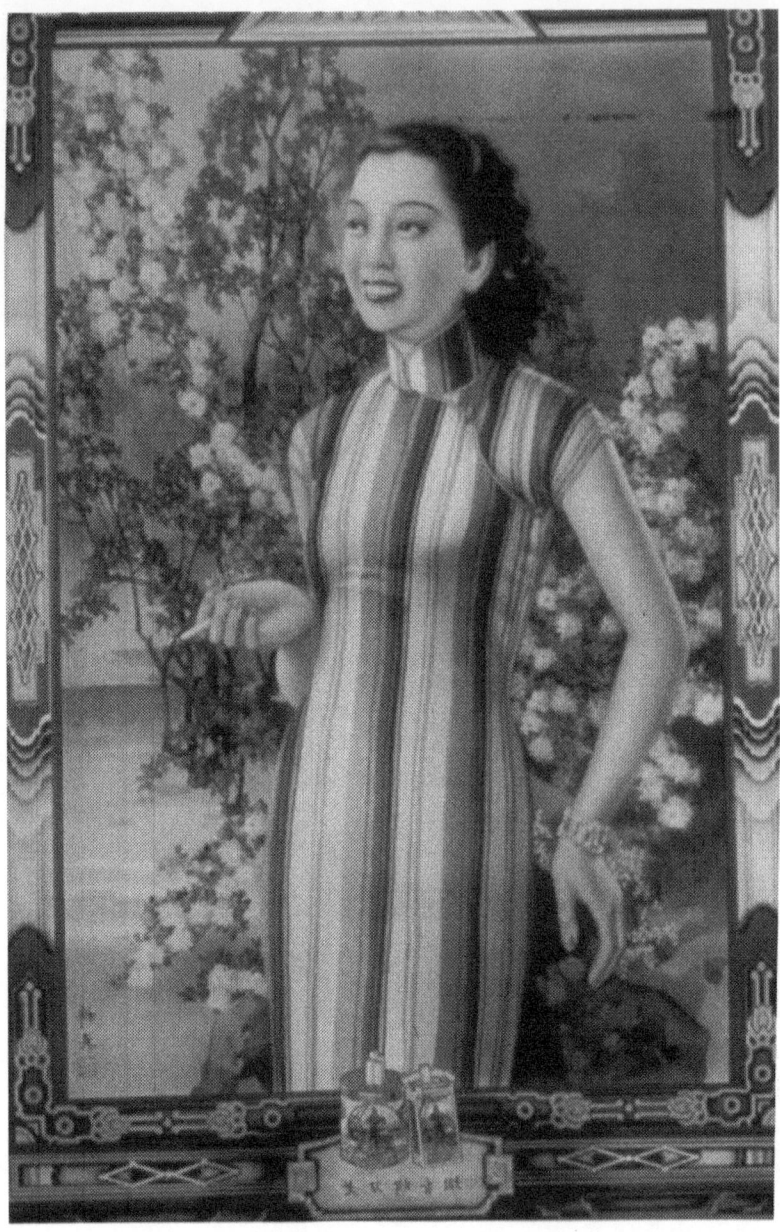

Fig. 10. Studio of Zhiying, advertising, undated. After Ng Chun Bong and others, *Chinese Woman and Modernity*, 45.

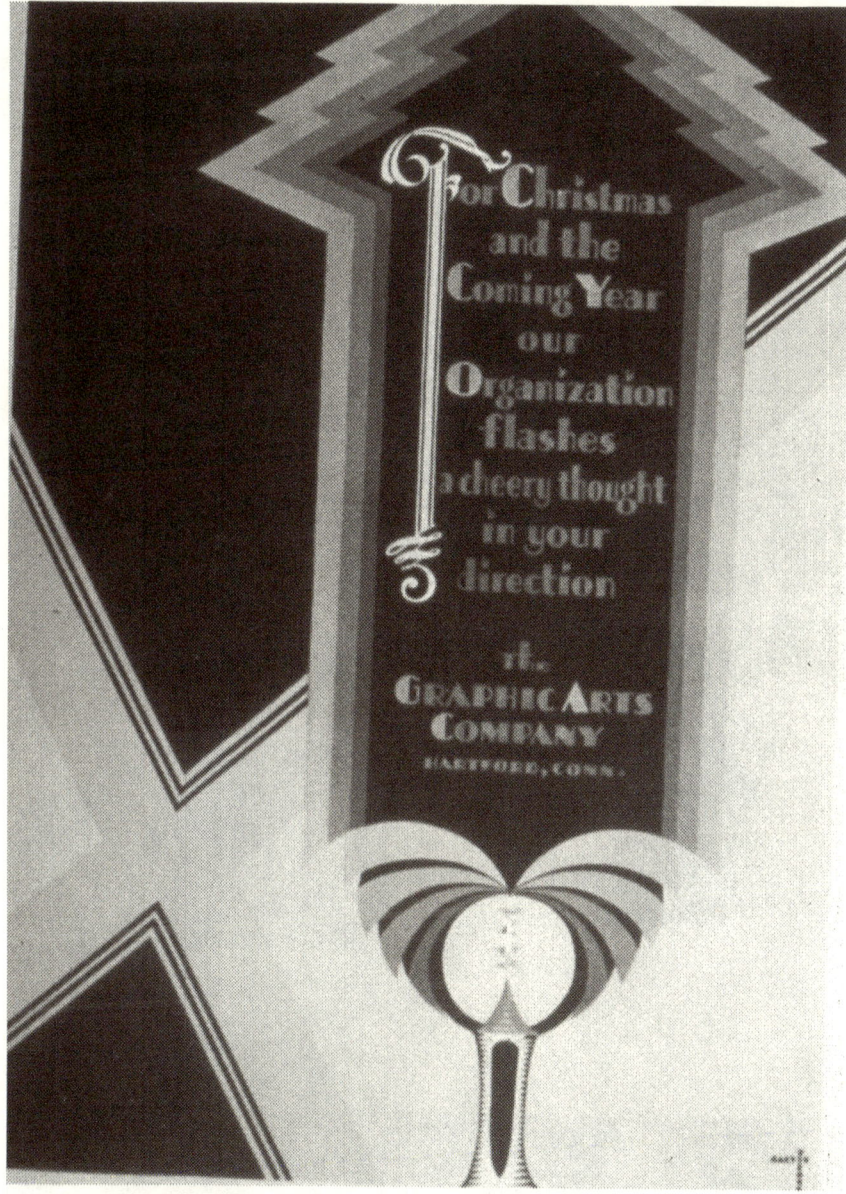

Fig. 11. Calvin Picone, Advertisement for an Art Studio, 1927. After Menten, *Advertising Art*, 35.

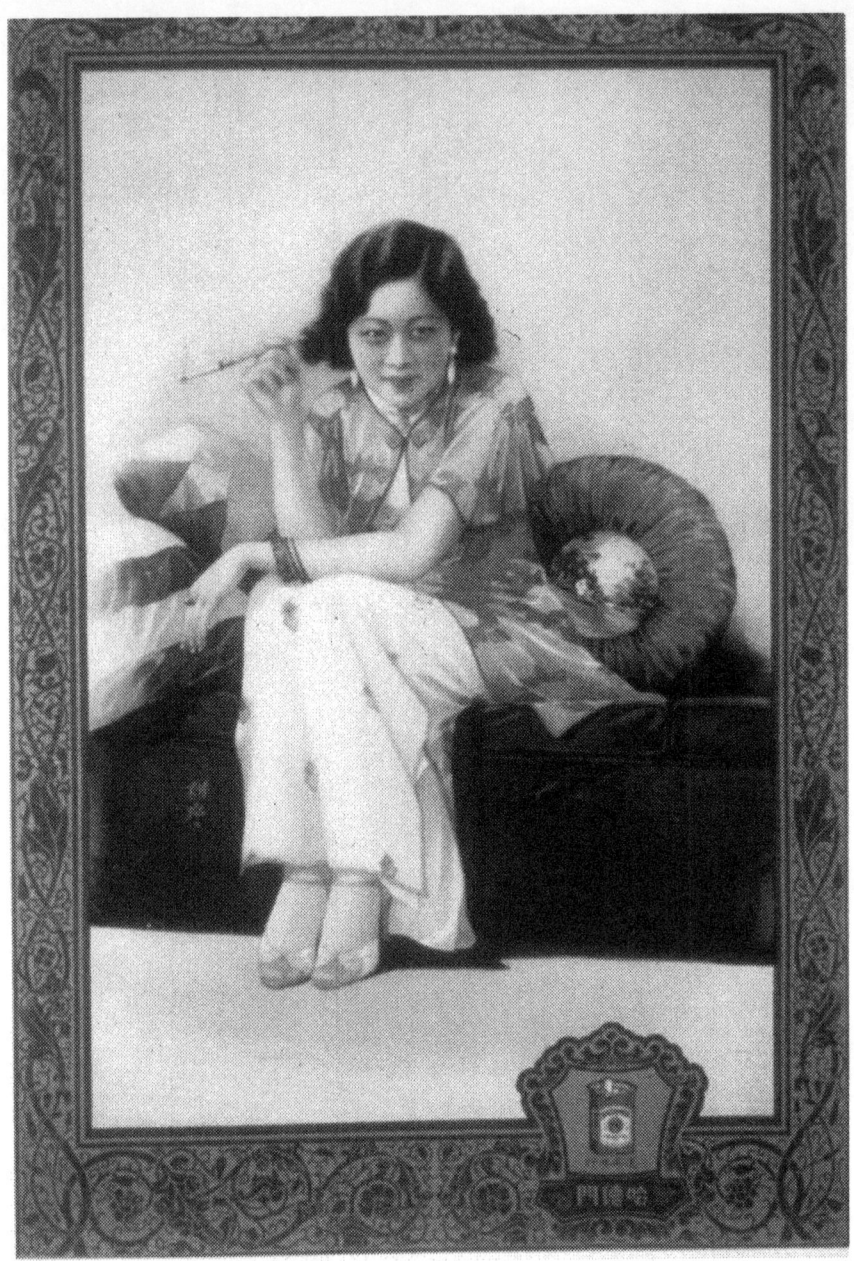

Fig. 12. Ni Gengye, advertisement, undated. After Zhang Yanfeng, vol. 1, 76.

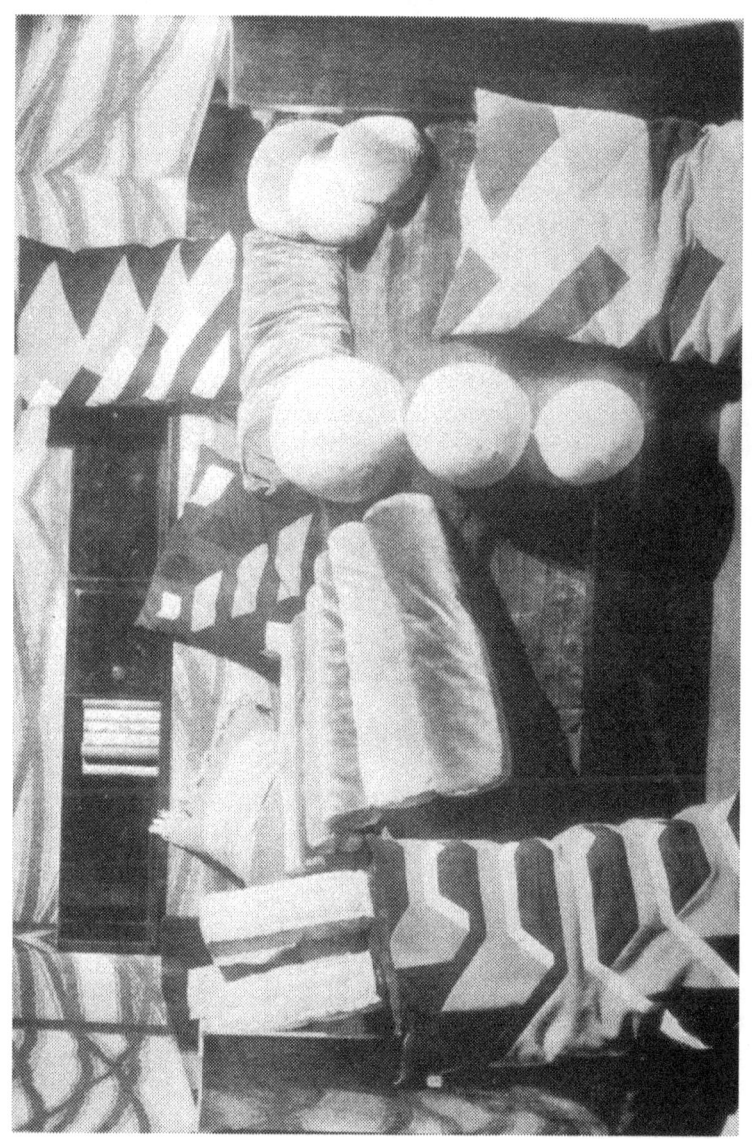

Fig. 13. Pillows by Madame Jean Tranchant. After Theodore Menten, *The Art Deco Style in Household Objects, Architecture, Sculpture, Graphics, Jewelry* (New York: Dover Publications, 1972), pl. 146.

Studio for the cigarette company Huacheng, shows a seated woman leaning one elbow on the top level of a stepped table (fig. 14). The table is
decorated with curved and rectangular patterns and on its lower level is a
steel and red enamel ashtray decorated with a crouching panther, whose
lithe streamlined anatomy is synonymous with power and speed, two
modern obsessions. This interior also boasts additional chevron and triangular patterns on the chair upholstery and another table has tubular steel
supports and more angular decoration. Artists' abilities to render interiors
varied. The background in an advertisement by Hu Weimin, for example,
is a jumble of unrelated forms and patterns (fig. 15). On the other end of
the scale is an especially well-integrated Art Deco interior rendered by the
Zhiying Studio for a Hatamen cigarette ad (fig. 16). Among the furnishings is a stepped table with a shining surface, holding a metal and enamel
ashtray. Another piece of furniture ornamented with rectangular panels is
visible behind the seated woman. Affixed to the wall to her left is a lighting fixture of a two-tiered soft white material (perhaps glass), relieved by
two diagonal strips. Directly behind the woman is a large, round mirror
and to the left of the mirror is a slender bud vase filled with red flowers.
The room reflected in the mirror is rendered in a pattern of vertical rectangles. Such complex Western interior settings seen in Chinese calendar
posters were copied from Western advertisements and other foreign pictorial sources.[10] In all probability the inspiration for the Art Deco interior
of the Zhiying Studio picture was the room designed by Joseph Urban in
1935 (fig. 17).

A number of other calendar posters have easily recognizable touches
of Art Deco furnishings. Women are sometimes seated in chairs covered
with fabrics in abstract patterns, and these chairs may be accompanied
by other Art Deco furnishings. In one instance there is a bookend on the
nearby table of stepped-block design.[11] In another example, a room screen
is decorated with triangle patterns that echo the angular patterns of the
upholstered chair.[12] In a third illustration, a woman is seated on a low
table supported by bent metal legs, a rare example of the curved metal
furniture that became popular in the West in the 1930s.[13] In yet a fourth example, a woman sits in front of ornamental blocks decorated with nested
semicircles; these in all probability are not pieces of actual furniture, but
an ornamental background used for fashion photography.[14]

In an ad for an electrical appliance company, a model dressed in Nile
green is seated in a photographer's chair, a special piece of furniture that
had a high arm on one side upon which the woman could rest her arm
and strike a comely pose (fig. 18). Such photographers' chairs began to be
used about 1925. The example here is modernized by being pale blue with
white designs and rust-colored edges. The sunburst motif at the corners,

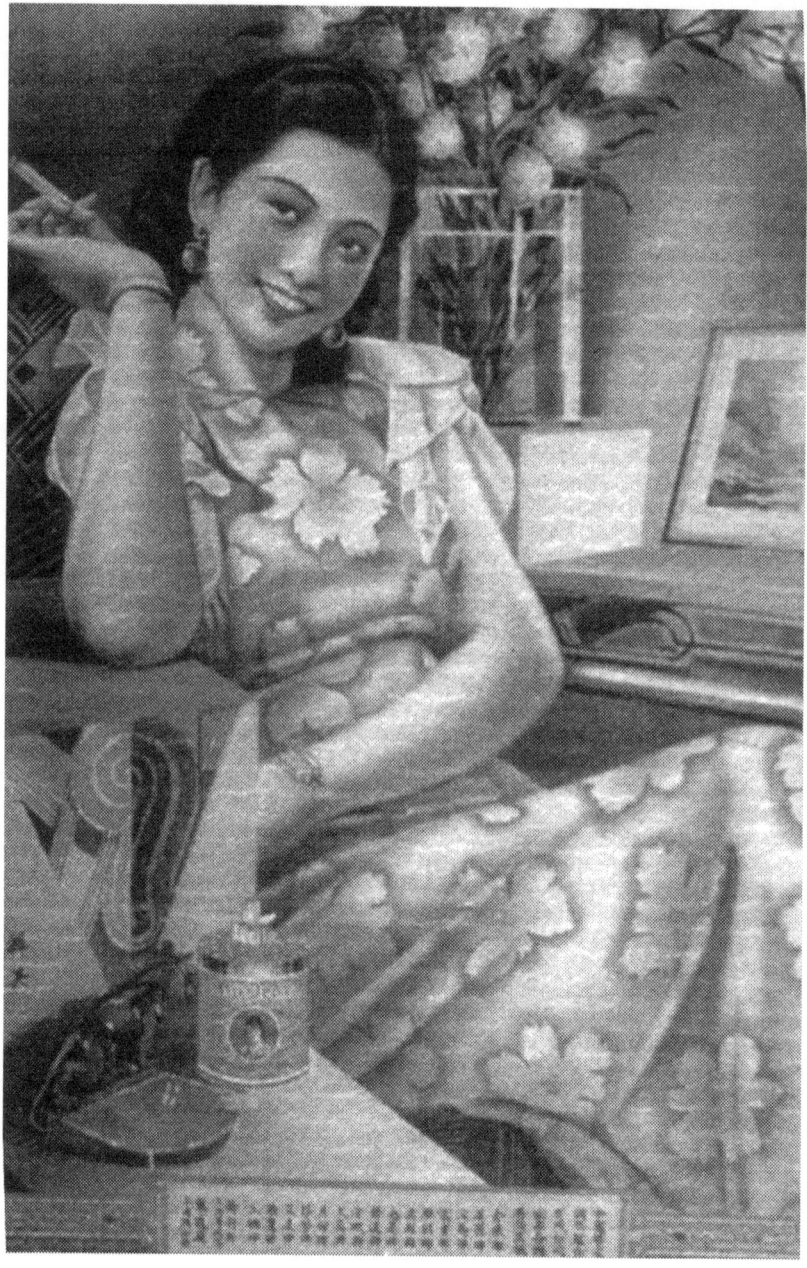

Fig. 14. Studio of Zhiying undated. After Zhang Yanfeng, vol. 2, 78.

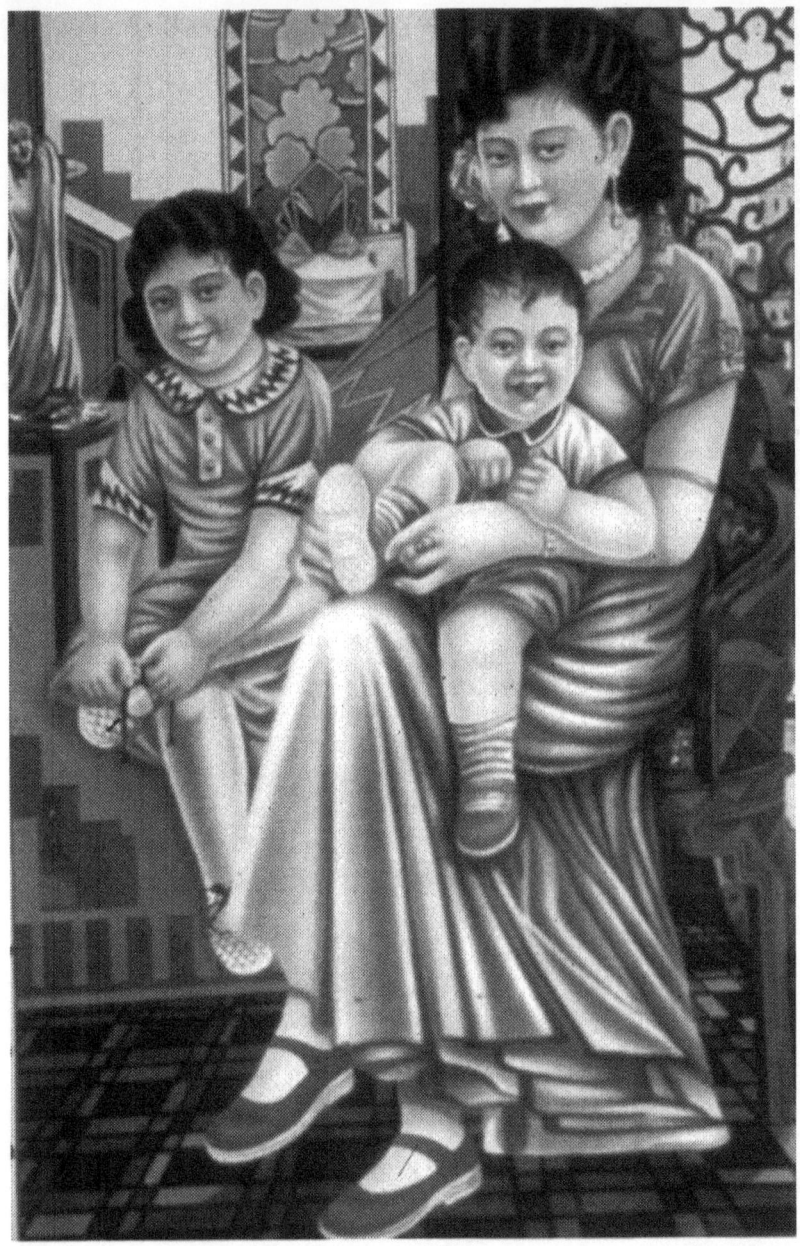

Fig. 15. Hu Weimin, advertising, undated. After Ng Chun Bong and others, *Chinese Woman and Modernity*, 22.

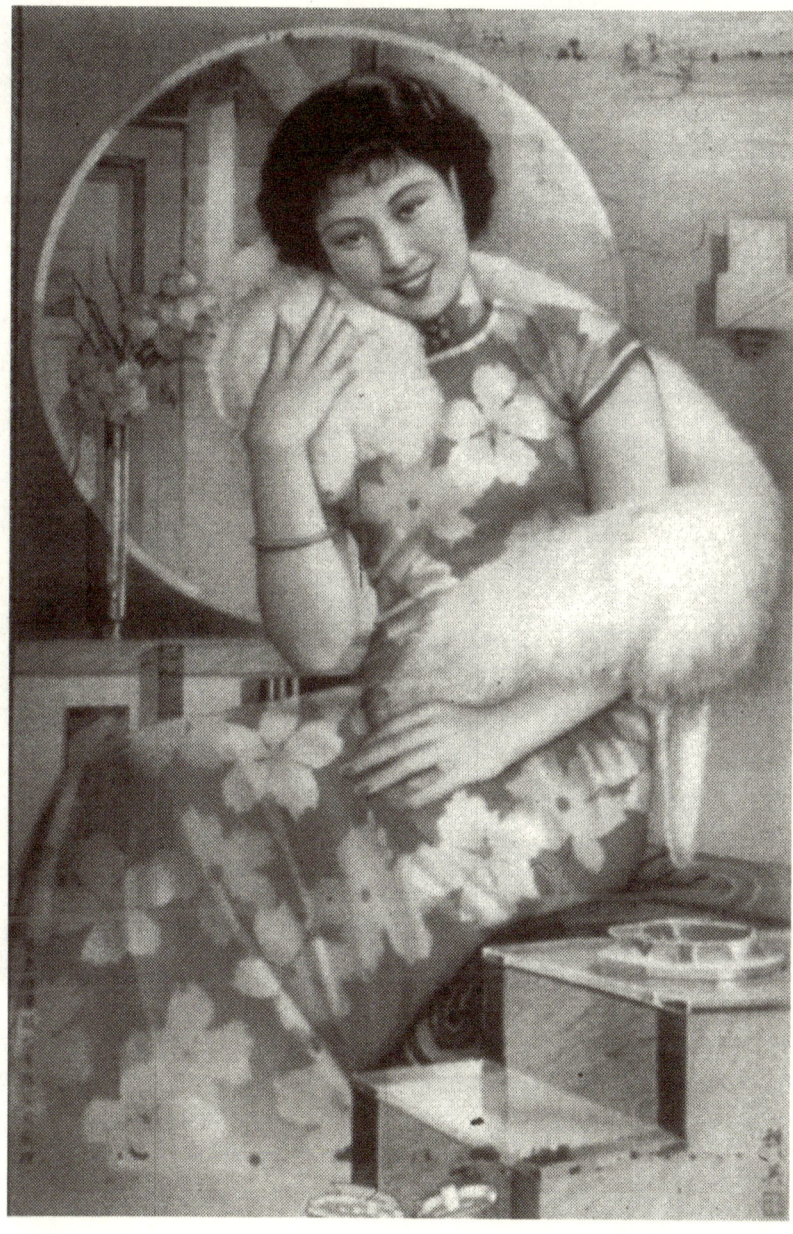

Fig. 16. Studio of Zhiying, advertising, 1930s After Zhang Yanfeng, vol. 1, 16.

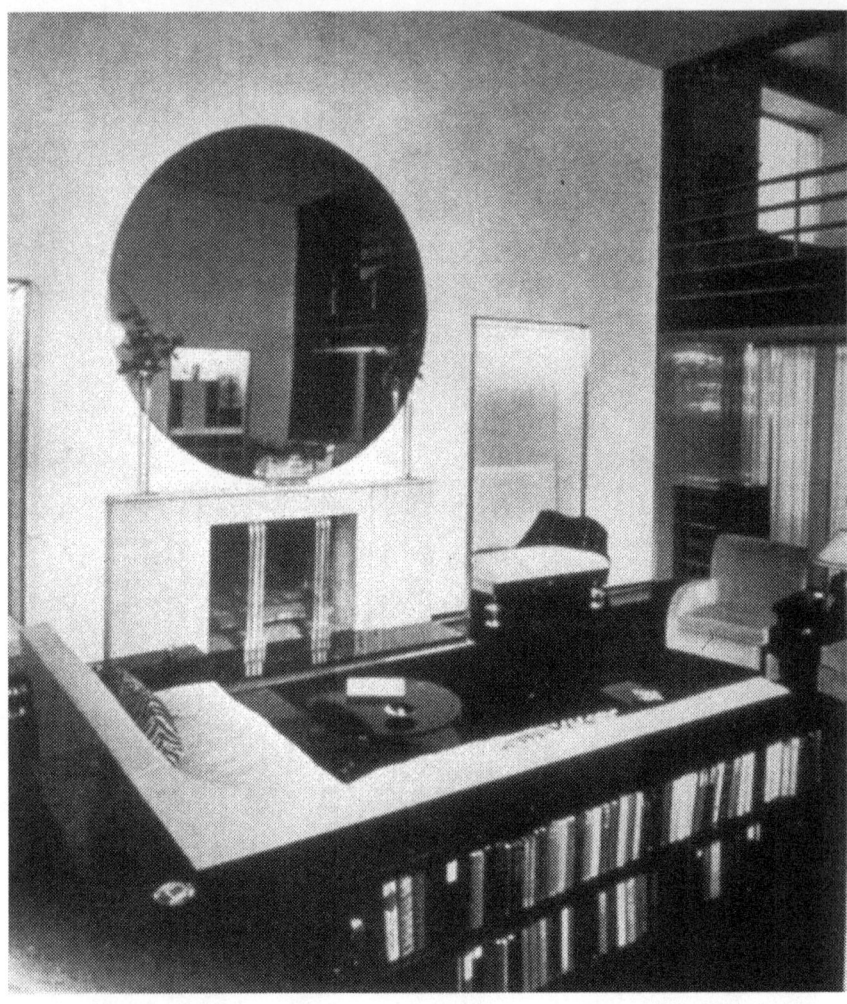

Fig. 17. Joseph Urban, Interior of Apartment designed for Miss Katherine Brush, about 1935. After Martin Battersby, *The Decorative Thirties* (New York: Walker and Company, 1971), p. 118.

a common Art Deco motif, is a rare example in a Chinese context. In the background is a column with a fluted base (a motif that became popular in furniture design of the late 1920s), and the walls are further decorated with birds and abstract designs in blue and white. These designs might very well represent the props for a photographer's studio or perhaps painted backdrops. This equipment appears in the background of several calendar posters, as in the example by Hu Huimin (fig. 19) and in one from a set of four painted by the Zhiying Studio for Weiming Batteries (fig. 20).[15] These props were used for actual photographs of movie stars, like photographs published in *Meishu shenghuo* of Chen Yanyan, modeling the latest mode (fig. 21). In both the fashion photographs and the calendar posters, these abstract background patterns lend an Art Deco flavor to the picture.

In China, the impact of Art Deco poster composition is seen in a limited number of advertisements placed in *Meishu shenghuo* mostly in 1934, but its effect upon the layout of calendar posters was, with one exception, almost nonexistent. Only one calendar poster obviously influenced by Art Deco advertising design has been discovered so far (fig. 22). Here the picture has been divided into three triangles, formed by two symmetrical diagonal lines drawn from the midpoint of the top border to each lower corner. In the large central triangle is the figure, whereas text occupies the two flanking triangles. An immediate prototype might be the automobile advertisement in figure 23.

Art Deco typography, on the other hand, had a major impact on the calendar poster. Until the arrival of Art Deco calligraphy forms in the late 1920s, the calligraphy printed on calendar posters was *kaishu* style, in either its printed or brush forms; occasionally large seal script was employed. However, the extreme Art Deco forms of calligraphy—which included shadowing around each stroke of a character, the conversion of *dian* ("dots") into geometrically accurate forms of perfect squares, triangles, or circles—are effects impossible to achieve easily with the brush. These Art Deco forms of Chinese characters are seen in the calendar posters of figures 7, 8, and 18. Geometric features are best produced by means of modern printing methods and thus reflect a technological achievement that was among the goals of those who sought to modernize China in the first half of the twentieth century. Art Deco calligraphy was not limited to calendar posters of pretty modern women, but also was seen in calendar posters illustrating famous Chinese stories or legends, as in a depiction of a scene from *Hongloumeng*, where a label for the Qidong Tobacco Company is in Art Deco style calligraphy.[16] Sometimes the urge to be artistically creative with calligraphy overcame legibility, as in the example in figure 24. After 1949, Art Deco calligraphy styles seem to have disappeared in China, usually replaced by Mao Zedong's calligraphic style.[17]

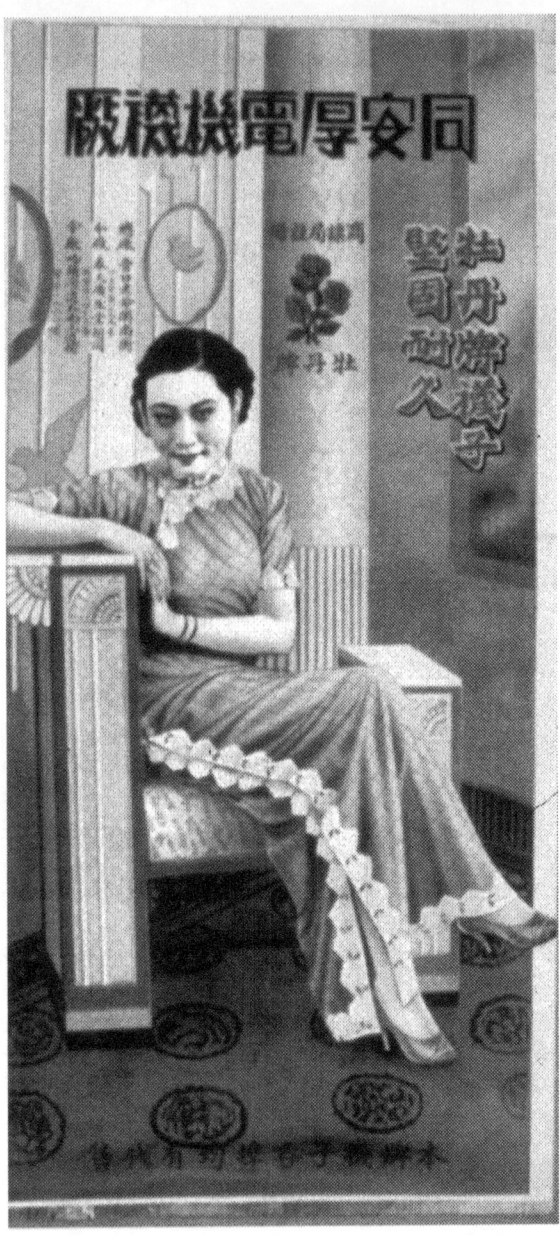

Fig. 18. Anonymous, advertising. SMC Publishing, Inc., collection.

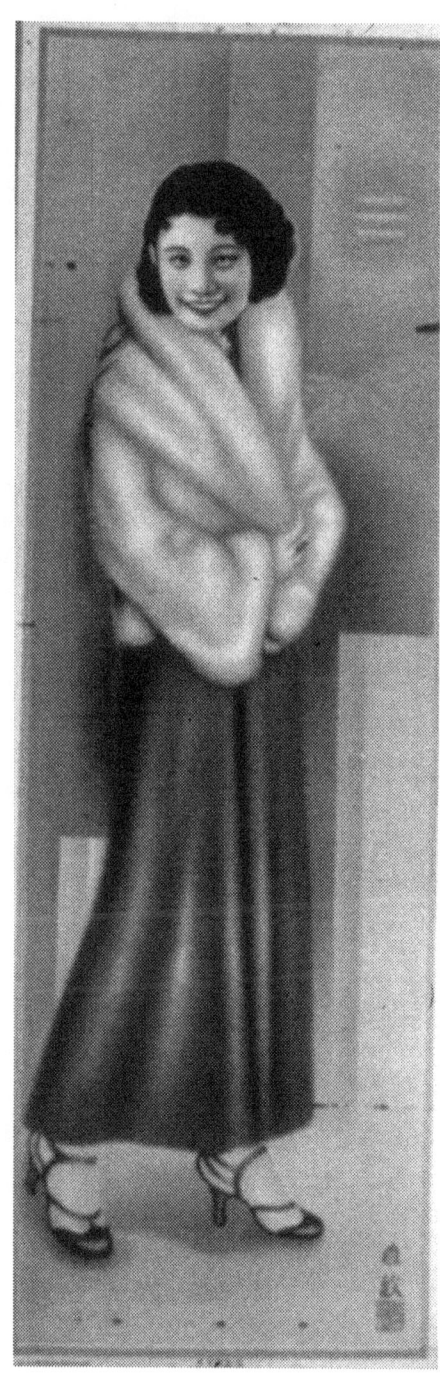

Fig. 19. Hu Wemin, advertising.
SMC Publishing, Inc., collection.

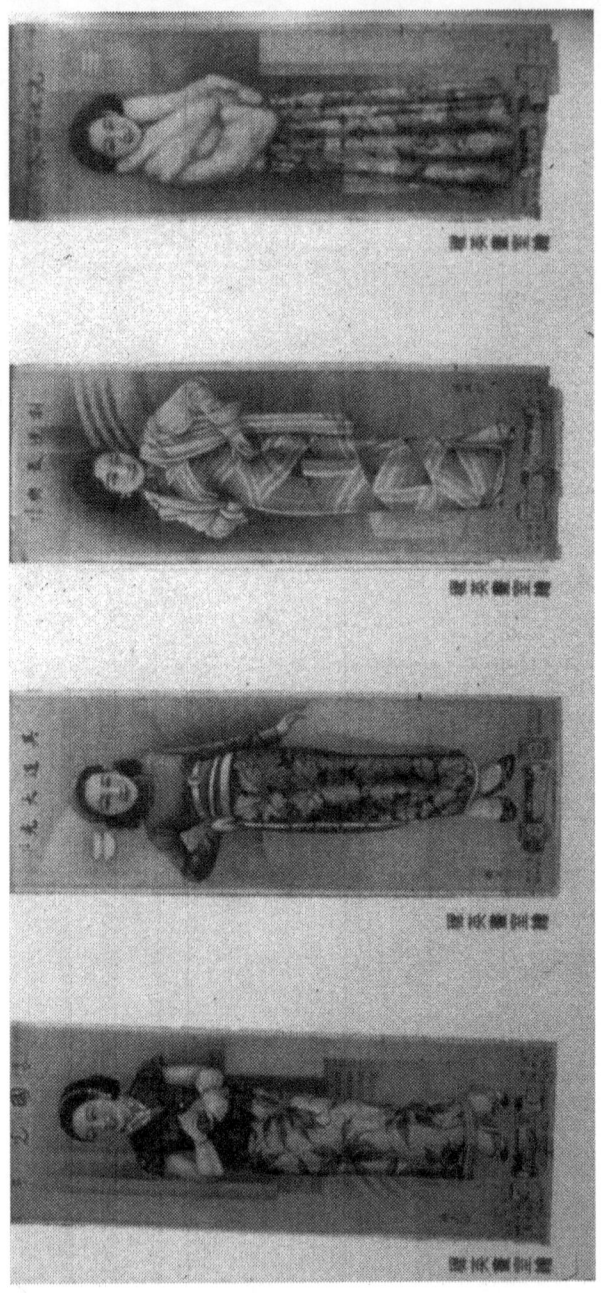

Fig. 20. Studio of Zhiying, undated. After Zhang Yanfeng, vol. 2, 109.

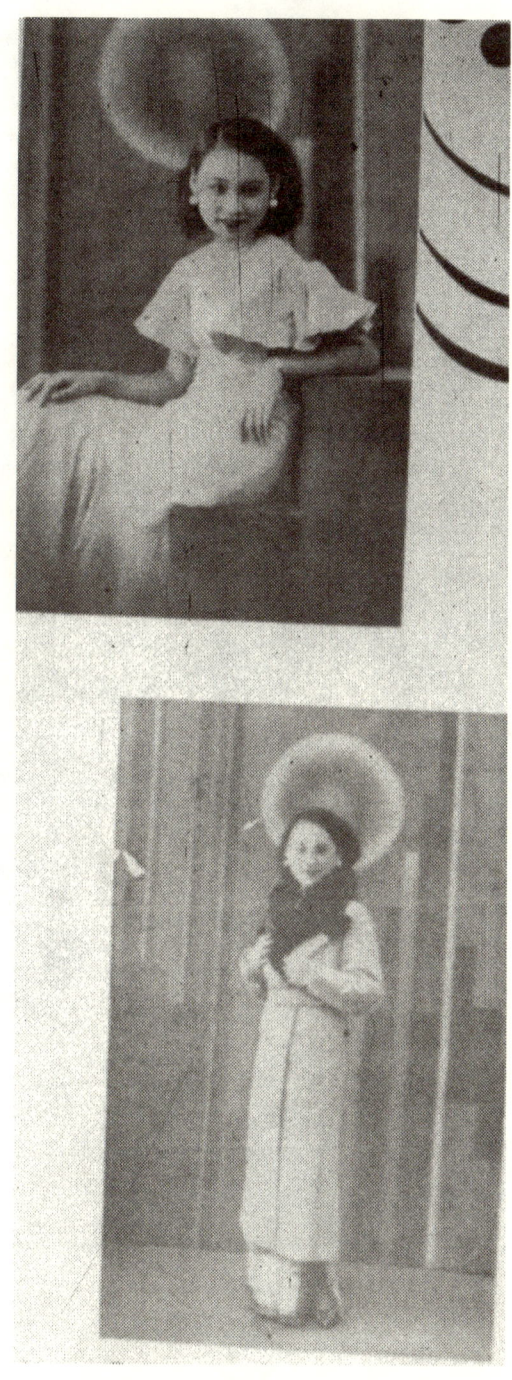

Fig. 21. After *Meishu shen-ghuo*, 2 (May 1934) and 3 (June 1934).

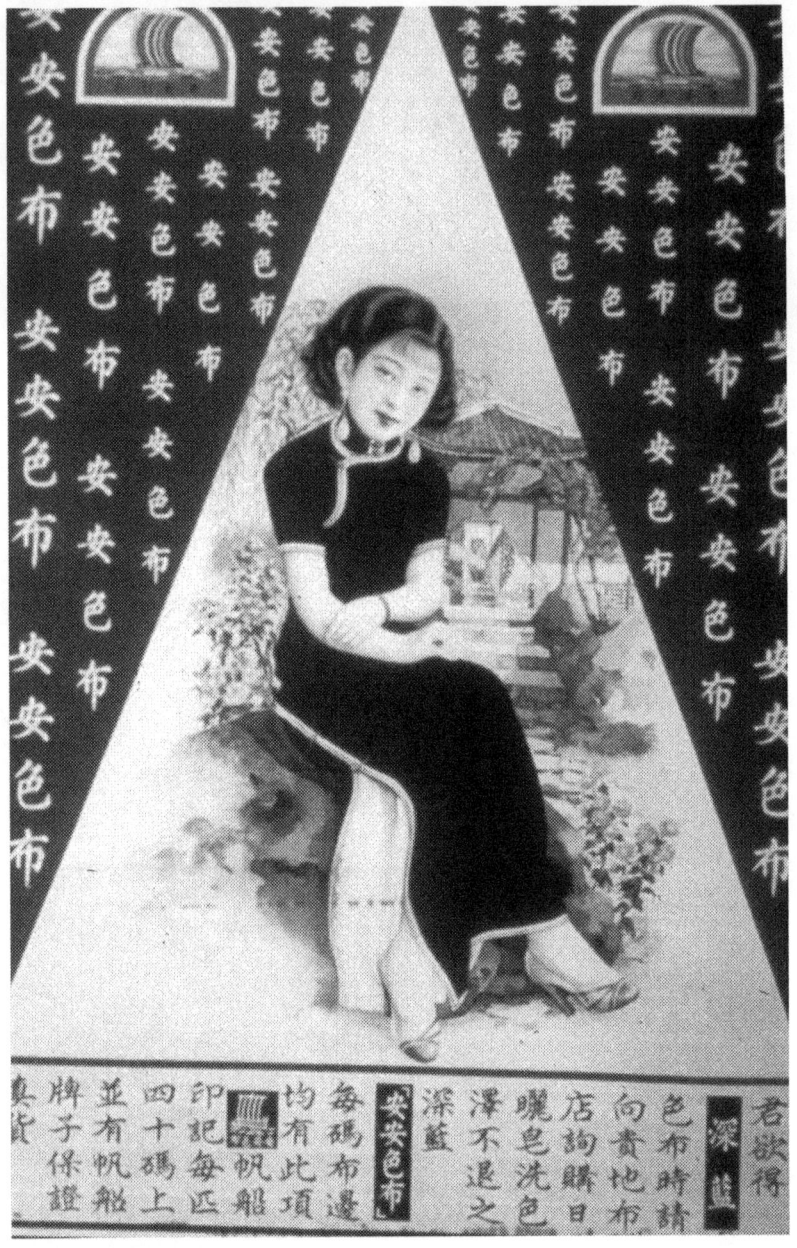

Fig. 22. Anonymous, advertising. After Ng Chun Bong and others, *Chinese Woman and Modernity*, 51.

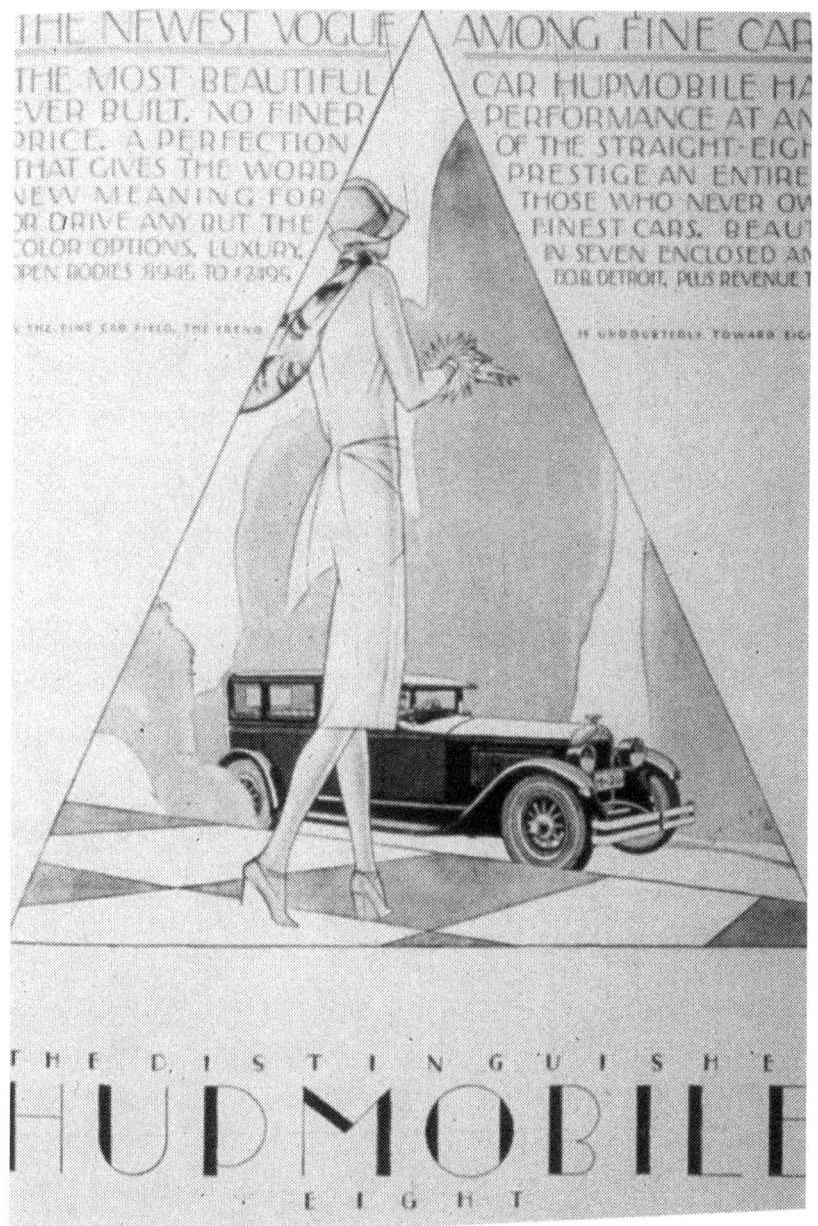

Fig. 23. Stults, Advertisement for Hupmobile, 1926. After Menten, *Advertising Art*, 322.

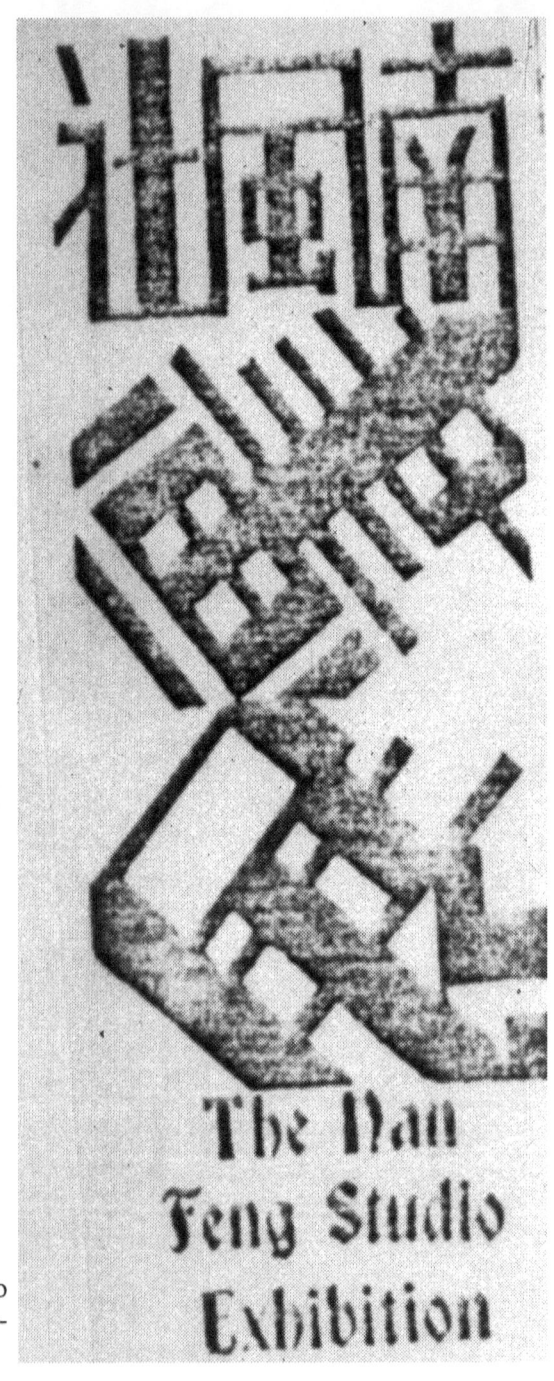

Fig. 24. Extreme Art Deco typography. After *Liangyou* 67 (July 1932): 15.

Hu Boxiang's 1930 calendar poster for Hatamen cigarettes is extraordinary for its thorough and harmonious integration of Art Deco style (fig. 25). The lovely woman portrayed in this picture is identified by some as the famous movie actress Ruan Lingyu (1910–1935). The blue and orange colors and the striped pattern of her *qipao* fabric have no precedents in Chinese costume. The color combination of blue and orange and the stripes that cut the garment into geometric shapes are all favored by Art Deco. Traditional Chinese garments often accentuated the neck, cuffs, and hem with floral or other decorative patterns, but here they are ornamented by wide, undecorated bands, the decoration at the side ending in a broad chevron, a key Art Deco pattern. Ruan wears the so-called Art Deco rose on her shoulder. Since the calendar poster is designed as a hanging scroll, it is supplied with a simulated mounting fabric. The design of this "mounting" is entirely Art Deco in concept and color. It is an abstract pattern of discs, arcs, and bars in the approved Art Deco blue and orange hues. The designer of this "mounting fabric" pattern probably was Zhang Guangyu, a Shanghai Art Academy graduate. He took great care in designing this pseudo-mounting, introducing subtle changes and variations on the basic pattern shapes. On the right side of the image the mounting design is constructed of connected bars; on the left side of the image, of discs and curved forms. Above the central image the design is composed of connected arcs and bars. The intricate frame that surrounds the calendar (fig. 26) at the bottom of the scroll seems to imitate some sort of wrought metalwork (fig. 27). It consists of highly stylized birds, pointed leaves, and flower forms. A related metalwork design frames a panel with small seal characters above the central image and extends to either side to underline the characters expressing wishes for a happy and prosperous new year. It is entirely possible that Zhang's exposure to Western art and his training in modern design at the Shanghai Art Academy enabled him to create this exceptionally sophisticated border. The characters expressing wishes for a happy new year, as well as those for the brand name of Hatamen, are rendered in the highly decorative Art Deco style, and were probably prepared by yet a third person, a specialist in art calligraphy.

By 1930, at least four art schools in the Shanghai area had design (*tu'an*) departments: the Dongfang Art Academy, the Shanghai Art Academy, Xinhua Art Academy, and the National Art Academy of Hangzhou. Chen Zhifo, upon his return in 1924 from studying in Japan, taught commercial design at the Dongfang Art Academy and later at other schools in Shanghai and Guangzhou. He won a wide reputation as a designer, publishing four books on design basics.[18] Hong Qing, the head of the design department at the Shanghai Art Academy, an architect with an interest in architectural decoration, studied in Paris; he later taught at the Xinhua Art

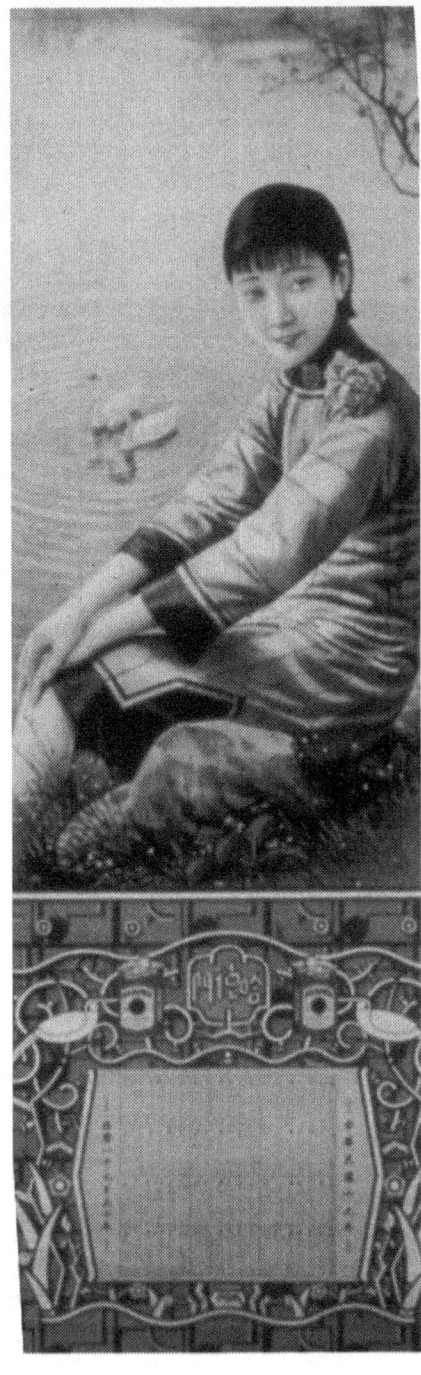

Fig. 25. Hu Boxiang, advertising, 1930. After Ng Chun Bong and others, *Chinese Woman and Modernity*, 41.

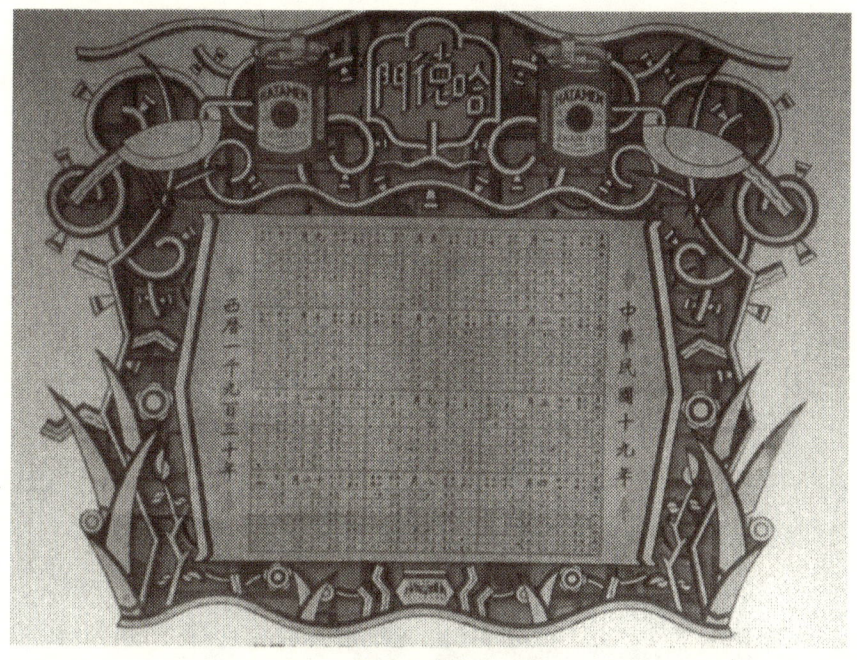

Fig. 26. Detail of figure 25. After Zhang Yanfeng, vol. 2, 54.

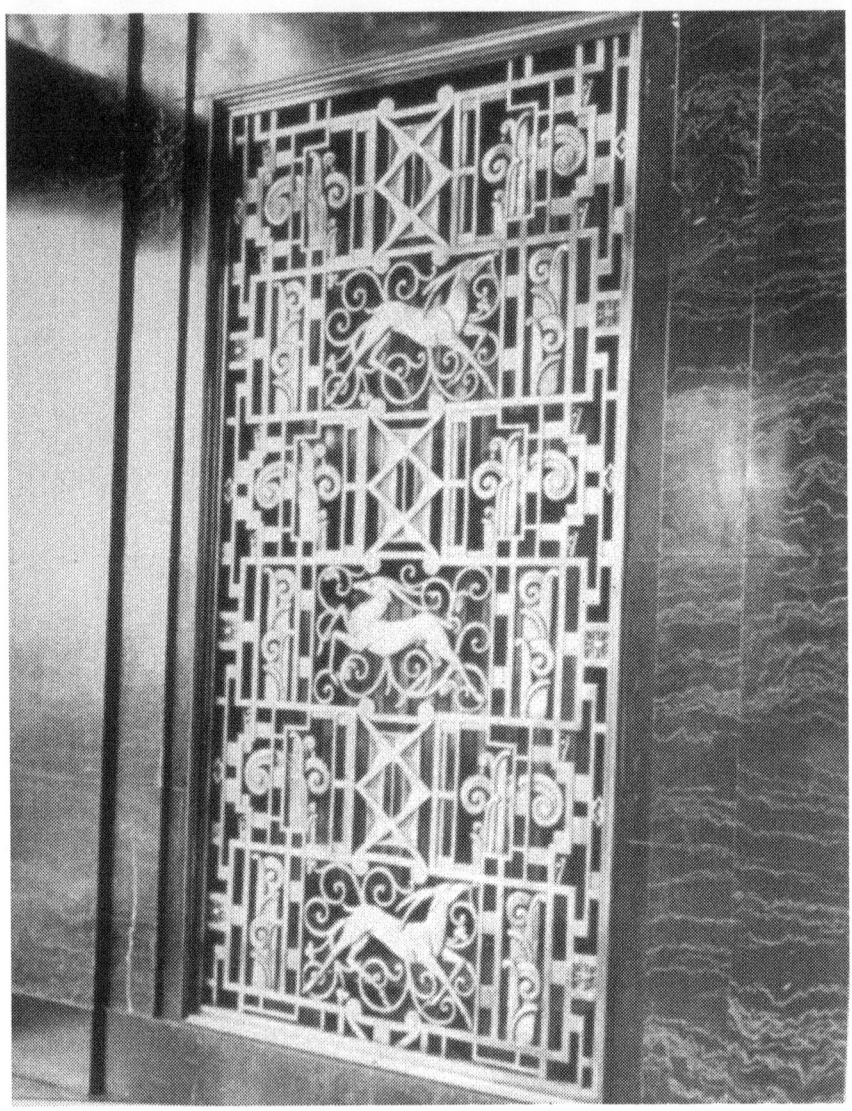

Fig. 27. Rubush and Hunter: Bronze grille, Circle Tower Building, India-
napolis, Indiana, 1929–1930. After Alastair Duncan, ed., *The Encyclopedia of
Art Deco* (New York: E. P. Dutton, 1988), frontispiece.

Academy.[19] Two of the professors in the design department of the National Art Academy in Hangzhou had also studied in France. Lei Guiyuan went to Paris in 1929 and returned to Hangzhou in 1930; he later also published several books on design.[20] Wang Ziyun was interested in architectural sculpture; he studied Western art at the Shanghai Art Academy and then went to France to train, among other places, at the École Nationale Superieur des Arts Décoratifs.[21] A third faculty member of the National Art Academy of Hangzhou, Sun Fuxi, spent the years between 1920 and 1924 in Paris.[22] Upon their return these experts were instrumental in bringing Art Deco ideals into China. They gave their pupils solid training in design principles. One of the most famous designers in China, Zheng Yuebo, was a graduate of the National Art Academy of Hangzhou; he later headed the design department at the Xinhua Art Academy.[23]

The achievements of the students and staff of the National Art Academy of Hangzhou were made known beyond the gates of the academy when the periodical press reproduced photographs of their works. In 1932, a selection of advertisement designs and decorations for lacquer and china wares, along with something called "literary decorations," created by members of a Hangzhou National Art Academy studio, were featured in *Liangyou*.[24] The stylized forms of animals and humans represented in these works, along with numerous geometric patterns, reveal a competent understanding of Art Deco–design principles. In 1936, five decorative works by Lei Guiyuan were illustrated in *Liangyou*.[25] They included the drawing for a reception room, a model for a memorial tower (in abstract stepped blocks), drawings of wall decoration and two designs of elongated figures. During 1934, several issues of the art journal *Meishu shenghuo* reproduced Art Deco furniture and household objects and other items by both Chinese and Western designers. Commercial design attained national recognition as a legitimate art when it was designated a category for entries in the 1937 National Art Exhibition in Nanjing.[26]

The upscale magazines *Liangyou* and *Meishu shenghuo* and the art exhibitions reached a limited segment of society, one that already professed an interest in the arts. Nevertheless, on all other social levels as well, Art Deco was a fact of modern life in the China of the late 1920s and 1930s and its presence simply could not be ignored or avoided. It was so prevalent that people of all walks of life were exposed to it, whether they recognized it as such or not. For the fashionable at the top of the social scale who totally absorbed Western modes, Art Deco design was accepted as the proper style for their dress and accessories as well as for the furnishings of their homes and apartments. Even those who were less committed to becoming entirely Western could not avoid the Art Deco designs that had seeped into their physical surroundings. Artists provided book covers announc-

ing the titles of novels written by modern writers in dynamic Art Deco letters that the intelligentsia must have found attractive and "modern."[27] Art
Deco calligraphy permeated all aspects of Chinese popular culture and
the urban landscape. The urban dweller was surrounded with Art Deco
and modernist abstract, geometric designs. Sides of buses carried Art Deco
advertising placards; the covers of movie magazines sold at open-air stalls
displayed their names in Art Deco styles (fig. 28), newspapers carried advertisements and announcements in Art Deco calligraphy. As discussed
above, the architecture, decoration, and offerings of cinemas were steeped
in Art Deco patterns (figs. 3 to 9). For the ordinary person, the sumptuous
and elegant Art Deco clothing and furnishings seen in the movies probably represented a level of luxury perhaps admired but acknowledged
as unattainable. From this perspective, the Art Deco elements in calendar
posters were just one more way in which the Chinese eye was made aware
of modern art. In some instances, as in the picture by Hu Boxiang with
the border by Zhang Guangyu (fig. 25), the calendar poster was a bridge
between the elite art school and the street picture stall, where it was seen
by even the most lowly.

This initial effort to identify examples of Art Deco and modernistic art
in Chinese calendar posters reveals that their absorption of Art Deco was
sporadic and erratic. Undoubtedly, this is due to the nature of the calendar poster and its audience. In both China and the West, a basic require-
ment for a calendar poster is that the primary subject must be presented
in a representational fashion. Thus, calendar posters always provided
highly accurate pictures for their public. Apparently, the Chinese happily
acquired a calendar with a few Art Deco or modernist motifs incorporated into stylish dresses or jewelry, or easily accepted a few abstract background patterns borrowed from the fashion photographer's studio (which
lent a degree of modern reality to the scene), or tolerated Art Deco frames
around central images, because these elements did not intrude into the
main picture or detract from the human figure. Art Deco might have been
a mainstay in the art academy and the movie world, but the introduction
of Art Deco motifs and modernist styles in the pictorial calendars brought
abstract art forms directly to the streets of Shanghai for all to see.

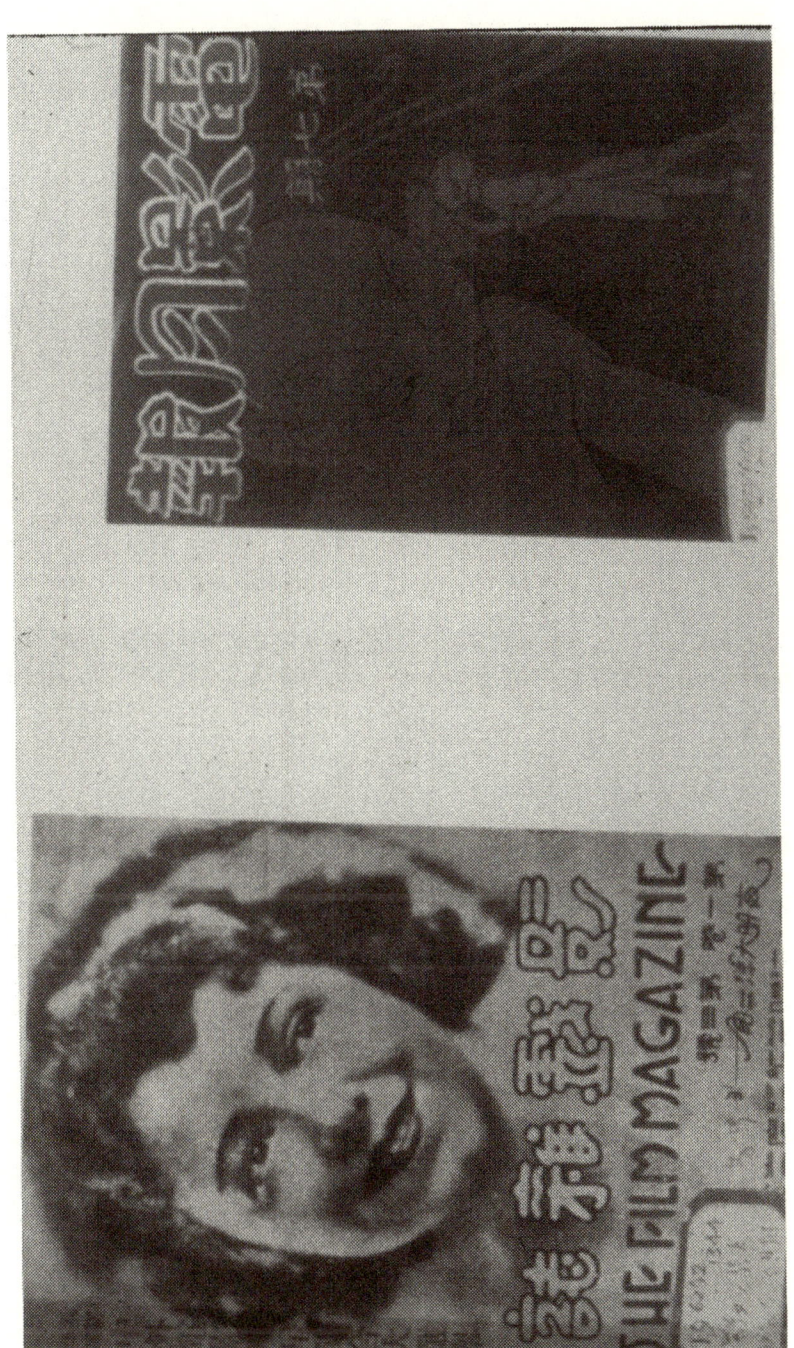

Fig. 28. Movie magazine covers, 1930s. After *Zhongguo dianying tuzhi*, p. 61.

Notes

1 Many of the dresses worn by the women in the calendar posters also reflect Art Deco styles. However, because fashions and accessories change so rapidly, they pose special research problems. Art Deco feminine fashions in the Chinese calendar posters will be dealt with in a later paper.

2 Bevis Hillier, *The World of Art Deco*, exh. cat., The Minneapolis Institute of Arts, 1971 (New York: E. P. Dutton, 1971), 39.

3 Bevis Hillier and Stephen Escritt, *Art Deco Style* (London: Phaidon Press, 1997), 41.

4 Ibid., 24–25.

5 Ibid., 19; Dan Klein, Nancy A. McClelland, and Malcolm Haslam, *In the Deco Style* (New York: Rizzoli, 1986), 113.

6 Klein et al, *In the Art Deco Style*, 8; Ellie Laubner, *Fashions of the Roaring 20s* (Atglen, PA: Schiffer Publishing, 1996), 25.

7 Alistar Duncan, ed., *Encyclopedia of Art Deco* (New York: E. P. Button, 1988), 68–69.

8 Ibid., 82.

9 Issue 9 (December 1934), n.p.

10 In one instance, the modern interior in a picture by Xie Zhiguang, is an exact replica of an interior depicted in an advertisement booklet published by Blabon's linoleum floor-covering firm located in Philadelphia.

11 Yi Bin, ed., *Lao Shanghai guanggao* (Shanghai: Shanghai huabao, 1995), 62.

12 Zhang Yanfeng, *Lao yuefengpai guanggaohua* (Taipei: Hansheng, 1996), 2:101.

13 Ibid. 2:73.

14 Ibid. 2:119.

15 See ibid., 2:109 and 110.

16 Ibid., 1:28.

17 Interestingly, however, the famous Shanghai calendar poster artist Xie Zhiguang used Art Deco–flavored characters for his signature on his Chinese paintings made during the 1960s and 70s.

18 *Zhongguo meishu nianjian*, 82 (chap. 1, n. 31).

19 Ibid., 48.

20 Ibid., 97.

21 Ibid., 6–7.

22 Ibid., Shi 2, 5, 19–20; Zhuan, 6–7, 97, 59.

23 Ibid., 109.

24 Issue 67 (July 1932): 14.

25 Issue 122 (Nov. 1936): 39.

26 *Jiaoyubu diyici chuanguo meishu zhanlanhui zhuanji disanzhong* (Shanghai: Commercial Press, 1943).

27 See Scott Minick and Jiao Ping, *Chinese Graphic Design in the Twentieth Century* (London: Thames and Hudson, 1990), 44–63.

10
The Park Hotel in Shanghai:
A Metaphor for 1930s China

Lenore Hietkamp

The image Shanghai presents to the world is one of the city's most compelling features today, relayed through a diverse mixture of architectural styles. When journalists cover the current fast pace of developments, the background they paint is the strange contrast of fantastic new skyscrapers on one side of the Huangpu River, and older buildings from classical Western traditions on the opposite bank along the famous Bund. A built environment of Western imagery is evidence of cultural interactions in a cosmopolitan city, from whence come the Pudong New Development Area, the Bund, and the foreign settlement areas. Conscious manipulations of Shanghai's architectural profile during the nineteenth and early twentieth centuries, and again today, make the study of its buildings, and in particular the Park Hotel on Nanjing Road, a gateway into the city's local, national, and international history and culture (fig. 1).

Long familiar to the eyes and minds of Shanghai residents, the Park Hotel (1931–34), remained unchallenged in height for fifty-five years. A photograph from around 1935 shows it rising 284 feet over the racecourse and its surroundings on Nanjing Road (fig. 2). It maintained this visual dominance from 1934 until the early 1980s, when changes in economic policy and national politics enabled the construction of tall buildings once again.[1] The fundamental reason for its familiarity is simply that for a whole generation it was the tallest building in Shanghai. Behind its towering visibility, however, looms a building that epitomizes in two important ways the period in which it was built. With Chinese owners, a Hungarian architect, modern technology, a hybrid style, and materials from China, Europe, and America, the Park Hotel grew out of a cosmopolitan Shanghai. The result, on the one hand, represents the quest for a new China, pursued by certain Chinese groups during this period, a quest fertilized by Western education and molded by the variety of cultural interactions in the crucible of Shanghai. The city's unique social, cultural, and political environment attests to attempts by an elite Chinese community to integrate Western

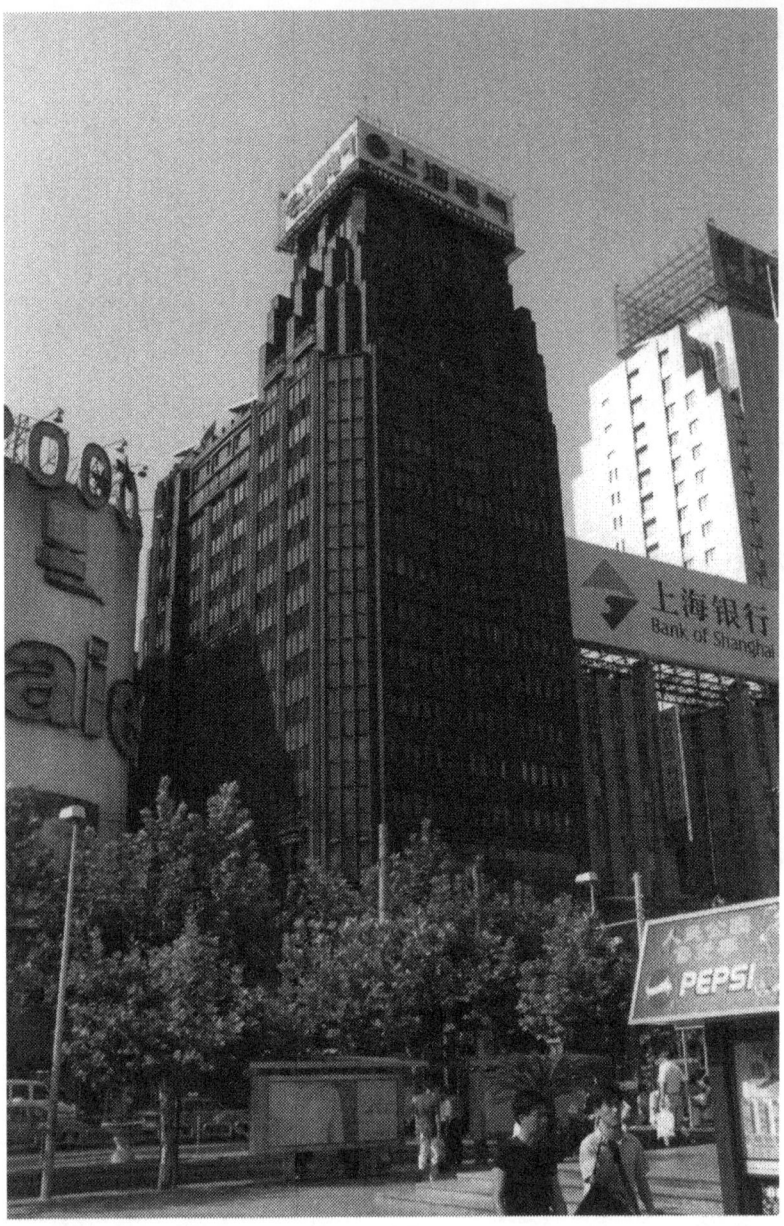

Fig. 1. Park Hotel, Shanghai. Photo credit: Lenore Hietkamp, 1998.

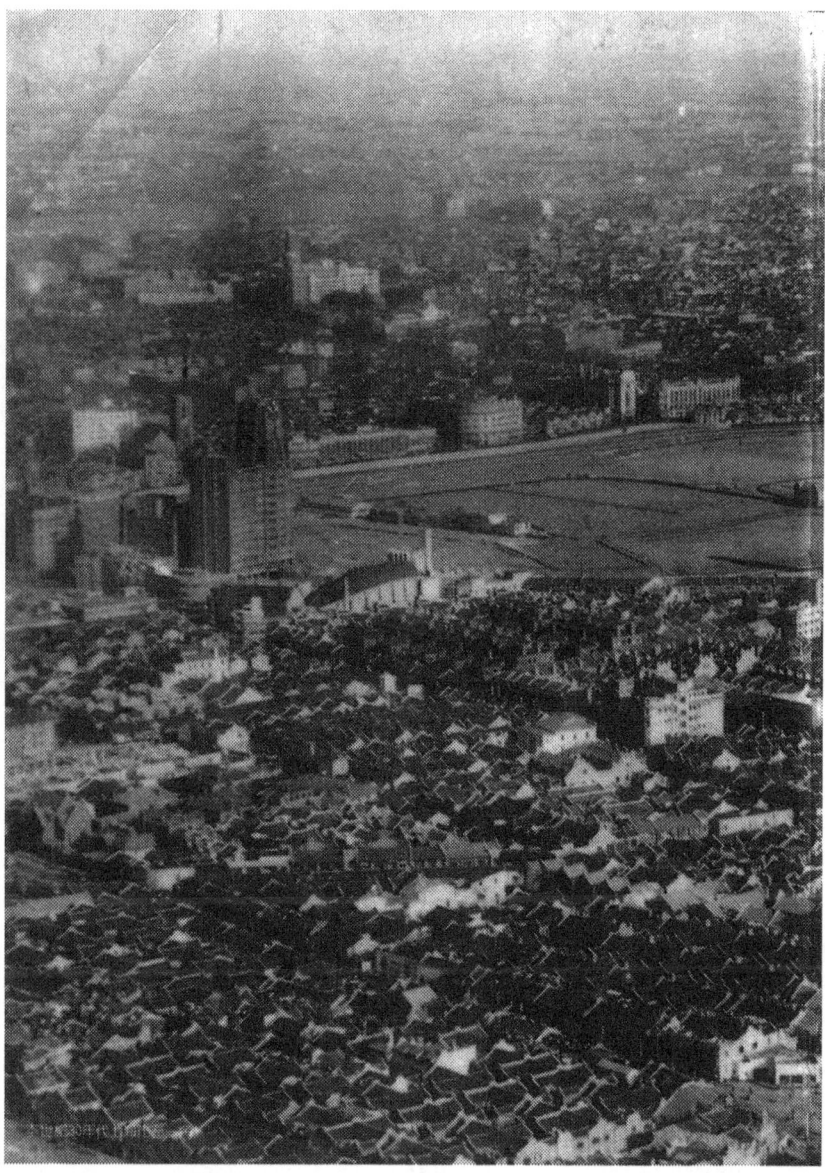

Fig. 2. Shanghai, circa 1935; view of north section of racecourse. Reproduced from Deng Ming and Zhou Zhende, eds., *Survey of Shanghai 1840s–1940s* (Shanghai: Shanghai People's Fine Arts Publishing House, 1993), frontispiece.

ideas into a new Chinese identity implicit in the absorption of Western ideas and imagery.[2] The process of implementing Western imagery into the hotel's design, however, makes the building a legacy of architectural design that must be analyzed separately from the hotel's symbolic status. Located in a city geographically removed from the European and American sources of much of Shanghai's 1920s and 30s architecture, the hotel was proclaimed the tallest building between London and Tokyo. The hybrid style of this skyscraper illustrates the freedom available to architects in Shanghai to appropriate elements from around the world, and the cosmopolitan culture of Shanghai that embraced these elements.

The Park Hotel, by the architect Laszlo Hudec (1893–1958), is still a vivid composition of color, line, and artistically rendered silhouette. The interior has been greatly altered, but the façade remains intact. The hotel projects warmth and comfort through the rich dark browns and blacks of its façade. Black granite clads the front of the first two stories but the somber color is moderated by the polished granite's reflective surface. The granite wraps around the corners in a smooth, streamlined, Art Deco motif, neatly packaging the eighty-foot width of the building. Vertical triangular piers appearing above the second floor create a strong upward movement. A vitrified tile pattern of burnt-umber lozenges covers the building from the third story up. The verticals then step inward and culminate in a sky- line cut sharply by the pointed remains of the piers. At the pinnacle, the original gold ball and flagpole top a small octagonal room with windows on all sides. Around the setback area have been added marquis supports for advertising sold by the hotel's current owner, the Jin Jiang Interna- tional Management Group.

The hotel's historic value is celebrated in small but widespread de- tails in the interior. The tiny graphic in the form of a Chinese junk, evi- dent in the hotel's advertisements of the 1930s, which firmly associates the hotel with its original Chinese owners, now adorns matchboxes and the sheer curtains on the windows (figs. 3 and 4). In particular, the sepia drawing used on various types of packaging highlights the hotel's form. It has been abstracted into another graphic logo, this one emphasizing the vertical stripes of the façade. In a renovation of 1997, a different retro–Art Deco simplification of the exterior design is repeated throughout the in- terior (fig. 5).[3] These original and recent variations on the outward design make an unequivocal statement that the Park's history is inextricably con- nected with its imagery and that the management thus finds this imagery worthwhile for advertising. It is the hotel's historic and enduring shape, the message conveys, that has become an integral part of the Shanghai landscape.

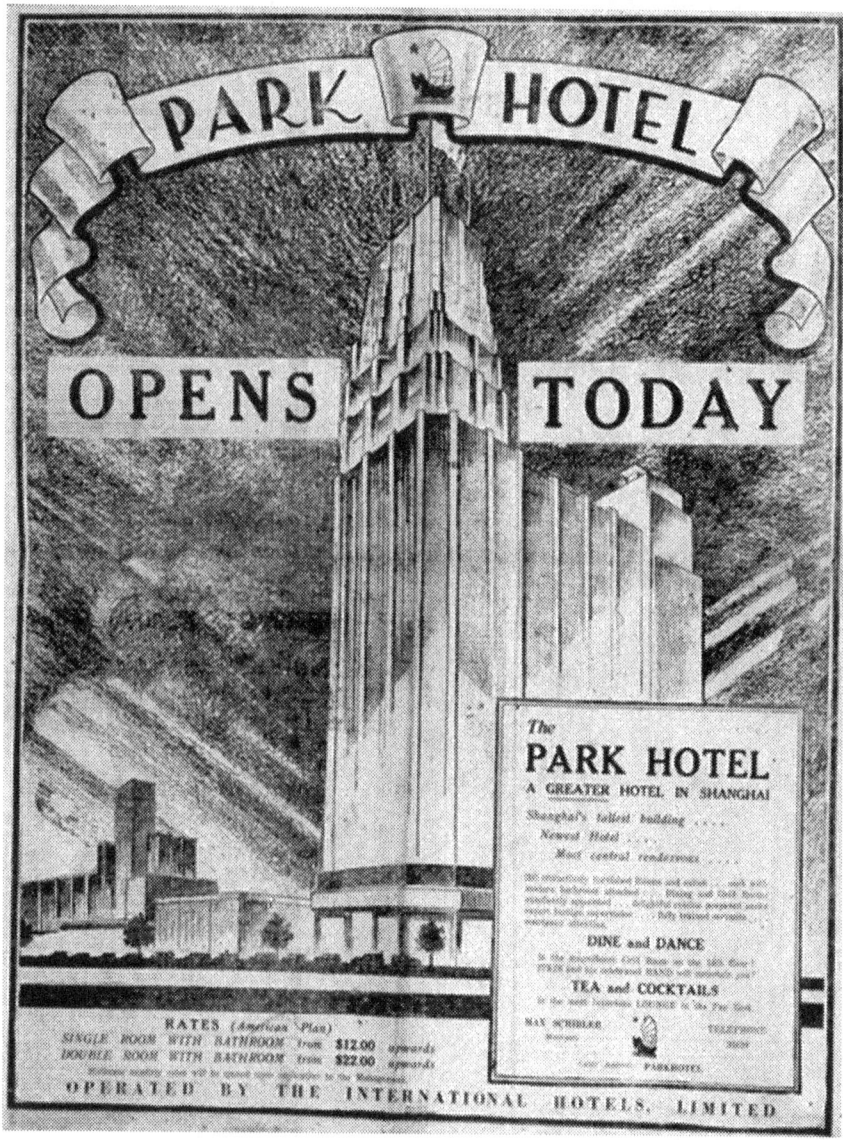

Fig. 3. Park Hotel opening ad. Note Chinese junk graphic in banner. Reproduced from *China Press*, 1 December 1934, p. 26.

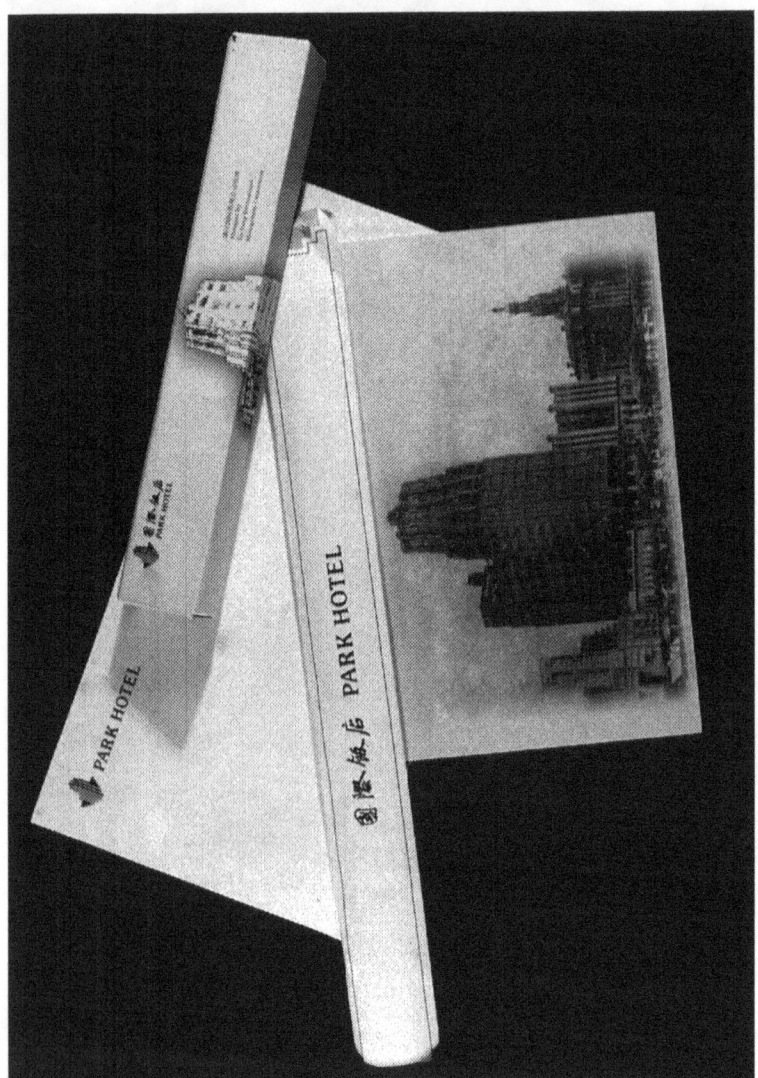

Fig. 4. Matchbox and toothbrush packaging, showing Chinese junk and old drawing of the Park Hotel. Photo credit: Lenore Hietkamp, 1999.

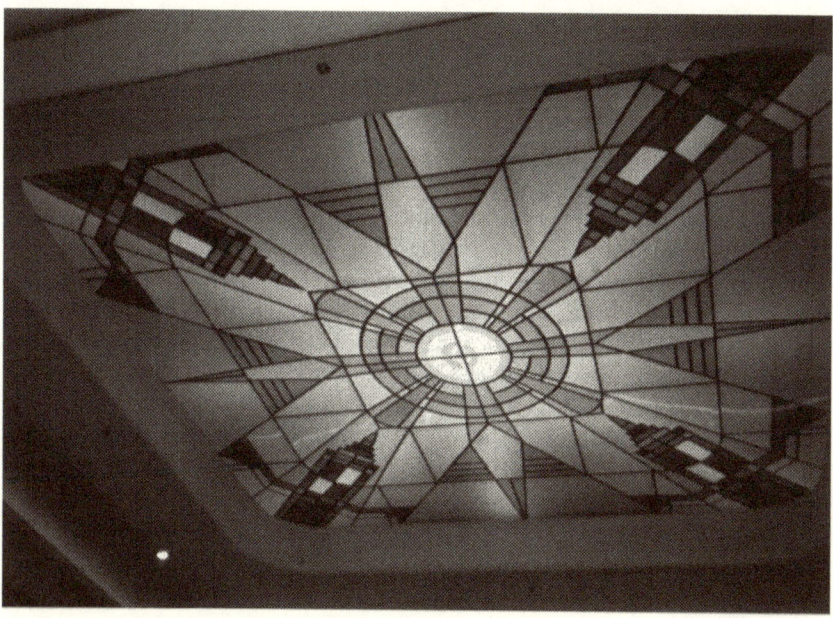

Fig. 5. Renovated stained glass ceiling design over former dance floor, 13th floor, Park Hotel; 1997 renovation. Photo credit: Lenore Hietkamp, 1998.

If the hotel is a metaphor for its time, it must first be understood as a symbol. In his recent examination of ethics and architecture, Karsten Harries says that a building can be a symbol because it represents, or "re-presents," its makers' worldview. Elements inherent in a building's function, style, and construction can be used as signs that convey particular meanings. Like lines on a map, individual components guide the viewer to an understanding of the whole, depending on the viewers' prior understanding of the meaning behind such signs.[4] In the case of the Park Hotel, design components and technology are aids in understanding the perspectives of both the owners and the architect. These elements are Western in origin, but were arrived at through the sanction of Chinese owners and the implied contribution of Chinese contractors. They are thus comprehensible to foreigners in Shanghai and an international audience, but also to Chinese who were part of an emerging modern Shanghai culture.

In the broader visual culture of Shanghai, the Park Hotel is embedded in a longstanding association between architecture and fine arts. Function and form are intimately connected. Ivan Gaskell includes architecture in his "history of images," defined as the study of visual elements in "a visual environment which are or have been valued for reasons other than their ostensible practical purpose."[5] As a hotel, the Park Hotel functioned, and still does, within a Western architectural typology, signifying through its associations with models of the type in Europe and America the intent to engage in a hospitality industry with Western standards. Through the bank that occupied the first floor and basement, it also functioned as an unusual dual-purpose building without precedent—a Shanghai hybrid. Highly visible, it communicates through accessible signifiers that are both seen and experienced: style, height, and function. On Nanjing Road, that important site of commercial and cultural exchange, the advertising value of a skyscraper hotel and bank made concrete the fashionable pursuit of modern ideas and technology in China.

Architecture, says Magali Sarfatti Larson, "occurs locally, in specific contexts. . . . On the one hand, we have architects putting into practice ideas that make up the discourse of the discipline. On the other hand, we have external forces—economic, political, social, and cultural movements—bearing down with more and more specific effects upon the practice of architecture."[6] As an external force, Shanghai of the 1920s and 30s was the arena from which China was launched into a global orbit. The modernizing role of Shanghai is illustrated by the development of commercialization of material culture within the city, a process recently examined by Wen-hsin Yeh. Under the municipal safety nets existing in the various foreign concessions—to which many Chinese were drawn during ongoing periods of civil strife outside Shanghai—Western goods and education began to change the lifestyles of Chinese residents. Western cultural products, identified as signs of modernity, were adapted by Chinese who could afford them, displacing traditions that were becoming increasingly problematic to Chinese living amid the parade of wealth purveyed by a minority of foreigners.[7] These commercial transactions occurred mainly on Nanjing Road, the Park Hotel's address. Social historian Xu Dingxin has called this process the "Nanjing Road Phenomenon." The conspicuousness of commerce and society on this street produced a novel commercial culture that combined new styles of product display, new standards of quality control, and new attitudes in customer service. These changes turned shopping into such a pleasant experience that Shanghai residents subsequently viewed a shopping trip not as a chore but as a diversion, not as an economic transaction but as a cultural consumption.[8]

The other major aspect of the Park Hotel's significance, its contribution to architectural history, is also grounded within the modernizing Chinese culture of Shanghai and its interaction with foreigners. The Hungarian architect, Laszlo Hudec, created a hybrid of styles considered appropriate for the expression of a building owned by wealthy, influential Chinese bankers.[9] Although the ultimate responsibility for the structure probably belonged jointly to both architect and Chinese owners, the choice of style is a direct reflection of the architect's Eastern European background and his professed interest in interpreting architectural traditions. However, the study of a building should not be simply a catalogue of the ins and outs of style, but must recognize that architecture is a complex art embracing form and function, symbol and social purpose, technique and belief. Hudec's solution brings into focus the cultural milieu of Shanghai's elite as purveyors of imagery that raised their profile in Shanghai through references to Western symbols of luxury and status: the skyscraper hotel and the technology needed to build it. Shanghai's wealth and geographical isolation, along with its different communities with regional ties, resulted in a built environment that emphasized visual presentation. Many architects found this environment stimulating, so that, for example, fashionable Art Deco runs riot through the architecture of this period, evident in Tess Johnston's photographic documentation of the Western architecture in Shanghai.[10] The spread of American urban culture in the 1920s and 30s in particular is important for studying the Park Hotel. Thus the Park Hotel stands as a beacon of the spread of Western architectural ideas during a key period in the history of modern architecture.

Background to the Park Hotel

The Park Hotel was built during an era of such prosperity and change in China that Marie-Claire Bergère has called it the golden age of the Chinese bourgeoisie. In this period, 1911 to 1937, traditional elements persisted in some quarters but the expansion of modern business produced an increasingly wealthy and powerful urban elite.[11] The hotel's owner, the Joint Savings Society (herein referred to as the JSS), had previously commissioned Laszlo Hudec to build its expensive banking headquarters at the corner of Sichuan and Hankou Roads.[12] Many of the men on the Society's fourteen-member board of directors were part of a wealthy group of elite Chinese who flourished during this golden age. The life of the JSS directly marks the beginning and ending of this period, from the founding of its four constituent banks in the early 1910s to their union in 1923 and the completion of the hotel in 1934.[13]

The JSS's formation and success also echo the complex network of Shanghai bankers and businessmen about whom much has been written.[14] Parks Coble notes the close ties between the banks comprising the JSS; the directors, who founded their own banks or were important players in local business, were well-known in Shanghai. They sat on many boards, reflecting the widespread practice of doing business through associations. They also formed a significant portion of the financiers from Zhejiang and Jiangsu provinces, a group that "so completely dominated Shanghai business and banking that [their] names became interchangeable with the terms 'Shanghai financiers' and 'Shanghai capitalists,' or 'Zhejiang-Jiangsu capitalists'."[15] Modern Chinese banks, as opposed to traditional "old-style" banks, held the majority of securities in China;[16] and six of the top ten banks holding eighty percent of all deposits were represented by the fourteen members comprising the JSS board of directors.[17] Some of these associated themselves with the Nationalist party in the belief that the Nationalists "would provide strong central leadership for the unification of the nation and the reconstruction of the economy."[18] They financially supported Chiang Kai-shek's war efforts and some were members of the "Political Study Group," active in creating policy for the Nationalist government. Membership in this group earned two of them full-page biographies in a confidential publication by the Chinese Communist Party in 1945.[19] Others on the JSS board included the vice-president of the semi-private Bank of Communications, an ex-minister of foreign affairs, and the ambassador to the USSR.[20] All these activities are evidence of increasing use of Western economic and political systems by a powerful group of Chinese at the top levels of Shanghai's Chinese community.

In Shanghai's international districts, the saturation of the physical landscape with Western architecture and of the business milieu with Western economics made manifest power then inherent in associations with Western society. By studying new sciences and ideas learned in the West, many Chinese believed they would gain the knowledge necessary to solve China's overwhelming problems and provide the country with the tools to operate in the global arena—a faith in science that closely echoed the idealism of contemporary architects in Western countries. This became a key pursuit of the new Chinese youth at the end of the Qing dynasty, who grew into roles such as those of the bankers on the Park Hotel's board of directors. The solution to China's "backwardness" that the Park Hotel symbolizes was "scientism," a philosophy adapted from the machine age society of the West and grounded in readings on social Darwinism. All aspects of the universe were rationally knowable, scientism assumed.[21] To Chinese students, the ability to use scientific methods was seen as characteristic of a democratic society, employed by the scientists and thinkers of the West to discover better ways of living for all. The Chinese writer Hu Shi claimed that democracy, a whole new system of morals, in effect a "new religion," originated from modern American life. Hu Shi's opening essay in Charles Beard's anthology *Whither Mankind: A Panorama of Modern Civilizations* compares Eastern and Western civilizations. Believing in the power of the individual aided by machines, he advised China's students to travel to the West to study "the knowledge and methods of the natural sciences. This is the road of hope, whereas the other road, that among old books and papers, leads nowhere."[22] Other well-known figures writing in this anthology, such as Bertrand Russell, John Dewey (both of whom frequented China's university lecture halls), and Lewis Mumford, added their views on the effects of modern science on everyday life in essays ranging from running a government to raising a family.[23]

The owners of the Park Hotel followed the trend of seeking China's reform through their own business ventures, which were founded upon Western models.[24] Many of the men on the hotel's board of directors were educated in America or Japan in law, economics, and agriculture. Chinese businessmen in Shanghai, Bryna Goodman has found, with strong loyalties to birth or ancestral places (usually outside Shanghai), "gave war-torn and devastated rural areas access to the wealth of Shanghai" by using foreign methods, particularly after the 1911 revolution. New banks often grew out of a perceived need for economic development in rural areas, initiating or helping fund bank branches and businesses.[25] The Chinese press in Shanghai lauded Chinese businessmen in Shanghai for being "farsighted" in their industrial efforts (in combination with education), which would result in an improvement of living conditions for the peasant masses.[26] Eventually, the successful rise of the Chinese Communist Party would follow the failure of the bourgeoisie to effect actual, significant change among those masses. Meanwhile, the bourgeoisie's perception of their role as patriotic modernizers, defined by the economic advantages their efforts afforded China, justified the concentration of wealth in Shanghai and the continued evolution of banking practices between 1911 and 1937, based on foreign models.

The intent to aid China and the hope to realize profit on a huge invest-ment are factors intimately connected to the eventual rise of a modern, Western-style hotel. The JSS was formed to stabilize China's economy and bring in a tidy profit at the same time; it grew at a phenomenal rate after its inception in 1923.[27] The Park Hotel was undoubtedly an investment of capital earned by the society, yet it was also a venue for the induction of Chinese youth into another modern venture: the hospitality industry. A hotel with international standards could attract international tourists and wealthy Chinese travelers. The International Hotel Company, Lim-ited, established by the JSS with several of the same board members, ex-isted to "erect and maintain" the Park Hotel according to world standards, and to provide a hotel school for local Chinese students. Presumably the school's students would be visible in the hotel, affirming the hotel's status as Shanghai's first foreign-style establishment under complete Chinese ownership and operation.[28] The Park's Chinese comptroller, Myron D. Ling, had worked in a well-known California hotel and graduated from the University of Shanghai's business administration course in 1931. He explained in the *China Weekly Review* how a Chinese hotel industry patronized by foreign visitors would allow China to benefit from the sector's great potential. "No step should be neglected," he wrote a week before the hotel opened for business, "that would in any way induce the foreigner to spend his money in China."[29]

The hotel was intended to appeal to both Chinese and foreign clientele. Chinese ownership, and the nineteenth-floor suite devoted to the sole use of one of the board members, clearly illustrates its attraction to Chinese customers. Closer proximity than the Cathay on the Bund to the main railway station in northern Zhabei provided access to areas further inland, and likely eased the need to target a competitive foreign tourist market. The restaurant services, however, catered directly to an international clientele. The kitchen area on the second floor was designed with the "meeting of East and West" in mind. Special steam tables in the food preparation areas indicate that "every effort [was] made to please people of all nationalities."[30] This policy proved to be popular; when the roof garden on top of the thirteenth floor behind the tower was converted into a covered dance floor in 1935, two new kitchens were added on the fourteenth floor to supply diners in the adjoining grill room. The kitchen on the east side created Chinese dishes, whereas foreign food came from the west kitchen; after dining, "east and west [would] meet as the guests mingle[d] on the dance floor." This idea came from the hotel's manager, Z. L. Loo, who also designed unique solid-silver serving platters for Chinese meals, instead of the traditional Chinaware.[31]

A brochure published at the time of the hotel's completion highlights the services and luxuries available, with an emphasis on the hotel's intended international appeal. It is illustrated with elegant drawings of people, recognizable as neither foreign nor Chinese, most in Western dress, grouped around drawings of the hotel's interior. A tour department advertising its services on two of the brochure panels is an obvious attempt to promote Chinese culture. The offer of visits to different government and cultural buildings in Shanghai is supported by a drawing and a photograph of such famous sites as the old Longhua Pagoda (symbolic of Ancient Cathay) and the newly constructed Chinese Civic Center, a concrete structure with Chinese architectural characteristics that clearly expressed the spirit of the new China (fig. 6).

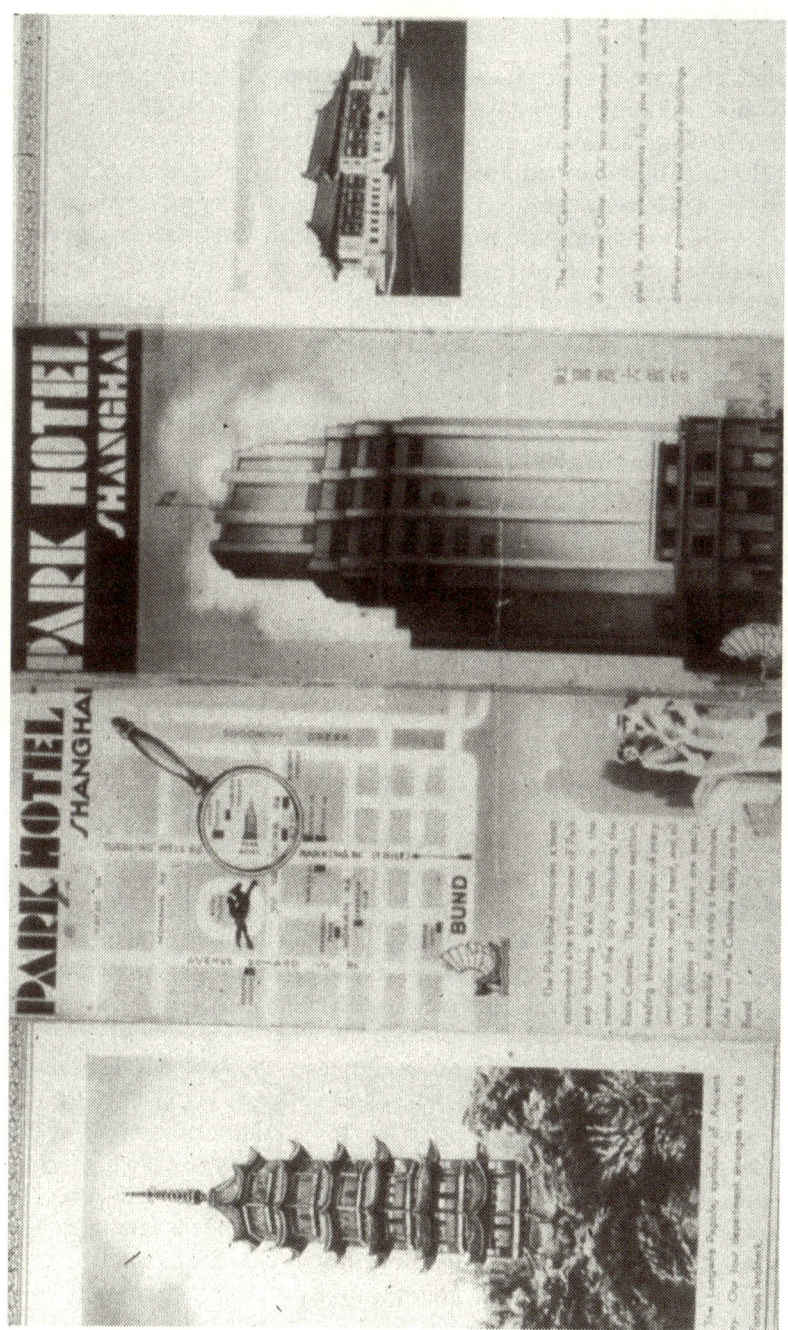

Fig. 6. Park Hotel brochure, circa 1934. From copy in possession of the author.

Laszlo Hudec in Shanghai

The hotel's architect, Laszlo Hudec, brought to the project unique qualities directly affecting the hotel's design and image. Hudec was born in Hungary in 1896. After his architectural training at the University of Budapest from 1910 to 1914, he joined the Austro-Hungarian army to fight on the Russian front. He was captured and sent to Siberia, from which he escaped in 1918. Traveling south to Harbin (Ha'erbin) and Shanghai, he lied about his origins to disguise the fact that he came from a country that had just lost a war, maintaining he was from Latvia, to explain his unfamiliar language to those foreigners he encountered.[32] At some point, the truth lost its edge, for by the 1930s Hudec's luxurious home in Shanghai had become a well-known social centre for expatriate Hungarians, and Hudec himself became the honorary consul for Hungary in Shanghai.[33] When he first arrived, he worked with an American architect, R. A. Curry, and by 1925 had established his own architectural practice. The Park appeared at the peak of his productive period; by 1931 he was a well-respected architect with at least twenty-four projects completed in Shanghai. Before the Communist takeover of 1949 he left the city and eventually retired in California, where he died in 1956.

The reasons behind the choice of a foreign architect for the Park Hotel illustrate the cosmopolitan profile of the JSS. Hudec appears to have been an obvious choice; not only was he well established, but he had already worked for the JSS, designing its head office on the corner of Hankou and Sichuan Roads in 1928 (fig. 7). In this project, the JSS wrote in 1929 that it had found Hudec's services to be "eminently satisfactory."[34] In addition to this project, approximately half of his oeuvre consists of significant projects for members of the Chinese community. The Moore Memorial Church of 1926, the Zhabei Waterworks and Power Station of 1929, the Zhabei funeral chapel of 1932, and three modern theaters were for, respectively, a Chinese Methodist congregation, the Chinese Municipality of Greater Shanghai, a Catholic Chinese funerary society, and a Chinese theater company.[35]

There were many architects in Shanghai to choose from, especially newly trained though less experienced Chinese ones.[36] L. C. Sun, for example, worked for Hudec and is listed as "the architect of the JSS" in the *China Press* of December, 1934. Although Sun's assistance may have contributed to the project, drawings of the hotel in the Hudec Collection are by Hudec, and it may be safely assumed that Hudec was the principal designer.[37] The experienced Hudec not only was professionally active in Shanghai but kept abreast of architectural developments around the world. In 1927 he traveled to America to see the architecture of the New

World, not settling for the information in architectural journals available in Shanghai; during a trip to Germany in 1931, he studied new materials in building technology.

That he "was popular with the Chinese," as his widow says, is evident, but there was more behind his selection than an appreciation for his skill or personality. A photograph places Hudec and two American architects in the company of Chinese architects and builders at a banquet given by the director of the Voh Kee Construction Company in honor of American architect Henry K. Murphy. Jeffrey Cody says this banquet "suggests a professional camaraderie between foreign and Chinese architects which was highly unusual," undoubtedly a testimony to Murphy's "missionary work" in striving to understand and absorb Chinese architecture and communicate it to his foreign colleagues.[38] Murphy had devoted much of his career in China to trying to define a Chinese style of architecture while using new technology—a quest that continues to this day for Chinese architects.[39] Most of Hudec's work for his Chinese clients, however, contains few, if any, identifiably Chinese elements. There is only the occasional gently scalloped edge on a roofline; perhaps the silhouette of his Grand Theatre façade can be likened to that of a pagoda. The mutual disinclination to socialize between foreigners and Chinese, noted by many "old China hands," including Hudec's family, points to an unusual business relationship commemorated by the banquet and photograph.[40]

Hudec's Hungarian nationality and his wife's German heritage may have helped bridge to some degree the social barrier between Chinese residents of Shanghai and the foreigners from treaty nations. The Chinese businessmen, from whose ranks Hudec received his commission, fought against the serious inequalities on the municipal council. However, the Chinese majority held no sway over the minority of members of treaty-holding nations in Shanghai. Only foreigners could vote for representation on Council, and only for representation by treaty nations.[41] To the Chinese bourgeoisie, which never easily accepted the privileges of treaty nations or "imperialists," Hudec's nationality held a particular significance: Hungarians never enjoyed official consular, or treaty, status. Residents from treaty-holding nations counted on legal protection under extraterritoriality. Without it, as a Hungarian, Hudec had to be cautious. Although Hudec's British and German in-laws made possible the kind of privileged, extensive social life prized by Shanghailanders, the German connection was important in Chinese international relations after the First World War.[42] By the mid-1920s, Germany had regained its long-standing business relations with China after losing the privileges of a treaty nation in the Treaty of Versailles in 1919.[43] It became the first European country to conduct business with China on an equal basis after the First World

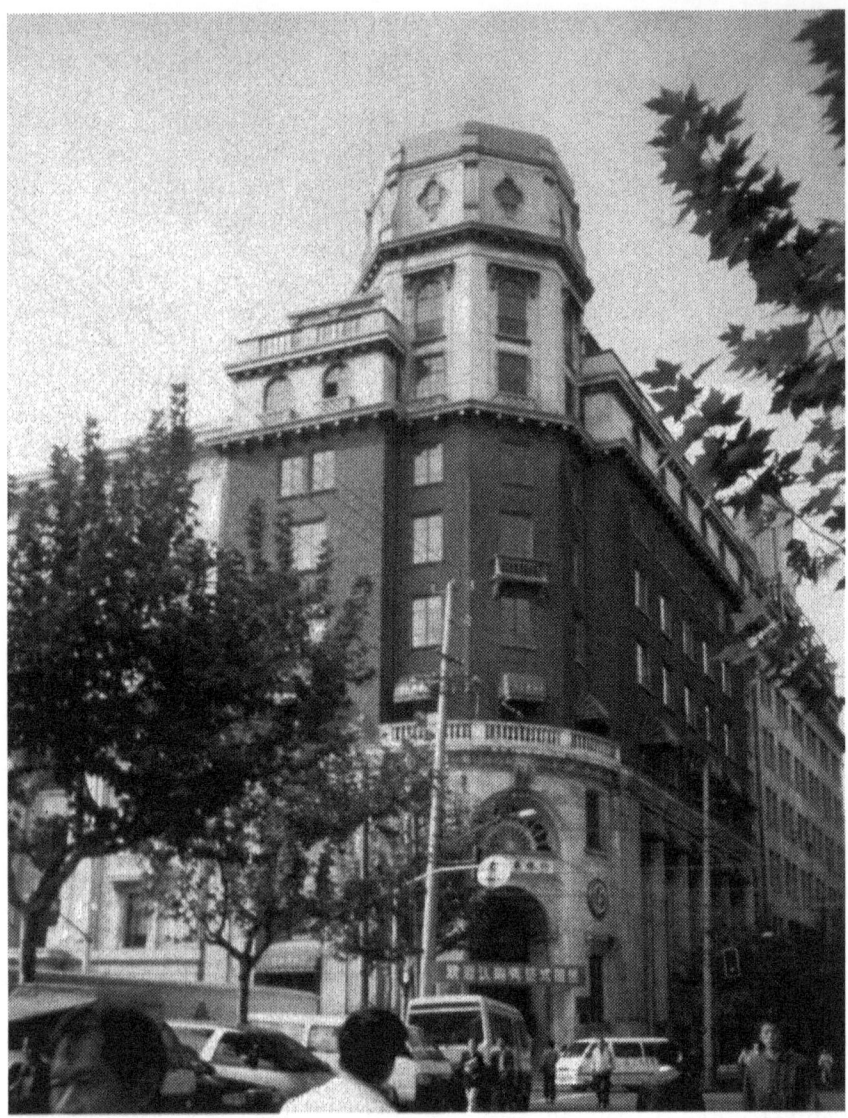

Fig. 7.   Former Joint Savings Society Building, corner of Sichuan and Hankou Roads, Shanghai. Photo credit: Lenore Hietkamp, 1998

War. When the Second World War brought to Shanghai Germany's Japanese allies, the enemy of many of the nations in the international community, Hudec's nationality enabled him and his family to avoid internment. In fact, Hudec appears to have practiced his profession somewhat in isolation from his British colleagues. He certainly had none of the lucrative British commissions that characterize the Bund. Nevertheless he was an extremely successful, prolific architect.

The Hotel's Site

Hudec's employment by Chinese businessmen indicates the hotel directors' complicity with a capitalist ideology in which foreign-style architecture was the generally accepted means of establishing a particular kind of physical presence in Shanghai. Their capital, however, was only superficially connected to China's well-being because it was held by an elite, bourgeois class, whose presence was evident in the many new buildings arising in the vicinity of the hotel.[44] The site on Bubbling Well Road opposite the racecourse was a good choice for a hotel that catered to an international and Chinese clientele with money to spend. It is about two miles west of the Bund, but the services and types of rooms offered by the Park Hotel put it in an apartment-hotel category popularized in New York by buildings such as the Shelton Hotel, the tallest hotel in the world when it was built in 1924, and the Panhellenic Tower of 1928, acclaimed for its innovative design within a skyscraper envelope. This expensive building type required close proximity to areas of leisure and recreation to which its clientele, transient and long-term guests, were drawn.[45] Since Shanghai was a tourist destination on popular steamship routes that traversed the world, people would disembark and stay for lengthy periods.[46] The nature of foreign business in Shanghai, where companies from abroad set up branch offices, also dictated the necessity for hotels offering the luxuries of home to visiting or temporarily relocated staff.

During its construction, the hotel was called the new Joint Savings Society Building, a confusing repetition of the name of the first building, of 1928, on Sichuan Road. By the time of its completion, however, the hotel was known as the Park, perhaps to locate it within the broad international circle of famous hotels with that name.[47] The name also refers to its location. By 1931, Bubbling Well Road had long been a major artery between downtown Shanghai and outlying areas (fig. 8). Just east of the racecourse, it became Nanjing Road (the crossing street that runs along the east side of the former racecourse was Xizang Road), but until 1862 adjoining stretches of Nanjing Road from the Bund to a point west of Xizang Road were called Park Lane and Mooloo Road.[48] *Park Lane* referred to the street's origins in the early days of the treaty port as a stretch of lane or bridle path extending from the waterfront area into the parklike vicinity that is now the racecourse.[49] Later, that road became Bubbling Well Road west of Xizang Road, and Nanjing Road to the east, terminating at the Bund. The park area eventually became the racecourse, Shanghai's social centre, and the name of Park Lane was transferred to the street alongside the hotel site, perpendicular to Nanjing Road. In the late 1920s, the racecourse area sported a foreign YMCA beside the hotel, a swimming pool, several hotels around the racecourse, and all kinds of activity on the racecourse itself.[50] The undated booklet commemorating and advertising the hotel's opening promoted the races as "an integral part of Shanghai business life and the ideal place for a man to display his wealth and compete for prestige."[51] Continuing past the racecourse, Bubbling Well Road extended west to the outskirts of the International Settlement and beyond to unpoliced territory, the "poshest part of town in which to live for Chinese and foreigners"; where, in fact, Hudec's family lived.[52] The migration of homeowners to this area, away from the increasing traffic congestion and noise of the crowded Bund area, made this location of the apartment hotel, at a transitional point on the road out of the business centre, ideal.

The Tall Building in Shanghai

The hotel made an imposing landmark on the otherwise low Shanghai horizon (figs. 8 and 9). A young I. M. Pei used to play pool beside the racecourse as a teenager, an excuse, he says, to catch the excitement of the Park Hotel under construction.[53] He was so impressed by the feat it represented that he was inspired to become an architect and is now one of the world's most famous. Local foreign newspaper coverage proclaimed the Park the tallest building on four continents, the tallest between London and Tokyo and a great source of pride for the dynamic city. The only other building to approach the Park Hotel in height was the Broadway Mansions, another hotel that was completed in the same year on the Bund, with contributions from the same foundation engineer who worked on the Park Hotel.[54] The Park must be seen as a conscious manipulation of economic determinants to create not just a modern hotel, but a significantly tall building.

Hudec maintained that a high building was financially more viable than a low one.[55] The erection of a tall building on Shanghai soil was no small achievement, however. The hotel's owners had to be convinced by the architect that a tall building would be in their best interests, and the Shanghai Municipal Council's safety concerns had to be appeased.

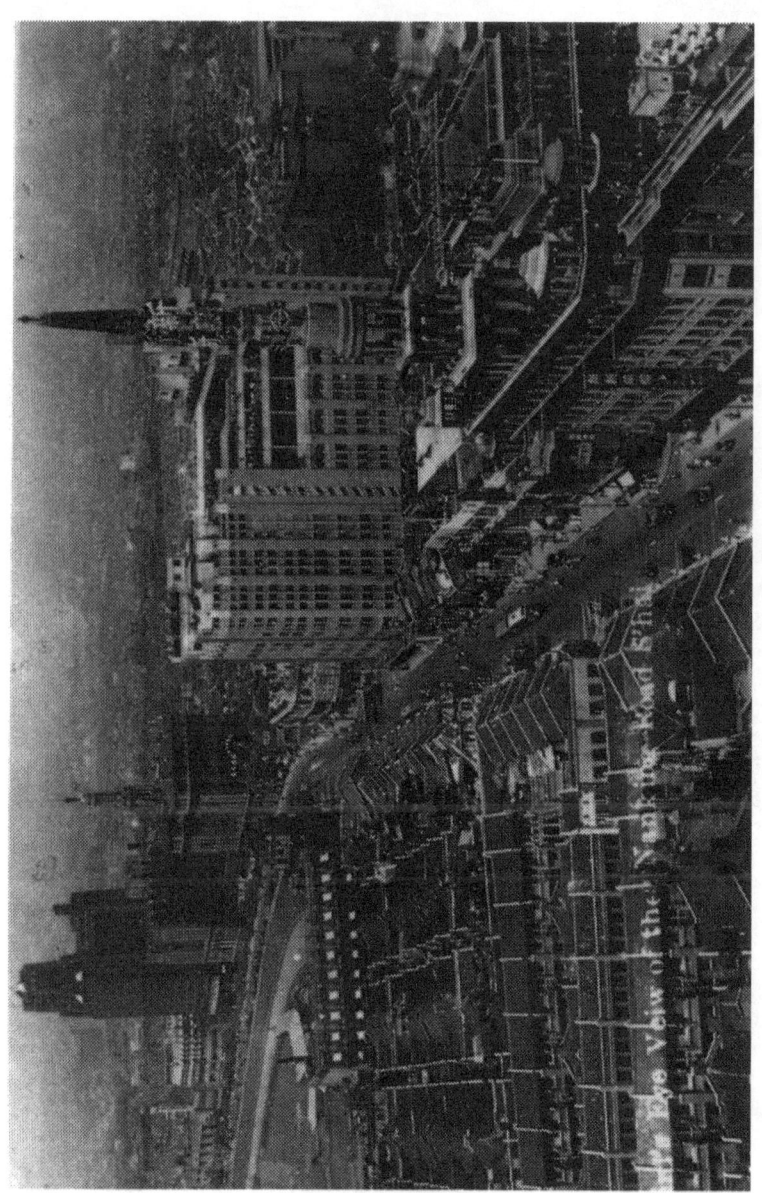

Fig. 8. Park Hotel and Nanjing Road in 1930s. Reproduced from Deng Ming and Zhou Zhende, eds., *Survey of Shanghai 1840s–1940s* (Shanghai: Shanghai People's Fine Arts Publishing House, 1993), p. 67.

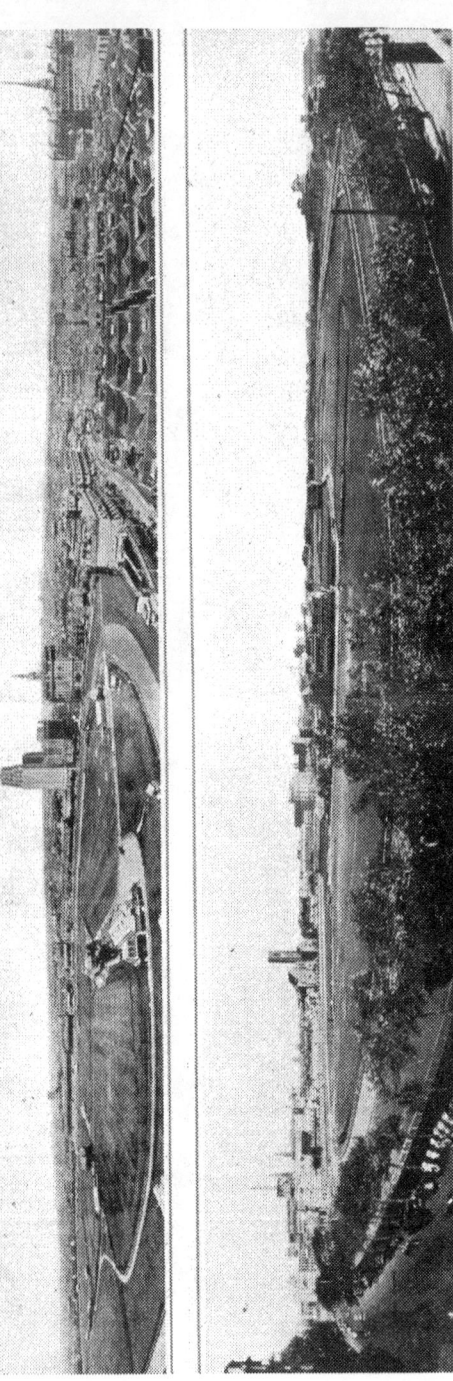

Fig. 9. Top: view of racecourse with drawing of hotel model set in. Bottom: View of racecourse from Park Hotel site. Reproduced from *Facts About the Park Hotel*, n.d. Hudec Collection, University of Victoria Special Collections.

Despite the difficulties, reported the *China Press* in 1931, by funding the project the owners were expressing the belief that "if anything happens to Shanghai land values it will result in a rise instead of a decline. They have the greatest confidence in the future of this city, and prove it by their move in building the tallest structure on four continents."[56] The price of land in Shanghai at the time is undoubtedly reflected in the small acreage the hotel occupies, with a frontage of only about eighty feet extending back in a solid T shape to the next street.[57] The contrast in overall size between it and the grandiose conceptions of other hotels planned for Bubbling Well Road facing the racecourse also suggests the effect of increasing real estate prices. One plan, published in a local paper in 1929, was for a horizontally oriented hotel with 560 rooms.[58] Another drawing, known only through an undated newspaper clipping in the Hudec archive, was also of a huge, horizontally massed building dubbed the "Monster Hotel," conceived by the masters of New York's immense Grand Central Station, Warren & Wetmore.[59]

These massive designs and that of the Park Hotel, the tallest building in Shanghai, represent a crucial period in China's history, when the "golden age of the Chinese bourgeoisie" in Shanghai was at its pinnacle. Tall buildings are signs of growing corporate power; that the JSS had enough capital to fund a tall building indicates the increasing wealth of the Chinese capitalist class. The tall building also indicates change in the economic life of a city. Because escalating land prices increase the number of stories needed to spread the cost of the lot, the tallest buildings generally appear at the end of a boom cycle.[60] In the first nine months of 1929, two years before the hotel was begun, the rate of building in Shanghai had exceeded the yearly average for the previous five years.[61] The idea for the Park Hotel skyscraper was likely conceived some years before 1931, for Hudec was sketching skyscrapers in New York in 1927, and construction of the hotel was well underway in 1931, anticipating completion in 1933 (the tenth anniversary of the JSS).[62] The paralyzing worldwide depression, debilitating much of the world by 1929, was held at bay in Shanghai until around 1932, due in large part to the stability of Shanghai's banking institutions, supported by the "Shanghai capitalists." Coble explains that in a departure from the downward trend of world economics, Shanghai banking actually expanded in nearly all areas from 1928 to 1932. The "severity of rural depression and accompanying rural unrest led the rural wealthy to deposit their money in Shanghai banks," whose far-reaching credit departments and rural branches had been visible in rural areas since the mid-1910s.[63] The Park Hotel is therefore also an indicator of the future of modernization on rural areas.

Although the architect emphasized the economic determinants of the hotel's height, denying any association with the symbolism of skyscrapers as "aspirations of mankind," there were already signs of these aspirations among tall buildings that the cosmopolitan Chinese residents of Shanghai clearly understood. In contrast to traditional Chinese architecture, where horizontal buildings and planning characterize city growth, Shanghai's business district raised row upon row of multiple-storied buildings. In fact, Hudec intended a design that would eclipse its closest rivals. Clues in his archive suggest that the architect was fully aware that height was important in Shanghai and that he was probably mindful of the major impact the hotel would have on the Shanghai skyline. In a damaged clipping found on the back of a photograph of the Park Hotel, a model of the Bank of China (completed in 1937) has been carefully measured in pencil (with a height marked of 219 feet), as has the Cathay Hotel beside it (212 feet; fig. 10). Another drawing puts the Park Hotel beside the major buildings along the Bund, complete with height measurements. This may have been a presentation drawing for the clients, to help them visualize the unprecedented height of 284 feet, but this information along with the clipping suggests a wish to create a parallel with the more distant icons of Shanghai along the Bund, perhaps even to create a second Bund along the racecourse equal in iconic symbolism (fig. 11). In addition to referring to the height of buildings on the Bund, early designs of the Park suggest the form of the already famous Cathay Hotel, now called the Peace Hotel. One drawing echoes not only the shape of the Cathay but also the row of colonnaded arches at the ground story, which an early design of the Park Hotel also incorporated (figs. 12 and 13). Against such a formidable competitor, which targeted the same international clientele as the Park Hotel—"foreign visitors, who can not adapt themselves to the Chinese, [who] will therefore have to stay in the European hotels, whether satisfactory or not"—it is not surprising the Park looked so similar to the Cathay in early conceptions.[64]

In the course of constructing a distinctly tall building, Hudec had to jump several hurdles. As in other cities such as New York, which instituted by-laws in 1916 to deal with problems implicit in tall-building construction, the height was of concern to Shanghai officials for various reasons. Hudec had to convince the Shanghai Municipal Council that its height would not be a handicap in case of fire, and that it would not affect the stability of buildings around it.[65] The concern for fire safety was common at the time, since the fastest exit from upper stories was by elevators, which could fail in the event of fire. In the Park, new technology in the form of eleven thousand fire sprinklers appeased this concern. As a final concession to the Municipal Council, although of little actual value to the

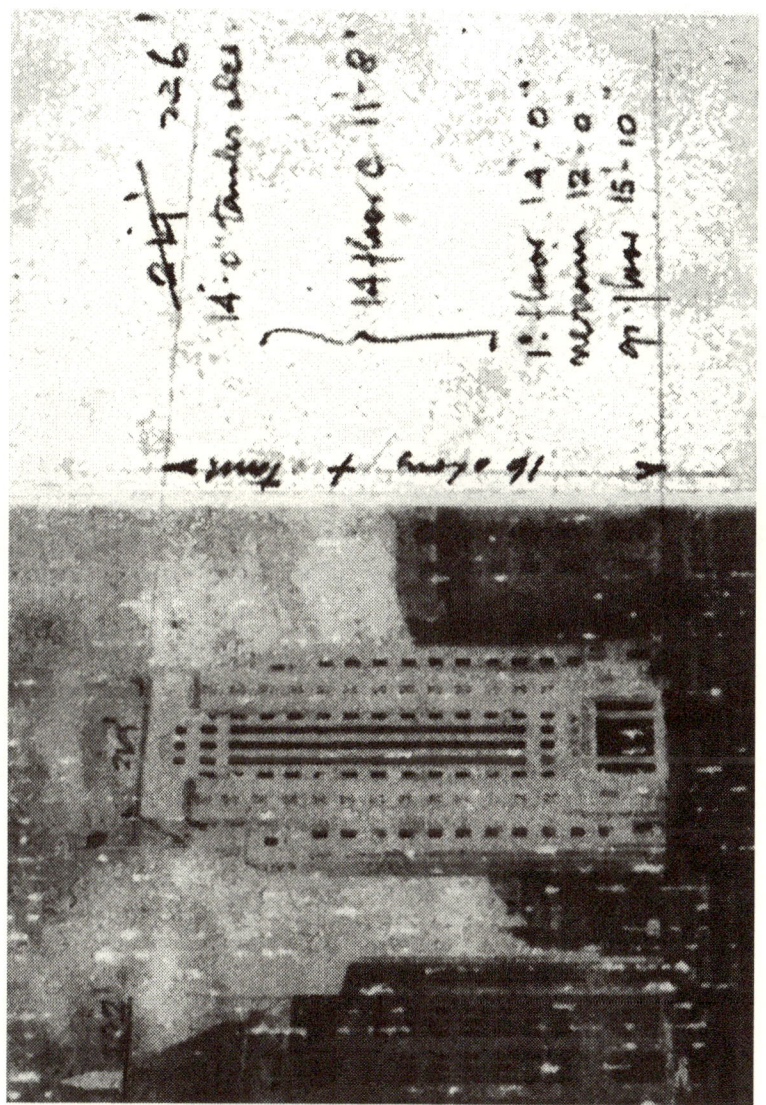

Fig. 10. Clipping with measurements of Bank of China model and Cathay Hotel. Sketch by L. E. Hudec. Hudec Collection, University of Victoria Special Collections.

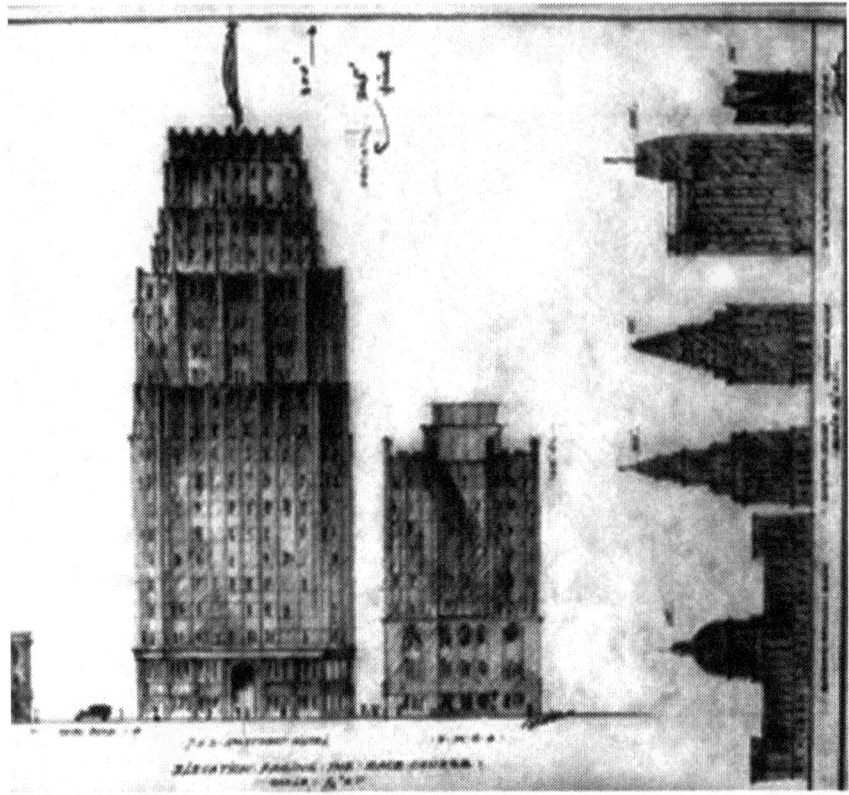

Fig. 11. The Park Hotel compared with the foreign YMCA, Cathay Hotel, Customs House, and Hong Kong and Shanghai Bank. Sketch by L. E. Hudec. Hudec Collection, University of Victoria Special Collections.

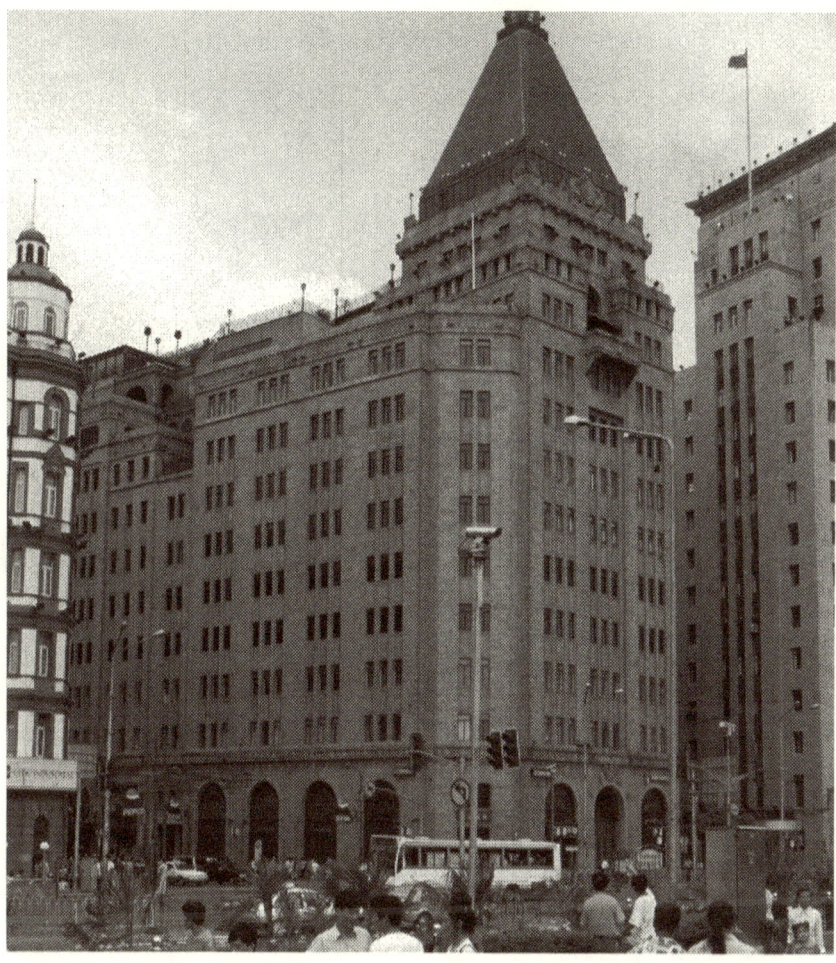

Fig. 12. View down Nanjing Road from the Bund; the former Cathay extends down the right. Photo credit: Lenore Hietkamp, 2001.

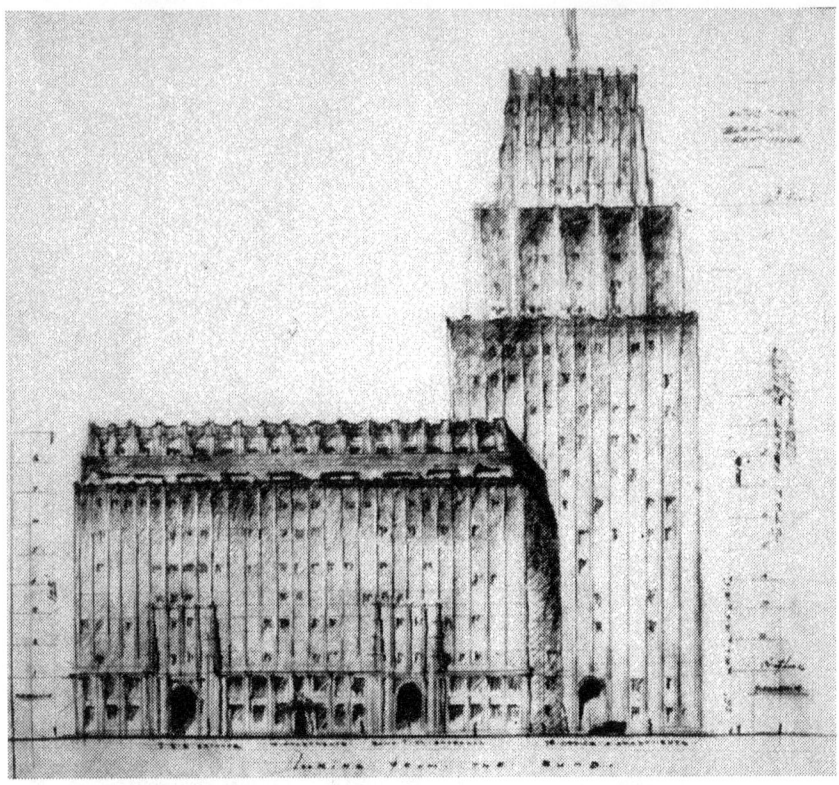

Fig. 13. Early drawing of the Park Hotel, Elevation "Looking from the Bund." Sketch by L. E. Hudec. Hudec Collection, University of Victoria Special Collections.

hotel, a tiny octagonal fire observation room was included on the roof— ostensibly the best location to view the city. In actuality not much can be seen because the structure is set in too far from the edge of the hotel's roof and the windows are too small.

In addition, Hudec had to fight the Council to allow the Park's un-precedented height because Shanghai's soil up to then was thought to be unable to support substantial vertical pressure. In his concern for the building's stability, Hudec and his engineers made unsurpassed efforts to counteract the dangers of heavy buildings sinking on Shanghai's swampy soil. In 1939, settlement occurred for some buildings at the rate of one inch per year.[66] Test borings Hudec or the engineer, B. J. Lindskog, made at the location of Hudec's 1928 building for the JSS suggest that, perhaps as early as 1927, Hudec was determined to build a tall building on that site. There, at the corner of Sichuan and Hankou Roads, they found that typical sandy Shanghai soil to a depth of 200 feet offered no resistance to the vertical weight tall structure, so the risk of building to unprecedented height there was too great. Test borings at the Park's current site, however, determined at least some resistance at 135 feet to vertical pressure. The additional measures of a floating raft, deep steel pilings, soil displacement for a basement that more than equaled the calculated weight of the build-ing above ground, and a light structural steel of a new German-developed alloy demonstrate concentrated efforts to make the tall building feasible. There was also concern for risk to adjacent buildings from the changes to soil structure around a tall building. This issue was resolved by using a new type of water-tight steel-sheet piling around the foundation's perim-eter.[67] Lindskog, the hotel's structural engineer, wrote an article disprov-ing the "old bogey" of Shanghai's architectural community (that the soil could not support a tall building) and summarizing the achievements the hotel's foundation represents.[68] Despite these achievements, it appears that Hudec's solutions were not incorporated into the Council's proposed revisions to building rules for foundations in 1936.

The Hotel's Hybrid Style

An American skyscraper would seem to have been the inevitable model for a tall building in a city that saw itself as progressive as Shanghai did in the late 1920s. Travel to America by architects and the publication and wide distribution of American cultural and technical innovations contributed to a European and worldwide interest in America and its developments in architecture and culture. Far beyond Europe, American urban culture spread to cities such as Shanghai that from the 1930s began to bristle with Art Deco skyscrapers.[69] The Park Hotel, however, not only aspired to the American skyscraper aesthetic but occupied a place within modern Euro-pean architectural developments as well. This makes it greatly important for the study of the dispersion of architectural ideas beyond the sites of their geographical origin.

Shanghai's geographical isolation from the home countries of its foreign architects allowed a freedom of stylistic expression unknown to the European architects who reacted against a traditional stylistic heritage in the 1920s. By the late 1920s, the European architect in Shanghai's foreign community, wrote French architect R. A. Hamburger, was "not hindered in his perception by the rigors of tradition and rules of defined etiquette. The atmosphere of movement, change and excitement [in Shanghai] demand that the architect leave the ordinary path, forcing him to attempt experiments in order to arrive at the solution to multiple problems."[70]

The Park Hotel is part of this trend of experimentation, the contest to form imagery appropriate to the Shanghai architectural milieu where Hudec flourished. In designing a skyscraper, he could look to America for models, as he did in his travels there in 1927 and 1928, when he experienced the exuberant energy associated with the upward growth of America's dynamic cities, New York and Chicago. The number of skyscrapers erected in New York in 1926 was not to be surpassed until 1957. To the person on the street these skyscrapers, wrote an architectural critic in 1927, were "superhuman, seemingly conscious of their own mystic symbolism, [and] deliver[ed] America's message of a colossal reality, of a new life and its unbridled force."[71] Hudec also saw new buildings being erected in response to new forms of entertainment and technology; for example, 1927 was the year the talkies came to town.[72] He would eventually design at least three theaters in Shanghai, one in 1933 only two buildings away from the Park Hotel. A search for modern designs for modern buildings with modern functions typified Hudec's architectural environment.

In addition to generating innovative solutions to new functions, and rising to new degrees of construction, architectural design in New York of 1927 "may be regarded as the fulcrum on which the balance between the old and the new tipped with irrevocable finality in the favor of the latter."[73] The architect whom Hudec specifically cites as his inspiration, Raymond Hood, exemplifies this tension between traditional styles and new ideas, a tension encountered as architects attempted to express the modern ideals of the dynamic interwar period. The language of traditional baroque and classical styles was often applied to a façade stretched vertically, appropriate for corporate structures that earned the sobriquet *cathedrals of commerce.*[74] Hood designed the Chicago Tribune Building in 1924, in a competition whose significance to a generation of skyscraper designers cannot be emphasized enough.[75] All manner of expressions of height found their way into the widely publicized competition, but Hood's design, eventually executed, was essentially traditional in its gothicized façade.

In designing the Park Hotel Hudec said he strove for "an original interpretation of the new vertical-line style of architecture personified in American cities by Raymond Hood, famous U.S. artist."[76] For Hood's later skyscrapers, the American architect expanded the limits of the traditional style, turning away from ornament and traditional references to emphasize simplified vertical lines. From the expressive Gothic Chicago Tribune Building of 1924, to the brooding American Radiator Building of the same year, to the aggressively striped, more modernistic, Daily News Building of 1929–30 (the latter two in New York), Hood strove to find a vertical design that would best suit the new technology of the new machine-age society.[77] The abstraction of verticals to suit the height of a building became the accepted solution to the tall-building design, honed to greater degrees of refinement after Hood's time.

The verticals of the Park Hotel, however, are strongest on the model (fig. 14). The differences among the early drawings, the model, and the actual building—the drawings address massing and the model stresses verticality—reinforces the comparison between Hood and Hudec and their struggle to place the fulcrum between modern and traditional design (figs. 9, 12, 14, and 15). The Park's transformation from drawings to completed project, a process that illustrates its architect's growing understanding a skyscraper's vertical potential, corresponds to Raymond Hood's own transition from the decorative Gothic to abstract verticality in skyscraper aesthetic. Hudec understood that the quest for an appropriate tall-building design was also a quest to express not just new technology but human accomplishment. He said of his design, "I have tried to give the effect of vertical lines in the Joint Savings Society Building. Not only does this style make the building appear taller than it actually is but it adds grace, beauty and sensation of immense power."[78] He was seeking, then, to convey modern imagery of power by referring to an American skyscraper style.

As modern in style as Hudec and Hood professed their skyscrapers to be, they nevertheless perpetuated classical concepts. Both were constrained by the difficulty of introducing the scale of a tall building to the pedestrian city over which it looms. The solution was a classical three-tiered façade, a direct inheritance from widespread European-based Beaux-Arts sensibility of symmetry, balance, and logic often associated with Louis Sullivan. Sullivan, a pioneer of the modern tall building, recommended division into three horizontal sections: the first to appeal to the eye at ground level; the second to draw the eye upward; and the topmost to end in interesting interactions with the sky.[79] In the Park Hotel's case, grounding the first few floors in a horizontal design for the benefit of the pedestrian does not seem to have been of great concern since it overlooks the racecourse, and the details from bottom to top were less important than the effect of height. However, that he kept the received solution suggests the force of precedent on his design.

The factors affecting Hudec's design do not originate solely in America but reflect a complex combination of his own expressive aesthetics and his use of traditional styles. Between 1928 and 1934 Hudec undertook at least sixteen projects that, despite their distinctly modern features, creatively adapt traditional styles in what I call his gothic-modern phase. The two façades of the building housing the China Baptist Publication Society and

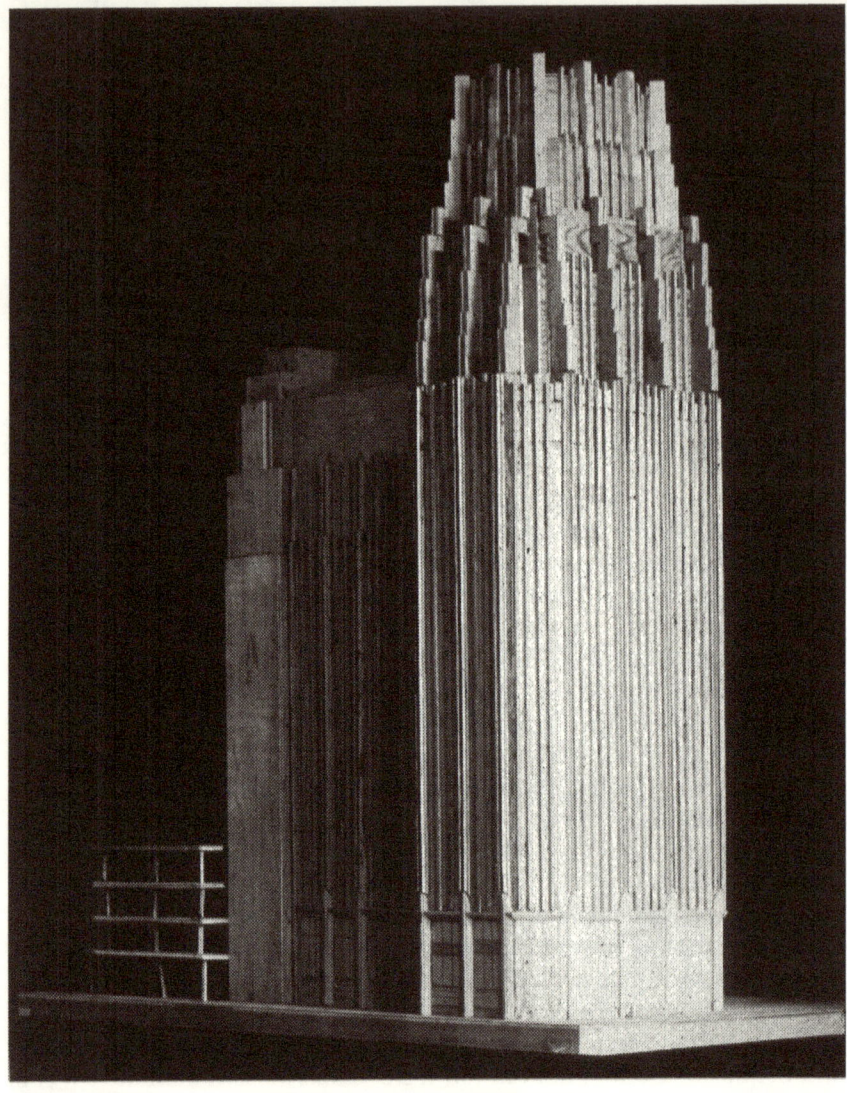

Fig. 14. Model of Park Hotel. Hudec Collection, University of Victoria Special Collections.

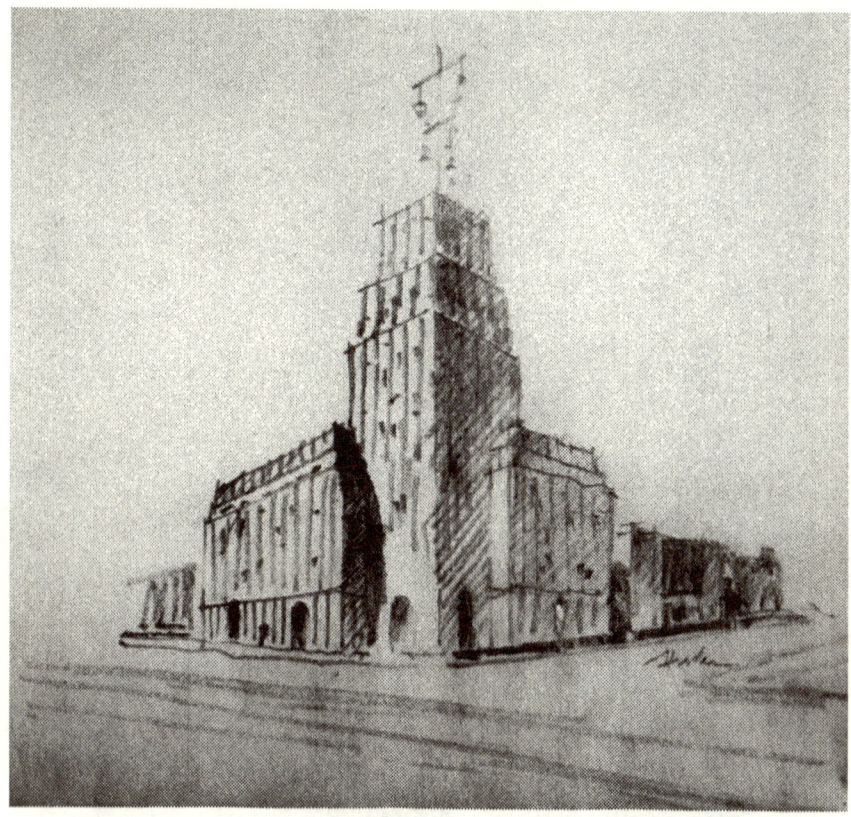

Fig. 15. Early design for Park Hotel. Sketch by L. E. Hudec. Hudec Collection, University of Victoria Special Collections.

Christian Literature, completed around 1930 and located one block behind the Bund between Yuanmingyuan and Bowuyuan Roads, illustrate some of these tendencies (figs. 16 and 17). Using the same dark burned-brick tile as found in the Park Hotel, Hudec created a dark, looming nine-story façade on the east side of the building. The striking silhouette against the sky, an exaggerated echo of the Park Hotel's, is produced by the culmination of sharp triangular shafts that begin at the base. The façade facing in the opposite direction, adorning the Christian Literature Society entrance, is a religious expression with a pointed arch of lighter brick extending from ground to cornice.

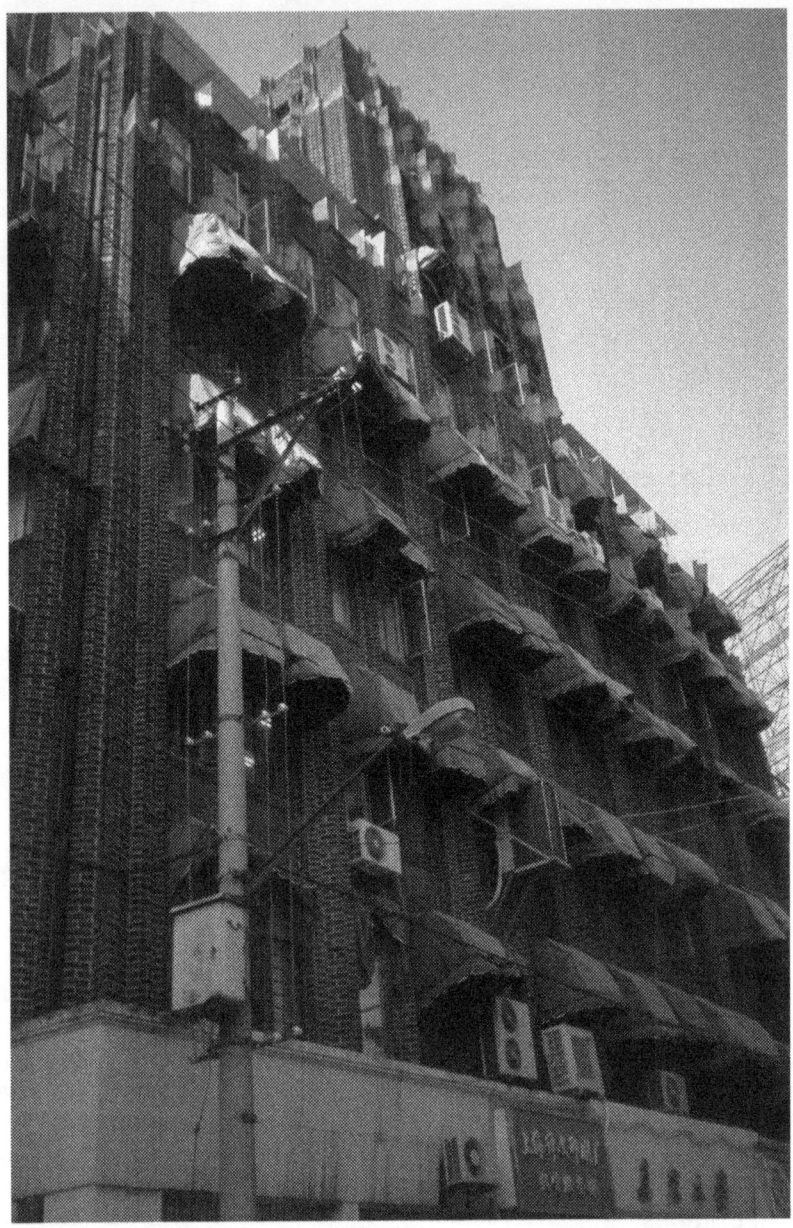

Fig. 16. China Baptist Publication Society and China Christian Literature Society building, Yuanmingyuan Road façade, 1930. L. E. Hudec, architect. Photo credit: Lenore Hietkamp, 2001.

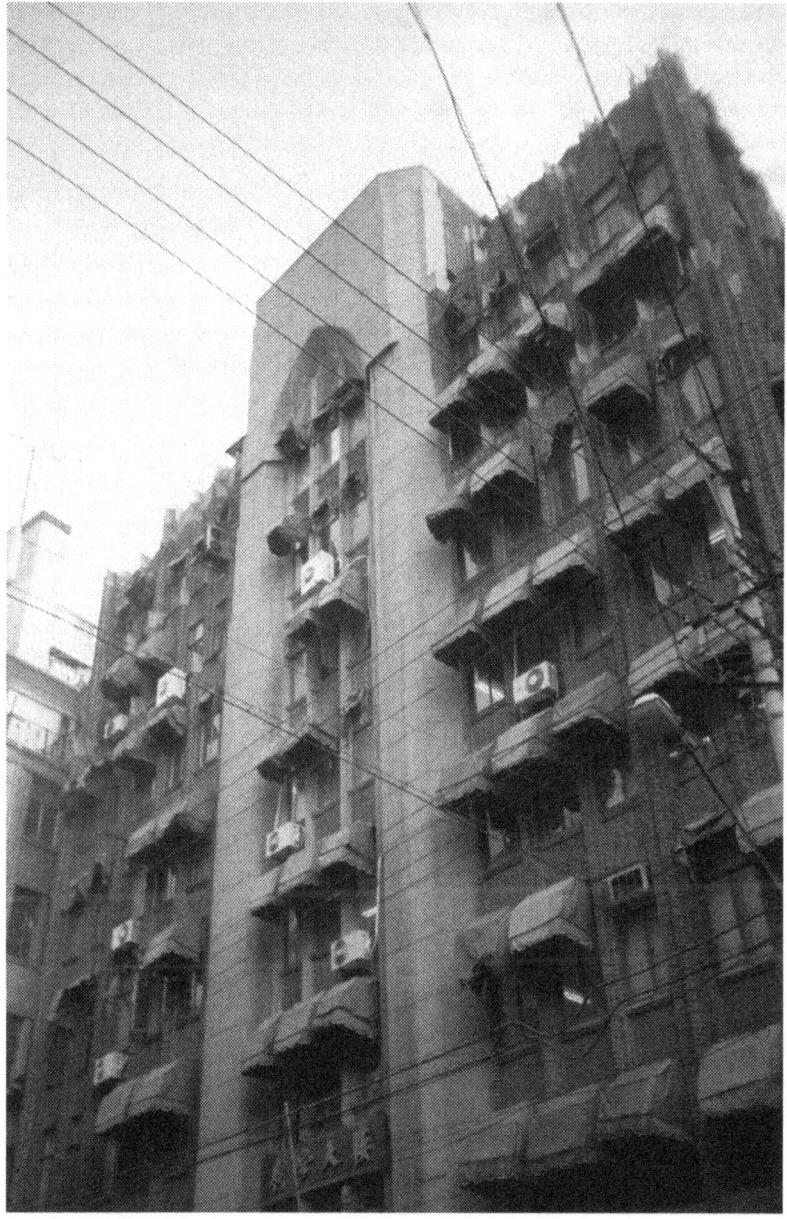

Fig. 17. China Baptist Publication Society and China Christian Literature Society building, Bowuyuan Road façade, 1930. L. E. Hudec, architect. Hudec Collection, University of Victoria Special Collections.

Such interest in the dynamic potential of a building's form, both to create aesthetic interest and to express its origin, not just its function, originates in German expressionism of the period before and just after the First World War. Notes on the best-known German expressionists appear in Hudec's sketchbook from his student days. As an organic art, architecture to the expressionists could borrow from the past any forms, colors, and textures that they felt conveyed the spiritual nature of buildings. Gothic references were popular since the style strongly associated architecture with spirituality, a preoccupation of the post–World War I period. The richly colored brick and stained glass of Gothic cathedrals created environments that uplifted troubled spirits. Interesting texture and color helped arouse emotion and induce positive psychological effects.[80] Torsten Warner, writing on German architecture in China, calls Hudec the only architect practicing expressionism in China. While Warner means to equate Hudec's "expressionism" with his creative ability rather than with German expressionism, Hudec's use of color and other visually appealing features combined with his deep interest in religion also closely paralleled the philosophy and principles of expressionist architects in Europe.[81] Richly detailed yet simply massed exteriors of almost all his buildings are enlivened through colored material: five-colored brick for the JSS building of 1928 on Sichuan Road; red and blue clinker brick for the German Protestant Church, no longer extant; alternating sepia and dark-brown, lozenge-shaped burnt tiles for the Park Hotel; red brick for the Moore Memorial Church, which still faces the old racecourse; and creamy tile for the Grand Theatre two doors up from the Park. In addition, the monumental and brooding drawings of the Park convey a basic pyramidal structure that seems a more important compositional element than the height of the building. It conveys an emotional quality similar to the many drawings by expressionist architects just after the First World War, drawings that were never realized in three dimensions (fig. 15).

Gothic color, part of a deeply embedded aesthetic, contributed to the Art Deco style that originated in Europe in the mid-20s, a style first publicly disseminated at the "Exposition Internationale des Art Décoratifs et Industriels Modernes" held in Paris in 1925.[82] Attention to tonal contrasts characterizes many Art Deco façades of 1920s skyscrapers. The startling black brickwork of Raymond Hood's American Radiator Building, of 1924, is a likely model for the Park's dark coloring, especially since Hudec would have seen it during his visit in 1927.

Art Deco may have originated in Europe, but it found popular expression in America, especially in New York City. Those years in which Hudec traveled to America, 1927 and 1928, marked a period in New York in which a few architects produced some of the most unusual buildings of the twentieth century, structures widely published and discussed. Art Deco ornament complemented many of the heroic skyscrapers because of its appeal to the imagination. It fascinated, and continues to fascinate, architects because it gives new life to working materials. Abstracted allusions to new technology such as steamships and railways illustrate humanity's lasting enchantment with its own ability to create materials with which to enrich daily life. Architectural surfaces are enhanced through old materials put to exotic use, or articulated through experimentation with newly available materials: metals and unexplored alloys, glass, plastics, and rubber, available in a wide range of patterns and colors.[83] In particular, Art Deco expressed an urban sophistication that meshed with the lifestyle of those living in the new apartment hotels.

Several buildings in New York are worth noting. The lobby of Raymond Hood's Daily News Building is clad in black glass and bronze; the upper reaches of the façade, in colored terra cotta. The first-floor exterior of the Chanin Building of 1926–29, whose interior Hudec sketched during his travels, was also clad in bronze and Belgian black marble. Accordingly, black granite faced Hudec's first three floors, black and pea-green marble adorned the public area on the first floor, and black opaque-glass columns and black-glass-topped counters provided accents in the banking hall (fig. 18). Shiny "metal rails, grills and neat stools" enhanced the bar (fig. 19).[84] They were not, however, the floral, curving, organic forms of the Chanin Building and other American buildings of the 1920s, but were instead geometric, often straight edged. The few original stylized features of the hotel's decor that still exist, particularly balcony railings and ventilation and security grills (fig. 20), are designed in vertical and horizontal lines of irregular length with an occasional curl, a pattern that apparently is repeated throughout the hotel in a variety of materials. Unpainted exterior railings, now oxidized to a warm red, are of Durametal, a nickel-silver alloy popular with Art Deco architects in the 1920s for its pliability.[85] Doors, staircase railings, and risers also carried the motif, as did the carpet and wall ornaments.[86] The flooring of colorful inlaid rubber demonstrated the latest advances in chemistry, while the terrazzo marble floor in the basement vault, lobby entrance, and dance floor off the grill room was fabricated by a local company that imported its machinery from America, England, and Germany. Tubular glass lamps from Czechoslovakia in the dance-floor ceiling looked vaguely space age, and the tubular metal chairs in the suites and banking space were clearly designs of the 1920s.[87]

The author of the grill-like motif found throughout the hotel is unknown. Whether it was Hudec—which is my guess—or one of his assistants, the use of the Art Deco style in Shanghai at that time was not unusual. In fact, among Chinese who embraced modernity, especially

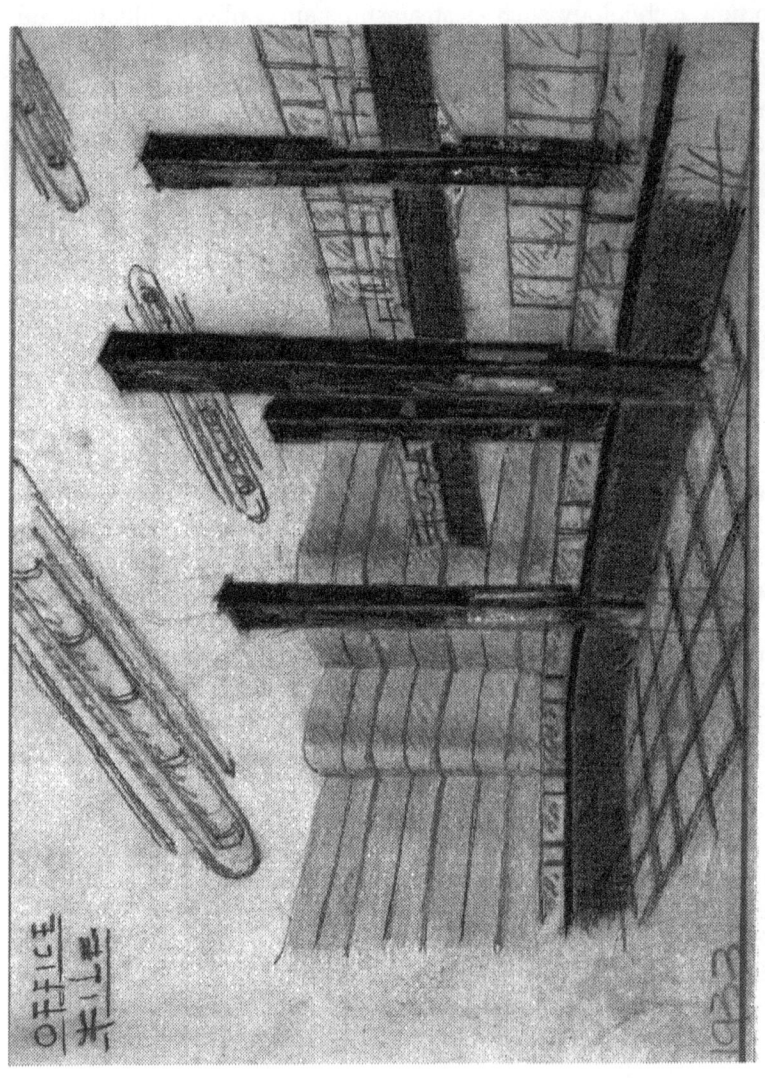

Fig. 18. Banking space, first floor and mezzanine, Park Hotel. Sketch by L. E. Hudec, 1933. Hudec Collection, University of Victoria Special Collections.

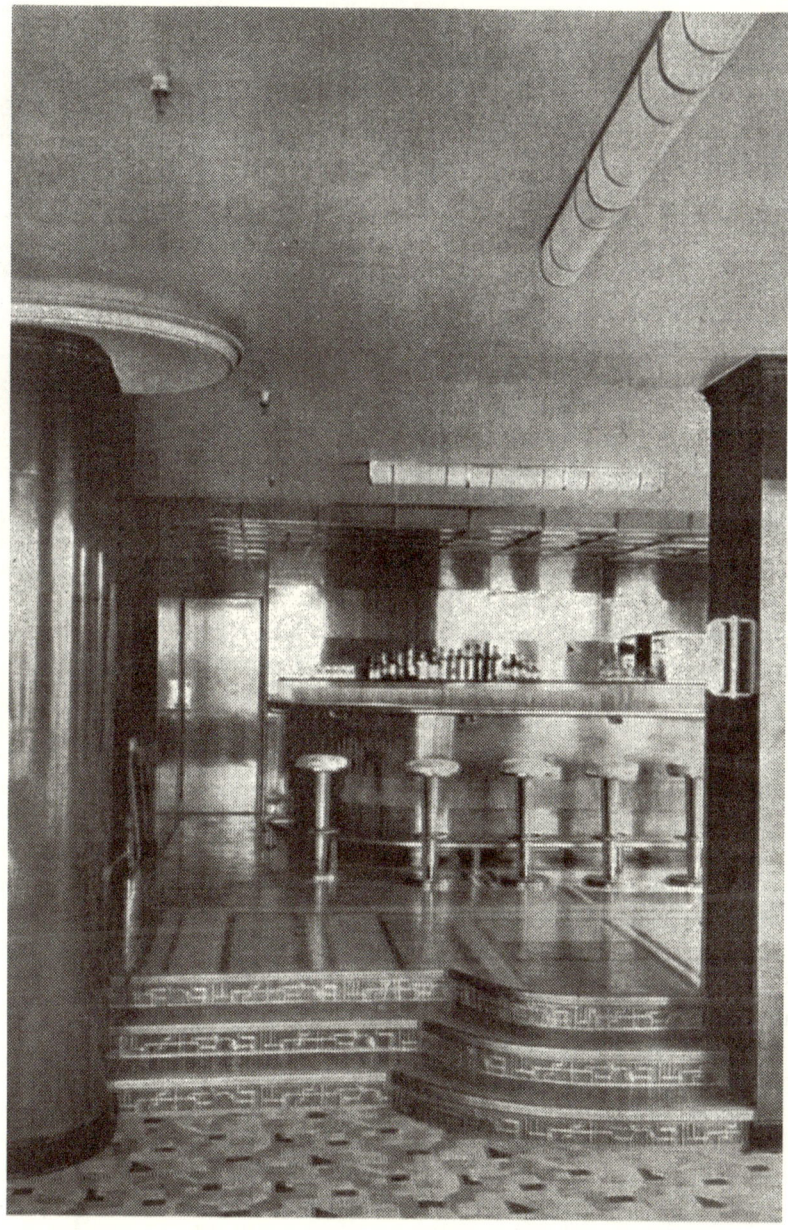

Fig. 19. Bar in Park Hotel. Reproduced from *Facts About the Park Hotel*, n.d. Hudec Collection, University of Victoria Special Collections.

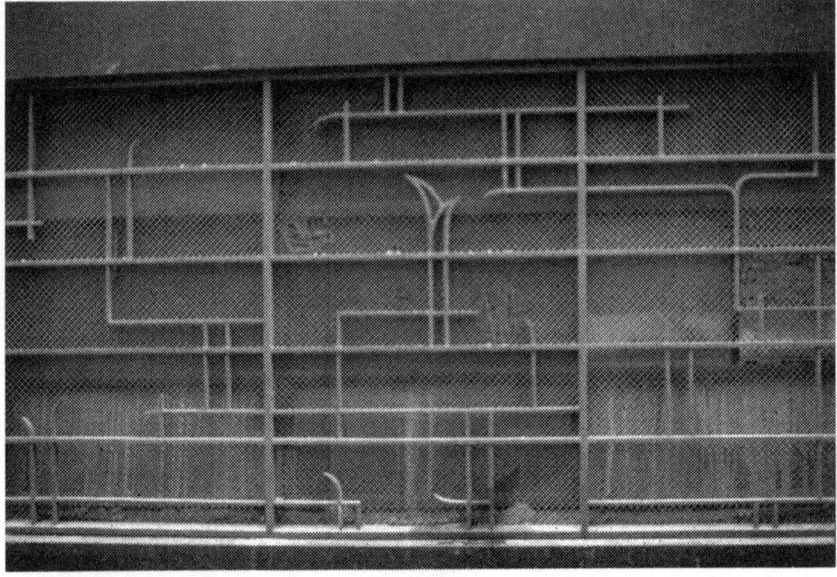

Fig. 20. Safety grill over basement window, Park Hotel. These grills were removed in 2000. Photo credit: Sunni Nishimura, 1997.

those in Shanghai, the Art Deco style was readily adopted as the fashion of the modern world and the global culture to which Shanghai aspired. Philosophical ideals of accessibility—notions originating in Europe and America—were key to the popularity of the style; the function of mass-produced products such as the automobile was suggested by Art Deco in graphic designs disseminated in a wide variety of venues. It became a major source for Chinese graphic design during the interwar period, when it evolved, as it did in other places around the world, into different regional modes. The Chinese entry in the Paris exposition of 1925 displayed work by Chinese artists who had studied in France. The few photographs available suggest that the Chinese entries showed a type of interior design that would soon be given the name Art Deco, taken from the title of the 1925 exposition.[88] By the 1930s, Chinese graphic artists had developed a distinct Shanghai Art Deco style. In it, traditional Chinese architectural ornamentation fused with the flattened space of Chinese painting, the clean lines found in articles used in daily life, and the rational study of geometric forms and perspective learned from the West.[89] The red lacquered columns and metallic-gold ceiling in the Park's grill room on the fourteenth floor were a flamboyant marriage of modern materials with a color scheme reminiscent of the broad applications of primary colors that characterized much of northern Chinese architecture. Red on architectural features indicated a wish for happiness and good fortune for the occupants, and yellow or gold, traditionally used for imperial architecture, signified power and wealth.[90] This type of decorative scheme, however, does not imply that only a Chinese clientele used this room; there was also a trend in Shanghai and elsewhere among foreigners toward interior decoration using exotic Chinese motifs, including moon doorways, lattice wood screens, and vivid paint on walls.[91]

The combination of European, American, and Chinese elements in the Park Hotel suggests a way to locate Hudec within the history of world architecture. Note first his German origins. Shanghai's economic status after the First World War was quite different from that of Germany. During postwar reconstruction, the German elite, needing both capital from which to rebuild their economy and models by which to rebuild their cities, sought outside sources that were deemed successful in representing a new, hopeful age.[92] Images of American skyscrapers were avidly studied in Germany throughout the 1920s, by way of exhibitions and publications on American architecture though few understood or wanted to build the vast symbols of capitalism.[93] Rather, neotraditionalist architects worked on their own hybrid buildings of traditional design, with modern attempts at height that served as status symbols for the corporate owners.[94]

The revival of tradition evident in the architecture by some of Hudec's generation sets it outside the work of avant-garde architects for whom the interwar period is best known. These architects in their turn strove to reconcile industrialism, society, and nature with mass-housing prototypes and futuristic city plans. Mostly European, these "heroes" reacted against the blind reuse of classical, gothic, Romanesque, and other traditional styles. They created buildings of such innovation that they dislodged the hold of previous traditions, laying down new definitions of architecture for the future.[95] Despite the distinctive "international style" that developed, the old and the new of this period cannot be polarized, for many architects began in one way and evolved into another, or they found virtues in the multitude of approaches to buildings of differing functions. The new ideas were well known to architects around the world. Germany was a wellspring of ideas during the early twentieth century; since 1900 it had been the "centre of European architectural thought," most notably the source of the Deutscher Werkbund, dating to 1907.[96]

Hudec made copious notes of the widely read volume *Das englische Haus* (1905), by the Werkbund's founder, Hermann Muthesius. This German architect advocated both appropriate form without excessive ornament to express function and the display of natural materials. Some of the ideas of this group helped form those of the widely influential Bauhaus, founded in 1919, whose ideal of pure functionalism is seen in Hudec's industrial architecture. One such example is his Union Brewery, whose strip windows, flat roof, and rectangular masses recall the factory aesthetic of the Bauhaus (fig. 21). This type of modernism spread across Europe and into America, and was embraced by many of Hudec's contemporary Hungarian and Czechoslovakian colleagues.[97] Hudec's familiarity with the work of these modern architects is evident from an issue found in the Hudec archive of the Czechoslovakian periodical *Tèr ès Forma*, in which one of his houses is featured. Some of Hudec's later houses in Shanghai, specifically the D. V. Woo house of 1936, and a house for Y. T. Shen, shown in a drawing in the Hudec Collection (fig. 22), show adaptations of the modern architecture, with flat white walls, long smooth lines, strip windows, and flat roofs.

The more modern, functional work of Hudec's later career never loses Hudec's flamboyant trademark. The D. V. Woo house shows in its curves, texture, and rich material the fancies of ornamentation that are the sum of remnants of Hudec's Central European heritage and his freedom to experiment, unique to Shanghai. The Park Hotel is also eloquent testimony to its architect's ability to adapt and synthesize a variety of sources. Hudec commented on how inspiration could be found in many places: "The architect may borrow from a hundred sources, but the result is his very own when he has fused all these component parts into one harmonious whole whose greatest characteristic . . . is its freshness and departure from all stilted and stereotyped old forms."[98]

Implications of the Park Hotel

The hotel's construction between 1932 and 1934 marked the end of an epoch during which luxury hotels around the world attracted Western travelers. These hotels abounded in Eastern countries along the major rail and water routes connecting Europe to destinations of "oriental fantasy." The nostalgia associated with these palaces of indulgence is captured in an equally lush book published in 1987. Surprisingly, the Park Hotel has been included among the entries featuring European designs that associated nineteenth-century traditions with luxury but excluded the modern designs of the twentieth. In one of the book's essays, Martin Meade notes that the "hallmark always intrinsic to [the] design of these hotel-palaces was the transposition and adaptation of their architecture, to the new scale of their specific location, to the climate and materials of the country and culture which they imposed themselves upon and with which, to some

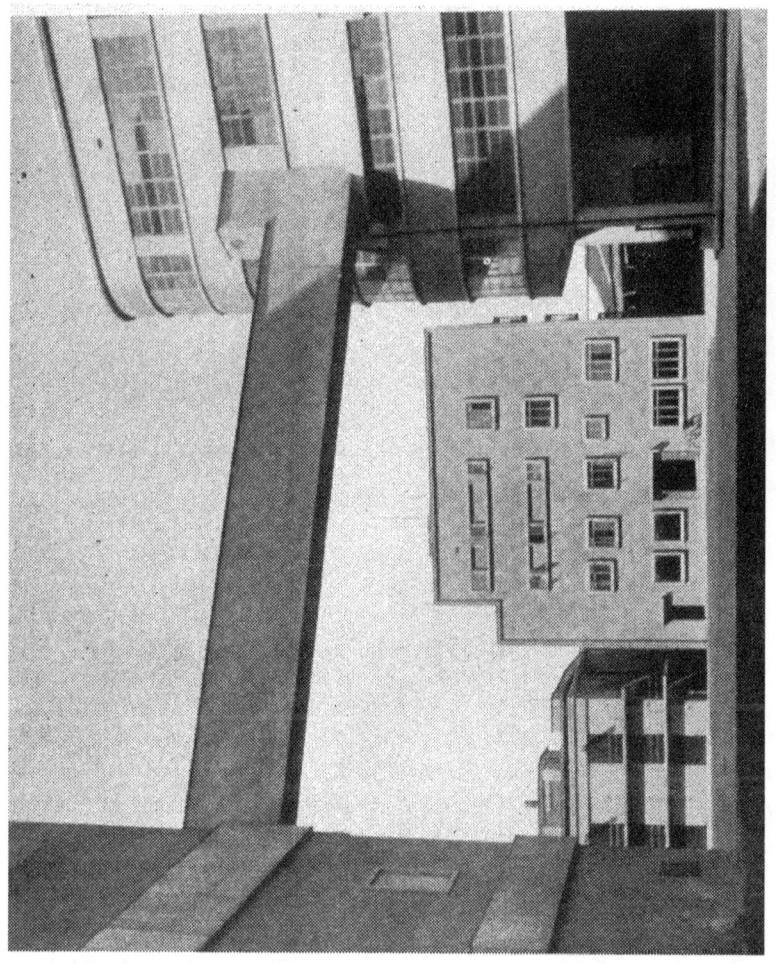

Fig. 21. Union Brewery, 1932–33. L. E. Hudec, architect. Hudec Collection, University of Victoria Special Collections.

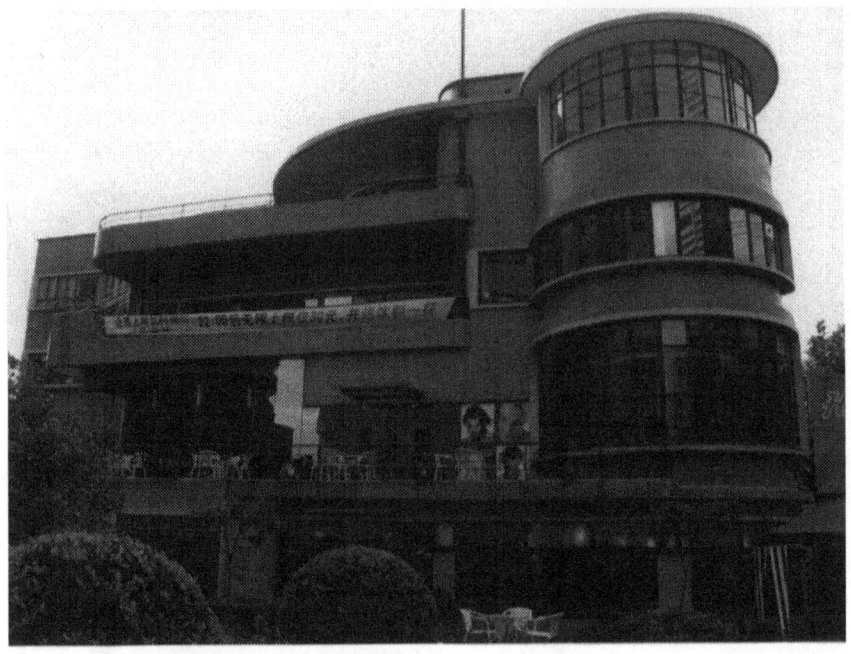

Fig. 22. Former D. V. Woo house, 1938. L. E. Hudec, architect. Photo credit: Lenore Hietkamp, 2001.

extent, they were integrated."[99] By making visual connections to the homes of their foreign clientele, the hotels brought to the exotic locations associations with class, comfort, and luxury.

A luxury hotel in Shanghai had to appeal across national borders, and to express the aspirations of its owners. The bankers who commissioned the Park Hotel took part in a move to be modern, or as Leo Lee translates, "to be consciously opposed to the old (*jiu*)."[100] The highly visible imagery from Western countries, synthesized by Hudec, coalesced in the Park Hotel as "the epitome of the urban world of consumption and . . . . a glamourous foreign-flavoured lifestyle."[101] Hybridity in architecture, however, points to a need to find elsewhere images and models on which to build, suggesting that Shanghai is a city of fanciful architecture belying the larger domestic reality of China.

The Western architecture of the 1920s and 30s was not intended to address Shanghai's social problems. Its architects, for the most part, were concerned with creating impressions. As the result of competitions for visibility and the manifestation of wealth and privilege, the Western image of the city hid the ordinary buildings and squalor of the densely populated areas. It was not a situation unique to Shanghai. Impressive structures in other cities, particularly New York, with its fleet of far bigger buildings, also belied endemic poverty. In Shanghai, however, there was a blatant attempt to create impressions and ignore more common, basic issues such as living conditions for the majority of the city's population.[102] During the planning stages for the solid, monumental Hong Kong and Shanghai Bank in 1919, a brief from the London head office advised, "Spare no expense but dominate the Bund."[103] The bank's dome, placed forward rather than over the building's centre, indeed looms over the Bund. And not just the Westerners subscribed to the promotion of dominance. A Chinese businessman of the day observed, "Why spend money on what no one sees?"[104]

Writers W. H. Auden and Christopher Isherwood had little good to say about the city's presentation in their joint observations, made while traveling in China in the mid-1930s and published in 1939:

> Seen from the river, towering above their couchant guardian warships, the semi-skyscrapers of the Bund present, impressively, the façade of a great city. But it is only a façade. The spirit which dumped them upon this unhealthy mud-bank, thousands of miles from their kind, has been too purely and brutally competitive. The biggest animals have pushed their way to the brink of the water; behind them is a sordid and shabby mob of smaller buildings. Nowhere a fine avenue, a spacious park, an imposing central square. Nowhere anything civic at all.[105]

These are strong words directed against a dynamic city, yet it could be argued that the Park Hotel tried to create civic space, albeit for an elite crowd. It faced the racetrack and catered to Chinese and Westerners alike. It was also some distance from the Bund, not part of the first impressions of the city to be seen from steamships coming up the Huangpu River from the Yangtse (Yangzi) River.

The vast gap between traditional and modern within their own ranks did not fail to concern the Chinese bourgeoisie. Carol Lynn Waara, examining art periodicals from the interwar period, describes a cartoon satirizing the pursuit of modern ways that existed in the midst of a country of old ways:

> [A] Westernized man in a top hat, representing China's banking community, apparently wedding a more traditional Chinese woman in high mandarin collar and simple, old-fashioned hair-

style, representing rural China. The caption reads, "Is eternal co-operation possible?"[106]

As both Bergère and Coble have shown, the bankers created their own associations in efforts to create equal business transactions between foreign and Chinese banks, both modern and old style. They tried to establish modern business ventures outside Shanghai, for reasons not necessarily purely capitalistic. The hotel itself shows an attempt to raise China to the higher standards of an international tourism industry. That they failed to effect real change outside of Shanghai, Bergère explains, was due more to the unstable central government than their own inability to see and address the problems around them. Shanghai was not a Chinese city—this is implied by notions that it lacked a strong architectural heritage or that the bourgeoisie behind the hotel's origins was weak in comparison to the needs of China. In fact, such conclusions, Yeh says, risk overlooking not only the transformation of the material foundation of urban life that was brought about by the forces of commerce, but also the very phenomenon of Shanghai modernity.[107] Just like the Park Hotel's towering presence, the evolution of a new modern culture in Shanghai was broadcast to a widening circle of Chinese society.[108] Thus, the façades of the city cannot be analyzed apart from the city as a whole; such a separation lends itself to pejorative interpretations. The façades must be seen in the light of circumstances from which they originated.

The visual effect of the Park could be part of an unintended civic role: it remained a landmark until taller buildings eclipsed it in the 1980s. As a building intended to impress viewers and communicate modern pursuits, the Park Hotel was compared with the Empire State Building, completed in 1931, in details such as rubber flooring and high-speed elevators.[109] But a deeper similarity points to a perception of the hotel in relation to its visual environment. Finished only three years before the Park, the Empire State took a "solitary stance" as the tallest building in the world, a "lonely symbol of the breakdown in logic that produced it," just as within its own sphere the Park Hotel did.[110] Other skyscrapers, because they reflect economic vicissitudes, are rarely alone. Even before the Second World War, the skyscraper-studded cityscapes of America were sites for explorations of style and practicable solutions to functional problems. Architectural historian Spiro Kostof asserts that skyscrapers are meant to be "admired from all sides and to command a large visual territory," but they were constantly eclipsed by closer, newer, and taller buildings. The American city, Kostof goes on, became "a collection of tall buildings concerned with the visual effect they are creating among others who posture in like manner, keen on holding a distinctive place in the skyline," challenging architects' creativity as cities continued to develop. In fact, he questions, if "for the starkest effect, the freestanding tower should rise alone in the center of the city-form . . . what modern institution might deserve such distinction?"[111] In Shanghai, that institution was the Joint Savings Society, the model of successful modern Chinese banks before the Communist takeover, enjoying its distinction through representation in a cityscape occasioned by a unique modernizing phenomenon.

Notes

Primary research material came from the Laszlo Hudec Collection of drawings, photographs, and newspaper clippings assembled by the architect and donated by his family to the University of Victoria's Maltwood Art Museum and Gallery. I am grateful to Martin Segger at the Maltwood Art Museum, Chris Petter at the University of Victoria's Special Collections, and Christopher Thomas, Astri Wright, and Kathlyn Liscomb in the Art History Department at the University of Victoria. This essay was written in 1999; since then, my conclusions have not changed in substance, but they are continually enriched and informed by new discussions that relate to the history of the Park Hotel, Shanghai's built environment, and the modern prerevolution aspirations of the Chinese entrepreneurs. One of these is Ackbar Abbas's essay, "Cosmopolitan De-scriptions: Shanghai and Hong Kong," in *Cosmopolitanism*, ed. Carol Breckenridge et al. (Durham and London: Duke University Press, 2002), 209–28, on the nature of cosmopolitanism peculiar to Hong Kong and Shanghai. The article discusses how spaces identified as cosmopolitan, of past or present, are negotiated as local or global. Abbas provides a larger context for my discussion of the nature of modern identity promoted by the Park Hotel, its owners, and its architect; I explore Abbas's arguments in relation to Hudec's work in Shanghai in more depth in a forthcoming essay in *Arts et Histoire de Chine* (Paris: Sorbonne Institute and Centre de Recherche sur L'Extrême-Orient de Paris [CREOPS]), vol. 2.

Invaluable recent research into documents of social history in Shanghai provides other perspectives on the hotel's function. In an important collection of essays about everyday life in early twentieth-century China, Brett Sheehan's social history of savings societies in China during this period characterizes the Joint Savings Society, the owner of the Park Hotel, as the largest of these societies, strengthening my claims about the hotel's significance; see "The Modernity of Savings, 1900–1937," in *Everyday Modernity in China*, ed. Madeleine Yue Dong and Joshua Goldstein (Seattle: University of Washington Press, 2006), chap. 4. In the same volume, Dong's essay on the China Travel Service (CTS) and the tourism industry in China, "Shanghai's Traveler" (chap. 6), offers a critical component to research on the Park Hotel. The social function of this tenant of the hotel, whose office opened in the Park Hotel's ground floor the year the hotel opened, fleshes out the experience of the Chinese visitors to the hotel. One can imagine the hotel's marketing department working in tandem with the CTS to offer the tour packages Dong discusses, and the hotel's concierge directing visitors to the agency's office.

My exploration of the hotel as an important part of Shanghai's identity is balanced by Lu Hanchao's work in *Beyond the Neon Lights: Everyday Shanghai in the Early Twentieth Century* (Berkeley: University of California Press, 1999) and by his more recent essay on material life in China, "Out of the Ordinary: Implications of Material Culture and Daily Life in China," in Dong and Goldstein, *Everyday Modernity*, chap. 1. Lu examines the life of everyday people in Shanghai—those who were most likely not to stay at the Park Hotel, or to have access to any of Hudec's architecture—and demonstrates that the life of the majority is often overlooked in the scholarly pursuit of a city's identity, no matter that the quest for identity was the primary goal of the city's wealthiest and most influential businessmen and politicians.

1 Shanghai, "City of Glitter and Ghosts," *The Economist*, 24 Dec. 1996–6 Jan. 1995, 40.

2 Wen-hsin Yeh, "Shanghai Modernity: Commerce and Culture in a Republican City," *China Quarterly* 150 (June 1997): 377.

3 The new motif of three parallel vertical lines does little to contribute to the hotel's uniqueness amid a large global family of ordinary American Art Deco buildings, and diverges from the hotel's original motifs, which were creative elaborations of vertical, horizontal, and circular lines. The latest interior renovations were completed in 1997 under the direction of an American designer.

4 Harries draws an analogy to map reading, where signs lead to paths that outline a definable territory (*The Ethical Function of Architecture* [Cambridge, MA: MIT Press, 1997], 98–99, 102–10).

5 "History of Images," in *New Perspectives on Historical Writing*, ed. Peter Burke (Cambridge, 1991), 169.

6 *Behind the Postmodern Façade: Architectural Change in Late Twentieth-Century America* (Berkeley: University of California Press, 1993), 67.

7 Yeh, "Shanghai Modernity," 381.

8 Ibid., 386. Paraphrased from Xu Dingxin's paper, "National Goods Advertising in Shanghai and Its Distinguishing Features, 1920s and 1930s," presented at the seminar "Consumer Culture in Shanghai," Cornell University, July 1995.

9 At the end of this note are the names of the board of directors, taken from an undated commemoration booklet, *An Oriental Skyscraper: The New Joint Savings Society Building* in the Hudec Collection. See my thesis, "The Park Hotel and Its Architect, Laszlo Hudec: A Metaphor for Pre-Communist China" (University of Victoria, March 1998), for further details of the board of directors, chap. 1 and app. B.

Some Chinese spelling of names, in square brackets, were found in Max Perleberg, *Who's Who in Modern China* (Hong Kong: Ye Olde Printerie, Ltd., 1954), 47, 240, 249–250; Howard L. Boorman, ed., *Biographical Dictionary of Republican China*, (New York: Columbia University Press, 1970), 1:192–96; 3:379–81, 427–29, 452–53; 4:50–52; George F. Nellist, ed., *Men of Shanghai and North China: A Standard Biographical Reference Work* (Shanghai: Oriental Press, 1933), 70, 75; Chinese Communist Party, *Biographies of Kuomintang Leaders*, John K. Fairbank, trans. (Cambridge, MA: Harvard University, mimeographed for private distribution by the Committee on International and Regional Studies, 1948), n.p.

The JSS board of directors consisted of Dr. W. W. Yen [Yen Hui-ching]; Dr. C. T. Wang [Wang Cheng-ting (Ju-tang)]; K. P. Chen [Chen Kuang-fu]; Y. F.

Kwei; Dr. D. C. Wu [Wu Ting-chang]; T. M. Chew [Chou Tso-min]; Y. Hou [Hu Yun]; Dr. Y. M. Chien [Chien Yung-ming (T. Hsin-chih)]; Fred C. Sze; Jean Z. Y. Horn; Sheng J. Wang; Z. L. Loo; L. S. Tan.

10 Tess Johnston and Deke Erh, *A Last Look: Western Architecture in Old Shanghai* (Hong Kong: Old China Hand Press, 1993).

11 Bergère says that the economy that developed at this time, consisting of dual business transactions in both traditional and modern practices, translated into the development of two very different economies (*The Golden Age of the Chinese Bourgeoisie, 1911–1937*, trans. Janet Lloyd [New York: Cambridge University Press, 1986], 25).

12 *Shanghai Times*, 7 May 1928, 1.

13 The name Joint Savings Society is used in contemporary English publications as well as in several different biographies in Boorman, *Biographical Dictionary*; see n. 8 above for page references. The four banks became known as the *Beisihang*, or the four northern banks (ibid., 3:427). Most private modern banks were assimilated by the Communist government after 1949 (John K. Fairbank, *The Great Chinese Revolution, 1800–1985* [New York: Harper & Row], 278).

14 For example, Bergère, *Golden Age*; idem, "The Other China: Shanghai from 1919–1951," in *Shanghai, Revolution and Development in an Asian Metropolis*, ed. Christopher Howe (New York: Cambridge University Press), 1981; idem, "The Political Failure of the Bourgeoisie," in *Cambridge History of China*, ed. John. K. Fairbank, vol. 12, *Republican China 1912–1949*, pt. 1 (New York: Cambridge University Press, 1983); Parks M. Coble Jr., *The Shanghai Capitalists and the Nationalist Government, 1927–1937* (Cambridge, MA: Council on East Asian Studies, Harvard University, 1980); Joseph Fewsmith, *Party, State, and Local Elites in Republican China: Merchant Organizations and Politics in Shanghai, 1890–1930* (Honolulu: University of Hawaii Press, 1985).

15 Coble, *Shanghai Capitalists*, 321 n. 79; 24–25, 276 n. 40. On the board of directors see n. 9 above.

16 After the fall of the Ching Dynasty, modern Chinese banks gradually replaced imperial and foreign banks as money lenders, and issued banknotes to old-style banks based on deposits placed in reserve. See Andrea Lee McElderry, *Shanghai Old-Style Banks (Ch'ien-chuang), 1800–1935: A Traditional Institution in a Changing Society* (Ann Arbor: Center of Chinese Studies, The University of Michigan, 1976), 16, 17, 133.

17 Chang Kia-ngau, "Toward Modernization of China's Currency and Banking, 1927–37" in *The Strenuous Decade: China's Nation-Building Efforts, 1927–1937*, ed. Paul K. T. Sih (New York: St. John's University Press, 1970), 137. In 1927, the total amount of deposits in modern banks was worth $360,000,000. Parks Coble explains that these leading banks held the largest number of securities in China (*Shanghai Capitalists*, 285 n. 23).

18 Fewsmith, *Local Elites*, 120–21.

19 Wu Ting-chang became Chiang Kai-shek's Minister of Industry in 1935, and Wang Cheng-ting was a member of the Central Executive Committee (Chinese Communist Party, *Biographies of Kuomintang Leaders*, n.p. [n. 9 above]).

20 Chien Yung-ming, Wang Cheng-ting, and Yen Hu-ching, respectively. (Nellist, *Men of Shanghai*, 70; Boorman, *Biographical Dictionary*, 3:362–64, 50–52 [both n. 9 above]).

21 D. W. Y. Kwok, *Scientism in Chinese Thought, 1900–1950* (New Haven: Yale University Press, 1965), 3. Not all Chinese believed advances in technology were beneficial to China; see for example the review of arguments for and against railroads in China, in Ralph Huenemann's *The Dragon and the Iron Horse: The Economics of Railroads in China, 1876–1937* (Cambridge, MA: Harvard University Press, 1984), 37. Leo Ou-fan Lee analyzes the development of the Chinese association with Western scientific ideas in "In Search of Modernity: Some Reflections on a New Mode of Consciousness in Twentieth-Century History and Literature," in *Ideas Across Cultures: Essays on Chinese Thought in Honor of Benjamin I. Schwartz*, ed. Paul A. Cohen and Merle Goldman (Cambridge, MA: Council on East Asian Studies, Harvard University Press, 1990).

22 Cited from "Methods and Materials for Study" by Kwok, *Scientism*, 95.

23 Bergère, *Golden Age*, 210 [n. 11 above]; Charles Beard, *Whither Mankind: A Panorama of Modern Civilizations* (New York: Blue Ribbon Books, Inc., 1928). Hu Shi adapted this essay, titled "The Civilizations of the East and the West," 1–25, in other versions such as "Let Us All Look at Ourselves in the Mirror," cited by Kwok, *Scientism*, 101, n. 34.

24 See above, n. 8, for Boorman's *Biographical Dictionary* entries on the numerous enterprises initiated by the board members.

25 Bryna Goodman, *Native Place, City and Nation: Regional Networks and Identities in Shanghai, 1853–1937* (Berkeley: University of California Press, 1995), 219. See also Boorman, *Biographical Dictionary*, 3:427; 1:194.

26 Marie-Claire Bergère, "Political Failure,12:768 (n. 14 above).

27 The reason given for the formation of the JSS is that the founding banks wanted to try stabilize note issue. On the history of the banknote problem, see my thesis, "Park Hotel," 18–19 (n. 9 above); McElderry, *Shanghai Old-Style Banks*, 17, 19 (n. 16 above); and Frank M. Tamagna, *Banking and Finance in China* (New York: International Secretariat, Institute of Pacific Relations, Publications Office, 1942), 15–16. From less than $1,500,000 in 1923, deposits in the JSS grew to almost $62,000,000 by 1932 ("Tallest Building between London and Tokyo Soon Ready," *Industrial Annual and Trade Review*, April 1933, 9).

28 *China Press*, 5 Nov. 1931, 3.

29 "New Chinese-Owned Park Hotel Will Be Operated on Foreign Lines," *China Weekly Review*, 10 Nov. 1934, 368.

30 "Nesson Will Hold Sway in Shanghai's Biggest Kitchen," *China Press*, 1 Dec. 1934, 16.

31 "Park Hotel's Sky Terrace Thrown Open," *China Press*, 4 Aug. 1935, n.p.

32 For a newly escaped prisoner of war, Hudec must have feared the possibility of encountering the strong sentiments felt by many international residents in China against Germans and allied nationals.

33 Most of the biographical material is taken from an unpublished manuscript by Dr. Ivan Kotsis in the Hudec Collection. Subsequent interviews with the architect's widow and three children shed light on Hudec's escape and the circumstances of the family's flight from Shanghai.

34 From a letter dated 9 April 1929, addressed to Mr. Singloh Hsu, General Manager of the National Commercial Bank, Shanghai, in the Hudec Collection.

35 For more details on these and other projects see my thesis, "Park Hotel,"

app. A, 107–10, chap. 1, 20–29, and throughout chap. 3.

36 By 1929 there were 44 architectural firms in Shanghai and 55 by 1934, mostly foreign, according to the *China Architects and Builders Compendium*, cited by Jeffrey W. Cody, "Henry K. Murphy, an American Architect in China, 1914–1935" (PhD diss., Cornell University, 1981)," 316 n. 6. See also Zhang Zaiyuan, "From West to Shanghai: Architecture and Urbanism in Shanghai from 184 to 1940," *A & U* 273 (June 1993): 96. Fifty-five Chinese architects, a statistic compiled from the Society of Chinese Architects' Membership List, 1933, are listed in Cody's dissertation in app. 2, "Directory of the 'First Generation of Chinese Architects,'" 351–55. The majority were trained in America, two at German schools and one at a Belgian School, as well as a few in schools at London and Paris. Only five Chinese architects are listed in Nellist's *Men of Shanghai* of 1933 (n. 9 above), a reference source apparently intended for foreign use, since its coverage of important Chinese is sketchy. It is likely that most of the Chinese architects listed above were employed in foreign firms.

37 *China Press*, 2 December 1934. Sun Lizhi was educated at the University of Illinois, and was a member of the Society of Architects. Other members of Hudec's team identified by this source are L. Matrai, J. L. Slaschov, and K. L. Egikoff.

38 Cody, "Henry K. Murphy," 316, 326.

39 Ibid., 313–14, fig. 55. On the extended debate over national style and modernism, see Robert Fan, "Efforts to Revive Chinese Architectural Beauty," *Shanghai Sunday Times*, Christmas 1929, n.p.; Liang Ssu-Ch'eng, "China's Architectural Heritage and Tasks of Today," *People's China*, November 1952, 31–36, reproduced in *China's Cultural Legacy and Communism*, ed. Ralph Croizier (New York, 1970), 256–64; and Wang Feng, "Debate Over Modern or Traditional Architecture in Beijing," *Beijing Review*, 9–15 September 1996, 17–19.

40 Hudec's son Martin recalls accompanying his father on visits to houses under construction for Chinese clients. The young child's mind was impressed with the number of bedrooms his father had to incorporate into his designs; when he asked his father why so many, he was told they were for the owners' wives (personal interview, 11 March 1997).

41 During the formulation of the Treaty of Versailles in 1919, the lack of recognition for China's participation in the war sparked the May Fourth Movement of 1919, a strong demonstration against the presence of foreign treaty powers. Coble says that the Chinese capitalists supported the anti-imperialist movements, although they were equally concerned with the potential dangers of further influence from the warlords prior to the Kuomintang takeover in 1927 (*Shanghai Capitalists*, 27 [n. 14 above]). This attitude contributed to the rise of Nationalist and Communist parties throughout the 1920s and 30s. See Bergère, "Shanghai, or the Other China," 13; Benjamin I. Schwartz, "Themes in Intellectual History: May Fourth and After," 402, 407; and Ernest P. Young, "Politics in the Aftermath of Revolution: The Era of Yuan Shih-Kai, 1912–1916," 269, all in *Cambridge History of China*, vol. 12 (n. 14 above).

42 He forbade Mrs. Hudec to drive after she got her license for fear of an accident that would launch them into some legal action in Chinese courts in which no consulate could intervene.

43 German-Chinese relations date to the 1750s. Although China had declared

war on Germany and Austro-Hungary in 1917, the reaction to the Treaty of Versailles eventually restored relations. Germany lost all imperialist trappings and all its concessions in China in 1919, and Germany's industrial interests gradually resumed, for they presented no threat to the Chinese (William C. Kirby, *Germany and Republican China* [Stanford: Stanford University Press, 1984], 16, 177).

44 Rhoads Murphy cites grim statistics of numbers of Chinese bodies picked up on streets in the International Settlement: 5,590 in 1935 and 20,746 in 1937 (*Shanghai: Key to Modern China* [Cambridge, MA: Harvard University Press, 1953], 12).

45 As an apartment hotel, the Park had rooms varying from singles with a bath to full suites with living rooms and kitchenettes. Robert Stern, Gregory Gilmartin, and Thomas Mellins, *New York 1930: Architecture and Urbanism between the Two World Wars* (New York: Rizzoli International Publications, 1987), 207–8.

46 Martin Meade, *Grand Oriental Hotels from Cairo to Tokyo* (n.p.: Vendome Press, 1987), chap. 1.

47 A famous contemporary one was the Park Hotel in New York. A search of Park Hotel on the Internet yields over 20,000 sites.

48 J. V. Davidson-Houston, *Yellow Creek: The Story of Old Shanghai* (London: Putnam, 1962), 80. G. Lanning and S. Couling explain that in 1862, 19 streets changed names from British to Chinese (*The History of Shanghai*, for the Shanghai Municipal Council [Shanghai: Kelly & Walsh, 1921], 451).

49 Pan Ling, *In Search of Old Shanghai* (Hong Kong: Joint Publishing Co., 1982), 54.

50 Betty Peh-T'i Wei, *Shanghai: Crucible of Modern China* (New York: Oxford University Press, 1987), 120; Harriet Sergeant, *Shanghai* (London: Jonathon Cape, 1991), 102–14.

51 *An Oriental Skyscraper: The New Joint Savings Society Building* (Shanghai, n.p., n.d.), 6.

52 Pan Ling, *In Search*, 65. Effects of the angle of the street at this site, combined with Shanghai's climate, are other possible reasons for the site, as explored in depth in my thesis, "Park Hotel," 45–48.

53 Telephone interview, 30 January 1996.

54 The Mansion's plans were changed in 1932 from 19 stories to 22, the same number as in the Park Hotel, but the Mansion was at least 20 feet shorter in total height, although the precise height of these buildings is not accurately documented. Zhang, "From West to Shanghai," 93 (n. 36 above), says the Mansion is 76.7 m, and the Park 83.8 m, while Torsten Warner, *Deutsche Architektur in China*, 132 (intro., n. 15), says the Park is 87 m. Warner's figure corresponds to reports at the time of the hotel's opening 284 or 285 feet, plus a 15-foot flagpole, bringing the total height to 300 feet.

55 *China Press*, 5 Nov. 1931, 3.

56 Ibid.

57 Unlike many other buildings, such as the Cathay Hotel, which appear large, but have their center cut out to serve as a light well.

58 "Grand Hotel Faces Race Course," *Shanghai Sunday Times Industrial Supplement*, 15 Dec. 1929, 40. It is not clear whether this design and the one in the next note were part of a competition for a large hotel on the site of the Park, or just

speculative designs for a nearby location.

59 "The Monster Hotel Which Is Shortly To Be Built Opposite the Racecourse," no citation information (Hudec Collection).

60 Carol Willis, *Form Follows Finance: Skyscrapers in New York and Chicago* (New York: Princeton Architectural Press, 1995), 166–67. On the morphology of central business districts and the cycles of tall buildings, see Willis's pt. 2, titled "Just Speculating: Observations on the Dynamics of CBDs," 145–86.

61 "1929 Proves Record Year for Local Building," *Shanghai Sunday Times Industrial Supplement*, 15 Dec. 1929, 19.

62 "22-Storey Building Facing Racecourse Tallest Skyscraper on 4 Continents," *China Press*, 5 Nov. 1931, 1.

63 Coble follows the course of the depression that eventually hit Shanghai in 1934 and 1935 after the erratic rise and fall of world silver prices (*Shanghai Capitalists*, 144–58, 299 n. 1 [n. 14 above]).

64 *Facts about the Park Hotel*, n.p. (Hudec Collection).

65 "Architect Hudec Wins Fight for Higher Shanghai Buildings," *China Press*, 1 December 1934, n.p.

66 Unspecified examples referred to in Bruno Kroker, "The Building Industry in Shanghai," *China Journal* 30 (May 1939): 317.

67 For the results of Hudec's test borings, related foundation material, and a provocative discussion during an international foundation engineering conference, see N. W. B. Clarke and J. B. Watson, "Settlement Records and Loading Data for Various Buildings Erected by the Public Works Department, Municipal Council, Shanghai," no. F12, 2:174–85, and Karl von Terzaghi, "Discussion of Papers No. F12 and F13 on Settlement of Structures in Shanghai, China," no. F21, 3:95, *Proceedings of the International Conference of Soil Mechanics and Foundation Engineering, June 22–26, 1936* (Cambridge, MA: Harvard University Press, 1936; repr. 1971).

68 "Old Bogey in Local Skyscraper Construction Disproved," *China Press*, 1 Dec. 1934, 1, 25.

69 Jean-Louis Cohen, *Scenes of the World to Come: European Architecture and the American Challenge 1893–1960* (Paris–Montreal: Flammarion, in conjunction with the Canadian Centre for Architecture, 1995), 15.

70 "L'Architecture en Chine," *L'Architecture d'Aujourdhui* 10 (Oct. 1938): X68.

71 L. B. Namier, "Skyscrapers," in *Skyscrapers and Other Essays* (Freeport, NY: Books for Libraries, 1927; repr. 1968), 1.

72 Stern, *New York 1930*, 259 (n. 45 above).

73 Robert Stern, *George Howe: Toward a Modern American Architecture* (New Haven: Yale University Press, 1975), 71.

74 A term first used to describe the Woolworth Building in New York (Paul Goldberger, *The Skyscraper* [New York: Knopf, 1981], 44).

75 Stern, *New York 1930*, 215.

76 "J. S. S. Building Facing Race Course," *China Press*, 5 Nov. 1931, 3.

77 These buildings can still be seen in Chicago and New York and are illustrated in many books. For the Chicago Tribune Building and the American Radiator Building see Goldberger, *Skyscraper*, 51, 60; the Daily News Building, Cervin Robinson and Rosemarie Bletter, *Skyscraper Style: Art Deco New York* (New York: Oxford University Press, 1975), fig. 35C.

78 Ibid.

79 From "The Tall Building Artistically Considered," cited by Robinson and Bletter, *Skyscraper Style*, 36.

80 On the different uses of texture, color, and material, see Wolfgang Pehnt, *Expressionist Architecture* (London: Thames Hudson, 1973), 87, 196–98.

81 Warner, *Deutsche Architektur in China*, 132 (intro., n. 15).

82 The interaction between American and European architecture is the theme of Cohen, *World to Come* (n. 69 above); that interaction is seen as the source of Art Deco in Robinson and Bletter, *Skyscraper Style*, 44–60.

83 William H. Jordy, *The Impact of European Modernism in the Mid-Twentieth Century* (Garden City, NY: Anchor Books, 1976), 80.

84 "Modern Home Helps in Furnishing New Hotel," *China Press*, 1 Dec. 1934, 18.

85 Thomas C. Jester, ed., *Twentieth Century Building Materials, History, and Conservation* (Washington, DC: National Park Service/McGraw-Hill, 1995), 60.

86 Similar themes can be found in Hudec's Grand Theatre two doors down, and in the D. V. Woo house of 1936, now the Shanghai Planning Institute.

87 *China Press*, 1 December 1934, 25.

88 For example, photos found in Craig Clunas, "Chinese Art and Chinese Artists in France 1924–25," *Arts Asiatiques* 44 (1989): 102.

89 Minick and Ping, *Chinese Graphic Design*, 36, 38, 44, 56 (chap. 9, n. 27).

90 Gin-Dijh Su, *Chinese Architecture Past and Contemporary* (Hong Kong: The Sin Poh Amalgamated [HK] Limited, 1964), 222–24; Fun Xinian, "Survey: Chinese Traditional Architecture," in *Chinese Traditional Architecture*, ed. Nancy Shatzman Steinhardt et al. (New York: China Institute in America, 1984), 14.

91 Illustrated, for example, in photographs of interiors for homes owned by foreigners, in G. L. Wilson, "Architecture, Interior Decoration, and Building in Shanghai Twenty Years Ago and To-day," *The China Journal* 12.3 (May 1930): 248–53.

92 Cohen, *World to Come*, 59–61 (n. 69 above).

93 Hugo Schnell, *Twentieth Century Church Architecture in Germany: Documentation, Presentation, Interpretation* (Munich–Zurich: Schnell & Steiner, 1974), 33.

94 For example, the Book Printing Works in Tempelhof, Berlin, 1924–26, by Eugene Schmohl, and Fritz Högers Hanover Advertiser Office, 1927, documented in Arnold Whittick, *European Architecture in the Twentieth Century*, vol. 2, pt. 3, *The Era of Functionalism* (New York: Crosby Lockwood & Son, 1953), pls. 3C, 311.

95 William J. R. Curtis, *Modern Architecture Since 1900* (Upper Saddle River, NJ: Prentice Hall, 1996), 15.

96 Leonardo Benevolo, *History of Modern Architecture*, vol. 2, *The Modern Movement* (Cambridge, MA: MIT Press, 1971), 380. The reason northern Europe was the birthplace of the avant-garde, suggests Benevolo, was that it lacked the type of precedents found in France and England's classical architecture; undoubtedly significant were the effects of war on the individual economies of smaller northern countries.

97 Janos Bonta, "Functionalism in Hungarian Architecture," in *East European Modernism: Architecture in Czechoslovakia, Hungary, and Poland Between the Wars, 1919–1939*, ed. Wojciech Lesnikowski et al. (New York: Rizzoli International Pub-

lications, 1995), 128–29.

98 *Shanghai Times*, 7 May 1928, n.p.

99 Meade, *Grand Oriental Hotels*, 212 (n. 46 above). The only other hotels included in this book that approach modernism in design are Frank Lloyd Wright's Imperial Hotel in Tokyo of 1914, and Shanghai's Cathay Hotel of 1927 and the Broadway Mansions of 1935.

100 "Grand Hotels and Palaces: The Dimensions of a Dream," *Grand Oriental Hotels*, 13.

101 Lee, "In Search of Modernity," 110 (n. 21 above).

102 Ibid., 121.

103 Former residents of Shanghai admit that blind eyes were turned to the hardships of the poor evident on city streets. See Sergeant, *Shanghai* (n. 50 above), for numerous personal recollections.

104 Ibid., 167. The "façadism" of today's constructions are regularly compared to those of the 1920s and 30s. For example, see Michael Leech, "Shanghai's Deco Shangri-La," *History Today* 43 (Sept. 1993): 5.

105 *Journey to a War* (1939; repr. London: Faber & Faber, 1973), 227.

106 "Arts and Life," 245 (chap. 7, n. 62).

107 "Shanghai Modernity," 381 (n. 2 above).

108 Ibid., 394.

109 See "Dunlop Rubber Floors Grace Parts of the J. S. S. Building," *Commercial Engineer* [Shanghai], Oct. 1934, 19.

110 Aaron Betsky, "Lost Horizons: The Birth and Death of the Skyscraper," *Architectural Design* 65 (July–Aug. 1995): 9.

111 *The City Shaped: Urban Patterns and Meanings Through History* (London: Thames and Hudson, 1991), 326. See also Cohen, *World to Come*, 11 (n. 69 above), on the development of skyscrapers in America and their implications in Europe.

Afterword

The Shanghai Gaze: Visual Culture and Images of Modernity

Wen-hsin Yeh

The essays in this volume, by art historians and literary scholars, examine a wide range of issues that pertain to visual culture and representation in Shanghai. Each essay makes a unique contribution to a set of questions, enriches our understanding, and opens up new vistas in studies of Chinese modernity.

This final essay builds on these insights and findings. I describe here the overall form and content of the visual culture suggested by the contributors to this volume. In addition, I raise a few questions about how studies of pictorial images can be fruitfully linked to an interdisciplinary approach to a study of Shanghai culture and society.

The Field Of Pictorial Production

Those somewhat familiar with the history of this period (1840s–1930s) will know that these were decades of major upheavals. Standard textbook accounts highlight the Opium War (1839–42), the Taiping Uprising (1850–64), the Sino-Japanese War (1894–95), the 1911 Revolution, the May Fourth Movement (1919), the May Thirtieth Movement (1925), the Northern Expedition (1926–28), and the War of Resistance (1937–45). The wars and revolutions, we learn, brought down governments and dramatically altered the lives of multitudes. It thus seems particularly intriguing that there seems to be little evidence, at least according to the contributors of this volume, of these political events translating themselves into significant turning points in art history. Instead, gradual social changes, effected by the opening up of the city to Western trade, the rise of merchant wealth, the movement of migrant population, and the appearance of women in public, converged to leave an indelible imprint on the visual landscape. One striking conclusion is that deep-seated structural shifts rather than momentary social upheavals changed the way pictures were made and used in nineteenth- and twentieth-century Shanghai.

The technology of imaging and pictorial reproduction, of course, underwent significant changes. The adoption of photography, the use of lithography, and the publication of newspapers in the second half of the nineteenth century dramatically altered not only how pictures were made but also how they were circulated. The application of this new visual technology enabled people, in an unprecedented way, to produce, reproduce, preserve, and gain access inexpensively to large quantities of images from a considerable distance. Pictures became just as important as texts, a complex tool to describe and represent the world surrounding modern Shanghai. They were valued, furthermore, as an effective medium to communicate with the less literate. A whole visual culture emerged and became a central part of urban life in Shanghai; it assumed a wide range of functions, including depiction, decoration, propagation, communication, and representation.

This insularity from politics and responsiveness to technological changes combined to lay the foundation of a new pictorial culture, notable in a number of ways. First, whether in subject matter or patron-client relationships, the production of art in Shanghai moved well beyond the confines and conventions of traditional literati painting. Instead of a galaxy of masters producing masterpieces that dealt with the transcendental and the universal, an array of painters and patrons emerged to produce drawings and representations that were mechanically reproduced for a given price. The very production and circulation of images pointed to the rise of new social organizations of art, formed on the basis of new relationships to the marketplace.

Visual art in modern Shanghai, furthermore, was not just about paintings for sale; it had everything to do with the physical transformation of Shanghai into a cosmopolitan metropolis. Graphic designs and architectural conceptions played a large part in the visual culture of an emerging urban society. The high-rise buildings and entertainment centers in Shanghai's financial and commercial districts in the 1930s, with their modernist lines and motifs, materially embodied the image of Chinese modernity. Here the interesting questions are not just about how the graphics were shaped and portrayed, but about the cultural transmission of these designs and their basic economic foundation.

The contributors to this volume have given us a rich variety of descriptions of the images that were produced. Taken together, the essays delineate the contours of a much-altered and expanded pictorial repertoire that appeared in the decades after the Opium War, and a field of pictorial production that displayed, roughly speaking, some of following characteristics.

Expansion in the range of aesthetic imagination and pictorial repertoire. Shanghai painters, as several essays in this volume have shown, went well beyond traditional categories to include new objects in their works. They painted new species of plants, flowers, birds, and animals that became known through handbooks and manuals via Sino-Western trade. Realistic depictions of new objects coexisted with imagined forms of demons, spirits, fairies, and ghosts. There was a new fascination with Western sojourners who had landed on the China coast. This fascination inspired new reflections, in turn, on how the Chinese might have appeared to foreign eyes. Figure paintings of this period displayed a new attention to details such as styles of clothing, items of accessories, facial features, and bodily postures, all of which were given new meaning as markers of cultural differences. We may conclude, based on this volume, that the pictorial images, seen in their totality, capture the visual richness of a bustling trading port that was filled with exotic objects of foreign origin.

Experimentation with new pictorial composition. Among the imports were European works of art and Japanese prints, which stimulated, as Jonathan Hay shows, new compositional schemes in Chinese paintings. Images of the Madonna and the child, for instance, inspired in Chinese paintings motifs that departed from traditional forms.[1]

Cross-breeding between visual genres. Photography and lithography brought changes in the reproduction of pictorial images. Hay shows that the composition of photographic portraitures often borrowed the established conventions of ancestral portraits, which had long been popular in affluent households. Studio portraitures, meanwhile, used props and established their own conventions of staging. These formulas in turn made their way into decorative poster portraits—advertisements that featured young women. One may thus trace a line from the painted portraits of ancestors, commonly used on ritual occasions, to the poster images of young women in the Republican period, primarily used for advertising. It would be interesting to examine, indeed, how the stern stares of the former eventually gave way to the coquettish smiles of the latter, which became the accepted norm in picture taking.[2]

The use of rich color for decorative purpose. The most popular paintings of the Shanghai School, as Shen Kuiyi observers, were those that impressed their viewers as sensual, pleasurable, colorful, and readily accessible. In contrast to the ink-and-brush landscape paintings of the literati, these images used new color schemes and brush work. Increasingly oversized, their display took up a much larger space than traditional paintings; they meant both to decorate and to impress. This art thus complemented the lifestyle of the city's new merchant elite and was the conspicuous display, in a sense, of new money.

The use of pictures for storytelling. Several essays describe how the albums and pictorials of nineteenth-century Shanghai depicted scenes of war, critiqued the conduct of national affairs, described urban life, narrated historical tales, and engaged in a variety of storytelling. The best known among these pictorials are no doubt those by Wu Youru, published in a three-volume set.[3] These pictorial images informed as well as entertained; they went hand in hand with narratives rather than poetry. For a popular audience, the authors argue, drawings of contemporary scenes and events potentially served journalistic as well as propagandistic functions. With lithography and the mass-publication of periodicals, these images gained broad circulation and emerged as a new medium in the building of an urban community of opinion.

The juxtaposition of a wide variety of images. Albums and collections often contain a wide range of images that show no apparent stylistic coherence. They were veritable emporia of images on display.

The saturation of public space with pictorial signs. Streets in commercial districts, as Hay shows, were saturated with shop signs combining calligraphy and pictures. Pedestrians walking down the street found themselves besieged by signs and banners vying for their attention.

Decorative images used in multiple aspects of everyday life. Pictorial images appeared in many places, including book covers, posters, calendars, and cigarette cards.[4] These pictures borrowed freely from European and Japanese designs, and went well beyond the traditional craft and handiwork that had displayed strong local and regional features. Calendar posters, for instance, were crowded with photographs and drawings of new imported goods. These posters, often adorned with elaborate border designs, were, as Laing shows, crammed with merchandizing messages. The posters thus helped to advertise new goods as they reached the hinterland.

This abundance of pictorial images, industriously produced, mechanically reproduced, and systematically distributed, significantly enriched the visual field of Chinese metropolitan life. The effect was particularly remarkable when combined with dramatic changes in cultural norms and social relationships. Looking at pictures and prints, ordinary people glimpsed things they had never before been allowed to see. Westerners collected photographs of "the Chinese" while Chinese circulated pictures of foreigners; housewives studied the images of prostitutes while prostitutes peered into the interiors of elite households. Gazes were deployed within these pictures from multiple vantage points to engage or to defy. In Ren Xiong's self-portrait, for instance, we see the artist looking out to meet the eye of the prospective viewer. By contrast, in the pictorial depiction of the fictional character Daiyu, the woman directs her eyes towards mid-space, thereby eluding any gaze of the prospective viewer that might threaten domination.[5] The essays in this volume provide a wealth of information about the deployment of gazes in the paintings of Shanghai. There was so much to be seen either literally or metaphorically in the daily lives of the city in those days, that viewing became entertainment and Shanghai itself was turned into a site of spectacle.

Shanghai as spectacle and a site of the "grand view" (*daguan*), with or without pejorative connotation, was a theme prominent in late nineteenth-century urban literature.[6] Guidebooks to the city, for instance, describe the courtesan quarters in the International Settlement and direct tourists there in the early evening hours in order to view the procession of high-class prostitutes, dressed in their finest clothing, coming and going in open carriages.[7] The spectacle was particularly sensational, as modesty had long prevented gentry women from displaying themselves in public. Another tourist attraction was the shops and department stores on Nanjing Road, which had spearheaded a consumer culture that permitted window shopping. To walk down Nanjing Road was to tour an emporium of goods and people foreign or domestic, novel or familiar, yet unfailingly a cause for curiosity and a source of amusement.[8]

Images of the city, readily reproduced and accessible, meanwhile, became a commodity. The use of photography and the advancement in printing technology facilitated the production and distribution of these images in large quantities. Postcard photos of the Bund advertised Shanghai's modern landscape far and wide. Prostitutes used their own photographs as token gifts as well as calling cards.[9] Fashion and tourism went hand in hand. Contemporary novels inform us that there was no greater humiliation for the proud son of a provincial elite than arriving in the city appearing like a country bumpkin. A privileged visitor could not jettison his silk gown fast enough in favor of a gabardine suit.[10] When seeing and being seen was the basis of a whole way of life, the city became at once a place for fashion and self-fashioning.[11]

Design Arts and Shanghai Cosmopolitanism

These emerging trends in Shanghai's urban culture, which were well in place before the turn of the century, received additional impetus in the first decades of the Republic, when the city underwent industrialization.[12] A new class of Chinese industrialists rose to wealth through light industries in textile, flour, matches, and tobacco. The abolition of the civil service examinations in 1905 removed the last hurdle for the development of a modern-style educational system. The creation of new-style banks, launched with official blessing during the final decade of the Qing, opened up additional opportunities for the advancement of a new breed of the educated.[13] The 1920s saw significant gains in the founding of colleges, banks, publishing houses, bookstores, newspapers, periodicals, factories, department stores, and other enterprises. Known as the golden age of the Chinese bourgeoisie, this was the period when middle-class elites began to make their presence felt in public affairs. During the interwar years a growing number of Chinese officials and students visited Europe and America. Ordinary people learned about the West through a steady stream of Western books in Chinese translation and by watching Hollywood films and by reading American sports magazines. The Shanghai municipal government embarked upon an extensive project to rebuild the Chinese part of the city in the image of a Westernized metropolis. More than ever before, Shanghai was tied to the West in business dealings and cultural interactions.

The essays by Laing and Hietkamp suggest that there was scarcely any lag between Shanghai and Paris for the spread of the latest fashion. Chinese students trained in European academies quickly brought home what they had learned abroad, such as Art Deco. Design arts became specialized subjects taught in academic institutes and training schools. What the elite academies endorsed as the latest fashion invariably spawned cheap copies in street stalls. Art Deco images and motifs traveled from European cities to Shanghai via Chinese and Westerners alike, be they students, tourists, architects, or businessmen. By the 1930s Art Deco designs and motifs had become ubiquitous inside a multitude of Shanghai dance halls, theaters, hotels, and luxurious private residences. For color, the choice of fabrics, the selection of materials, or the design of furniture, meanwhile, there were journals to inform housewives about how to be a discriminating consumer.[14] Shanghai's rich and sophisticated thus regarded their taste and style as fully in keeping with that of a world-class fashion and design industry.

Shanghai, meanwhile, had become a destination point in a global itinerary of tourism. In the heyday of grand tours aboard cruise ships, as Hietkamp's research shows, Shanghai came to be the port of the "Orient." To cater to this constituency, a group of Chinese bankers commissioned the construction of the palatial Park Hotel. When the hotel opened in 1934, it was noted, not only in English-language newspapers such as the *North China Herald*, but also in the cruise industry's roster of grand hotels. Apart from its Hungarian Jewish architect, its Art Deco design, its commanding height, and the banking wealth it represented, the hotel operated successfully because it was staffed by a team of Chinese employees who held undergraduate business degrees from the Shanghai Baptist College. The cosmopolitan sheen of Shanghai in the 1930s was not just a matter of local

Chinese becoming modern. It was also a systematic mobilization of the city's resources, cultural as well as financial, for the production of an "Orient" that would take its prescribed place in a Euro-centric world.

Women and Modernity

The Western presence and the Westernization of its educated elite, as many have pointed out elsewhere, posed major challenges to established Chinese culture and identity. The place of women represents a particularly difficult issue, for it impinges upon ethical norms in family relationships, and raises complicated questions about power and authority in the most intimate domains of human lives.

It is thus no wonder that women and modernity are prominent themes in pictorial representations in Shanghai. The issues took many forms, and were explored from a variety of perspectives, evident in Wu's album. There is, for instance, the lady of the house encountering the world of the machine as she sits sewing by a window opened to a space defined by bamboo trees. There is, highly visible in the public, a group of young women joining the audience of a play. There are scenes from home entertainment, where elaborately dressed women play billiards together under a chandelier, leaning forward against the large pool table, balancing their weight on their dainty feet.[15] Finally, in perhaps the most tangible portrayal of how the technology of modernity has redrawn the lines between public and private space, there are images of women reclining in the bedroom, dressed in Western-style clothing and tuning in the enticing voice of the radio. To enjoy the performance of a favorite storyteller, it was no longer necessary for a modern woman to venture into the world of teahouses or theaters. News and noises from that world had penetrated into the privacy of their inner chambers via radio broadcast.[16]

Pictorial images of women, of course, did not appear in a void. The way certain images became popularly acceptable while others faded away speak volumes about normative expectations of women and their place in Shanghai society. Shu-mei Shi argues that images of women had been produced primarily to meet the expectations of a predominantly male gaze. She further suggests that the way Chinese men looked at Chinese women had much to do with their self-awareness as Chinese in a colonial context. Whether we subscribe to her interpretive readings or not, Shi's analysis points to the social dynamics that helped to explain the production of certain images and their particular appeal.

The mixing of the conventional and the novel, the abstract and the concrete in these pictures, meanwhile, often send ambiguous messages. One may well argue that while "the machine in the garden" leads to a subversion of the age-old idyllic composition of the maiden weaving at home, its inclusion in this familiar motif no doubt contributes to the machine's indigenization. Drawings that depict the contrast between the jewel-bedecked rich in the house and the barefooted poor on the street, similarly, invite clichéd critiques of economic disparity. When used to portray the social distance between a modern middle-class housewife and a beggar woman, critique helps to structure the meaning of the drawing. But conventional critique, by its very conventionality, obscures the novelty of the injustice that was the product of two different cultural and economic systems. By making a novel condition so readily describable in conventional terms, the pictures help close off rather than open up new sensibilities to the full dimensions of the changing reality.

Images of women, in short, dominated a wide range of pictorial compositions at all levels of visual culture in Shanghai society. The public presence of women, both in person and via representations, was among the most visible signs of Chinese modernity. These "modern women" often located their modernity in the most tangible forms of material objects – bobbed hair, high heel shoes, telephone sets, cars—as well as in the intrusion of these objects into previously closed space. The objects, inert as they appeared to be, brought with them new sets of social relationships: a boyfriend on the arm, an employer at the mill, a voice via the phone, a savings account at the post office, and so forth. The objects, which both epitomized and enacted networks of social relationships, sometimes reinforced and other times undermined established relationships. More often than not, the presence of the material transforms other elements in the pictures, both tangible and intangible, visible and invisible. In addition to depicting the novelty of the material, modernity in the visual culture of Shanghai radically reconfigured social space and multiplied the perspectives of viewing. It was not just a matter of women appearing in public. Visual technology led to a breakdown of the divisions between the inner and the outer, the private and the public. It produced images of women inviting the public into the inner realm of their existence.

The Industrialization of Artistic Production

Visual culture in Shanghai in the 1930s, as we may deduce from the essays in this volume, was both rich in content and innovative in its confrontation with modernity. This new culture was itself the product of the reorganization of artistic production, a reorganization that followed industrial patterns. There were, for instance, advertising agencies that produced pictorial images to promote their products. Some of these were no more than one-man entrepreneurial operations. They built, nonetheless, complex businesses by working with craft studios, radio stations, newspapers, and periodicals, promoting goods through a combination of poster drawings, storytelling programs, and a variety of textual and pictorial ads.[17]

Graphic designs for textiles, handkerchief, pillows, sheets, quilts, and so forth, which traditionally had been the work of unmarried women weaving and embroidering at home, had become increasingly part of a machine-based industry. For instance, in the last decades of the Qing, in response to a sense of crisis about the loss of competitiveness of Chinese silk fabric in world market, Jiangsu gentry reformers decided to sponsor learning tours and send Chinese artisans to Japan to study patterns and designs. Back home in Jiangnan, these reformers funded institutes of sericulture as well as vocational training schools, and supplied graduates to an emerging Chinese-owned textile industry. Textile designs were no longer home based but instead part of an industrial process. The diverse local traditions of arts and crafts, textiles and embroidery, which had been sustained for centuries by the labor and imagination of young girls training for womanhood, eventually gave way to a professional craftsmanship that linked a national market to machine-produced textiles.[18]

Painting as a Profession

The professional organization of painting, similarly, underwent significant changes. The early masters of the Shanghai School of Painting moved about in literati circles and painted to complement the poems composed by their elite patrons. Their Republican descendants, by contrast, organized painting societies and presented themselves as professional painters. Biographical sketches of leading artists suggest significant differences in personal styles and demeanor between the nineteenth and twentieth centuries. The nineteenth-century master Ren Xiong, a man of humble origin from Ningbo, was known for his awkward manner and ill temper. His self-portrait depicts a man gazing out with irrepressible irreverence and uncertain intention. His portraitures include ugly figures and unhappy characters missing an eye or a limb. As Britta Erickson shows, Ren also painted demons and ghosts depicted in classical texts. In a way his figures often seem ill at ease, yet demanding recognition. Few appear apologetic despite their imperfection.

Ren Xiong's professional descendants of the Republican period formed painting societies and handled their affairs in a strikingly different manner. As Julia Andrews shows, they published journals, organized clubs, formed associations, elected officials, took part in national exhibitions, handed out awards, trained students, set criteria, and displayed foreign academic degrees. Unlike their Qing predecessors, they manifested a much higher degree of autonomy from the patronage of individual members of the social elite. Republican painters operated, instead, through elite networks as well as institutional sponsorships, and turned the production of art into the creation of market value. The Ministry of Education, meanwhile, organized national exhibitions and tried to assert its authority as an arbitrator of aesthetic value. State participation in this process not only contributed to the consolidation of the notion of a "national" arena of artwork and a "national" audience for its products; it also laid the ground for a politicized reading of art.

To sum up, several trends emerged in pictorial production in the century after the Opium War: professionalization, commercialization, popularization, and Westernization. There was a brisk demand for pictorial images by the urban elite, and this demand was readily met by easy access to quantities of reproduced images at an affordable price. The production and consumption of popular pictorial images enriched the visual dimensions of an urban existence that was tuned, by and large, to the imperatives of the marketplace.

The Dynamics Of Viewing

Trade and technology had combined, meanwhile, to create in Shanghai a veritable visual bonanza. This was, however, not just a matter of foreign imports and foreign cultures enlarging the inventory of new images. Seeing had, indeed, become an indispensable part of everyday life. Those with inquisitive eyes searched for new venues to break down visual barriers. New forms of business, ranging from global tourism to the paid use of distortion mirrors in amusement halls, thrived on this thirst for views and spectacles. Pictorial images were not only produced and disseminated in a new way; they came to be newly viewed and newly consumed.

With the introduction of paved roads, electric lighting, residential neighborhoods, public parks, and high-rise commercial buildings, the cityscape was transformed between the 1880s and the 1930s.[19] The monumentality of a building such as the Park Hotel was no doubt meant to impress rather than to commingle, to dominate rather than to communicate, to exclude rather than to include, to tower above rather than to stand with. Yet the city, by the mid-1930s, had become, thanks to the scores of tall buildings that etched its jagged skyline, a place of multiple vantage viewpoints. To vie for the panoramic view and to be visible from far and near, those who wielded corporate power sat on top of those major buildings of commanding height and regarded themselves as being in charge. But the view from the top was never quite the same as that from below, and those on the street certainly formed perspectives of their own. An Art Deco interior designer might have fixed his eyes on the latest trends in Paris and London. A migrant woman worker in a cotton mill, on the other hand, could not afford to take her eyes off the fast-rolling machine in the workshop.[20] To make sense of the visual culture in the city, one must not only keep in sight the incessant struggles between the high and the low, the near and the far. One must also confront the fragmented nature of the myriad images that were but parts of an evolving whole, and were gleaned from a variety of perspectives.

What, then, were the sensitivities that informed pictorial images produced in Shanghai? Whose sensitivities were they and what sorts of viewpoints did they adopt? How were the senses cultivated against the backdrop of Shanghai's variegated landscape and how did the individual locate his or her place in this shifting context? Modern Shanghai was at once a commercial entrepôt, an industrializing city, a Westernizing metropolis, and a colonial enclave. How was the Shanghai gaze disciplined to revere or to dismiss, to engage or to avert, to support or to subvert emerging systems of power? How, conversely, did commercialization and industrialization, colonialism and nationalism, manifest themselves in a new visual culture?

Much of the discussion in this volume has been about how the pictures looked and what had been produced. But visual culture is not just an inventory and a sum total of the images and designs produced. More important, it is also about the dynamics of seeing and viewing, and the positioning of pictorial images in relation to the viewing eye. Unless we reject the notion that things change over time, there were historical dimensions to the distinct patterns that structured the gaze and endowed the images with their normative significance. There were factors, both tangible and intangible, that trained and disciplined the viewing eye.

What sorts of discursive imperatives, both explicit and implicit, framed the views and rendered them intelligible? What were the sorts of expectations, whether crisply articulated or but-dimly perceived, that make some pictures appear natural and others unnatural, communicative, or inaccessible to a Shanghai audience in the past century? How did pictures complement or contradict relationships of power, contributing either to their consolidation or subversion? What, in short, were the politics of pictures and images produced in the midst of dramatic social changes?

The acts of seeing and viewing, similarly, were hardly innocent of social and political meaning. Did seeing and viewing, practiced in new ways by a growing number of people and facilitated by new visual technology, challenge the established structures of authority and erode traditional boundaries of spatial insularity? Did Shanghai urbanites broaden their vision as they encountered an enriched visual environment? What was the relationship between viewing and an altered understanding?

These are some of the questions that this volume inspires. These essays, by drawing our attention to the pictorial images and graphic designs, have opened up new vistas in our understanding of Chinese modernity. What we need to do next, on the foundation of this rich description of pictorial production, is to analyze the dynamics of viewing to recover its historical dimension.

Notes

1 See, for instance, Wu Youru, "Xi furen," in *Wu Youru huabao*, vol. 2, "Gujin baimei tu," shang, p. 1 (chap. 6, n. 7).

2 On poster paintings for commercial advertisements, see Sherman Cochran, "Marketing Medicine" (intro., n. 14) and *Big Business in China: Sino-Foreign Rivalry in the Cigarette Industry, 1890–1930* (Cambridge, MA: Harvard University Press, 1980).

3 Wu, *Wu Youru huabao*.

4 Julia Andrews, "Judging a Book" (intro., n. 6).

5 Wu, *Wu Youru huabao*, "huabao buyi," vol. 13, xia, p. 5. Daiyu is the heroine of the Qing fiction *Dream of Red Chamber*, by Cao Xueqin.

6 For a topical treatment of Shanghai literature in the 19th century, see David Der-wei Wang, *Fin-de-siècle Splendor: Repressed Modernities of Late Qing Fiction, 1849–1911* (Stanford: Stanford University Press, 1997).

7 Wu, *Wu Youru huabao*, "Haishang baiyan tu," vol. 3 shang: p. 19.

8 Yeh, "Shanghai Modernity" (chap. 10, n. 2).

9 On Shanghai prostitution, see Hershatter, *Dangerous Pleasures* (chap. 3, n. 16); Christian Henriot, *Shanghai Ladies of the Night: Prostitution and Sexuality in Nineteenth and Twentieth-Century China* (New York: Cambridge University Press, 1997); Catherine Vance Yeh, "The Life-Style of Four *Wenren* in Late Qing Shanghai," *Harvard Journal of Asiatic Studies* 57.2 (December 1997): 419–70.

10 Li Boyuan, *Wenming xiaoshi*, translated by Douglas Lancashire as *Modern Times: A Brief History of the Enlightenment* (Hong Kong: Research Center for Translation, Chinese University of Hong Kong, 1996).

11 These images were wonderfully captured in Wu, *Wu Youru huabao*, "Haishang baiyan tu," vol. 3, xia: pp. 8–9.

12 Bergère, *Golden Age* (chap. 10, n. 11).

13 On the transformation of the modern Chinese educated elite, see Wen-hsin Yeh, *The Alienated Academy: Culture and Politics in Republican China, 1919–1937* (Cambridge, MA: Council on East Asian Studies, Harvard University, 1990).

14 On housewives as consumers, see Susan Glosser, "A Contest for Family and Nation in Republican and Early Communist China, 1919–1952," (PhD diss., University of California at Berkeley, 1995).

15 Wu, *Wu Youru huabao*, "Haishang baiyan tu," vol. 3: xia, p. 12; shang, p. 5; shang, p. 9.

16 Carlton Benson, "From Teahouse to Radio: Story-Telling and the Commercialization of Culture in 1930s Shanghai" (PhD diss., University of California at Berkeley, 1996).

17 Cochran, "Marketing Medicine" (intro., n. 14), and Benson, "From Teahouse to Radio."

18 Bai Wei, "Wo toudao wenxue quan de chuzhong," in Lan Yunyue, ed., *Minguo cainu meiwen ji* (Beijing: Yanshan chuban she, 1995), 1:146–56.

19 Zhang Zhongli, ed., *Shanghai chengshi shi* (Shanghai: Shanghai Academy of Social Sciences Press, 1997).

20 On the ethnic composition and working conditions of industrial workers in Shanghai, see Emily Honig, *Sisters and Strangers: Women in the Shanghai Cotton Mills, 1919–1949* (Stanford: Stanford University Press, 1986), and Elizabeth J. Perry, *Shanghai on Strike: The Politics of Chinese Labor* (Stanford: Stanford University Press, 1993).

Contributors

JULIA ANDREWS is professor of art history at The Ohio State University. She is the author of *Painters and Politics in the People's Republic of China* (University of California Press, 1994) and coauthor of *A Century in Crisis: Tradition and Modernity in the Art of Twentieth-Century China* (The Guggenheim Museum, 1998), the catalog of a major exhibition bearing the same title.

BRITTA ERICKSON earned her doctoral degree in Art History from the Department of Art, Stanford University. Her articles on the paintings of Ren Xiong have appeared in *Stanford University Museum of Art Journal* and *Phoebus*. Now working as an independent scholar, she focuses on both the Shanghai School of Painting and contemporary Chinese art.

JONATHAN HAY is an art historian specializing principally in Qing dynasty and modern Chinese painting. Since 1990 he has taught at the Institute of Fine Arts, New York University, where he is currently associate professor. His recent articles include "Painters and Publishing in Late Nineteenth-Century Shanghai," "Marden's Choice" (on the contemporary American painter Brice Marden), and "Time Difference" (on contemporary Taiwanese painting). He is the author of *Shitao: Painting and Modernity in China* (Cambridge University Press, 2001).

LENORE HIETKAMP is a doctoral candidate in Chinese art at the University of Washington and an architectural historian specializing in Western architecture in Shanghai. About this topic she has presented numerous conference papers and public lectures, one of which is being published in the *Bulletin* of the Society for the Study of Architecture in Canada. She recently curated an exhibition on the architectural archive of Laszlo Hudec at the University of Victoria. She is also active in producing architectural tours to Shanghai.

JASON C. KUO is professor of art history at the University of Maryland. He is the author of *The Landscape Art of Wang Yüan-ch'i* (National Palace Museum, Taipei, 1981), *The Austere Landscape: The Paintings of Hung-jen*

(SMC Publishing in cooperation with University of Washington Press, 1991), *Word as Image: The Art of Chinese Seal Engraving* (China Institute in America, New York, 1992), *Rethinking Art History and Art Criticism* (National Museum of History, Taipei, 1996), and *Transforming Traditions in Modern Chinese Painting: Huang Pin-Hung's Late Work* (New York and Bern: Peter Lang, 2004), among others. In 1992–93, he was Director of the Summer Institute on the Art of Imperial China for College and University Professors funded by the National Endowment for the Humanities. He founded and directed the Summer Institute of Connoisseurship in Chinese Calligraphy and Painting (2001–2003) funded by the Henry Luce Foundation.

ELLEN JOHNSTON LAING is a research associate at the Center for Chinese Studies, University of Michigan, and was the Maude I. Kerns Professor of Oriental Art at the University of Oregon. She has published more than fifty scholarly articles in almost all major journals in Asian art. Her books include *An Index to Reproductions of Paintings by Twentieth-Century Chinese Artists*, revised edition (Center for Chinese Studies, University of Michigan, 1998) and *The Winking Owl: Art in the People's Republic of China* (University of California Press, 1988). Her recent book is *Selling Happiness: Calendar Posters and Visual Culture in Early-Twentieth-Century Shanghai* (University of Hawaii Press, 2004).

KUIYI SHEN is associate professor of Chinese art history at the University of California, San Diego. He is the coauthor of *A Century in Crisis: Tradition and Modernity in the Art of Twentieth-Century China* (The Guggenheim Museum, 1998), catalog of a major exhibition bearing the same title.

SHU-MEI SHIH is associate professor in the East Asian Languages and Cultures Department, Comparative Literature Department, and Asian American Studies Program at UCLA. Her articles have appeared in *Signs, Journal of Asian Studies, Positions,* and various anthologies. She also publishes in Taiwan, Hong Kong, and China. Her book on Chinese literary modernism in the context of global/local circuits of culture and politics in the early twentieth century, *The Lure of the Modern: Writing Modernism in Semicolonial China, 1917–1937,* was published by the University of California Press in 2001. She is currently working on a new book tentatively titled *Visuality and Identity across the Chinese Pacific.*

CARRIE WAARA is associate professor of history at the Castleton State College in Vermont. Her article "Invention, Industry, and Art: The Commercialization of Culture in Republican Art Magazines" appears in *Inventing Nanjing Road: Commercial Culture in Shanghai,* edited by Sherman Cochran (Ithaca, NY: Cornell University Press, 1999).

ROBERTA WUE is assistant professor of art history at Towson University. She is the author of several publications on painting, photography, visual culture, and advertising in nineteenth-century China.

WEN-HSIN YEH is professor of history at the University of California, Berkeley. She is the author of *The Alienated Academy: Culture and Politics in Republican China* (Harvard University Press, 1990) and *Provincial Passages: Culture, Space, and the Origins of Chinese Communism* (University of California Press, 1996). She is the editor of *Wartime Shanghai* (Routledge, 1998) and coeditor of *Shanghai Sojourners* (Institute of East Asian Studies, University of California, Berkeley, 1992). Her articles have appeared in *Journal of Asian Studies, Republican China,* and *The China Quarterly.*

YINGJIN ZHANG is professor of Chinese, comparative literature, and film studies at the University of California, San Diego. He is the author of *The City in Modern Chinese Literature and Film: Configurations of Space, Time, and Gender* (Stanford University Press, 1996), coauthor of *Encyclopedia of Chinese Film* (Routledge, 1998), and editor of *China in a Polycentric World: Essays in Chinese Comparative Literature* (Stanford University Press, 1998) and *Cinema and Urban Culture in Shanghai, 1922–1943* (Stanford University Press, 1999).

Index

www.ingramcontent.com/pod-product-compliance
Lightning Source LLC
Chambersburg PA
CBHW020723180526
45163CB00001B/91